Sharks Just Wanna Have Fun

Other Books by Jim Toomey

Sherman's Lagoon: Ate That, What's Next?
Poodle: The Other White Meat
An Illustrated Guide to Shark Etiquette
Another Day in Paradise
Greetings from Sherman's Lagoon
Surf's Up!
The Shark Diaries
Catch of the Day
A Day at the Beach
Surfer Safari
Planet of the Hairless Beach Apes
Yarns & Shanties (and Other Nautical Baloney)

Treasuries

Sherman's Lagoon 1991 to 2001:
Greatest Hits and Near Misses
In Shark Years I'm Dead: Sherman's Lagoon Turns Fifteen

Sharks Just Wanna Have Fun

The Thirteenth Sherman's Lagoon Collection
by Jim Toomey

Sherman's Lagoon is syndicated internationally by King Features Syndicate, Inc. For information, write King Features Syndicate, Inc., 300 West Fifty-Seventh Street, New York, NY 10019.

Sharks Just Wanna Have Fun copyright © 2008 by Jim Toomey. All rights reserved. Printed in Singapore. No part of this book may be used or reproduced in any manner whatsoever without written permission except in the case of reprints in the context of reviews. For information, write Andrews McMeel Publishing, LLC, an Andrews McMeel Universal company, 1130 Walnut Street, Kansas City, Missouri 64106.

08 09 10 11 12 TWP 10 9 8 7 6 5 4 3 2 1

ISBN-13: 978-0-7407-7387-7
ISBN-10: 0-7407-7387-9

Library of Congress Control Number: 2008923397

www.andrewsmcmeel.com

Sherman's Lagoon may be viewed on the Internet at
www.shermanslagoon.com.

─── **ATTENTION: SCHOOLS AND BUSINESSES** ───

Andrews McMeel books are available at quantity discounts with bulk purchase for educational, business, or sales promotional use. For information, please write to: Special Sales Department, Andrews McMeel Publishing, LLC, 1130 Walnut Street, Kansas City, Missouri 64106.

To my parents, for having a sense of humor.

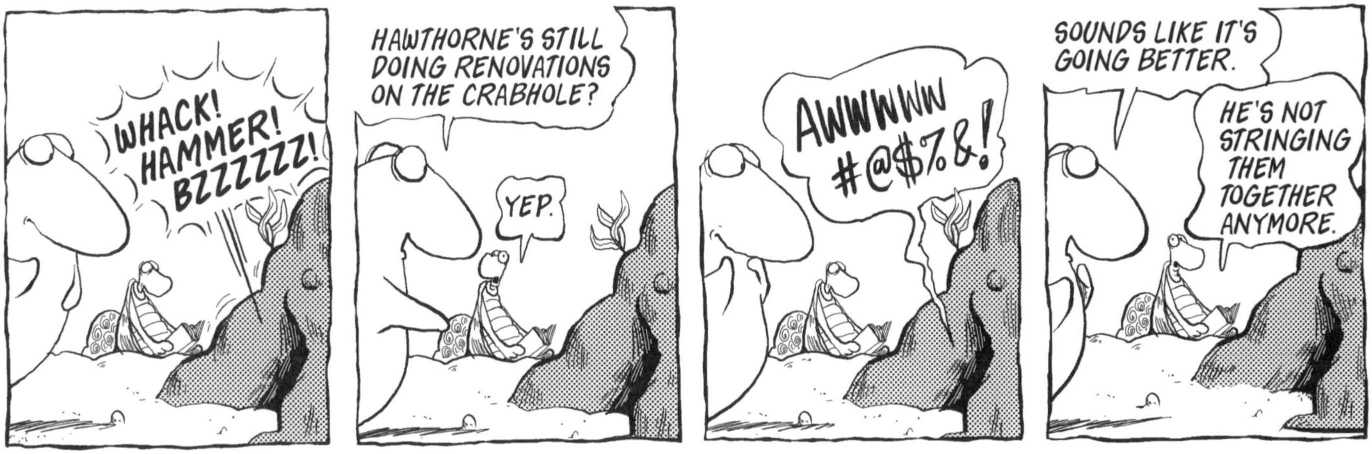
WHACK! HAMMER! BZZZZZZ!
HAWTHORNE'S STILL DOING RENOVATIONS ON THE CRABHOLE?
YEP.
AWWWWW #@$%&!
SOUNDS LIKE IT'S GOING BETTER.
HE'S NOT STRINGING THEM TOGETHER ANYMORE.

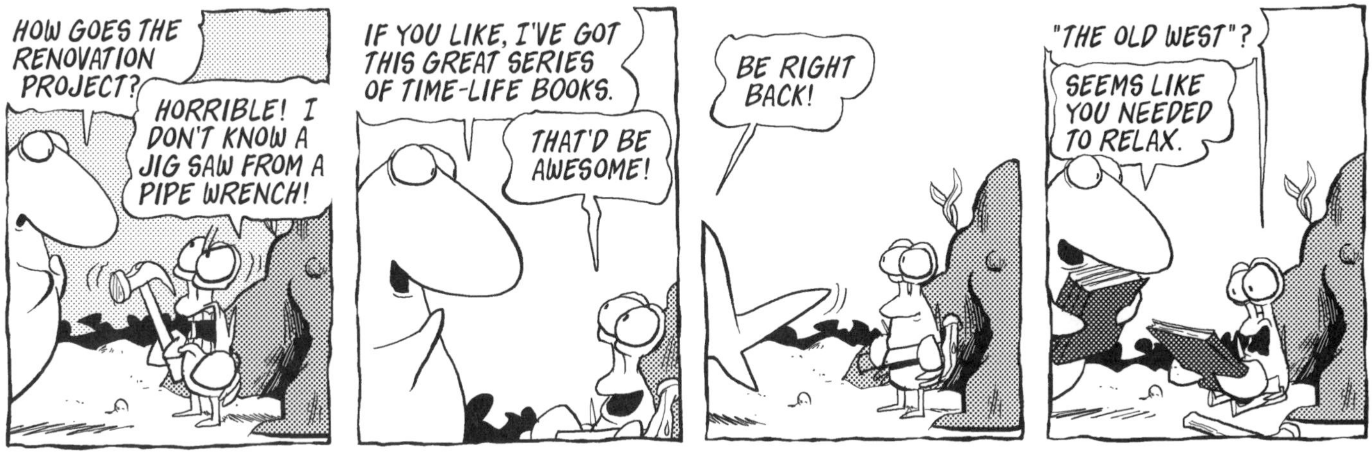
HOW GOES THE RENOVATION PROJECT?
HORRIBLE! I DON'T KNOW A JIG SAW FROM A PIPE WRENCH!
IF YOU LIKE, I'VE GOT THIS GREAT SERIES OF TIME-LIFE BOOKS.
THAT'D BE AWESOME!
BE RIGHT BACK!
"THE OLD WEST"?
SEEMS LIKE YOU NEEDED TO RELAX.

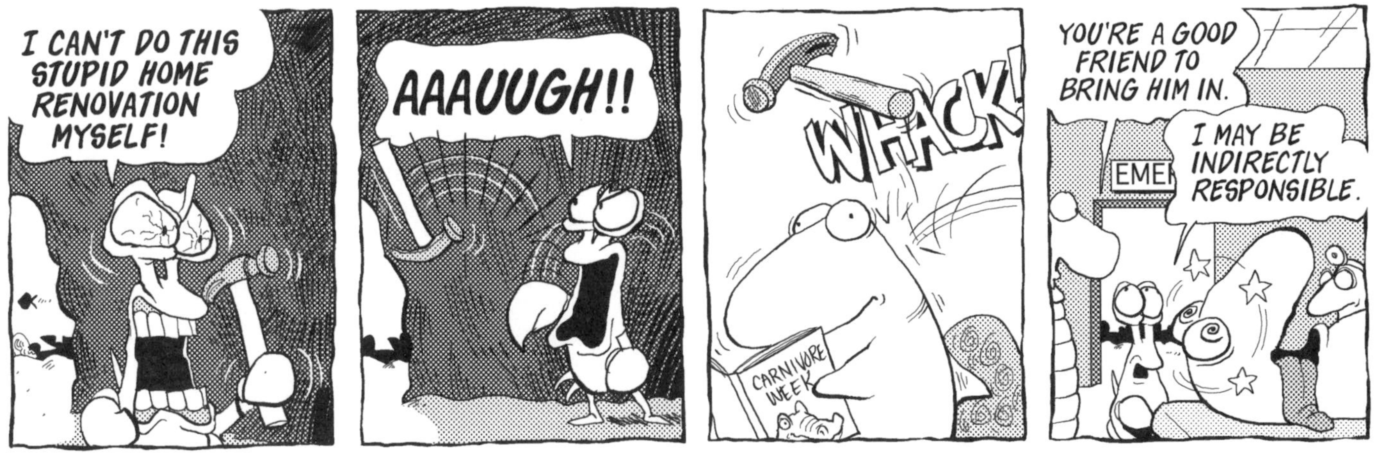
I CAN'T DO THIS STUPID HOME RENOVATION MYSELF!
AAAUUGH!!
WHACK!
CARNIVORE WEEK
YOU'RE A GOOD FRIEND TO BRING HIM IN.
EMER
I MAY BE INDIRECTLY RESPONSIBLE.

AS YOUR ARCHITECT, I SEE BIG THINGS FOR YOUR CRAB HOLE.

I SEE VAULTED CEILINGS AND HIGH ARCHWAYS.

I SEE A SPACIOUS SUNKEN LIVING ROOM.

I SEE IT COSTING AROUND $30,000.

I'LL SEE YOU TO THE DOOR.

SO, CARL, CAN YOU GIVE ME A PRICE ON THE RENOVATION WORK?

Carl's Contracting

OH, I'D SAY BETWEEN $500 AND $1000.

BOTH YOU AND I KNOW THAT MEANS IT'LL COST $1000... WHEN CAN YOU START?

TUESDAY OR WEDNESDAY... THURSDAY AT THE LATEST.

WHICH MEANS YOU'RE STARTING THURSDAY... WHEN WILL IT BE FINISHED?

Carl's Contracting

OH, ANYTIME BETWEEN NOW AND DOOMSDAY.

SEE YA THURSDAY, CARL.

Carl's Contracting

CARL, MY PLACE IS A DISASTER!

IT'S A WORK IN PROGRESS. YOU KNOW WHAT I MEAN?

THIS PLACE IS SUCH A CONSTRUCTION SITE, I CAN'T EVEN STAY HERE ANYMORE.

Carl's Contracting

YOU DON'T HAVE ANY FRIENDS WHO WOULD ENJOY YOUR COMPANY?

OF COURSE.

YOUR GUESTROOM LOOKS A LOT LIKE A DRYER.

LET ME JUST GET THOSE DIAPERS.

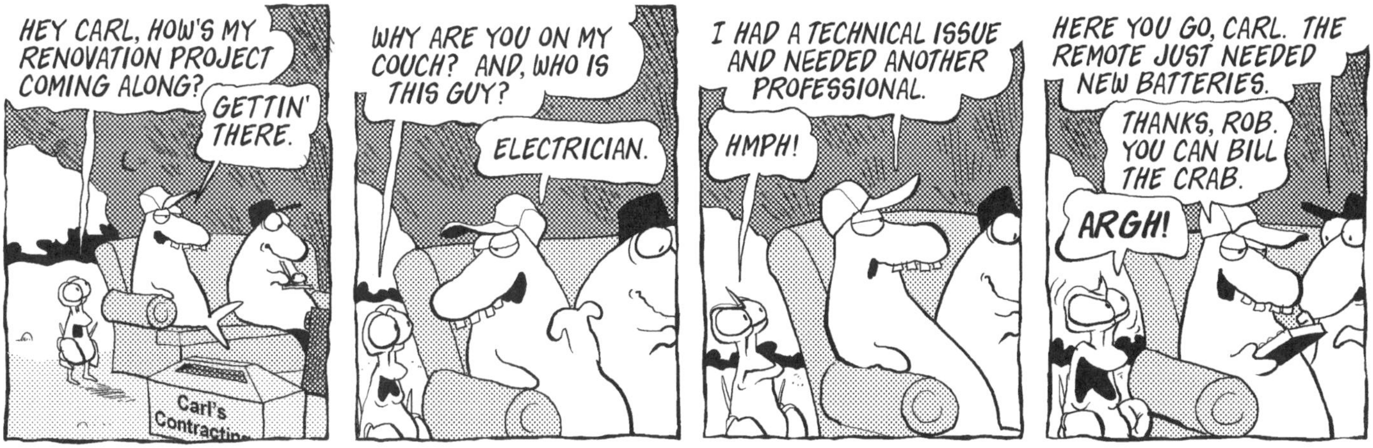
HEY CARL, HOW'S MY RENOVATION PROJECT COMING ALONG?
GETTIN' THERE.
Carl's Contracting
WHY ARE YOU ON MY COUCH? AND, WHO IS THIS GUY?
ELECTRICIAN.
I HAD A TECHNICAL ISSUE AND NEEDED ANOTHER PROFESSIONAL.
HMPH!
HERE YOU GO, CARL. THE REMOTE JUST NEEDED NEW BATTERIES.
THANKS, ROB. YOU CAN BILL THE CRAB.
ARGH!

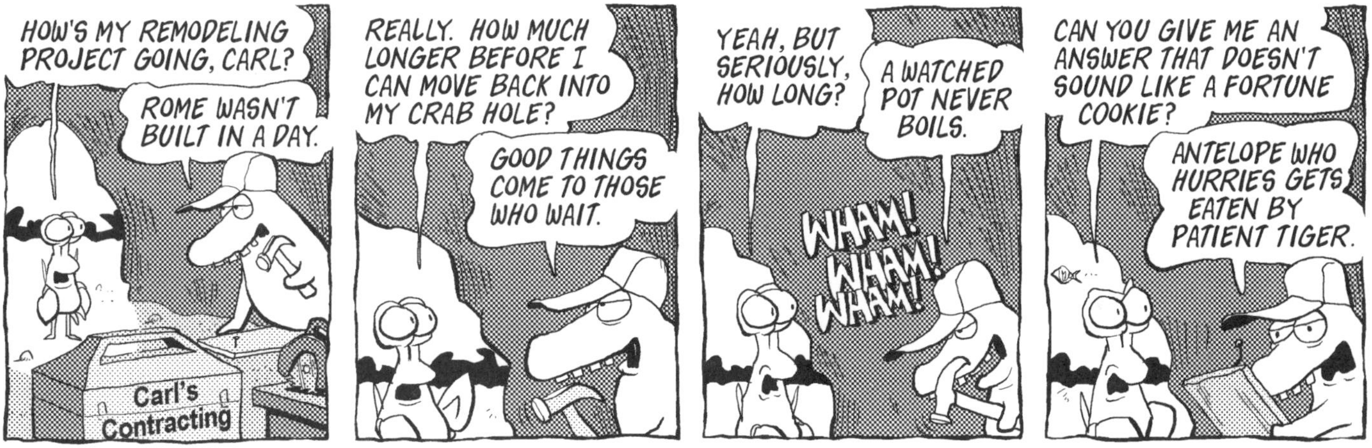
HOW'S MY REMODELING PROJECT GOING, CARL?
ROME WASN'T BUILT IN A DAY.
Carl's Contracting
REALLY. HOW MUCH LONGER BEFORE I CAN MOVE BACK INTO MY CRAB HOLE?
GOOD THINGS COME TO THOSE WHO WAIT.
YEAH, BUT SERIOUSLY, HOW LONG?
A WATCHED POT NEVER BOILS.
WHAM! WHAM! WHAM!
CAN YOU GIVE ME AN ANSWER THAT DOESN'T SOUND LIKE A FORTUNE COOKIE?
ANTELOPE WHO HURRIES GETS EATEN BY PATIENT TIGER.

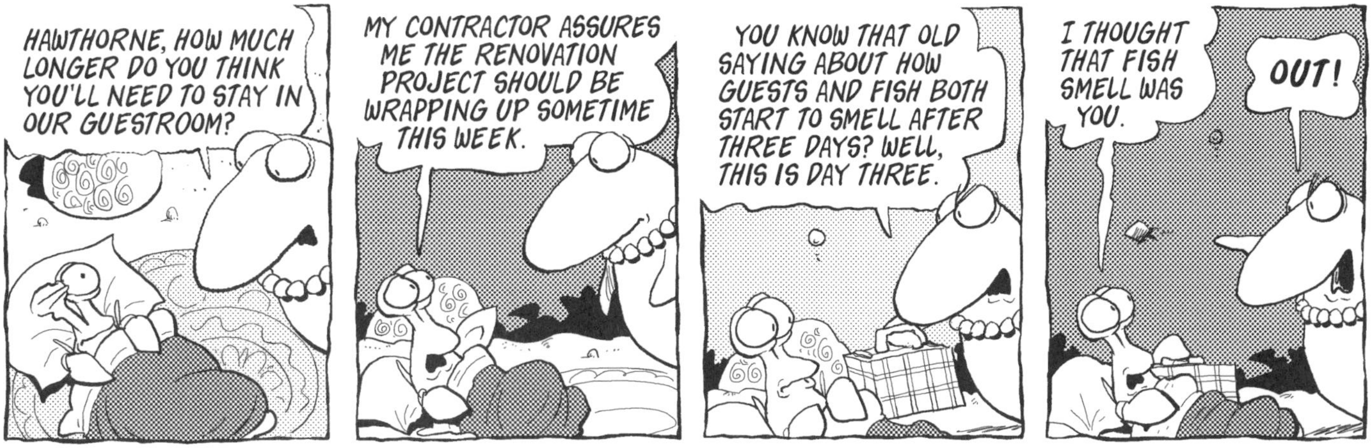
HAWTHORNE, HOW MUCH LONGER DO YOU THINK YOU'LL NEED TO STAY IN OUR GUESTROOM?
MY CONTRACTOR ASSURES ME THE RENOVATION PROJECT SHOULD BE WRAPPING UP SOMETIME THIS WEEK.
YOU KNOW THAT OLD SAYING ABOUT HOW GUESTS AND FISH BOTH START TO SMELL AFTER THREE DAYS? WELL, THIS IS DAY THREE.
I THOUGHT THAT FISH SMELL WAS YOU.
OUT!

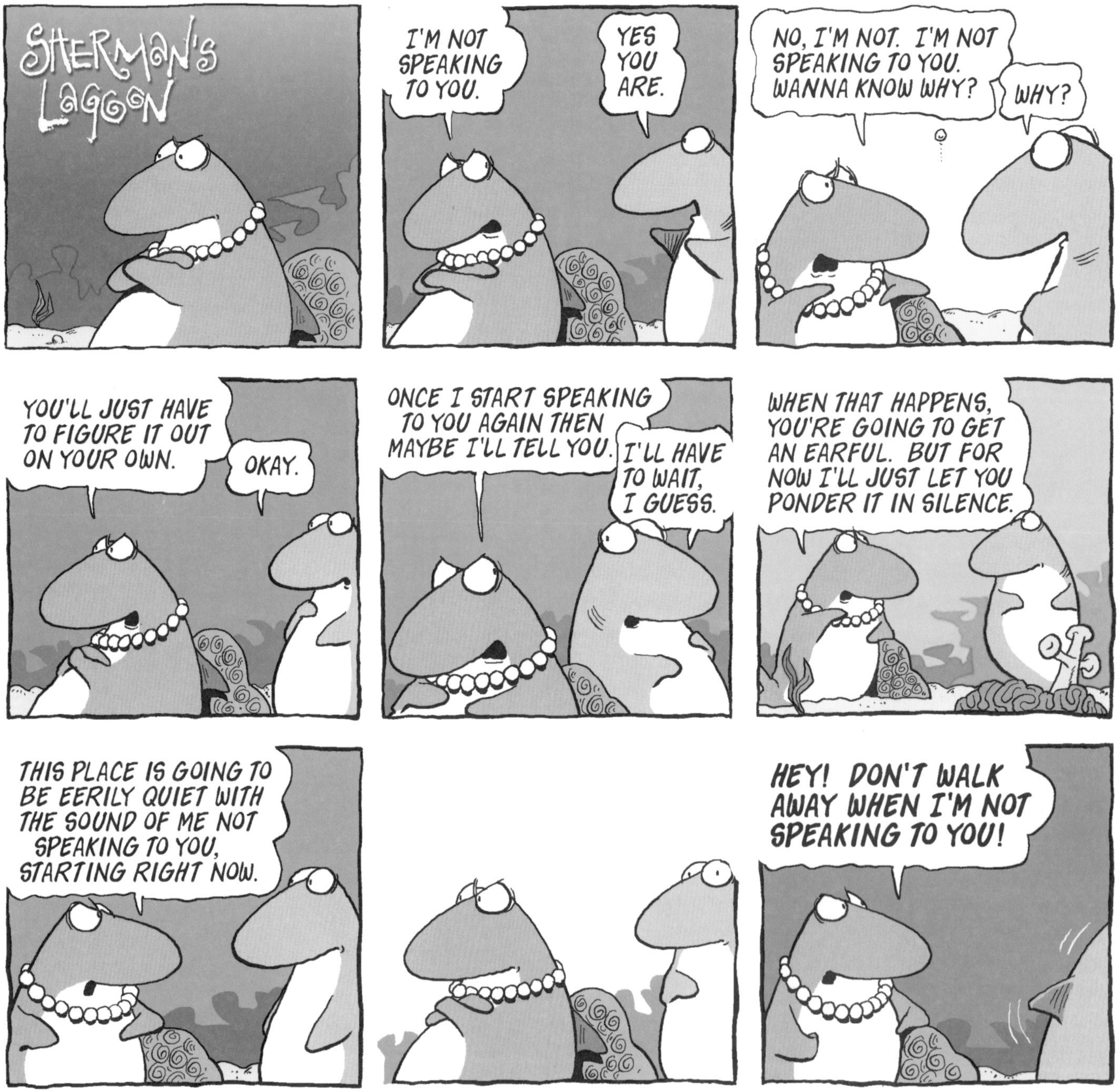
SHERMAN'S LAGOON
I'M NOT SPEAKING TO YOU.
YES YOU ARE.
NO, I'M NOT. I'M NOT SPEAKING TO YOU. WANNA KNOW WHY?
WHY?
YOU'LL JUST HAVE TO FIGURE IT OUT ON YOUR OWN.
OKAY.
ONCE I START SPEAKING TO YOU AGAIN THEN MAYBE I'LL TELL YOU.
I'LL HAVE TO WAIT, I GUESS.
WHEN THAT HAPPENS, YOU'RE GOING TO GET AN EARFUL. BUT FOR NOW I'LL JUST LET YOU PONDER IT IN SILENCE.
THIS PLACE IS GOING TO BE EERILY QUIET WITH THE SOUND OF ME NOT SPEAKING TO YOU, STARTING RIGHT NOW.
HEY! DON'T WALK AWAY WHEN I'M NOT SPEAKING TO YOU!

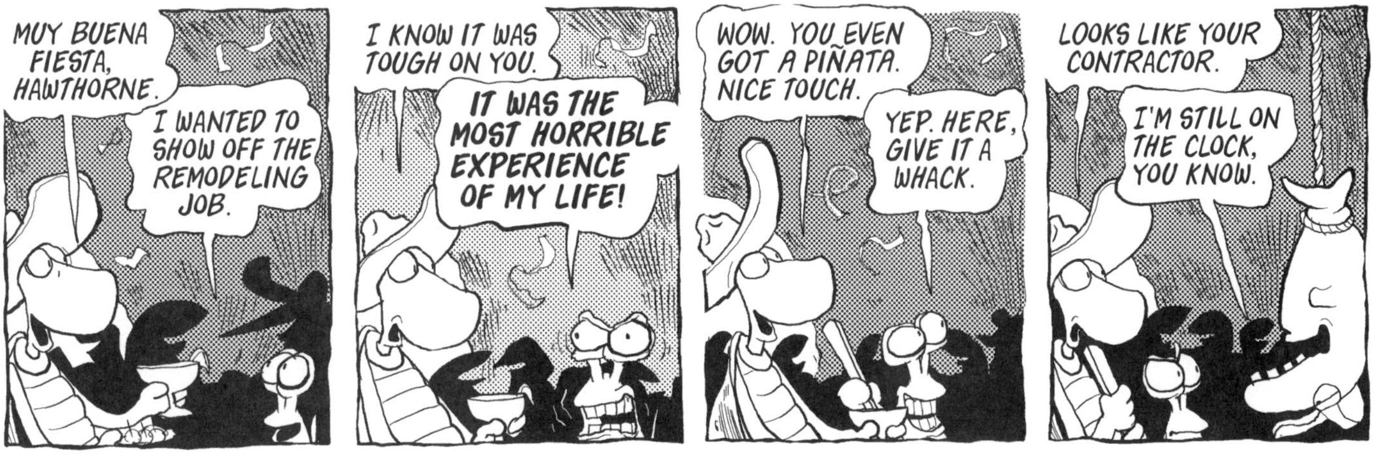
MUY BUENA FIESTA, HAWTHORNE.
I WANTED TO SHOW OFF THE REMODELING JOB.
I KNOW IT WAS TOUGH ON YOU.
IT WAS THE MOST HORRIBLE EXPERIENCE OF MY LIFE!
WOW. YOU EVEN GOT A PIÑATA. NICE TOUCH.
YEP. HERE, GIVE IT A WHACK.
LOOKS LIKE YOUR CONTRACTOR.
I'M STILL ON THE CLOCK, YOU KNOW.

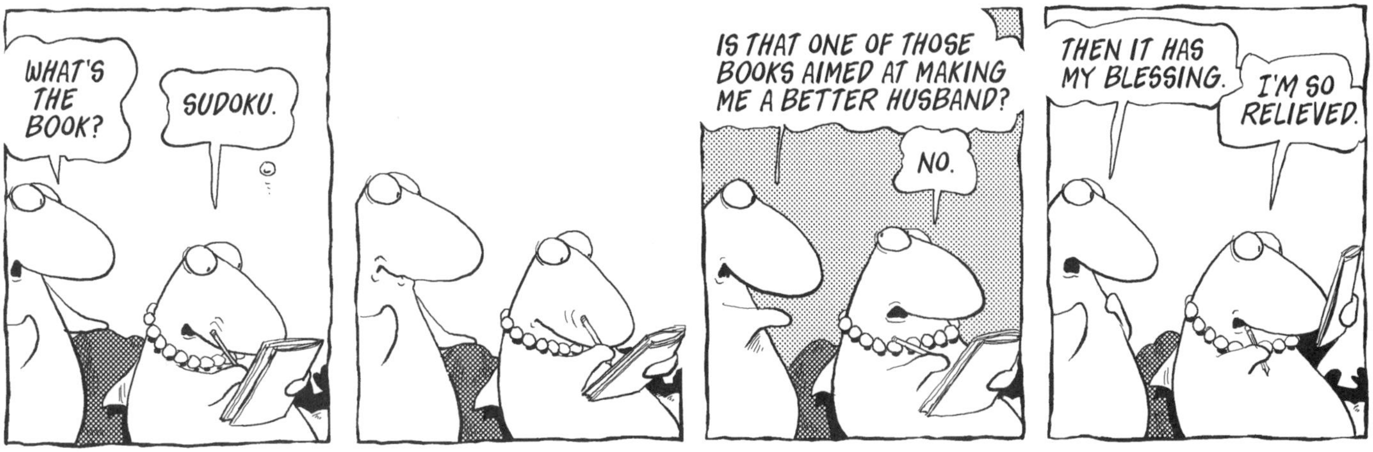
WHAT'S THE BOOK?
SUDOKU.
IS THAT ONE OF THOSE BOOKS AIMED AT MAKING ME A BETTER HUSBAND?
NO.
THEN IT HAS MY BLESSING.
I'M SO RELIEVED.

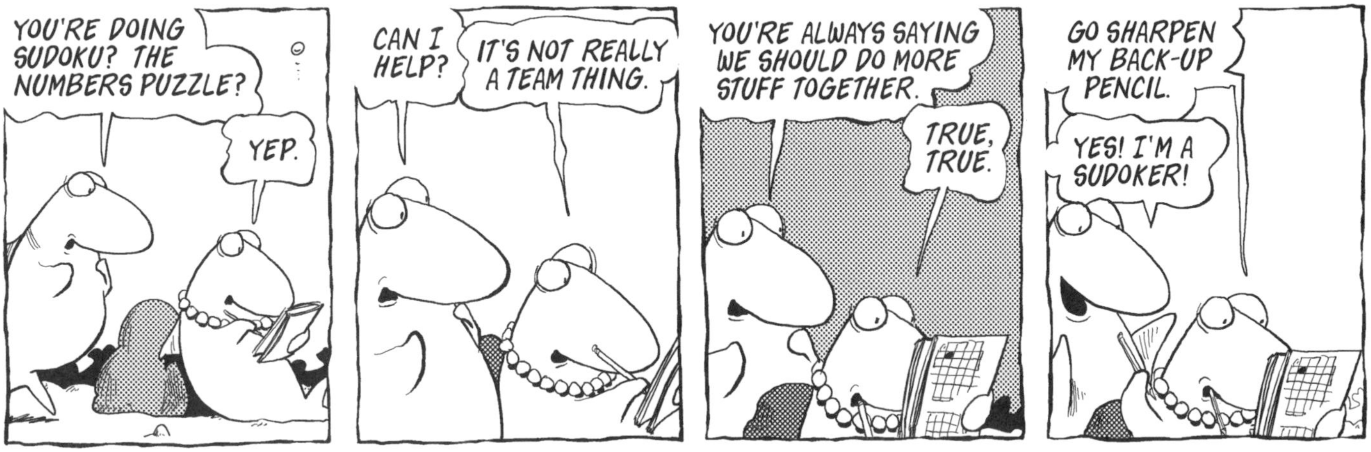
YOU'RE DOING SUDOKU? THE NUMBERS PUZZLE?
YEP.
CAN I HELP?
IT'S NOT REALLY A TEAM THING.
YOU'RE ALWAYS SAYING WE SHOULD DO MORE STUFF TOGETHER.
TRUE, TRUE.
GO SHARPEN MY BACK-UP PENCIL.
YES! I'M A SUDOKER!

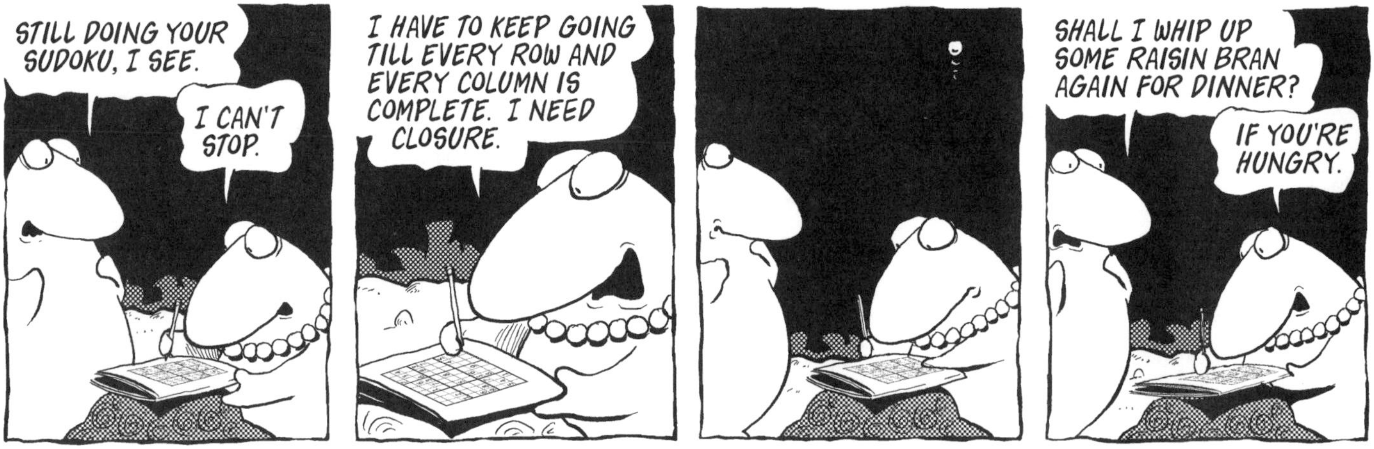
STILL DOING YOUR SUDOKU, I SEE.
I CAN'T STOP.
I HAVE TO KEEP GOING TILL EVERY ROW AND EVERY COLUMN IS COMPLETE. I NEED CLOSURE.
SHALL I WHIP UP SOME RAISIN BRAN AGAIN FOR DINNER?
IF YOU'RE HUNGRY.

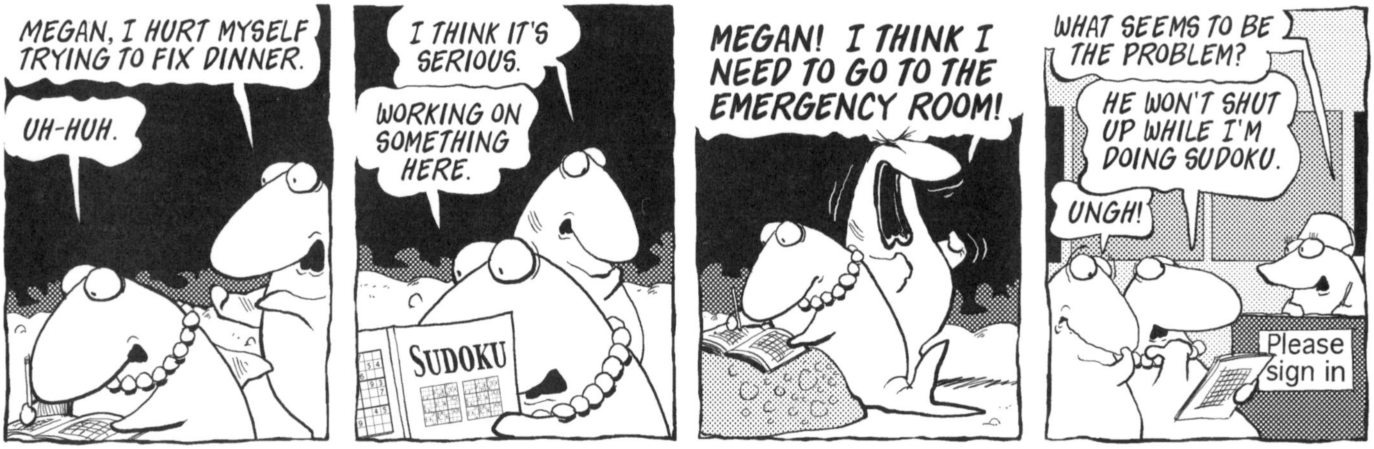
MEGAN, I HURT MYSELF TRYING TO FIX DINNER.
UH-HUH.
I THINK IT'S SERIOUS.
WORKING ON SOMETHING HERE.
SUDOKU
MEGAN! I THINK I NEED TO GO TO THE EMERGENCY ROOM!
WHAT SEEMS TO BE THE PROBLEM?
HE WON'T SHUT UP WHILE I'M DOING SUDOKU.
UNGH!
Please sign in

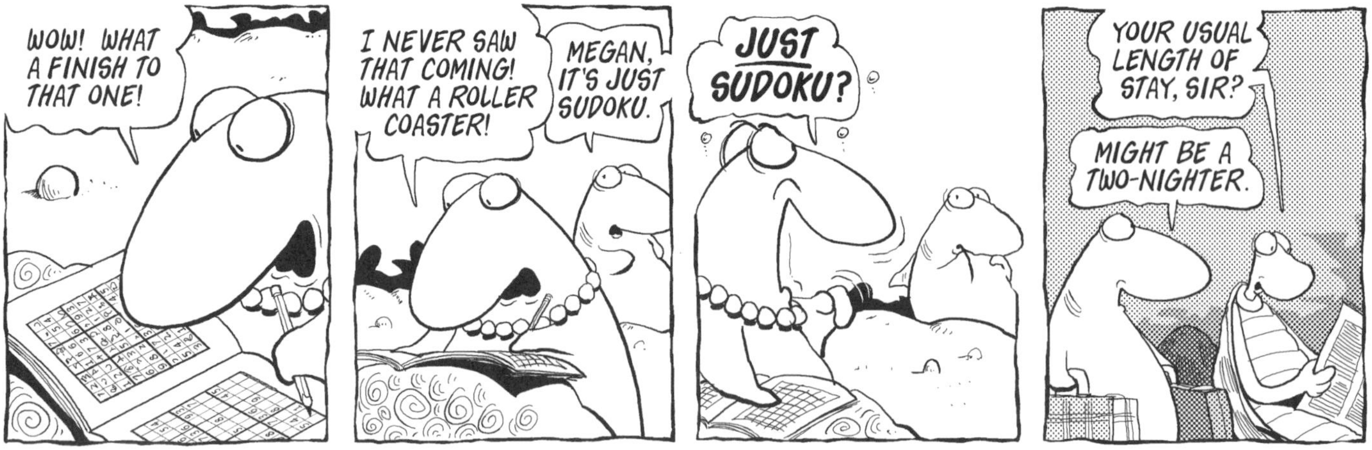
WOW! WHAT A FINISH TO THAT ONE!
I NEVER SAW THAT COMING! WHAT A ROLLER COASTER!
MEGAN, IT'S JUST SUDOKU.
JUST SUDOKU?
YOUR USUAL LENGTH OF STAY, SIR?
MIGHT BE A TWO-NIGHTER.

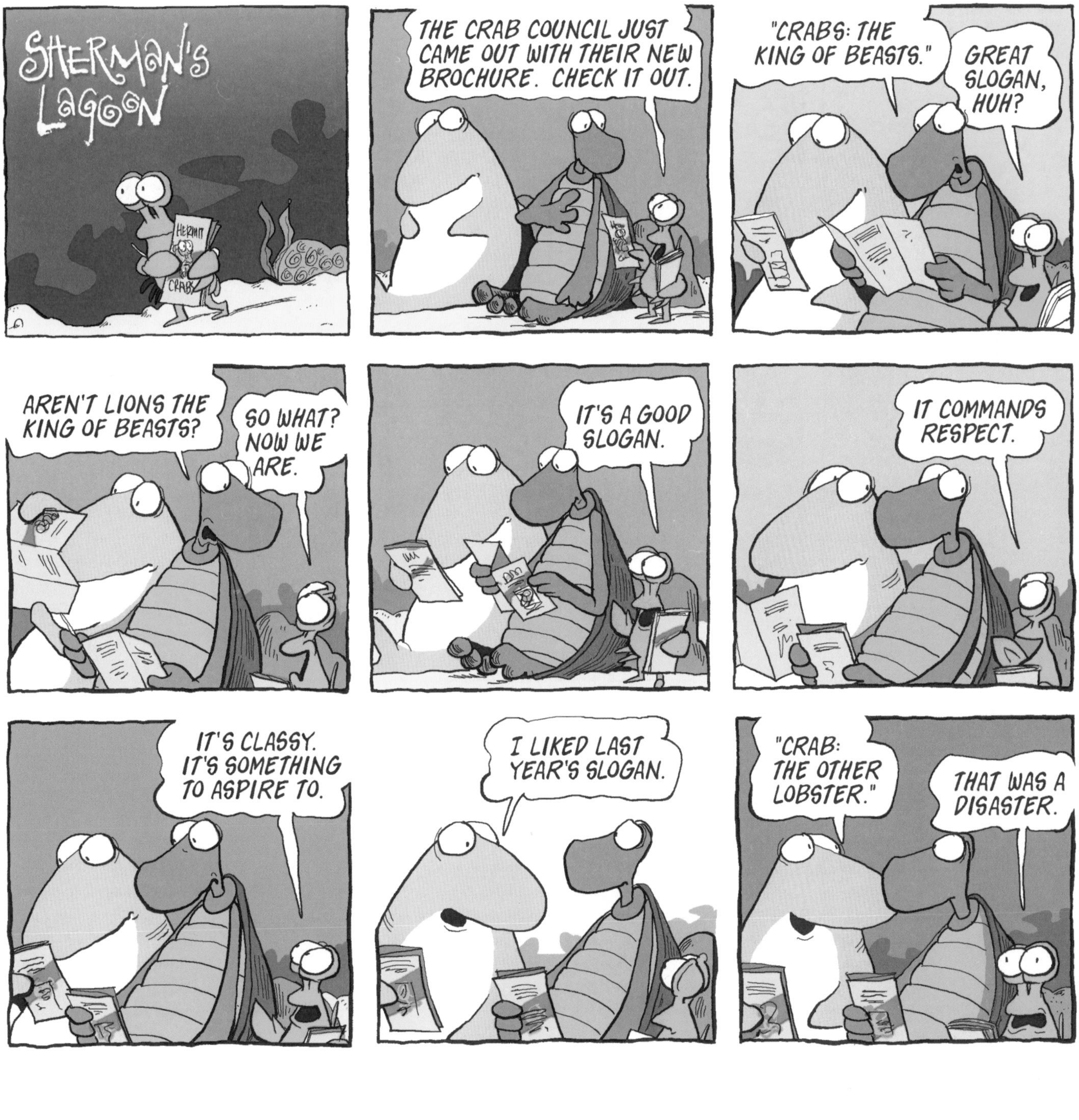
SHERMAN'S LAGOON
HERMIT CRABS
THE CRAB COUNCIL JUST CAME OUT WITH THEIR NEW BROCHURE. CHECK IT OUT.
"CRABS: THE KING OF BEASTS."
GREAT SLOGAN, HUH?
AREN'T LIONS THE KING OF BEASTS?
SO WHAT? NOW WE ARE.
IT'S A GOOD SLOGAN.
IT COMMANDS RESPECT.
IT'S CLASSY. IT'S SOMETHING TO ASPIRE TO.
I LIKED LAST YEAR'S SLOGAN.
"CRAB: THE OTHER LOBSTER."
THAT WAS A DISASTER.

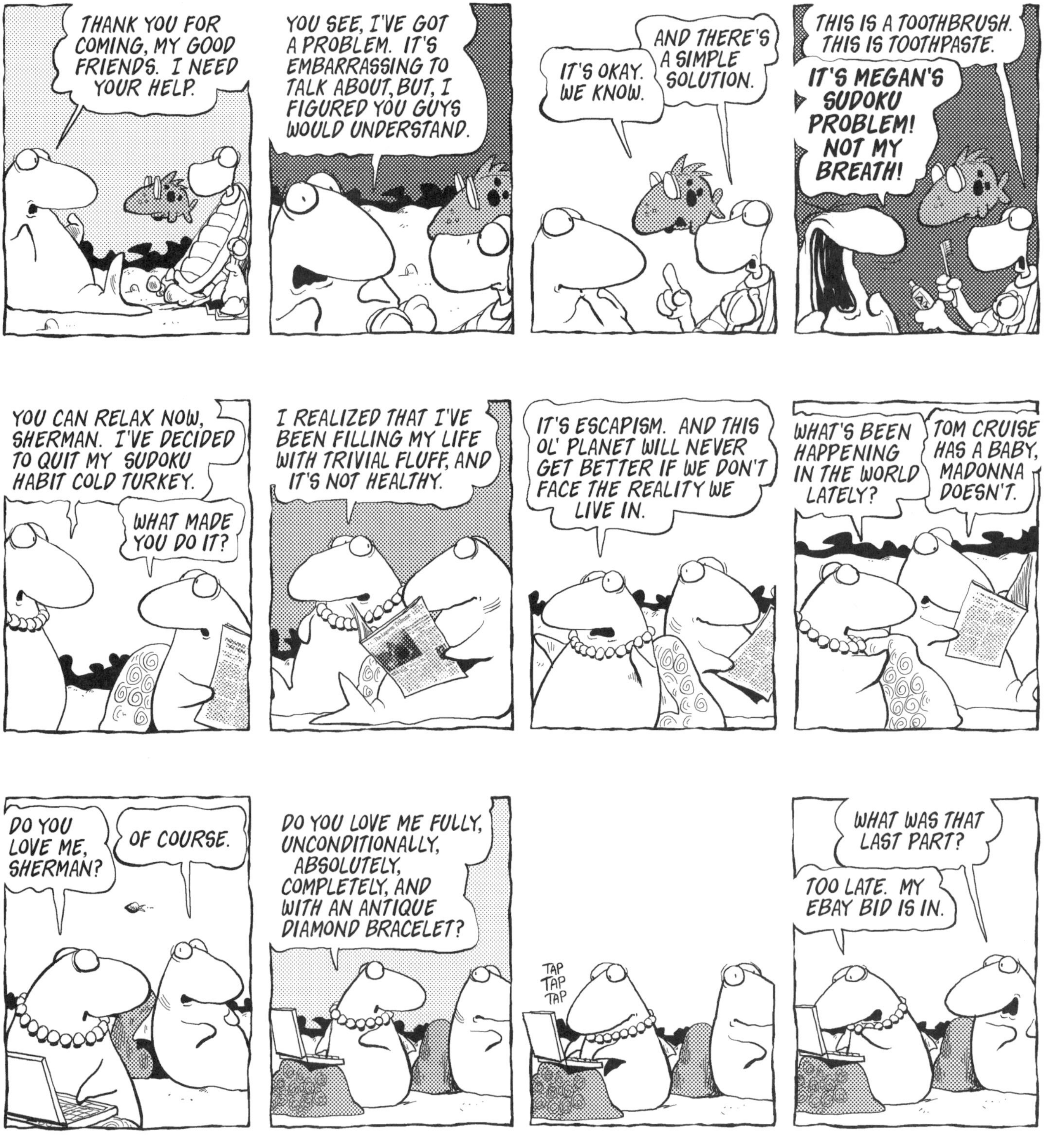
THANK YOU FOR COMING, MY GOOD FRIENDS. I NEED YOUR HELP.
YOU SEE, I'VE GOT A PROBLEM. IT'S EMBARRASSING TO TALK ABOUT, BUT, I FIGURED YOU GUYS WOULD UNDERSTAND.
IT'S OKAY. WE KNOW.
AND THERE'S A SIMPLE SOLUTION.
THIS IS A TOOTHBRUSH. THIS IS TOOTHPASTE.
IT'S MEGAN'S SUDOKU PROBLEM! NOT MY BREATH!
YOU CAN RELAX NOW, SHERMAN. I'VE DECIDED TO QUIT MY SUDOKU HABIT COLD TURKEY.
WHAT MADE YOU DO IT?
I REALIZED THAT I'VE BEEN FILLING MY LIFE WITH TRIVIAL FLUFF, AND IT'S NOT HEALTHY.
IT'S ESCAPISM. AND THIS OL' PLANET WILL NEVER GET BETTER IF WE DON'T FACE THE REALITY WE LIVE IN.
WHAT'S BEEN HAPPENING IN THE WORLD LATELY?
TOM CRUISE HAS A BABY, MADONNA DOESN'T.
DO YOU LOVE ME, SHERMAN?
OF COURSE.
DO YOU LOVE ME FULLY, UNCONDITIONALLY, ABSOLUTELY, COMPLETELY, AND WITH AN ANTIQUE DIAMOND BRACELET?
TAP TAP TAP
WHAT WAS THAT LAST PART?
TOO LATE. MY EBAY BID IS IN.

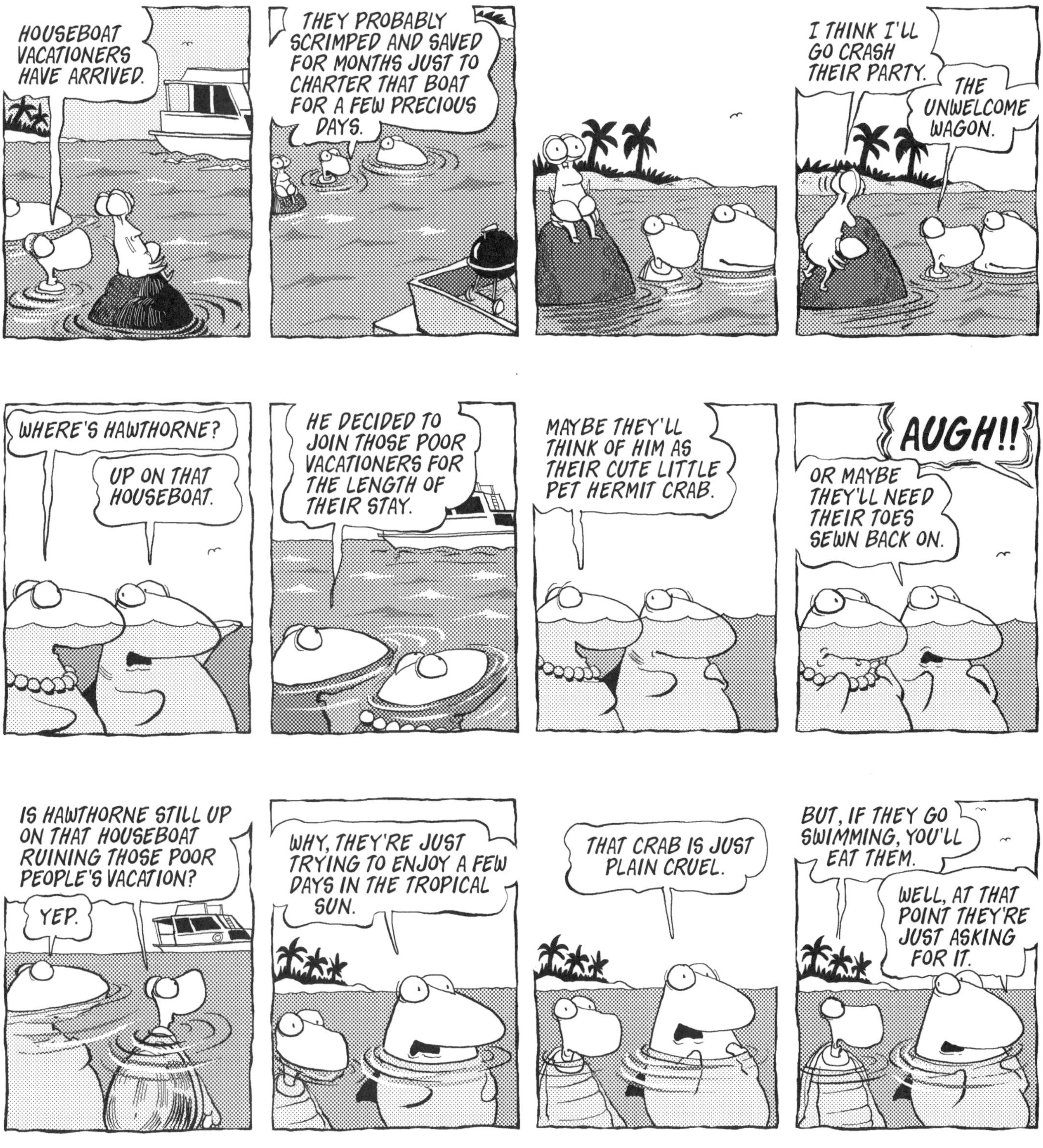
HOUSEBOAT VACATIONERS HAVE ARRIVED.
THEY PROBABLY SCRIMPED AND SAVED FOR MONTHS JUST TO CHARTER THAT BOAT FOR A FEW PRECIOUS DAYS.
I THINK I'LL GO CRASH THEIR PARTY.
THE UNWELCOME WAGON.
WHERE'S HAWTHORNE?
UP ON THAT HOUSEBOAT.
HE DECIDED TO JOIN THOSE POOR VACATIONERS FOR THE LENGTH OF THEIR STAY.
MAYBE THEY'LL THINK OF HIM AS THEIR CUTE LITTLE PET HERMIT CRAB.
AUGH!!
OR MAYBE THEY'LL NEED THEIR TOES SEWN BACK ON.
IS HAWTHORNE STILL UP ON THAT HOUSEBOAT RUINING THOSE POOR PEOPLE'S VACATION?
YEP.
WHY, THEY'RE JUST TRYING TO ENJOY A FEW DAYS IN THE TROPICAL SUN.
THAT CRAB IS JUST PLAIN CRUEL.
BUT, IF THEY GO SWIMMING, YOU'LL EAT THEM.
WELL, AT THAT POINT THEY'RE JUST ASKING FOR IT.

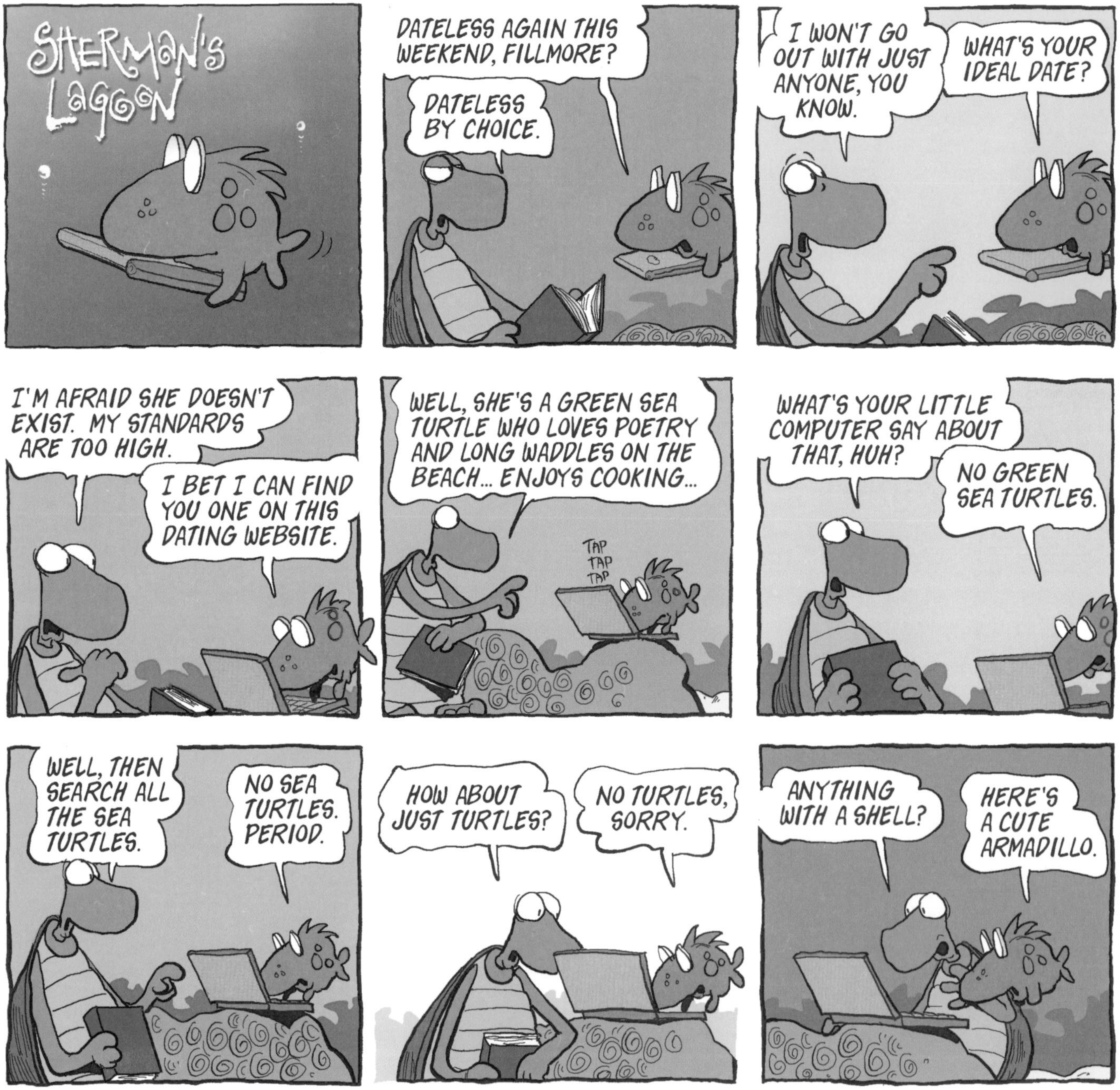
SHERMAN'S LAGOON
DATELESS AGAIN THIS WEEKEND, FILLMORE?
DATELESS BY CHOICE.
I WON'T GO OUT WITH JUST ANYONE, YOU KNOW.
WHAT'S YOUR IDEAL DATE?
I'M AFRAID SHE DOESN'T EXIST. MY STANDARDS ARE TOO HIGH.
I BET I CAN FIND YOU ONE ON THIS DATING WEBSITE.
WELL, SHE'S A GREEN SEA TURTLE WHO LOVES POETRY AND LONG WADDLES ON THE BEACH... ENJOYS COOKING...
TAP TAP TAP
WHAT'S YOUR LITTLE COMPUTER SAY ABOUT THAT, HUH?
NO GREEN SEA TURTLES.
WELL, THEN SEARCH ALL THE SEA TURTLES.
NO SEA TURTLES. PERIOD.
HOW ABOUT JUST TURTLES?
NO TURTLES, SORRY.
ANYTHING WITH A SHELL?
HERE'S A CUTE ARMADILLO.

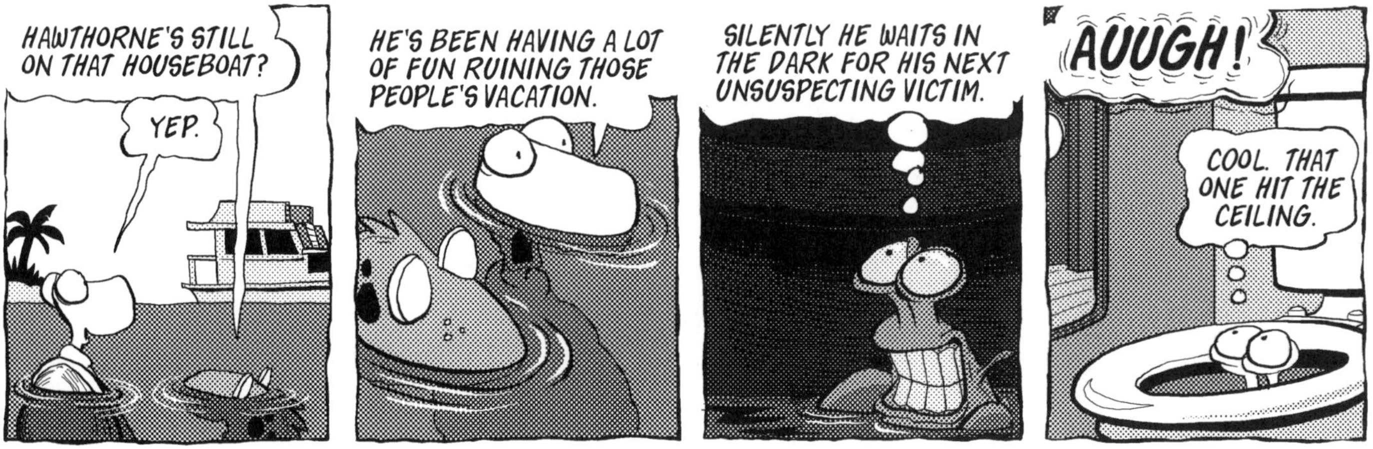
HAWTHORNE'S STILL ON THAT HOUSEBOAT?
YEP.
HE'S BEEN HAVING A LOT OF FUN RUINING THOSE PEOPLE'S VACATION.
SILENTLY HE WAITS IN THE DARK FOR HIS NEXT UNSUSPECTING VICTIM.
AUUGH!
COOL. THAT ONE HIT THE CEILING.

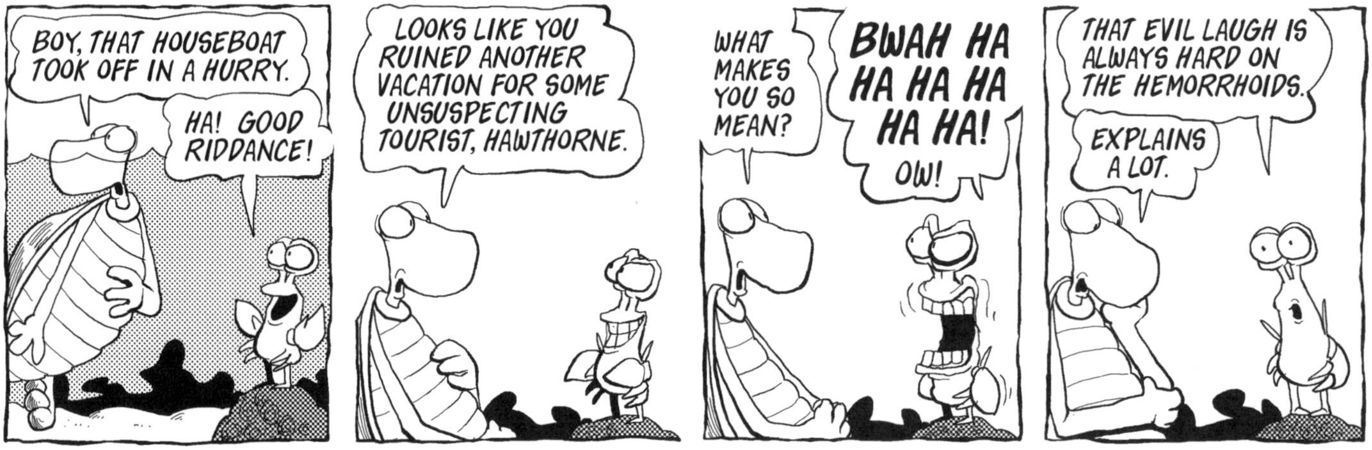
BOY, THAT HOUSEBOAT TOOK OFF IN A HURRY.
HA! GOOD RIDDANCE!
LOOKS LIKE YOU RUINED ANOTHER VACATION FOR SOME UNSUSPECTING TOURIST, HAWTHORNE.
WHAT MAKES YOU SO MEAN?
BWAH HA HA HA HA HA HA!
OW!
THAT EVIL LAUGH IS ALWAYS HARD ON THE HEMORRHOIDS.
EXPLAINS A LOT.

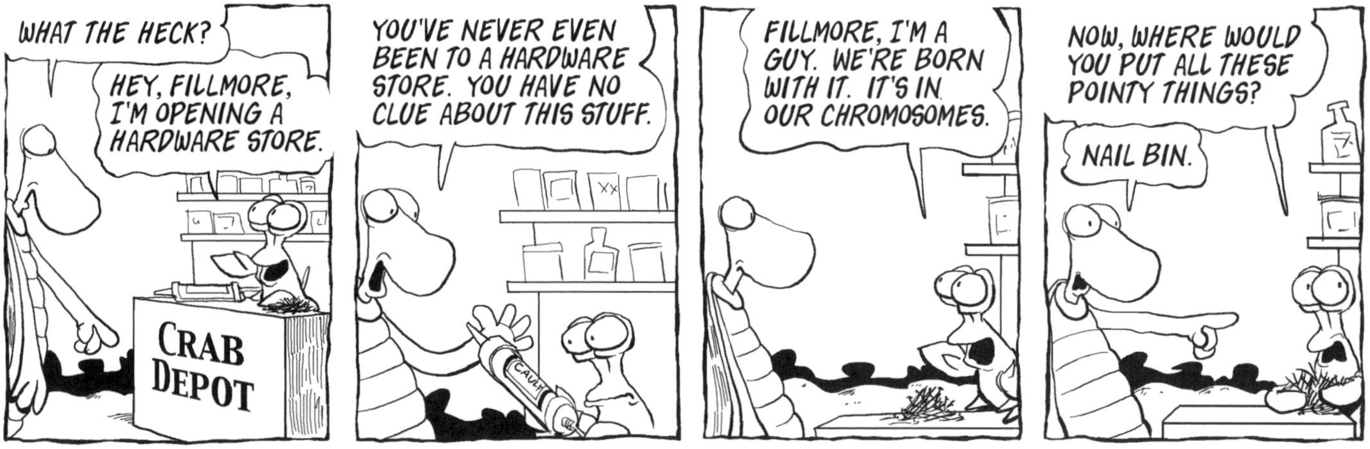
WHAT THE HECK?
HEY, FILLMORE, I'M OPENING A HARDWARE STORE.
CRAB DEPOT
YOU'VE NEVER EVEN BEEN TO A HARDWARE STORE. YOU HAVE NO CLUE ABOUT THIS STUFF.
FILLMORE, I'M A GUY. WE'RE BORN WITH IT. IT'S IN OUR CHROMOSOMES.
NOW, WHERE WOULD YOU PUT ALL THESE POINTY THINGS?
NAIL BIN.

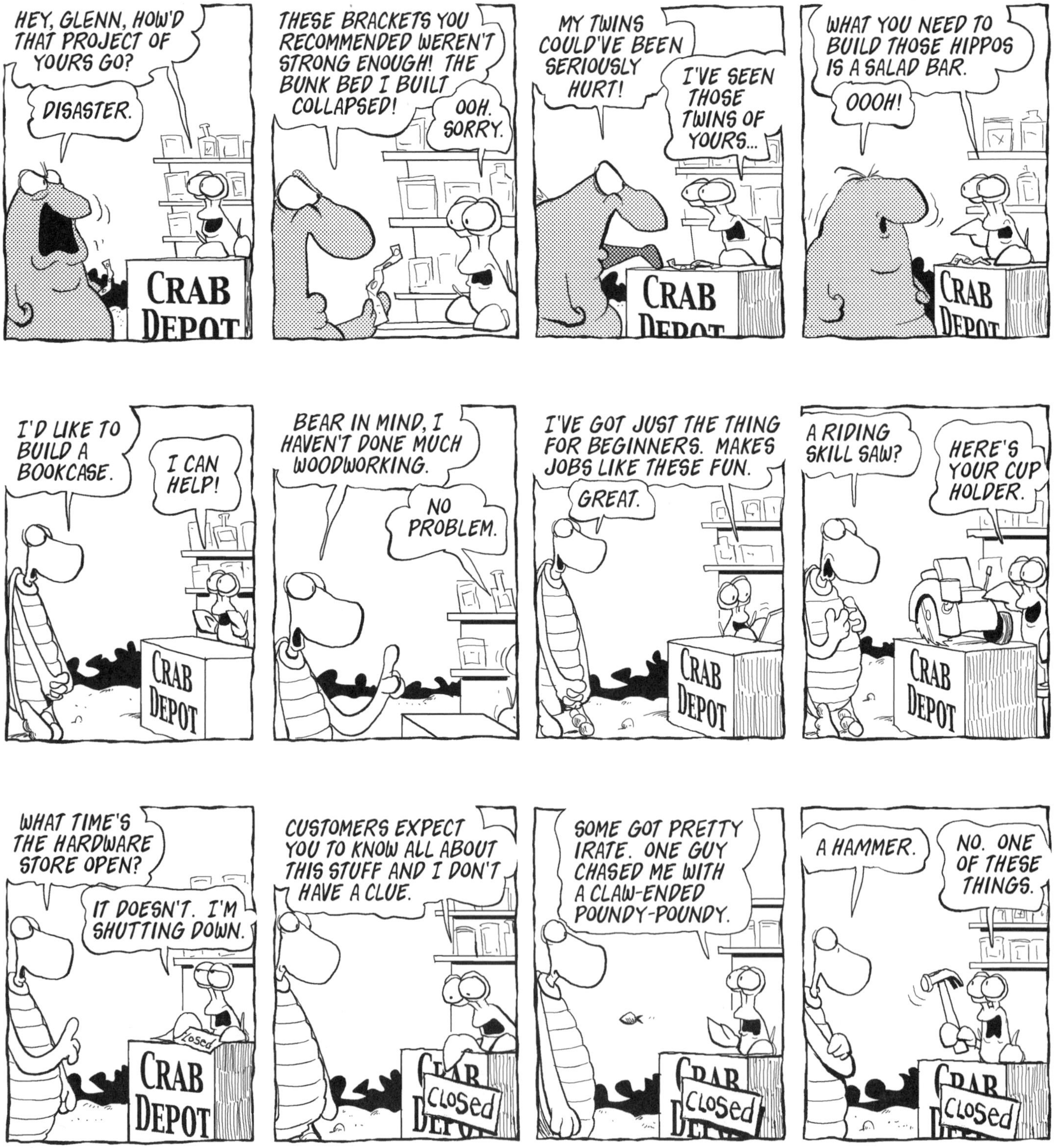
HEY, GLENN, HOW'D THAT PROJECT OF YOURS GO?
DISASTER.
CRAB DEPOT
THESE BRACKETS YOU RECOMMENDED WEREN'T STRONG ENOUGH! THE BUNK BED I BUILT COLLAPSED!
OOH. SORRY.
MY TWINS COULD'VE BEEN SERIOUSLY HURT!
I'VE SEEN THOSE TWINS OF YOURS...
CRAB
WHAT YOU NEED TO BUILD THOSE HIPPOS IS A SALAD BAR.
OOOH!
CRAB
I'D LIKE TO BUILD A BOOKCASE.
I CAN HELP!
CRAB DEPOT
BEAR IN MIND, I HAVEN'T DONE MUCH WOODWORKING.
NO PROBLEM.
I'VE GOT JUST THE THING FOR BEGINNERS. MAKES JOBS LIKE THESE FUN.
GREAT.
CRAB DEPOT
A RIDING SKILL SAW?
HERE'S YOUR CUP HOLDER.
CRAB DEPOT
WHAT TIME'S THE HARDWARE STORE OPEN?
IT DOESN'T. I'M SHUTTING DOWN.
Closed
CRAB DEPOT
CUSTOMERS EXPECT YOU TO KNOW ALL ABOUT THIS STUFF AND I DON'T HAVE A CLUE.
CLOSED
SOME GOT PRETTY IRATE. ONE GUY CHASED ME WITH A CLAW-ENDED POUNDY-POUNDY.
CLOSED
A HAMMER.
NO. ONE OF THESE THINGS.
CLOSED

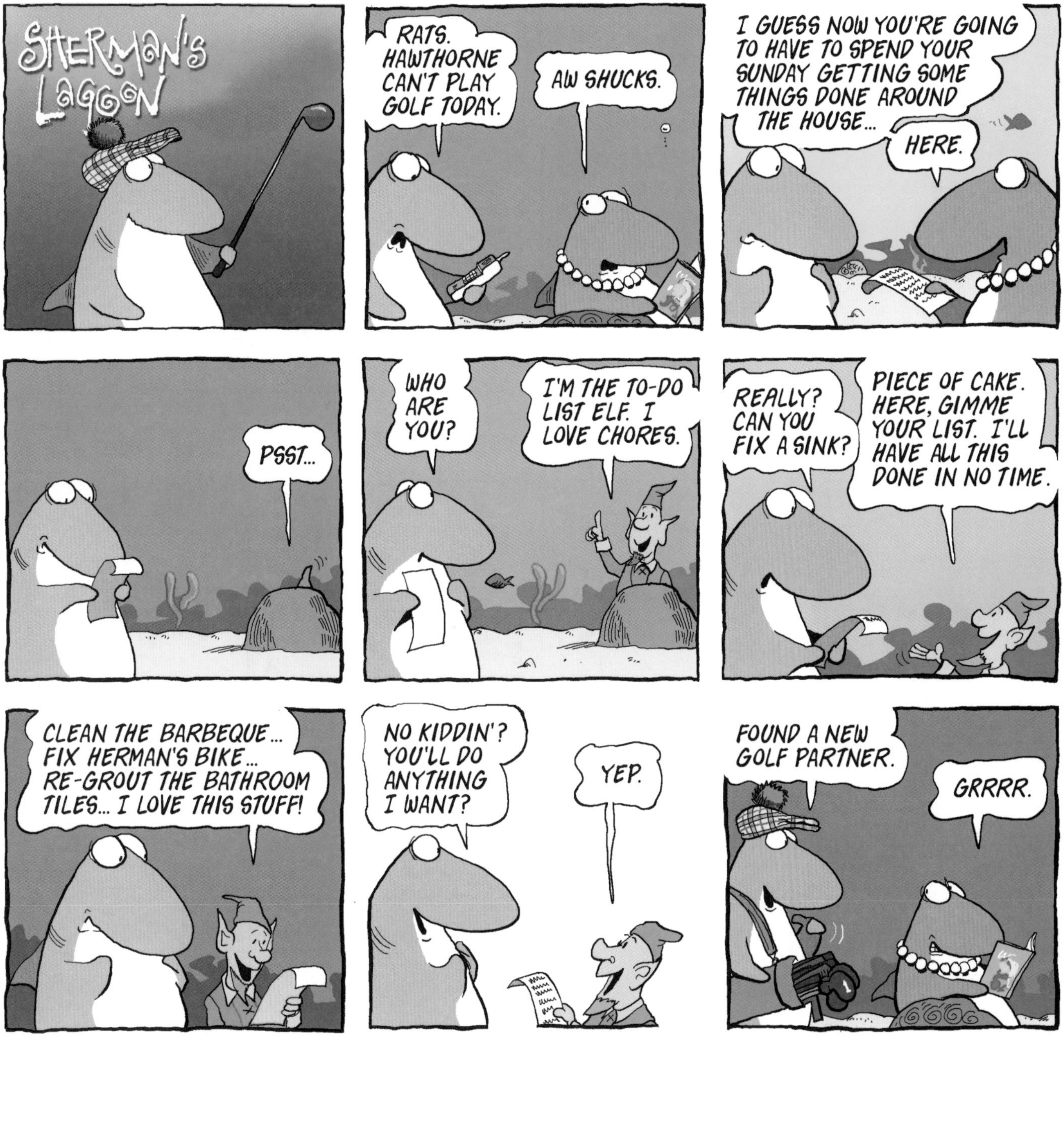
SHERMAN'S LAGOON
RATS. HAWTHORNE CAN'T PLAY GOLF TODAY.
AW SHUCKS.
I GUESS NOW YOU'RE GOING TO HAVE TO SPEND YOUR SUNDAY GETTING SOME THINGS DONE AROUND THE HOUSE...
HERE.
PSST...
WHO ARE YOU?
I'M THE TO-DO LIST ELF. I LOVE CHORES.
REALLY? CAN YOU FIX A SINK?
PIECE OF CAKE. HERE, GIMME YOUR LIST. I'LL HAVE ALL THIS DONE IN NO TIME.
CLEAN THE BARBEQUE... FIX HERMAN'S BIKE... RE-GROUT THE BATHROOM TILES... I LOVE THIS STUFF!
NO KIDDIN'? YOU'LL DO ANYTHING I WANT?
YEP.
FOUND A NEW GOLF PARTNER.
GRRRR.

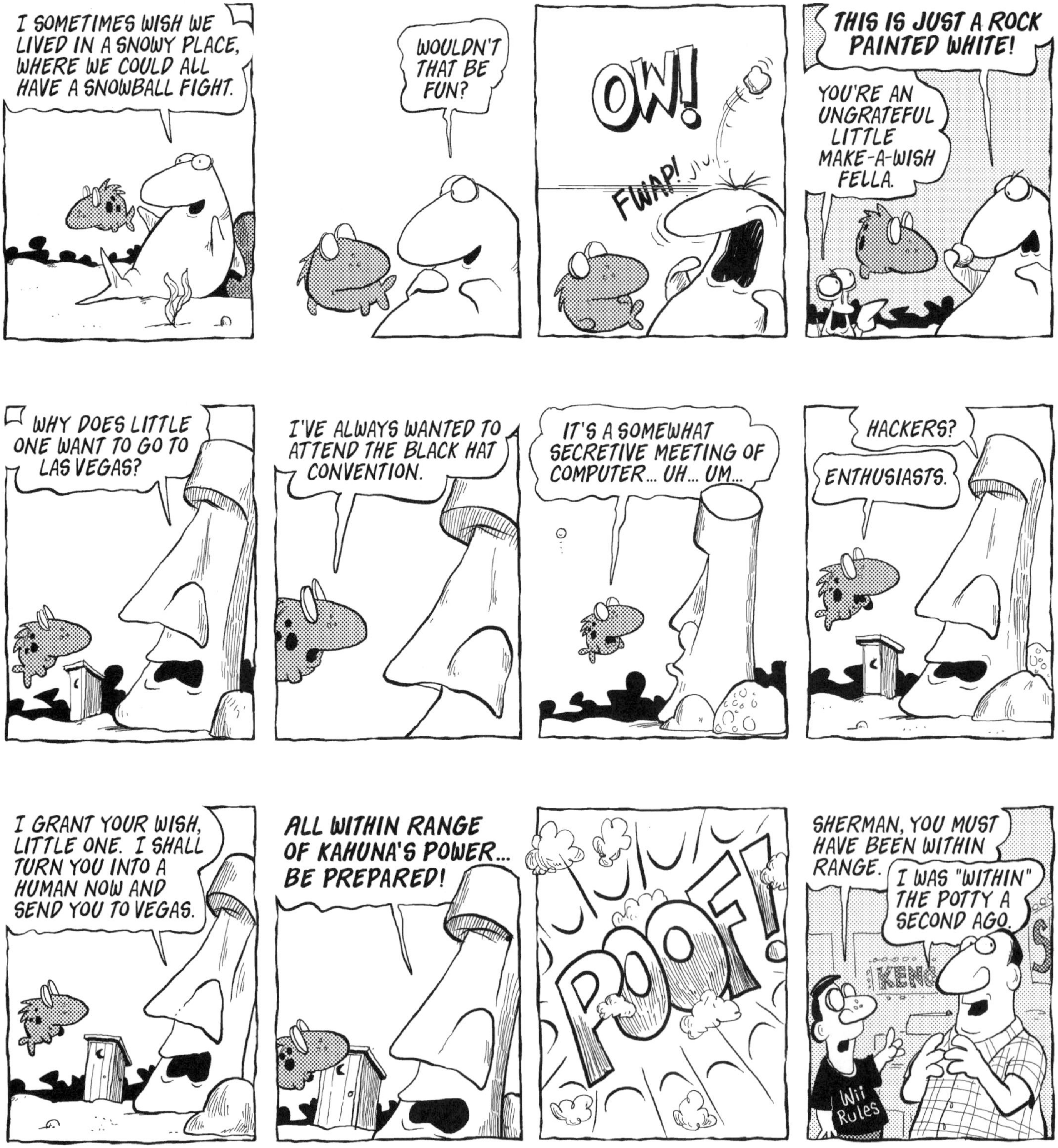
I SOMETIMES WISH WE LIVED IN A SNOWY PLACE, WHERE WE COULD ALL HAVE A SNOWBALL FIGHT.
WOULDN'T THAT BE FUN?
OW!
FWAP!
THIS IS JUST A ROCK PAINTED WHITE!
YOU'RE AN UNGRATEFUL LITTLE MAKE-A-WISH FELLA.
WHY DOES LITTLE ONE WANT TO GO TO LAS VEGAS?
I'VE ALWAYS WANTED TO ATTEND THE BLACK HAT CONVENTION.
IT'S A SOMEWHAT SECRETIVE MEETING OF COMPUTER... UH... UM...
HACKERS?
ENTHUSIASTS.
I GRANT YOUR WISH, LITTLE ONE. I SHALL TURN YOU INTO A HUMAN NOW AND SEND YOU TO VEGAS.
ALL WITHIN RANGE OF KAHUNA'S POWER... BE PREPARED!
POOF!
SHERMAN, YOU MUST HAVE BEEN WITHIN RANGE.
I WAS "WITHIN" THE POTTY A SECOND AGO.
KENO
Wii Rules

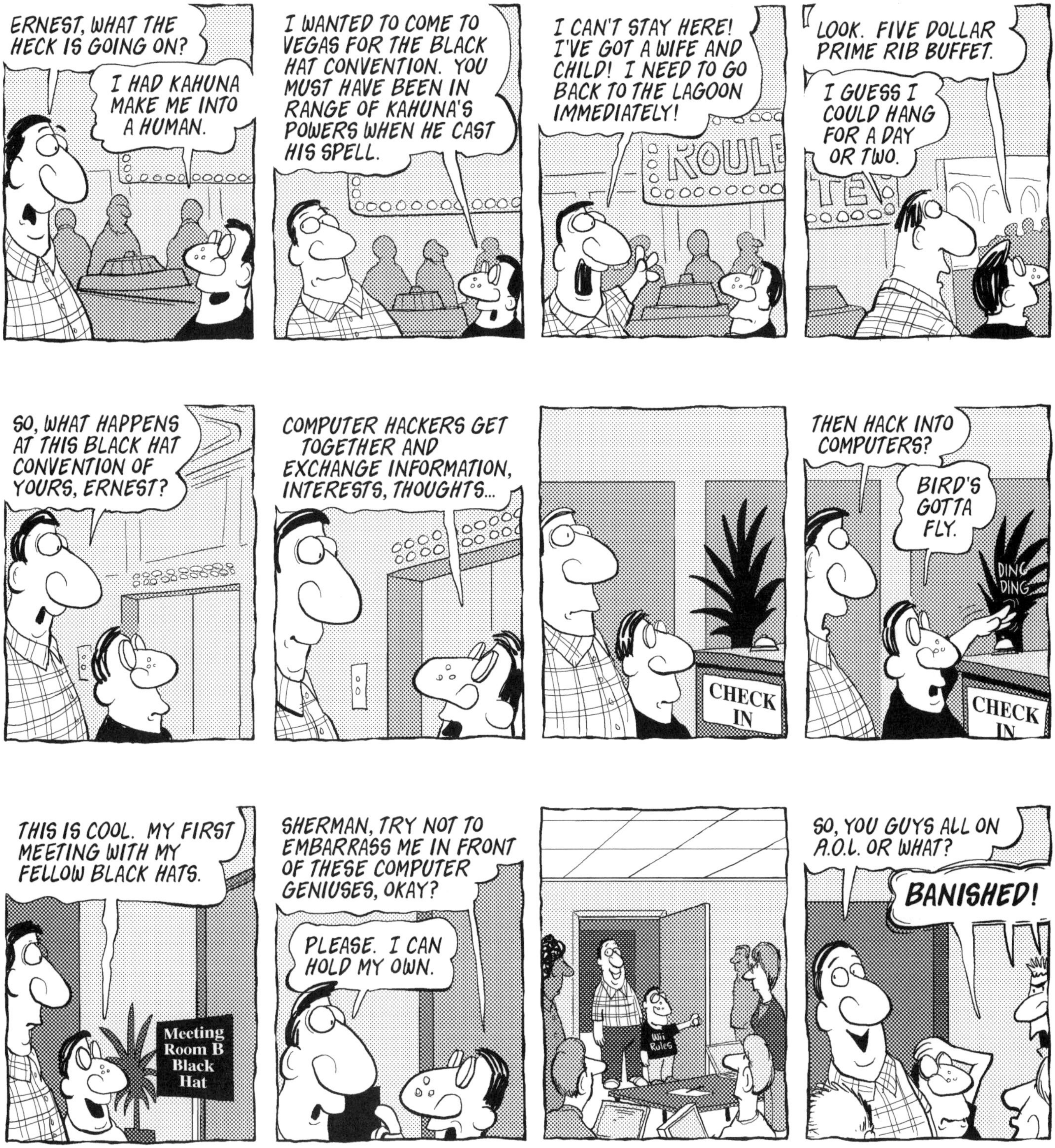
ERNEST, WHAT THE HECK IS GOING ON?
I HAD KAHUNA MAKE ME INTO A HUMAN.
I WANTED TO COME TO VEGAS FOR THE BLACK HAT CONVENTION. YOU MUST HAVE BEEN IN RANGE OF KAHUNA'S POWERS WHEN HE CAST HIS SPELL.
I CAN'T STAY HERE! I'VE GOT A WIFE AND CHILD! I NEED TO GO BACK TO THE LAGOON IMMEDIATELY!
LOOK. FIVE DOLLAR PRIME RIB BUFFET.
I GUESS I COULD HANG FOR A DAY OR TWO.
SO, WHAT HAPPENS AT THIS BLACK HAT CONVENTION OF YOURS, ERNEST?
COMPUTER HACKERS GET TOGETHER AND EXCHANGE INFORMATION, INTERESTS, THOUGHTS...
CHECK IN
THEN HACK INTO COMPUTERS?
BIRD'S GOTTA FLY.
DING DING
CHECK IN
THIS IS COOL. MY FIRST MEETING WITH MY FELLOW BLACK HATS.
Meeting Room B Black Hat
SHERMAN, TRY NOT TO EMBARRASS ME IN FRONT OF THESE COMPUTER GENIUSES, OKAY?
PLEASE. I CAN HOLD MY OWN.
SO, YOU GUYS ALL ON A.O.L. OR WHAT?
BANISHED!

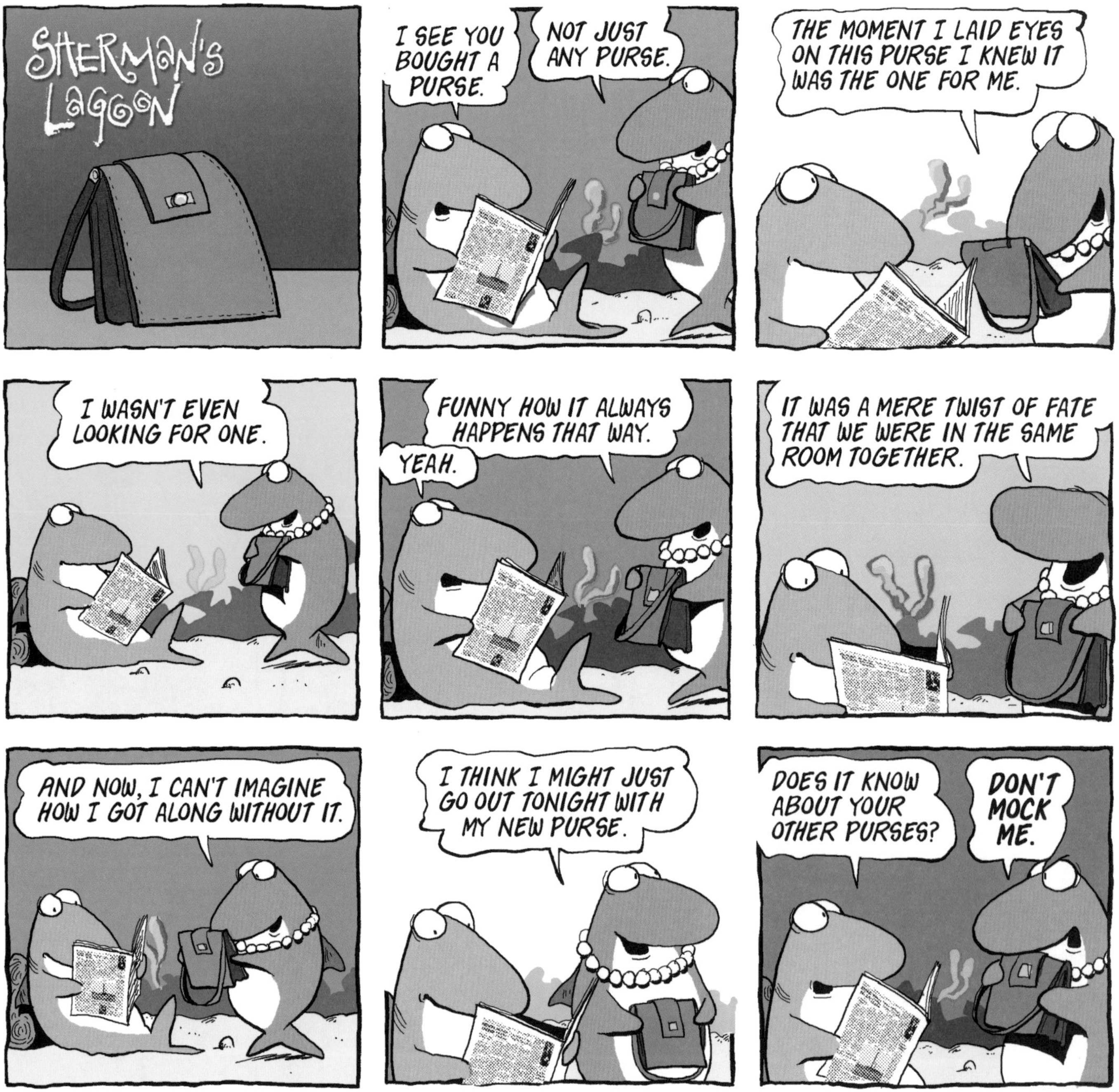
SHERMAN'S LAGOON
I SEE YOU BOUGHT A PURSE.
NOT JUST ANY PURSE.
THE MOMENT I LAID EYES ON THIS PURSE I KNEW IT WAS THE ONE FOR ME.
I WASN'T EVEN LOOKING FOR ONE.
FUNNY HOW IT ALWAYS HAPPENS THAT WAY.
YEAH.
IT WAS A MERE TWIST OF FATE THAT WE WERE IN THE SAME ROOM TOGETHER.
AND NOW, I CAN'T IMAGINE HOW I GOT ALONG WITHOUT IT.
I THINK I MIGHT JUST GO OUT TONIGHT WITH MY NEW PURSE.
DOES IT KNOW ABOUT YOUR OTHER PURSES?
DON'T MOCK ME.

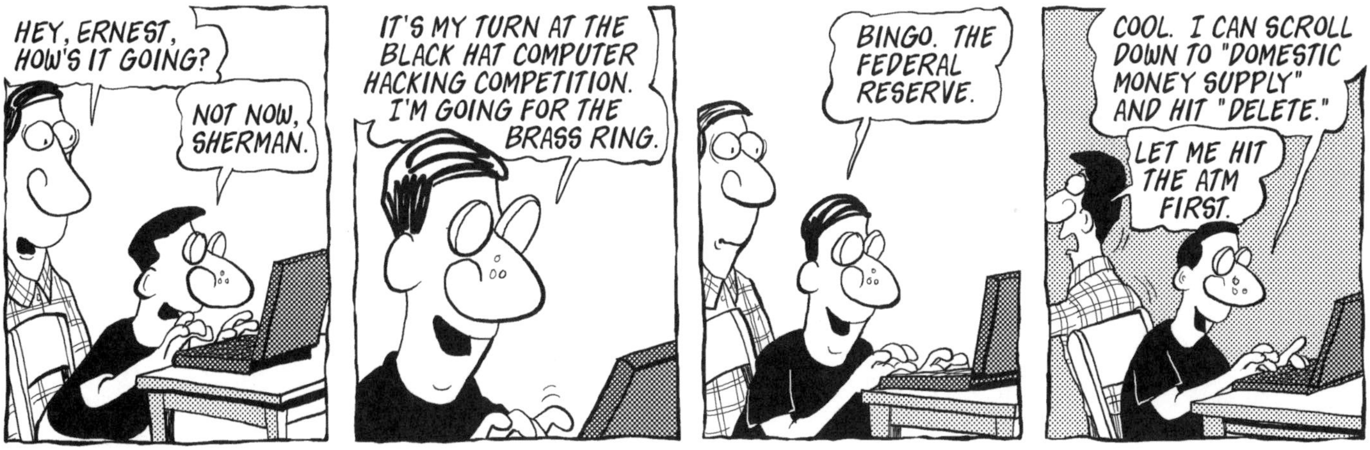
HEY, ERNEST, HOW'S IT GOING?
NOT NOW, SHERMAN.
IT'S MY TURN AT THE BLACK HAT COMPUTER HACKING COMPETITION. I'M GOING FOR THE BRASS RING.
BINGO. THE FEDERAL RESERVE.
COOL. I CAN SCROLL DOWN TO "DOMESTIC MONEY SUPPLY" AND HIT "DELETE."
LET ME HIT THE ATM FIRST.

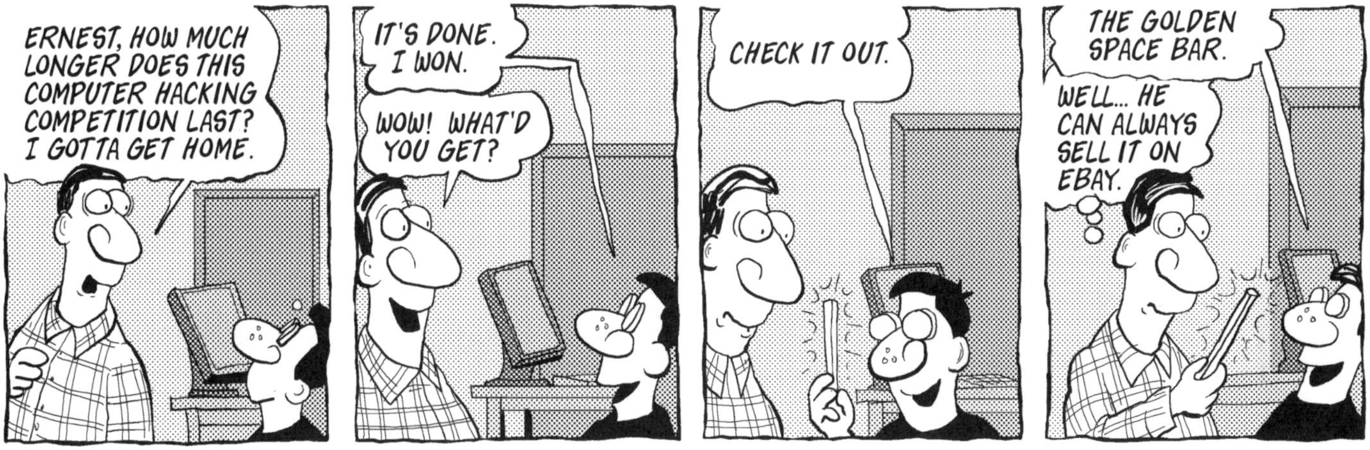
ERNEST, HOW MUCH LONGER DOES THIS COMPUTER HACKING COMPETITION LAST? I GOTTA GET HOME.
IT'S DONE. I WON.
WOW! WHAT'D YOU GET?
CHECK IT OUT.
THE GOLDEN SPACE BAR.
WELL... HE CAN ALWAYS SELL IT ON EBAY.

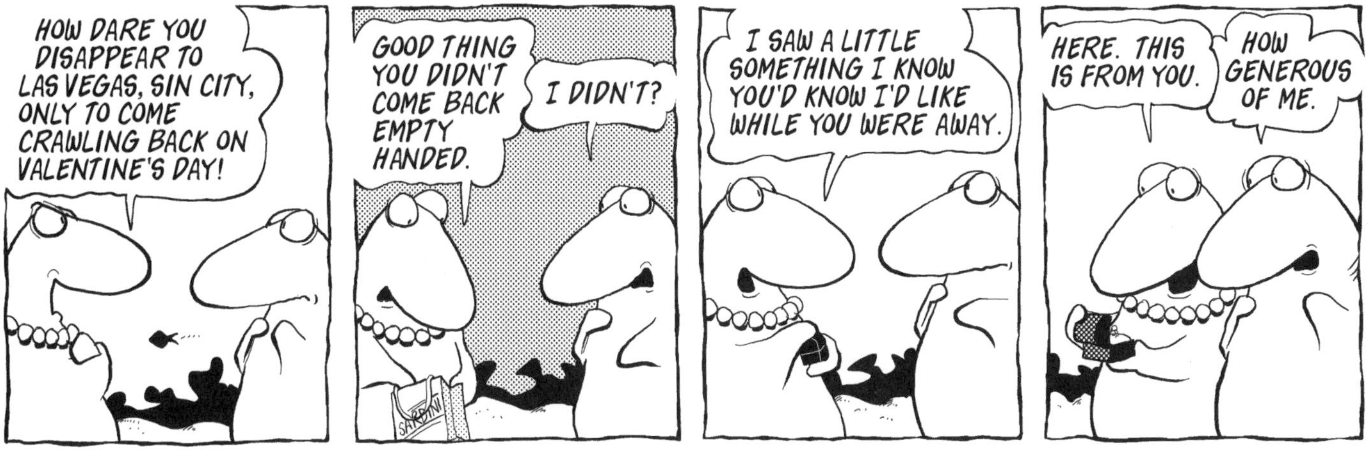
HOW DARE YOU DISAPPEAR TO LAS VEGAS, SIN CITY, ONLY TO COME CRAWLING BACK ON VALENTINE'S DAY!
GOOD THING YOU DIDN'T COME BACK EMPTY HANDED.
I DIDN'T?
SARDINI
I SAW A LITTLE SOMETHING I KNOW YOU'D KNOW I'D LIKE WHILE YOU WERE AWAY.
HERE. THIS IS FROM YOU.
HOW GENEROUS OF ME.

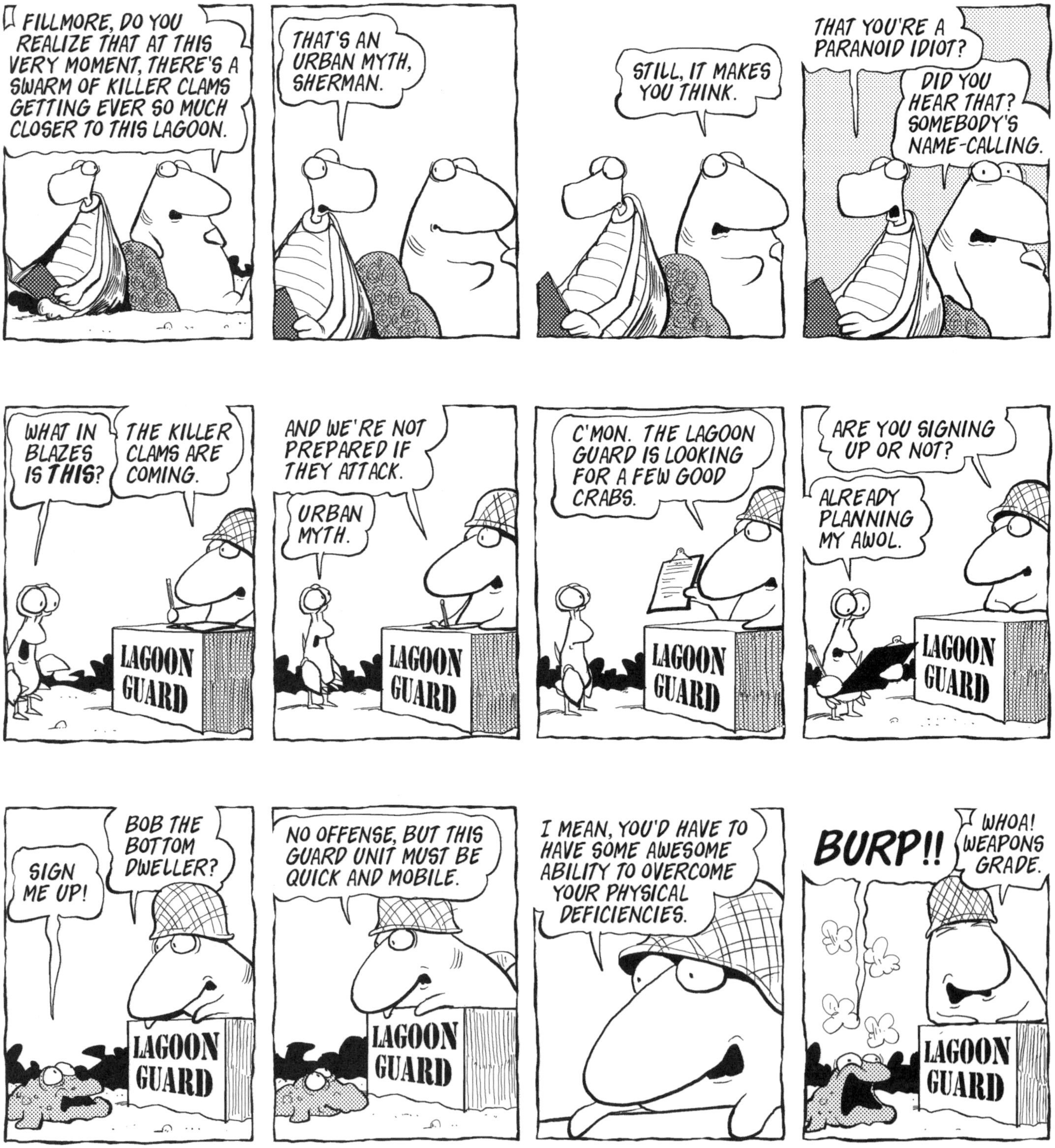
FILLMORE, DO YOU REALIZE THAT AT THIS VERY MOMENT, THERE'S A SWARM OF KILLER CLAMS GETTING EVER SO MUCH CLOSER TO THIS LAGOON.
THAT'S AN URBAN MYTH, SHERMAN.
STILL, IT MAKES YOU THINK.
THAT YOU'RE A PARANOID IDIOT?
DID YOU HEAR THAT? SOMEBODY'S NAME-CALLING.
WHAT IN BLAZES IS THIS?
THE KILLER CLAMS ARE COMING.
LAGOON GUARD
AND WE'RE NOT PREPARED IF THEY ATTACK.
URBAN MYTH.
LAGOON GUARD
C'MON. THE LAGOON GUARD IS LOOKING FOR A FEW GOOD CRABS.
LAGOON GUARD
ARE YOU SIGNING UP OR NOT?
ALREADY PLANNING MY AWOL.
LAGOON GUARD
SIGN ME UP!
BOB THE BOTTOM DWELLER?
LAGOON GUARD
NO OFFENSE, BUT THIS GUARD UNIT MUST BE QUICK AND MOBILE.
LAGOON GUARD
I MEAN, YOU'D HAVE TO HAVE SOME AWESOME ABILITY TO OVERCOME YOUR PHYSICAL DEFICIENCIES.
BURP!!
WHOA! WEAPONS GRADE.
LAGOON GUARD

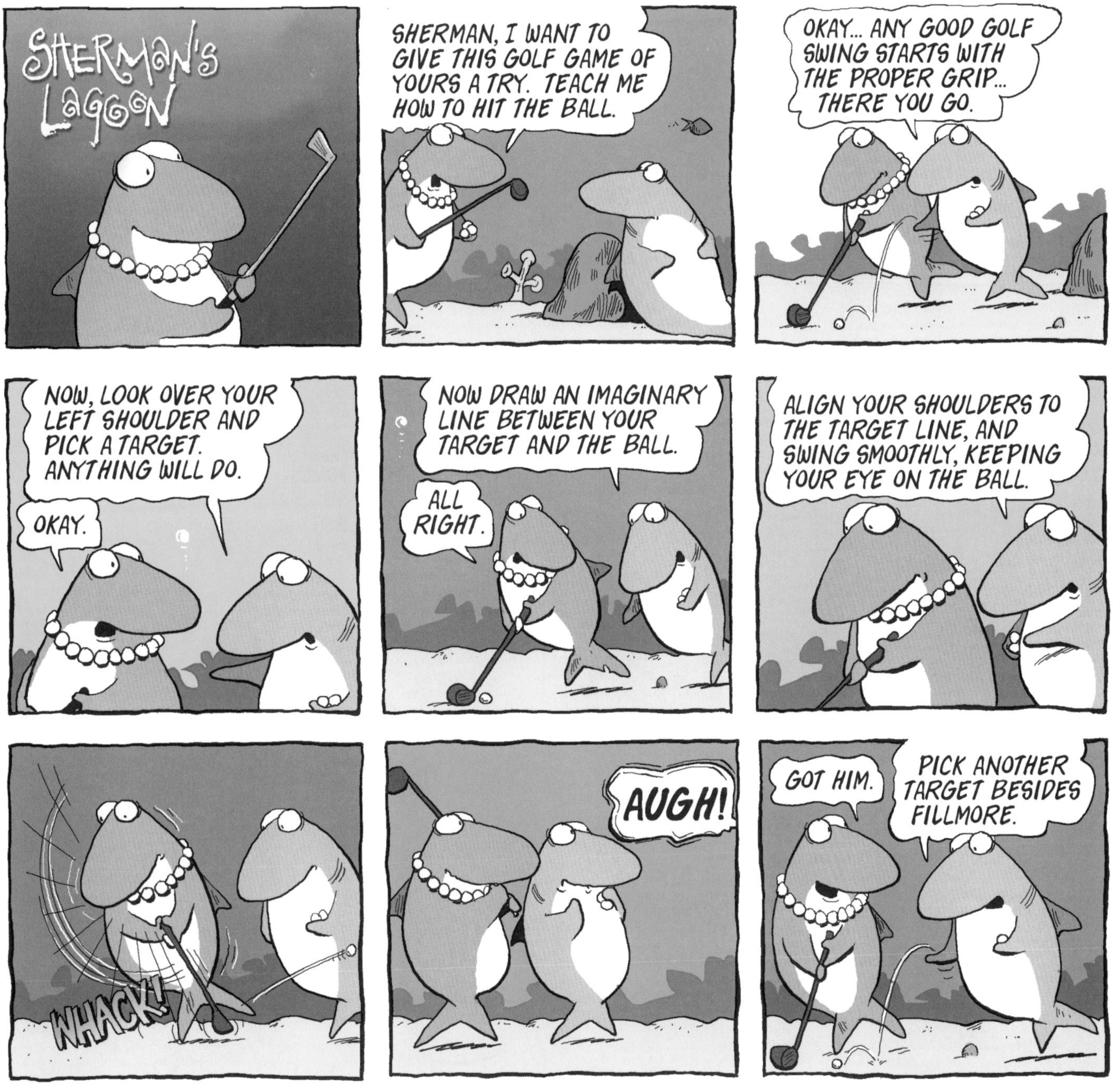
SHERMAN'S LAGOON
SHERMAN, I WANT TO GIVE THIS GOLF GAME OF YOURS A TRY. TEACH ME HOW TO HIT THE BALL.
OKAY... ANY GOOD GOLF SWING STARTS WITH THE PROPER GRIP... THERE YOU GO.
NOW, LOOK OVER YOUR LEFT SHOULDER AND PICK A TARGET. ANYTHING WILL DO.
OKAY.
NOW DRAW AN IMAGINARY LINE BETWEEN YOUR TARGET AND THE BALL.
ALL RIGHT.
ALIGN YOUR SHOULDERS TO THE TARGET LINE, AND SWING SMOOTHLY, KEEPING YOUR EYE ON THE BALL.
WHACK!
AUGH!
GOT HIM.
PICK ANOTHER TARGET BESIDES FILLMORE.

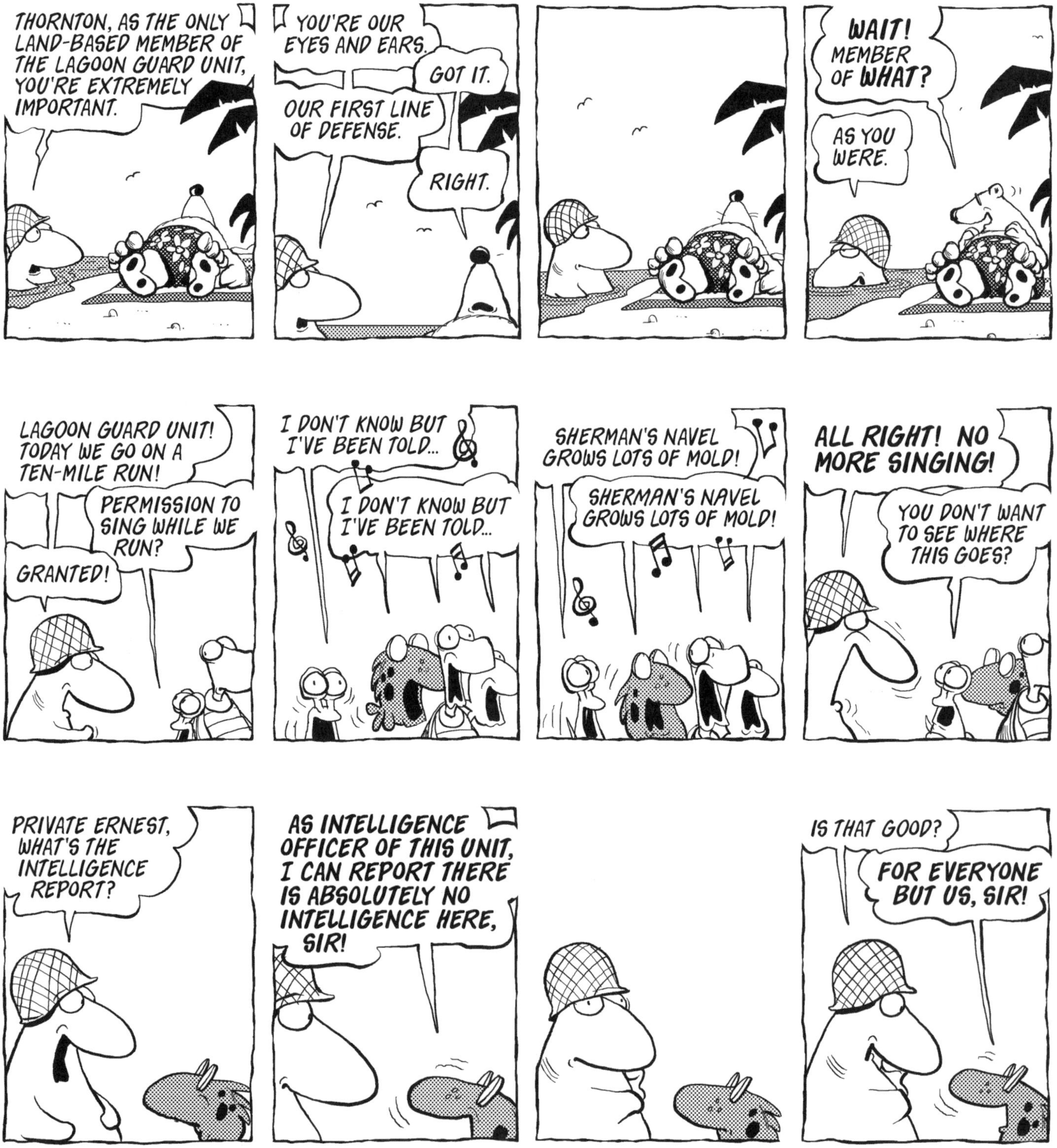
THORNTON, AS THE ONLY LAND-BASED MEMBER OF THE LAGOON GUARD UNIT, YOU'RE EXTREMELY IMPORTANT.
YOU'RE OUR EYES AND EARS.
GOT IT.
OUR FIRST LINE OF DEFENSE.
RIGHT.
WAIT! MEMBER OF WHAT?
AS YOU WERE.
LAGOON GUARD UNIT! TODAY WE GO ON A TEN-MILE RUN!
PERMISSION TO SING WHILE WE RUN?
GRANTED!
I DON'T KNOW BUT I'VE BEEN TOLD...
I DON'T KNOW BUT I'VE BEEN TOLD...
SHERMAN'S NAVEL GROWS LOTS OF MOLD!
SHERMAN'S NAVEL GROWS LOTS OF MOLD!
ALL RIGHT! NO MORE SINGING!
YOU DON'T WANT TO SEE WHERE THIS GOES?
PRIVATE ERNEST, WHAT'S THE INTELLIGENCE REPORT?
AS INTELLIGENCE OFFICER OF THIS UNIT, I CAN REPORT THERE IS ABSOLUTELY NO INTELLIGENCE HERE, SIR!
IS THAT GOOD?
FOR EVERYONE BUT US, SIR!

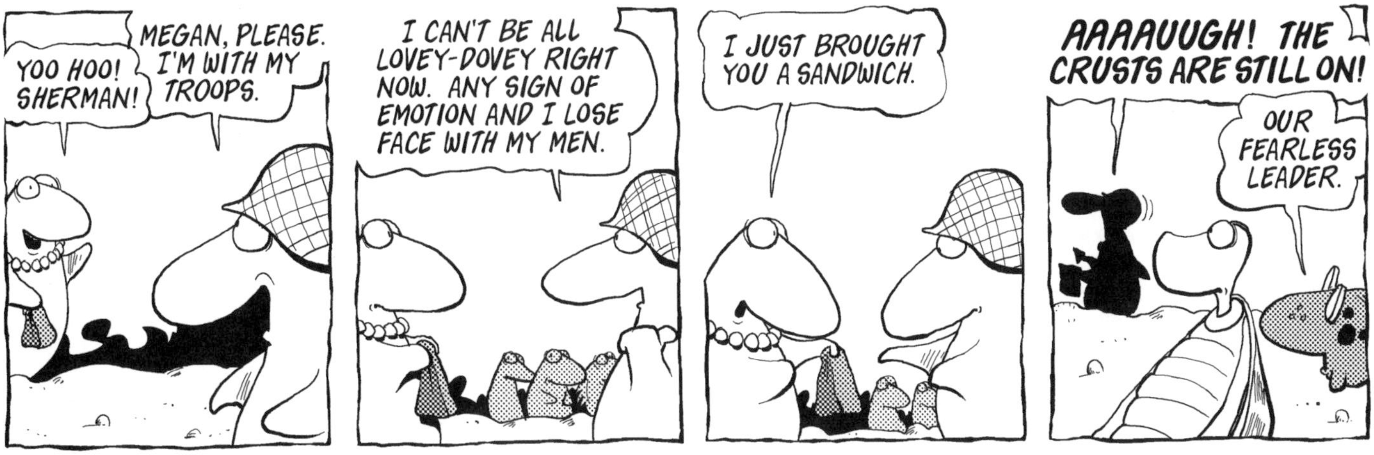
YOO HOO! SHERMAN!
MEGAN, PLEASE. I'M WITH MY TROOPS.
I CAN'T BE ALL LOVEY-DOVEY RIGHT NOW. ANY SIGN OF EMOTION AND I LOSE FACE WITH MY MEN.
I JUST BROUGHT YOU A SANDWICH.
AAAAUUGH! THE CRUSTS ARE STILL ON!
OUR FEARLESS LEADER.

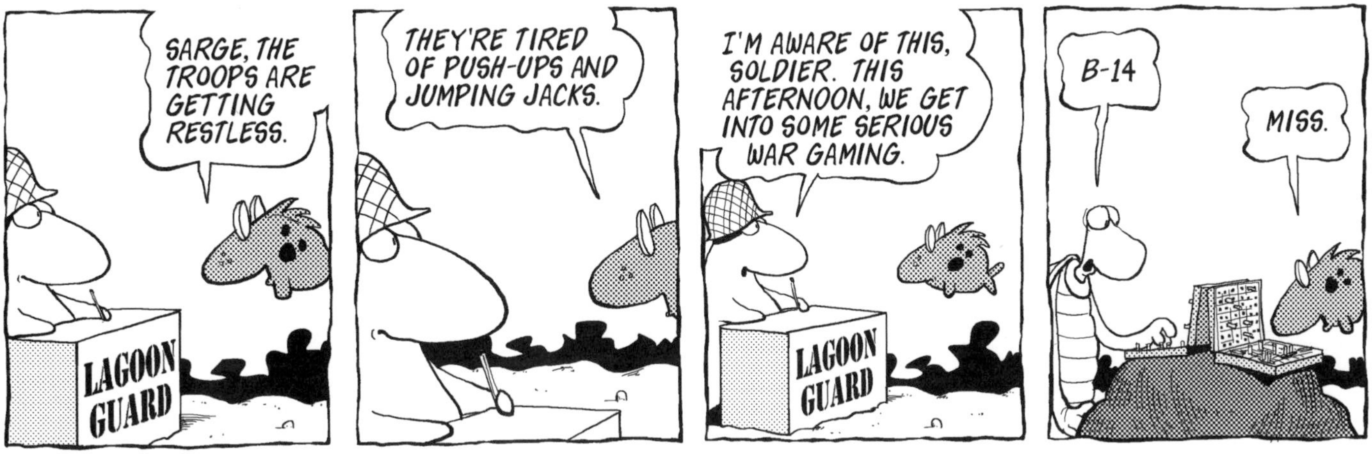
SARGE, THE TROOPS ARE GETTING RESTLESS.
LAGOON GUARD
THEY'RE TIRED OF PUSH-UPS AND JUMPING JACKS.
I'M AWARE OF THIS, SOLDIER. THIS AFTERNOON, WE GET INTO SOME SERIOUS WAR GAMING.
LAGOON GUARD
B-14
MISS.

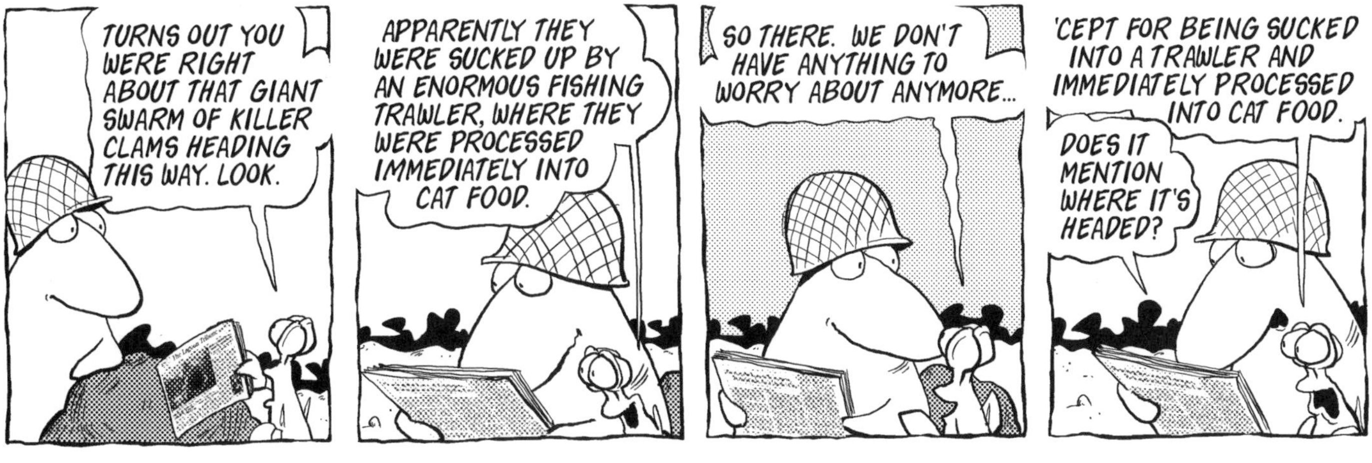
TURNS OUT YOU WERE RIGHT ABOUT THAT GIANT SWARM OF KILLER CLAMS HEADING THIS WAY. LOOK.
APPARENTLY THEY WERE SUCKED UP BY AN ENORMOUS FISHING TRAWLER, WHERE THEY WERE PROCESSED IMMEDIATELY INTO CAT FOOD.
SO THERE. WE DON'T HAVE ANYTHING TO WORRY ABOUT ANYMORE...
'CEPT FOR BEING SUCKED INTO A TRAWLER AND IMMEDIATELY PROCESSED INTO CAT FOOD.
DOES IT MENTION WHERE IT'S HEADED?

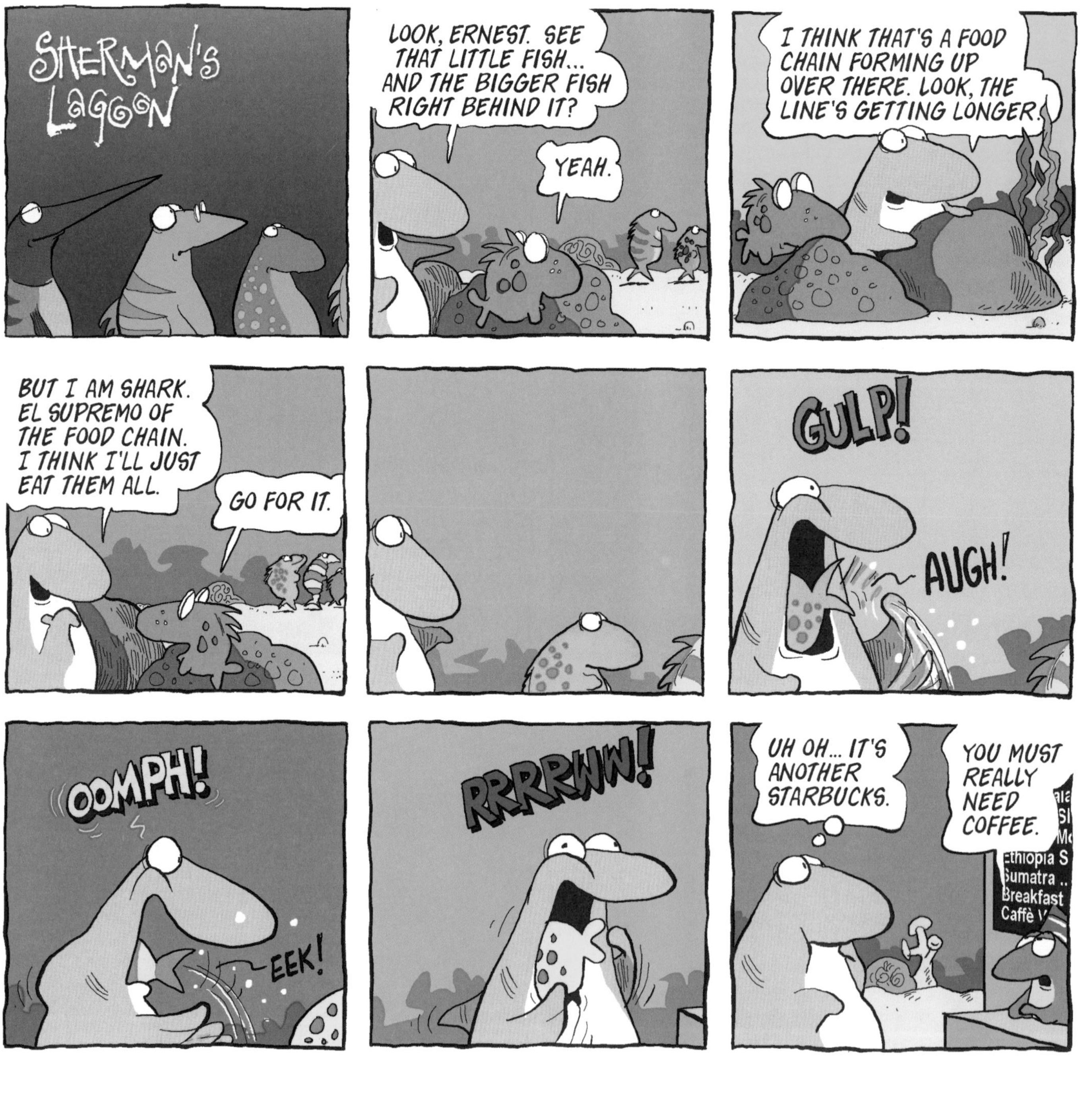
SHERMAN'S LAGOON
LOOK, ERNEST. SEE THAT LITTLE FISH... AND THE BIGGER FISH RIGHT BEHIND IT?
YEAH.
I THINK THAT'S A FOOD CHAIN FORMING UP OVER THERE. LOOK, THE LINE'S GETTING LONGER.
BUT I AM SHARK. EL SUPREMO OF THE FOOD CHAIN. I THINK I'LL JUST EAT THEM ALL.
GO FOR IT.
GULP!
AUGH!
OOMPH!
EEK!
RRRRWW!
UH OH... IT'S ANOTHER STARBUCKS.
YOU MUST REALLY NEED COFFEE.
Ethiopia
Sumatra
Breakfast
Caffè

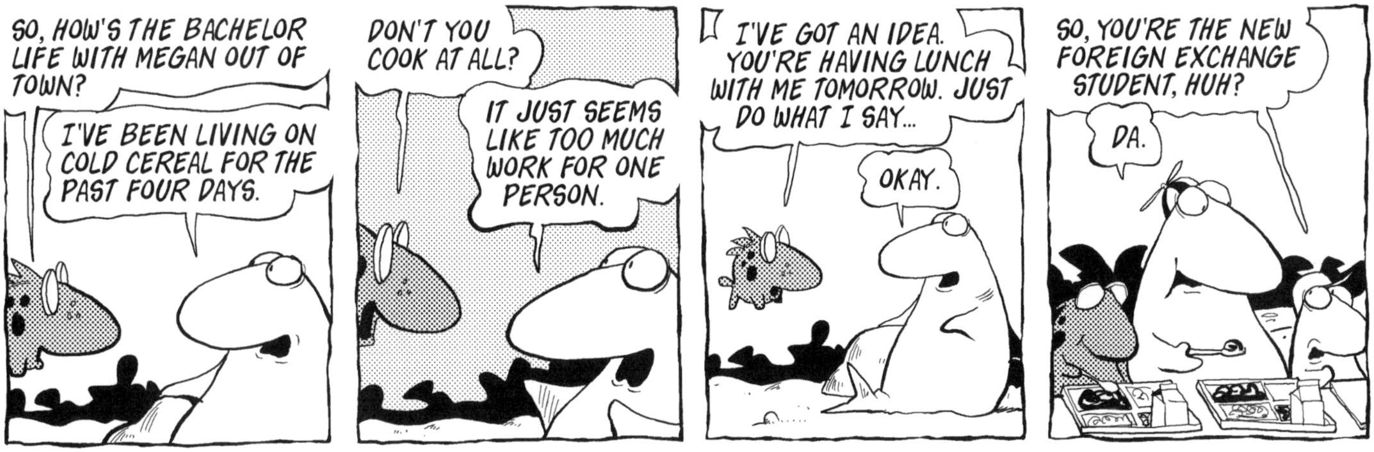
SO, HOW'S THE BACHELOR LIFE WITH MEGAN OUT OF TOWN?
I'VE BEEN LIVING ON COLD CEREAL FOR THE PAST FOUR DAYS.
DON'T YOU COOK AT ALL?
IT JUST SEEMS LIKE TOO MUCH WORK FOR ONE PERSON.
I'VE GOT AN IDEA. YOU'RE HAVING LUNCH WITH ME TOMORROW. JUST DO WHAT I SAY...
OKAY.
SO, YOU'RE THE NEW FOREIGN EXCHANGE STUDENT, HUH?
DA.

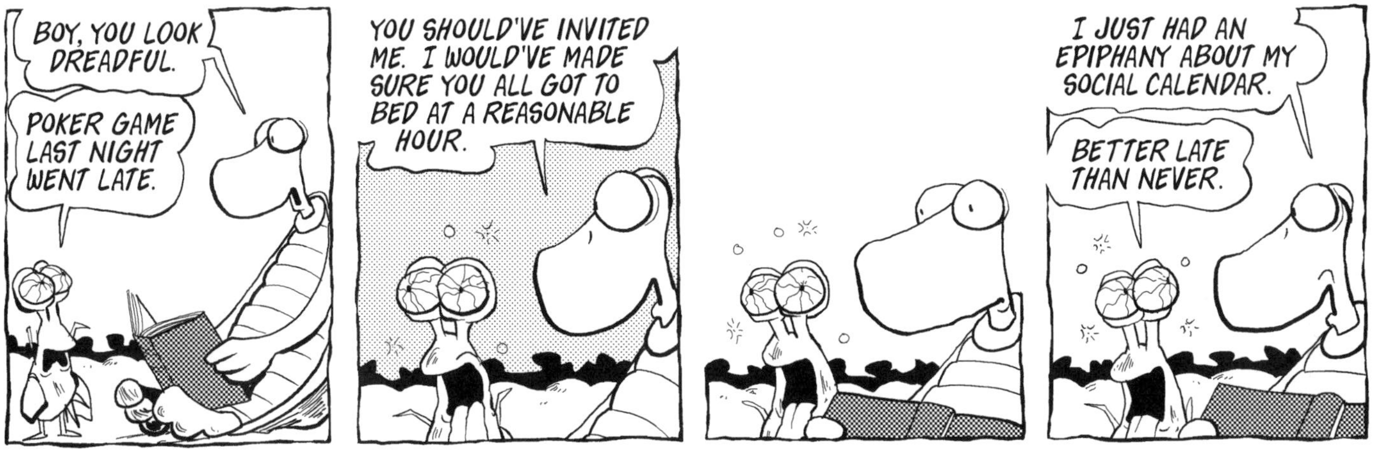
BOY, YOU LOOK DREADFUL.
POKER GAME LAST NIGHT WENT LATE.
YOU SHOULD'VE INVITED ME. I WOULD'VE MADE SURE YOU ALL GOT TO BED AT A REASONABLE HOUR.
I JUST HAD AN EPIPHANY ABOUT MY SOCIAL CALENDAR.
BETTER LATE THAN NEVER.

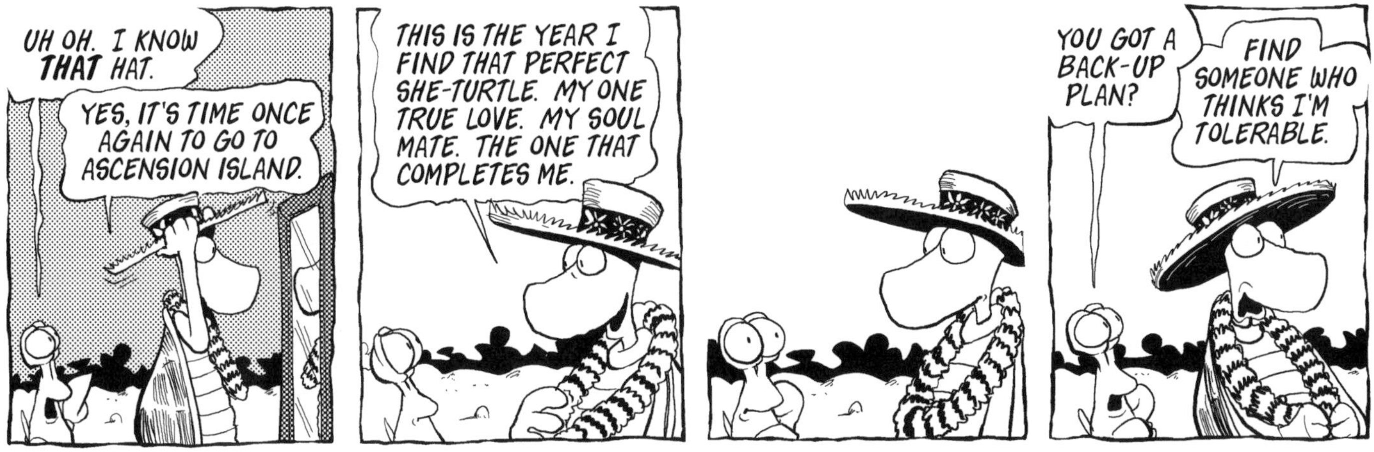
UH OH. I KNOW **THAT** HAT.
YES, IT'S TIME ONCE AGAIN TO GO TO ASCENSION ISLAND.
THIS IS THE YEAR I FIND THAT PERFECT SHE-TURTLE. MY ONE TRUE LOVE. MY SOUL MATE. THE ONE THAT COMPLETES ME.
YOU GOT A BACK-UP PLAN?
FIND SOMEONE WHO THINKS I'M TOLERABLE.

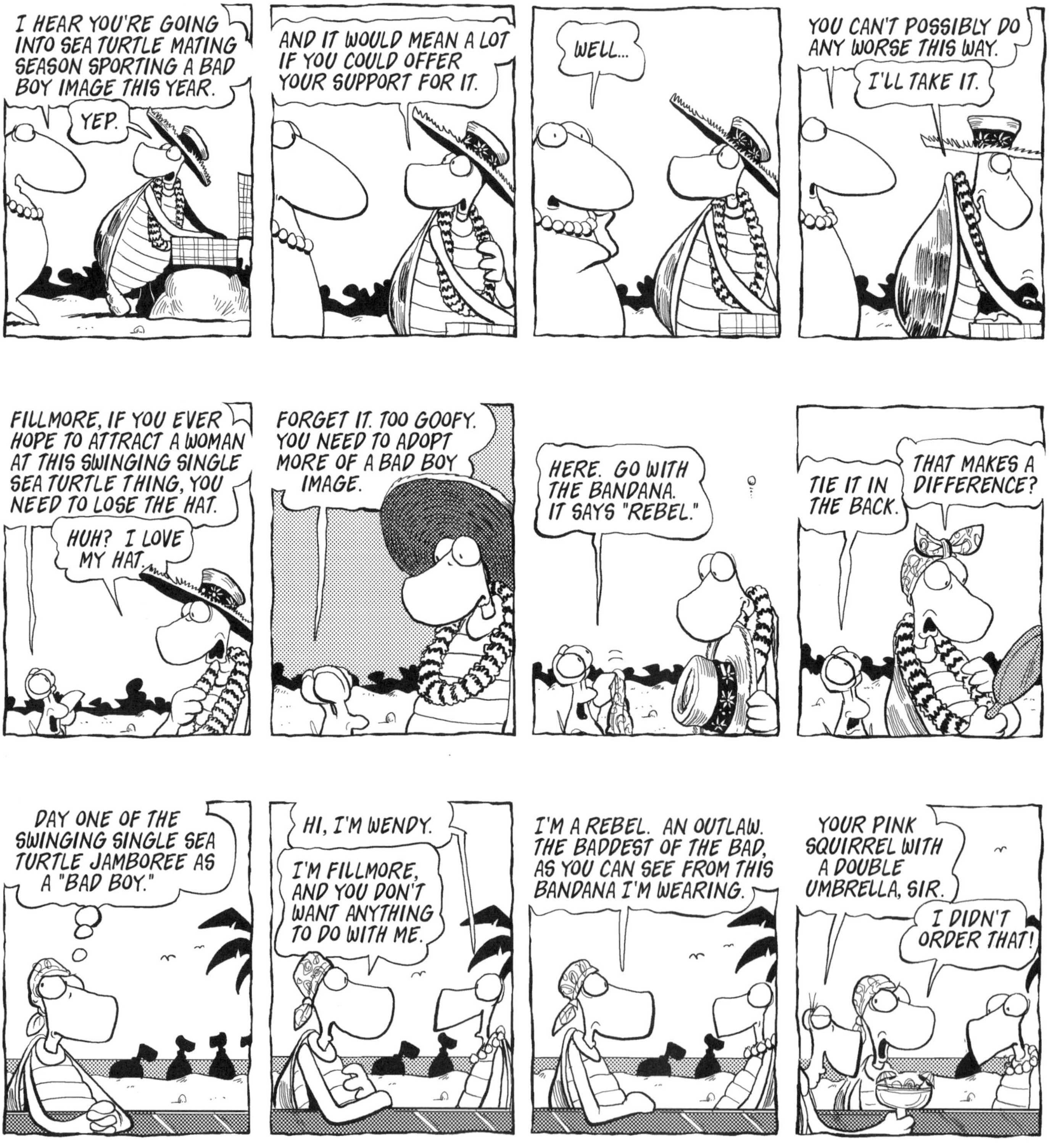
I HEAR YOU'RE GOING INTO SEA TURTLE MATING SEASON SPORTING A BAD BOY IMAGE THIS YEAR.
YEP.
AND IT WOULD MEAN A LOT IF YOU COULD OFFER YOUR SUPPORT FOR IT.
WELL...
YOU CAN'T POSSIBLY DO ANY WORSE THIS WAY.
I'LL TAKE IT.
FILLMORE, IF YOU EVER HOPE TO ATTRACT A WOMAN AT THIS SWINGING SINGLE SEA TURTLE THING, YOU NEED TO LOSE THE HAT.
HUH? I LOVE MY HAT.
FORGET IT. TOO GOOFY. YOU NEED TO ADOPT MORE OF A BAD BOY IMAGE.
HERE. GO WITH THE BANDANA. IT SAYS "REBEL."
TIE IT IN THE BACK.
THAT MAKES A DIFFERENCE?
DAY ONE OF THE SWINGING SINGLE SEA TURTLE JAMBOREE AS A "BAD BOY."
HI, I'M WENDY.
I'M FILLMORE, AND YOU DON'T WANT ANYTHING TO DO WITH ME.
I'M A REBEL. AN OUTLAW. THE BADDEST OF THE BAD, AS YOU CAN SEE FROM THIS BANDANA I'M WEARING.
YOUR PINK SQUIRREL WITH A DOUBLE UMBRELLA, SIR.
I DIDN'T ORDER THAT!

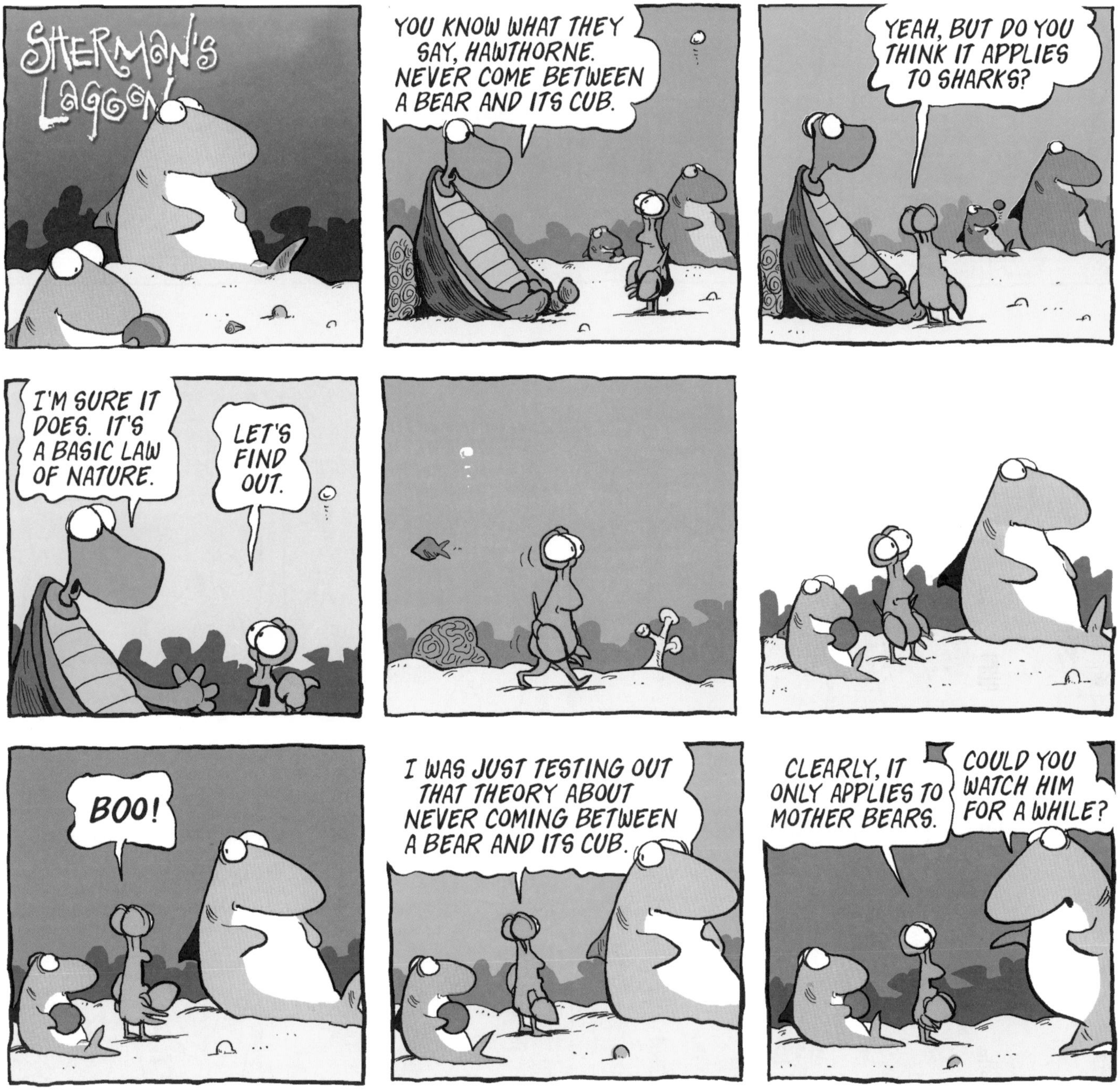
SHERMAN'S LAGOON
YOU KNOW WHAT THEY SAY, HAWTHORNE. NEVER COME BETWEEN A BEAR AND ITS CUB.
YEAH, BUT DO YOU THINK IT APPLIES TO SHARKS?
I'M SURE IT DOES. IT'S A BASIC LAW OF NATURE.
LET'S FIND OUT.
BOO!
I WAS JUST TESTING OUT THAT THEORY ABOUT NEVER COMING BETWEEN A BEAR AND ITS CUB.
CLEARLY, IT ONLY APPLIES TO MOTHER BEARS.
COULD YOU WATCH HIM FOR A WHILE?

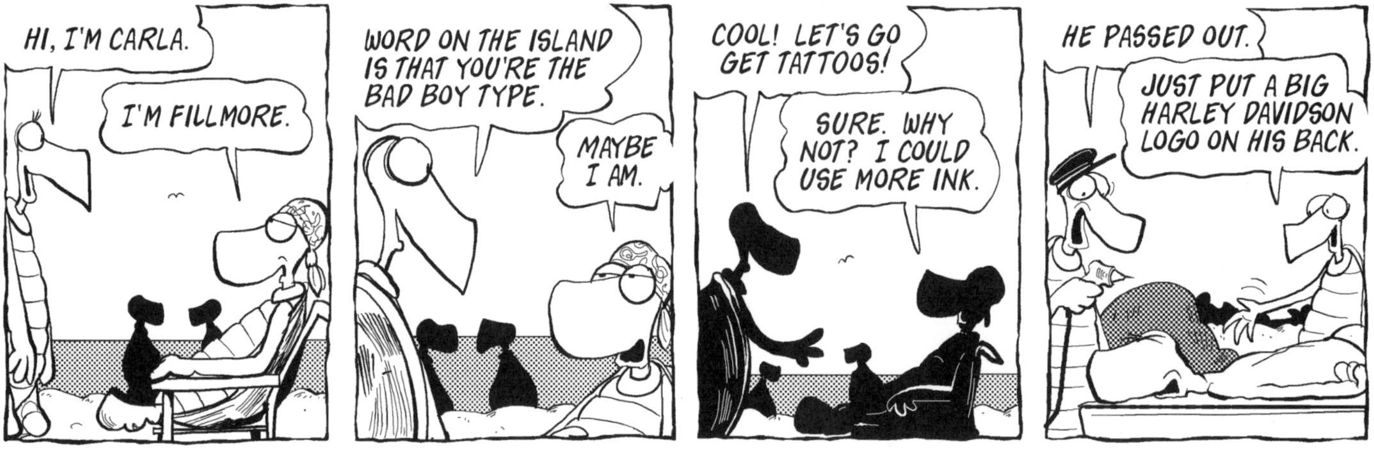
HI, I'M CARLA.
I'M FILLMORE.
WORD ON THE ISLAND IS THAT YOU'RE THE BAD BOY TYPE.
MAYBE I AM.
COOL! LET'S GO GET TATTOOS!
SURE. WHY NOT? I COULD USE MORE INK.
HE PASSED OUT.
JUST PUT A BIG HARLEY DAVIDSON LOGO ON HIS BACK.

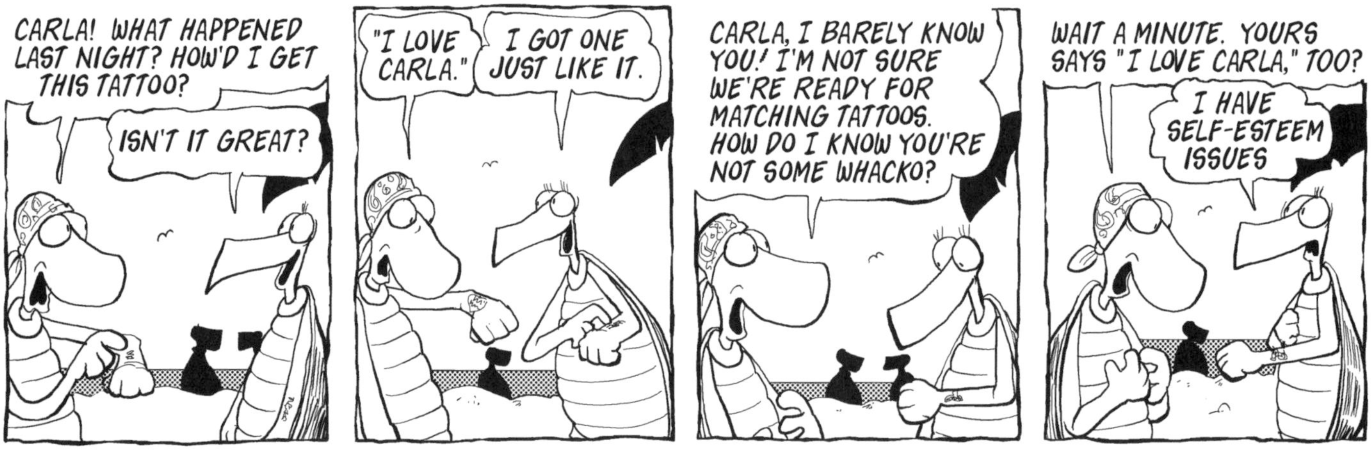
CARLA! WHAT HAPPENED LAST NIGHT? HOW'D I GET THIS TATTOO?
ISN'T IT GREAT?
"I LOVE CARLA."
I GOT ONE JUST LIKE IT.
CARLA, I BARELY KNOW YOU! I'M NOT SURE WE'RE READY FOR MATCHING TATTOOS. HOW DO I KNOW YOU'RE NOT SOME WHACKO?
WAIT A MINUTE. YOURS SAYS "I LOVE CARLA," TOO?
I HAVE SELF-ESTEEM ISSUES

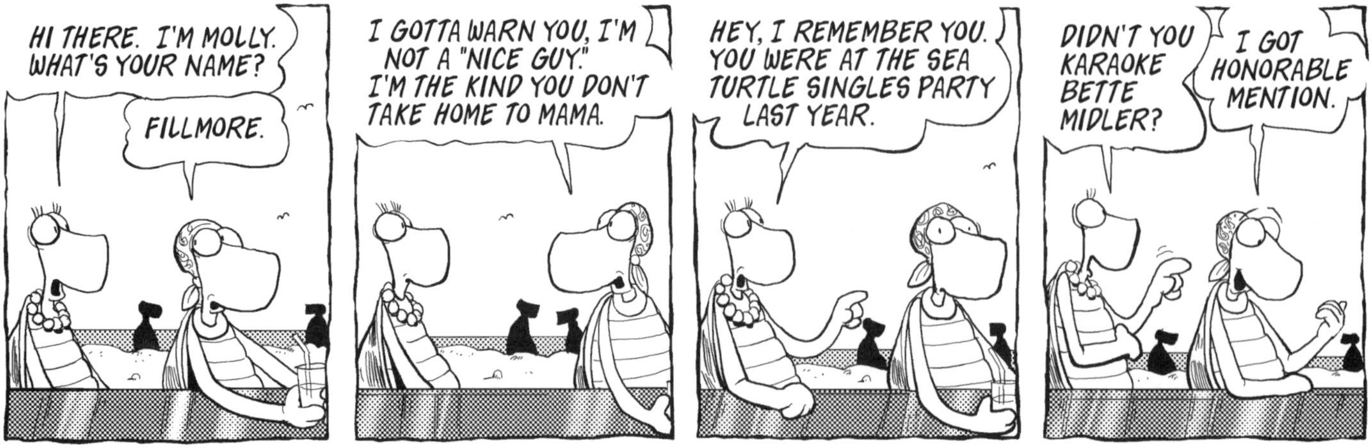
HI THERE. I'M MOLLY. WHAT'S YOUR NAME?
FILLMORE.
I GOTTA WARN YOU, I'M NOT A "NICE GUY." I'M THE KIND YOU DON'T TAKE HOME TO MAMA.
HEY, I REMEMBER YOU. YOU WERE AT THE SEA TURTLE SINGLES PARTY LAST YEAR.
DIDN'T YOU KARAOKE BETTE MIDLER?
I GOT HONORABLE MENTION.

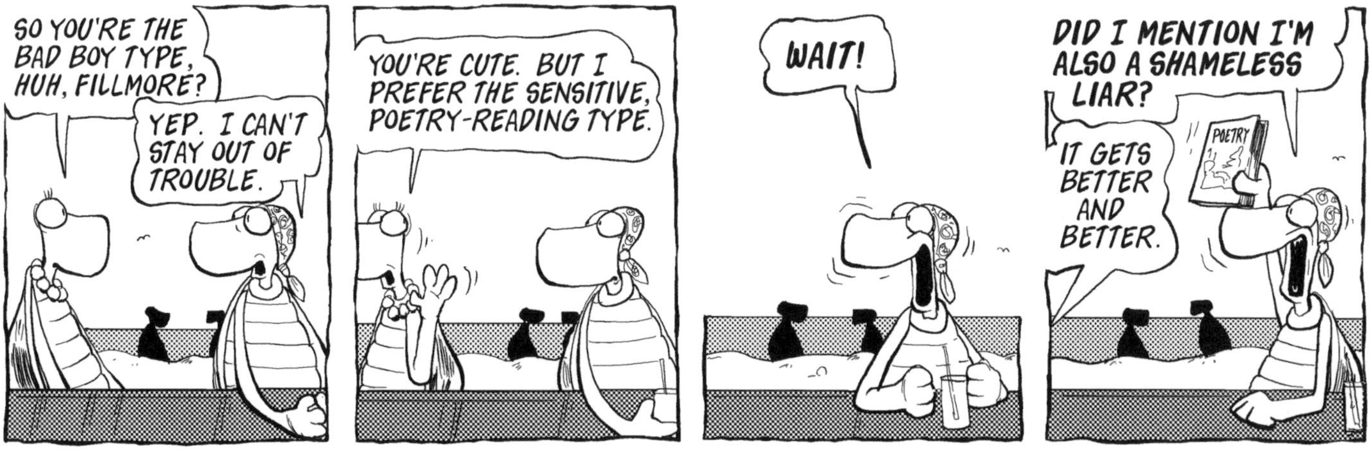
SO YOU'RE THE BAD BOY TYPE, HUH, FILLMORE?
YEP. I CAN'T STAY OUT OF TROUBLE.
YOU'RE CUTE. BUT I PREFER THE SENSITIVE, POETRY-READING TYPE.
WAIT!
DID I MENTION I'M ALSO A SHAMELESS LIAR?
IT GETS BETTER AND BETTER.
POETRY

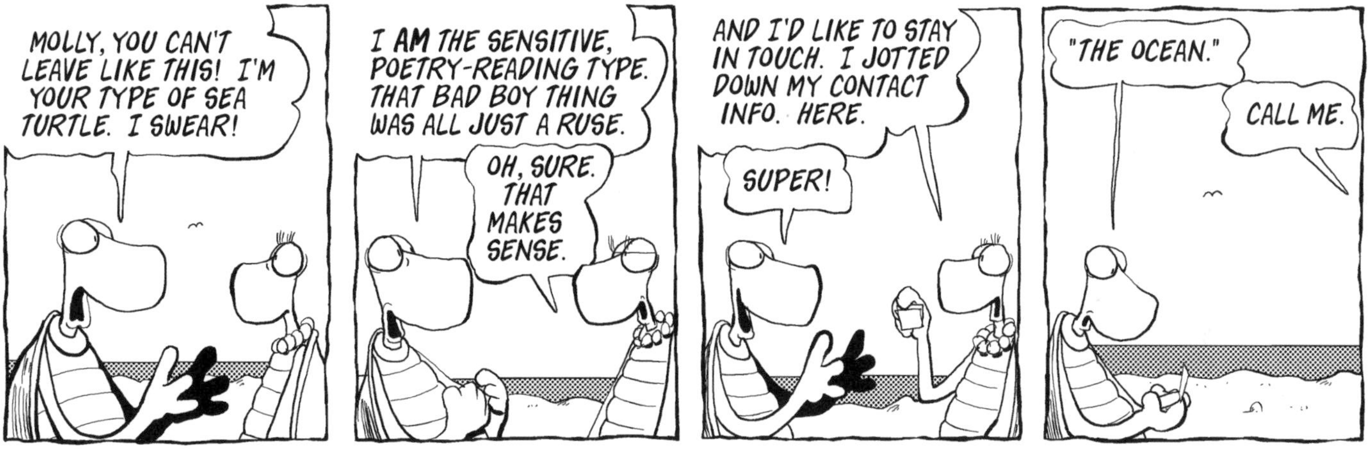
MOLLY, YOU CAN'T LEAVE LIKE THIS! I'M YOUR TYPE OF SEA TURTLE. I SWEAR!
I AM THE SENSITIVE, POETRY-READING TYPE. THAT BAD BOY THING WAS ALL JUST A RUSE.
OH, SURE. THAT MAKES SENSE.
AND I'D LIKE TO STAY IN TOUCH. I JOTTED DOWN MY CONTACT INFO. HERE.
SUPER!
"THE OCEAN."
CALL ME.

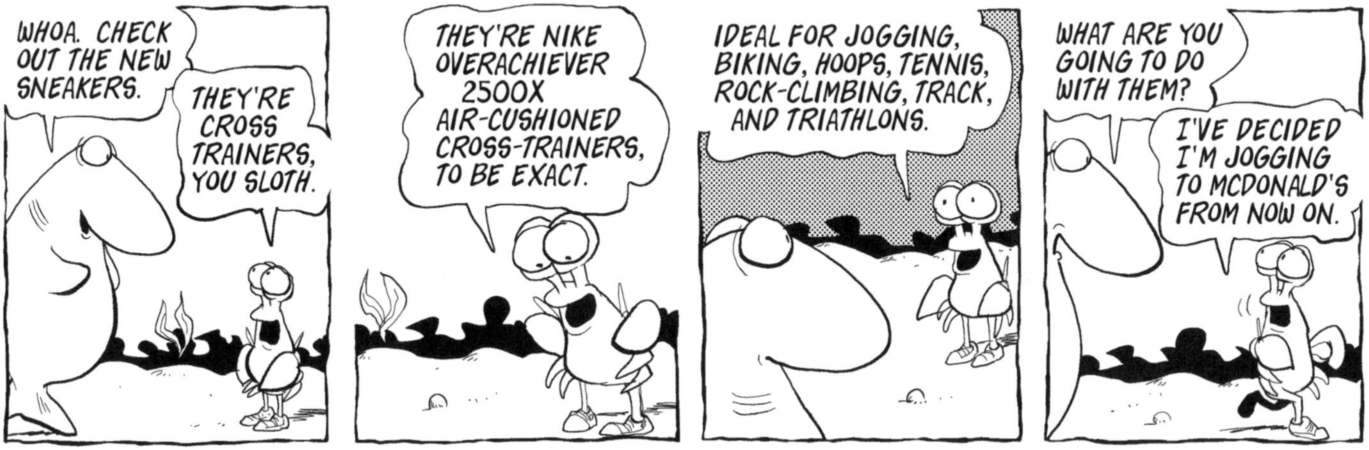
WHOA. CHECK OUT THE NEW SNEAKERS.
THEY'RE CROSS TRAINERS, YOU SLOTH.
THEY'RE NIKE OVERACHIEVER 2500X AIR-CUSHIONED CROSS-TRAINERS, TO BE EXACT.
IDEAL FOR JOGGING, BIKING, HOOPS, TENNIS, ROCK-CLIMBING, TRACK, AND TRIATHLONS.
WHAT ARE YOU GOING TO DO WITH THEM?
I'VE DECIDED I'M JOGGING TO MCDONALD'S FROM NOW ON.

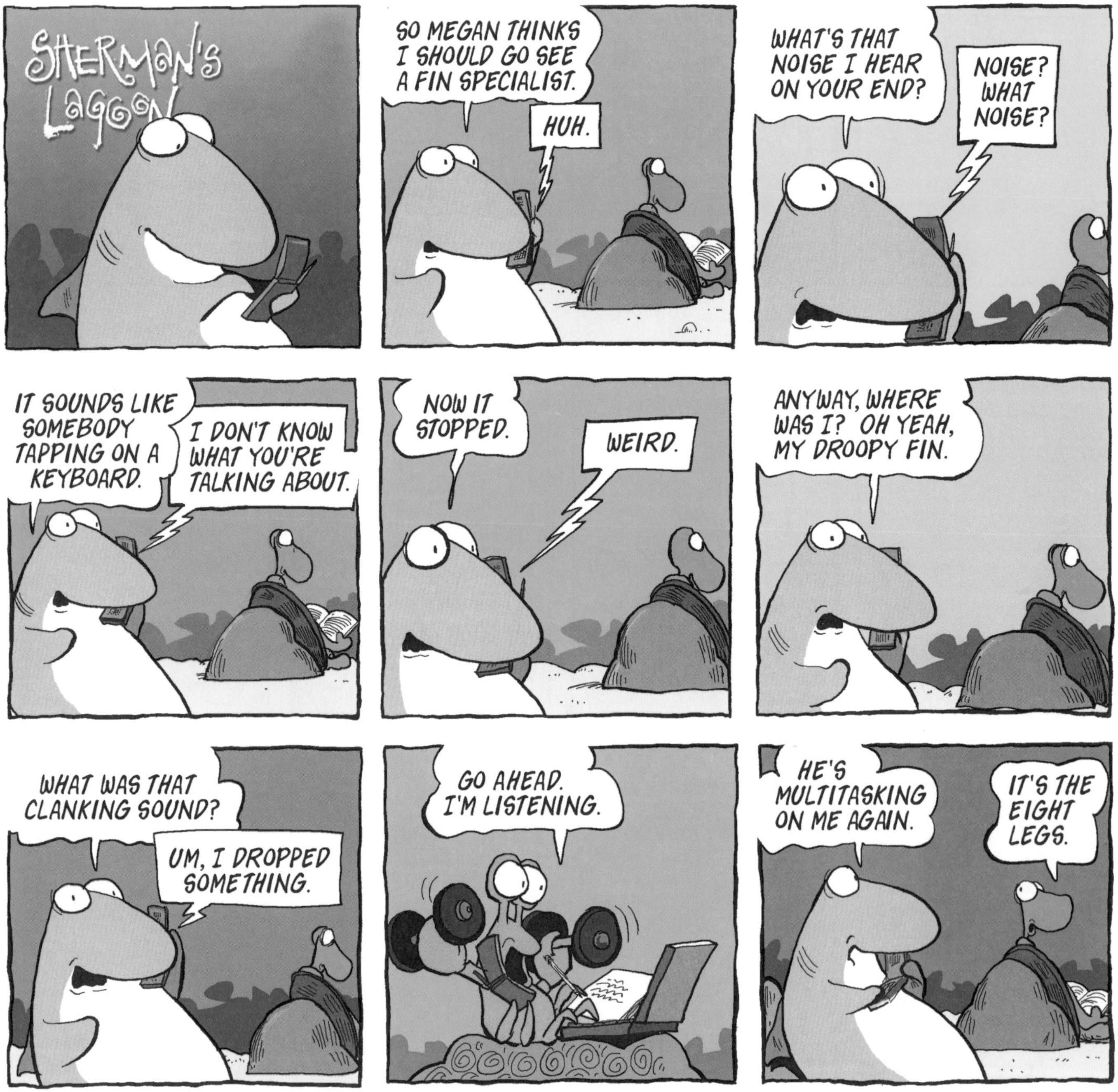
SHERMAN'S LAGOON
SO MEGAN THINKS I SHOULD GO SEE A FIN SPECIALIST.
HUH.
WHAT'S THAT NOISE I HEAR ON YOUR END?
NOISE? WHAT NOISE?
IT SOUNDS LIKE SOMEBODY TAPPING ON A KEYBOARD.
I DON'T KNOW WHAT YOU'RE TALKING ABOUT.
NOW IT STOPPED.
WEIRD.
ANYWAY, WHERE WAS I? OH YEAH, MY DROOPY FIN.
WHAT WAS THAT CLANKING SOUND?
UM, I DROPPED SOMETHING.
GO AHEAD. I'M LISTENING.
HE'S MULTITASKING ON ME AGAIN.
IT'S THE EIGHT LEGS.

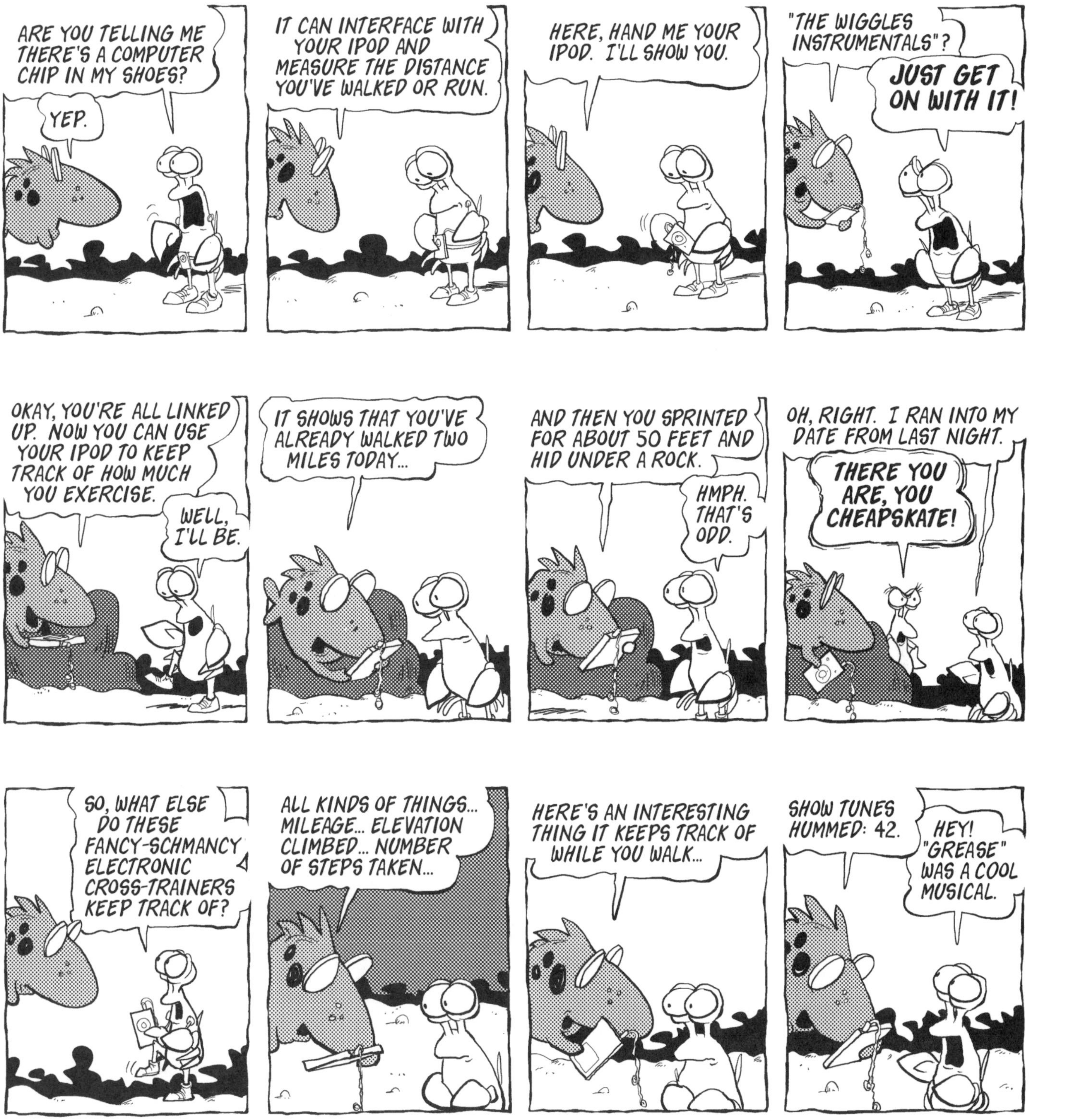
ARE YOU TELLING ME THERE'S A COMPUTER CHIP IN MY SHOES?
YEP.
IT CAN INTERFACE WITH YOUR IPOD AND MEASURE THE DISTANCE YOU'VE WALKED OR RUN.
HERE, HAND ME YOUR IPOD. I'LL SHOW YOU.
"THE WIGGLES INSTRUMENTALS"?
JUST GET ON WITH IT!
OKAY, YOU'RE ALL LINKED UP. NOW YOU CAN USE YOUR IPOD TO KEEP TRACK OF HOW MUCH YOU EXERCISE.
WELL, I'LL BE.
IT SHOWS THAT YOU'VE ALREADY WALKED TWO MILES TODAY...
AND THEN YOU SPRINTED FOR ABOUT 50 FEET AND HID UNDER A ROCK.
HMPH. THAT'S ODD.
OH, RIGHT. I RAN INTO MY DATE FROM LAST NIGHT.
THERE YOU ARE, YOU CHEAPSKATE!
SO, WHAT ELSE DO THESE FANCY-SCHMANCY ELECTRONIC CROSS-TRAINERS KEEP TRACK OF?
ALL KINDS OF THINGS... MILEAGE... ELEVATION CLIMBED... NUMBER OF STEPS TAKEN...
HERE'S AN INTERESTING THING IT KEEPS TRACK OF WHILE YOU WALK...
SHOW TUNES HUMMED: 42.
HEY! "GREASE" WAS A COOL MUSICAL.

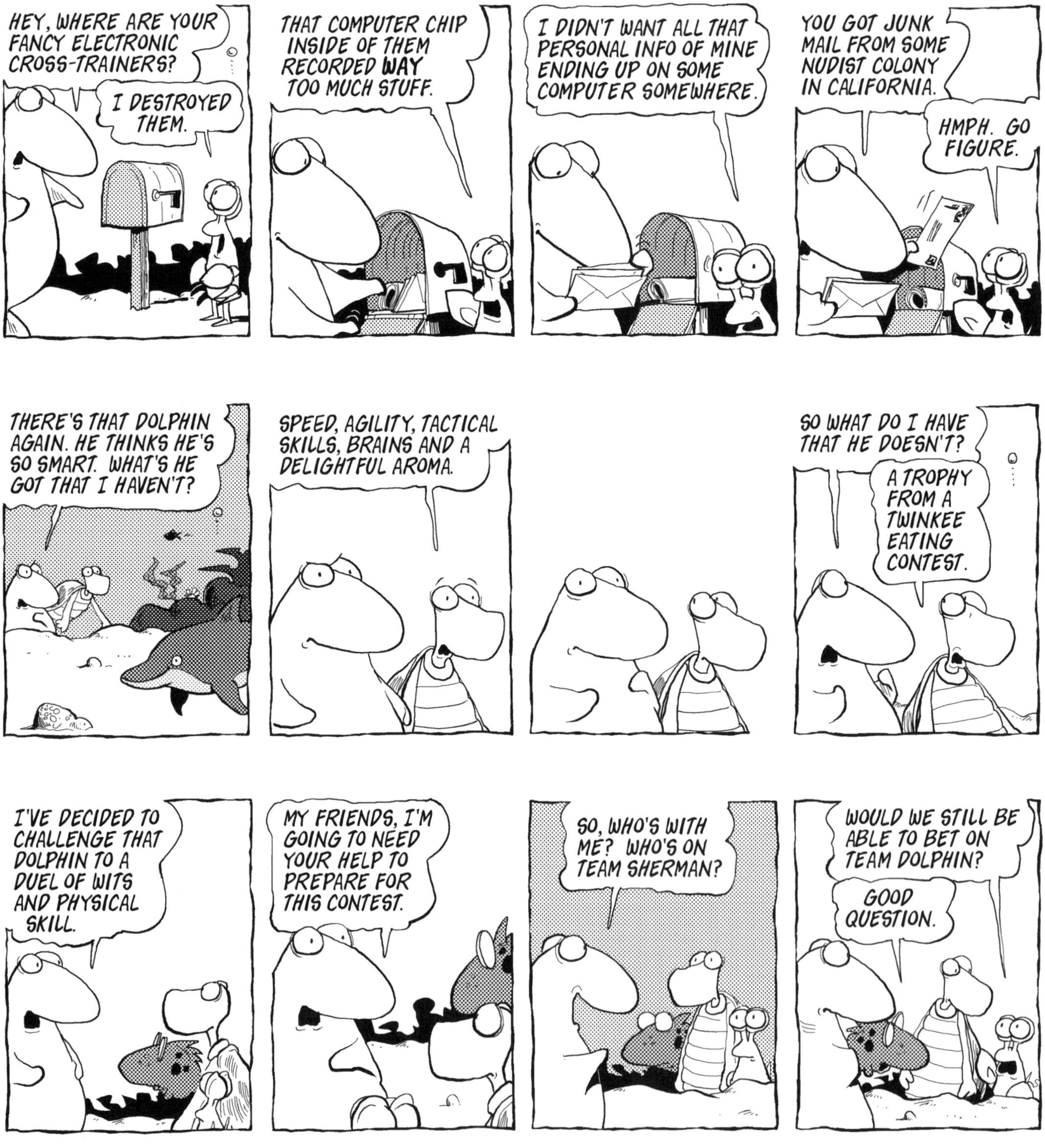
HEY, WHERE ARE YOUR FANCY ELECTRONIC CROSS-TRAINERS?
I DESTROYED THEM.
THAT COMPUTER CHIP INSIDE OF THEM RECORDED WAY TOO MUCH STUFF.
I DIDN'T WANT ALL THAT PERSONAL INFO OF MINE ENDING UP ON SOME COMPUTER SOMEWHERE.
YOU GOT JUNK MAIL FROM SOME NUDIST COLONY IN CALIFORNIA.
HMPH. GO FIGURE.
THERE'S THAT DOLPHIN AGAIN. HE THINKS HE'S SO SMART. WHAT'S HE GOT THAT I HAVEN'T?
SPEED, AGILITY, TACTICAL SKILLS, BRAINS AND A DELIGHTFUL AROMA.
SO WHAT DO I HAVE THAT HE DOESN'T?
A TROPHY FROM A TWINKEE EATING CONTEST.
I'VE DECIDED TO CHALLENGE THAT DOLPHIN TO A DUEL OF WITS AND PHYSICAL SKILL.
MY FRIENDS, I'M GOING TO NEED YOUR HELP TO PREPARE FOR THIS CONTEST.
SO, WHO'S WITH ME? WHO'S ON TEAM SHERMAN?
WOULD WE STILL BE ABLE TO BET ON TEAM DOLPHIN?
GOOD QUESTION.

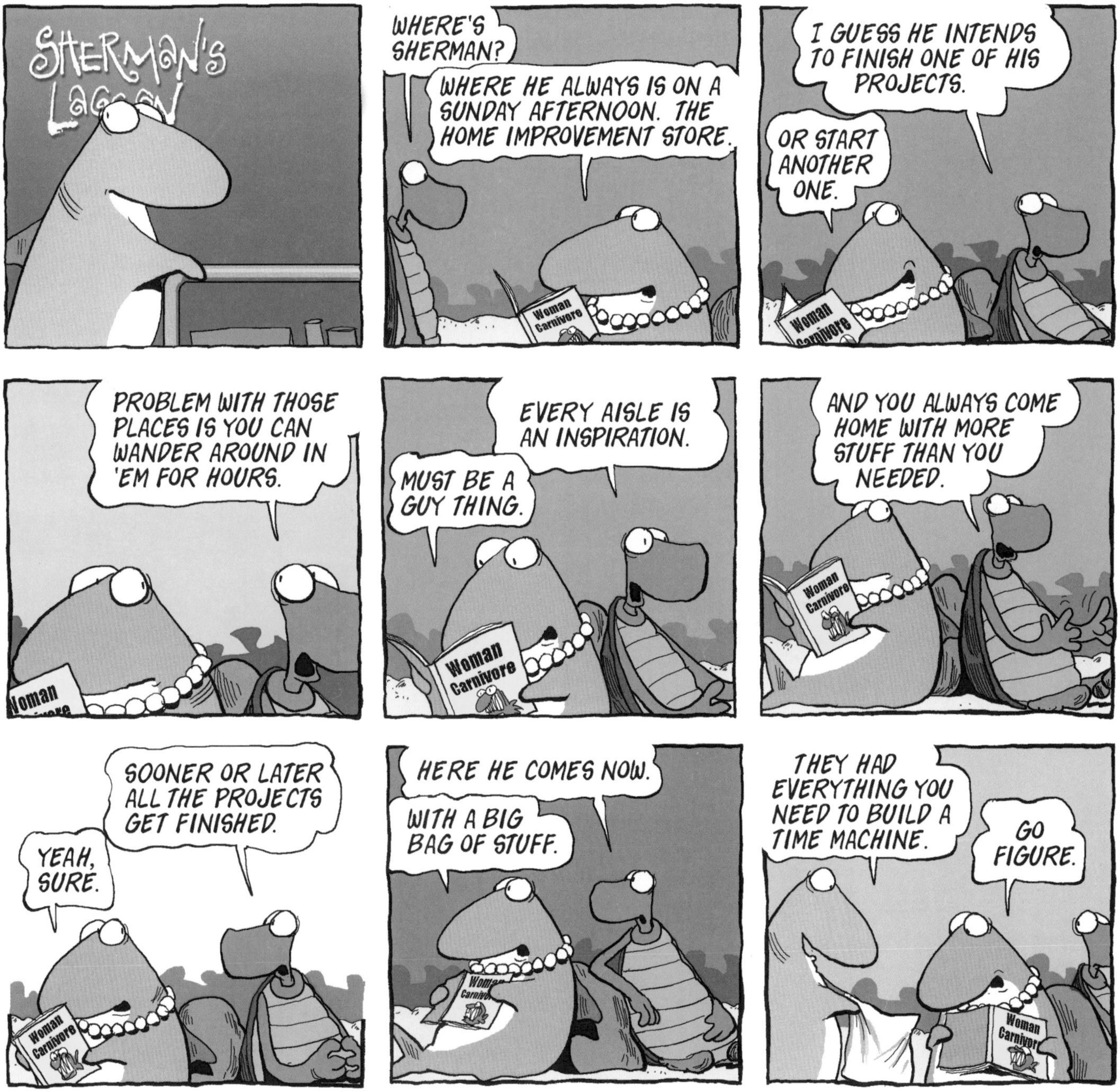
SHERMAN'S LAGOON
WHERE'S SHERMAN?
WHERE HE ALWAYS IS ON A SUNDAY AFTERNOON. THE HOME IMPROVEMENT STORE.
Woman Carnivore
I GUESS HE INTENDS TO FINISH ONE OF HIS PROJECTS.
OR START ANOTHER ONE.
Woman Carnivore
PROBLEM WITH THOSE PLACES IS YOU CAN WANDER AROUND IN 'EM FOR HOURS.
EVERY AISLE IS AN INSPIRATION.
MUST BE A GUY THING.
Woman Carnivore
AND YOU ALWAYS COME HOME WITH MORE STUFF THAN YOU NEEDED.
Woman Carnivore
SOONER OR LATER ALL THE PROJECTS GET FINISHED.
YEAH, SURE.
Woman Carnivore
HERE HE COMES NOW.
WITH A BIG BAG OF STUFF.
THEY HAD EVERYTHING YOU NEED TO BUILD A TIME MACHINE.
GO FIGURE.
Woman Carnivore

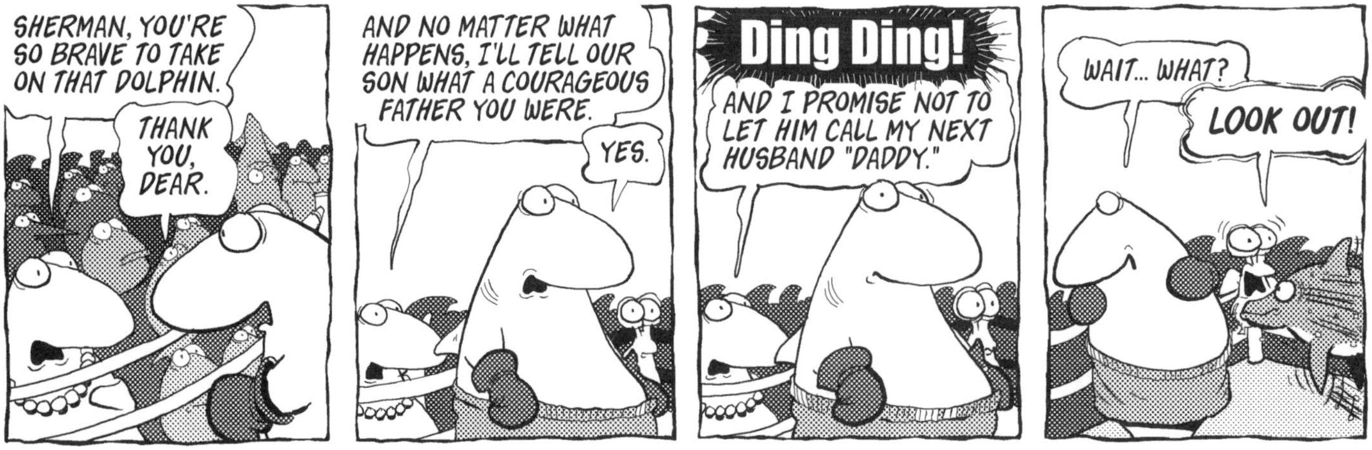
SHERMAN, YOU'RE SO BRAVE TO TAKE ON THAT DOLPHIN.
THANK YOU, DEAR.
AND NO MATTER WHAT HAPPENS, I'LL TELL OUR SON WHAT A COURAGEOUS FATHER YOU WERE.
YES.
Ding Ding!
AND I PROMISE NOT TO LET HIM CALL MY NEXT HUSBAND "DADDY."
WAIT... WHAT?
LOOK OUT!

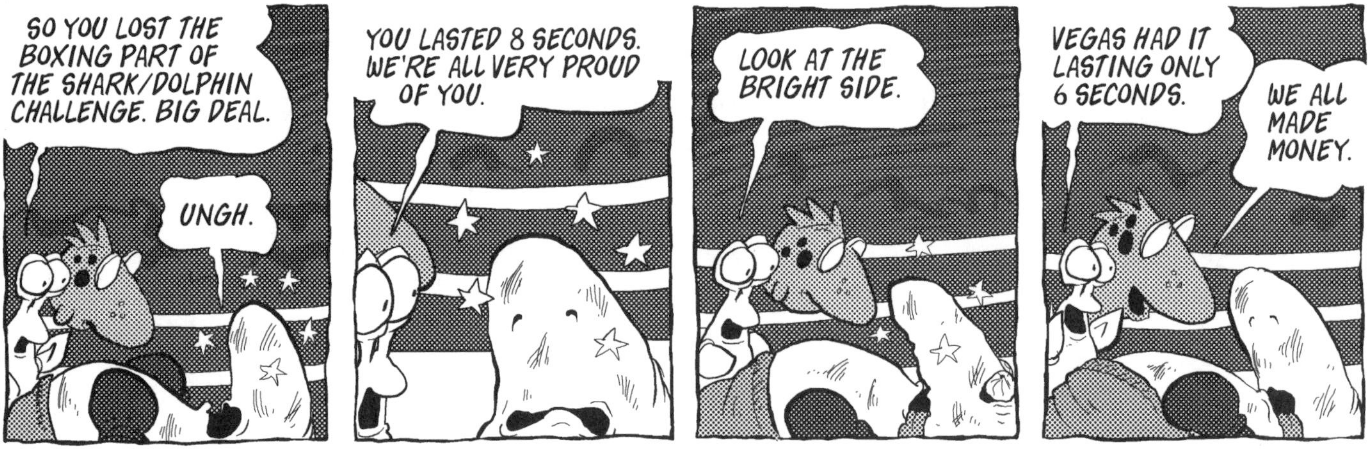
SO YOU LOST THE BOXING PART OF THE SHARK/DOLPHIN CHALLENGE. BIG DEAL.
UNGH.
YOU LASTED 8 SECONDS. WE'RE ALL VERY PROUD OF YOU.
LOOK AT THE BRIGHT SIDE.
VEGAS HAD IT LASTING ONLY 6 SECONDS.
WE ALL MADE MONEY.

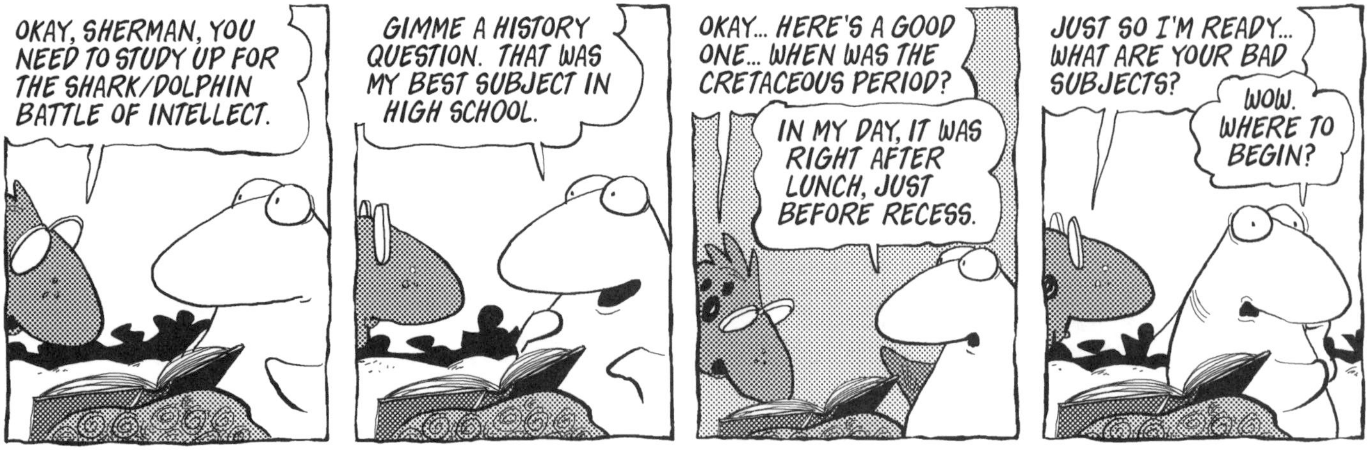
OKAY, SHERMAN, YOU NEED TO STUDY UP FOR THE SHARK/DOLPHIN BATTLE OF INTELLECT.
GIMME A HISTORY QUESTION. THAT WAS MY BEST SUBJECT IN HIGH SCHOOL.
OKAY... HERE'S A GOOD ONE... WHEN WAS THE CRETACEOUS PERIOD?
IN MY DAY, IT WAS RIGHT AFTER LUNCH, JUST BEFORE RECESS.
JUST SO I'M READY... WHAT ARE YOUR BAD SUBJECTS?
WOW. WHERE TO BEGIN?

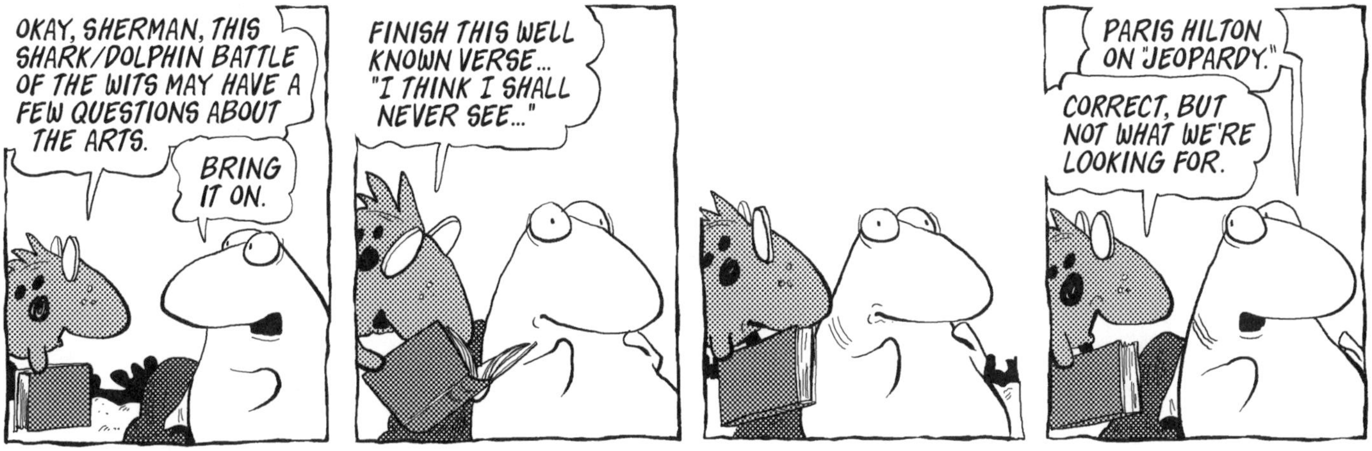
OKAY, SHERMAN, THIS SHARK/DOLPHIN BATTLE OF THE WITS MAY HAVE A FEW QUESTIONS ABOUT THE ARTS.
BRING IT ON.
FINISH THIS WELL KNOWN VERSE... "I THINK I SHALL NEVER SEE..."
PARIS HILTON ON "JEOPARDY."
CORRECT, BUT NOT WHAT WE'RE LOOKING FOR.

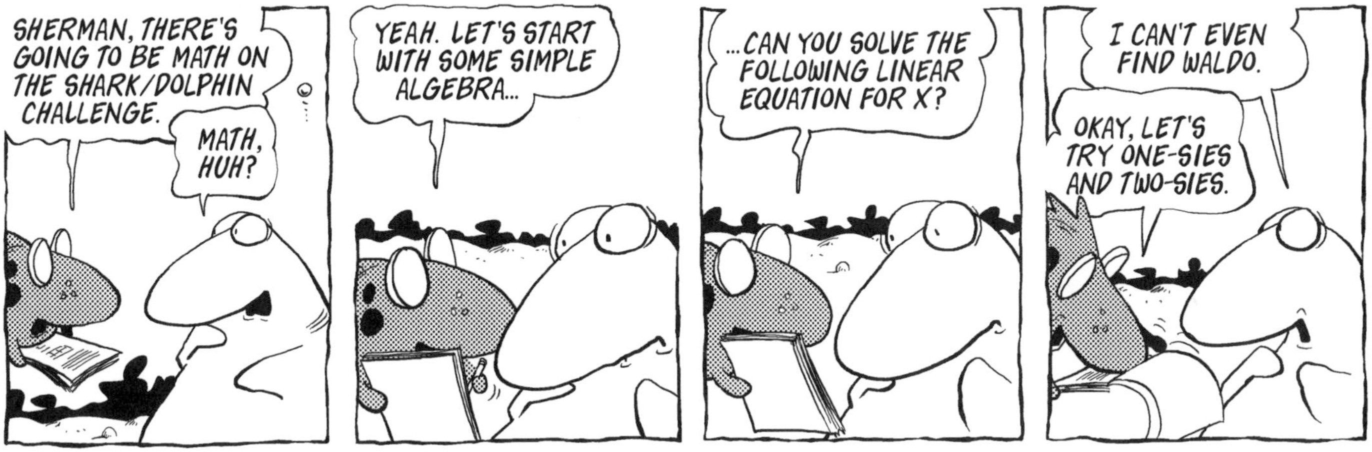
SHERMAN, THERE'S GOING TO BE MATH ON THE SHARK/DOLPHIN CHALLENGE.
MATH, HUH?
YEAH. LET'S START WITH SOME SIMPLE ALGEBRA...
...CAN YOU SOLVE THE FOLLOWING LINEAR EQUATION FOR X?
I CAN'T EVEN FIND WALDO.
OKAY, LET'S TRY ONE-SIES AND TWO-SIES.

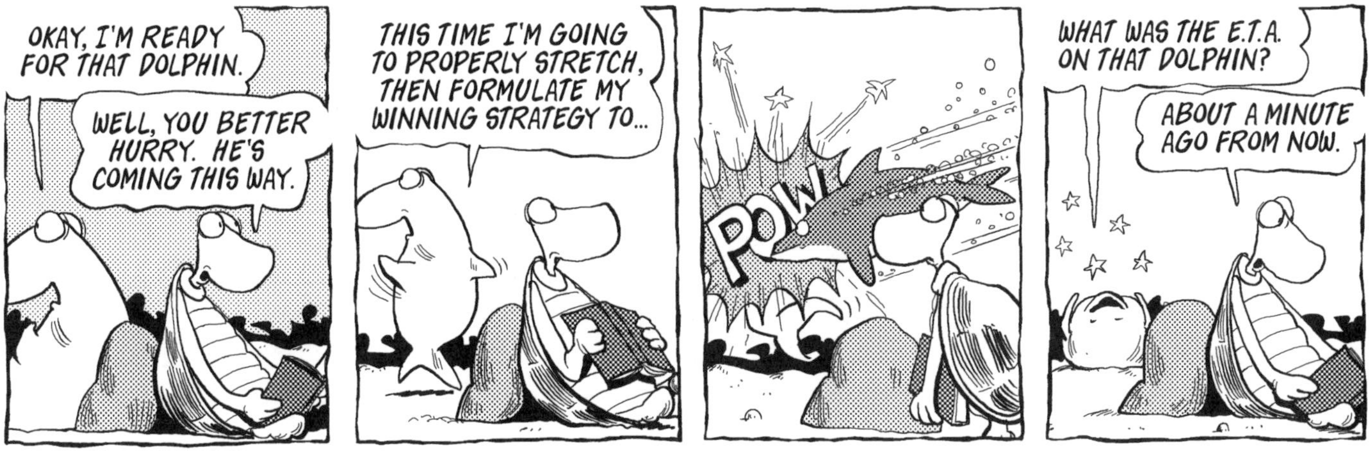
OKAY, I'M READY FOR THAT DOLPHIN.
WELL, YOU BETTER HURRY. HE'S COMING THIS WAY.
THIS TIME I'M GOING TO PROPERLY STRETCH, THEN FORMULATE MY WINNING STRATEGY TO...
POW
WHAT WAS THE E.T.A. ON THAT DOLPHIN?
ABOUT A MINUTE AGO FROM NOW.

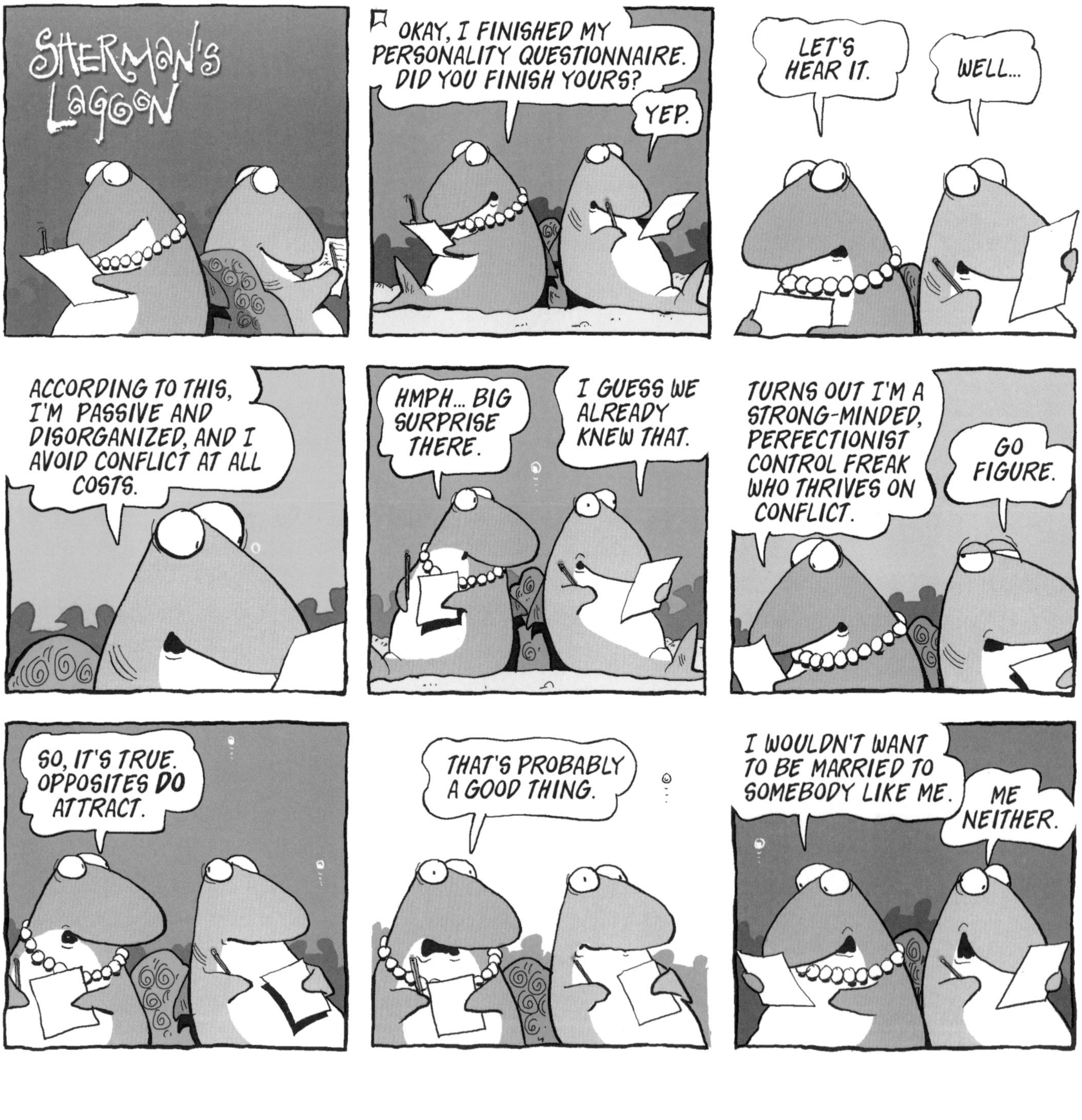
SHERMAN'S LAGOON
OKAY, I FINISHED MY PERSONALITY QUESTIONNAIRE. DID YOU FINISH YOURS?
YEP.
LET'S HEAR IT.
WELL...
ACCORDING TO THIS, I'M PASSIVE AND DISORGANIZED, AND I AVOID CONFLICT AT ALL COSTS.
HMPH... BIG SURPRISE THERE.
I GUESS WE ALREADY KNEW THAT.
TURNS OUT I'M A STRONG-MINDED, PERFECTIONIST CONTROL FREAK WHO THRIVES ON CONFLICT.
GO FIGURE.
SO, IT'S TRUE. OPPOSITES **DO** ATTRACT.
THAT'S PROBABLY A GOOD THING.
I WOULDN'T WANT TO BE MARRIED TO SOMEBODY LIKE ME.
ME NEITHER.

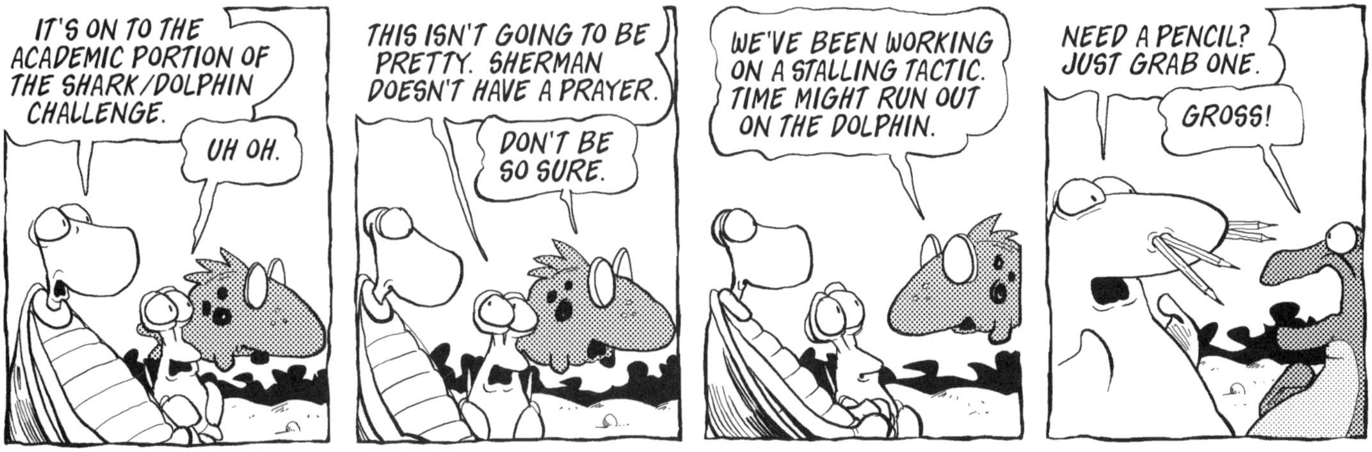
IT'S ON TO THE ACADEMIC PORTION OF THE SHARK/DOLPHIN CHALLENGE.
UH OH.
THIS ISN'T GOING TO BE PRETTY. SHERMAN DOESN'T HAVE A PRAYER.
DON'T BE SO SURE.
WE'VE BEEN WORKING ON A STALLING TACTIC. TIME MIGHT RUN OUT ON THE DOLPHIN.
NEED A PENCIL? JUST GRAB ONE.
GROSS!

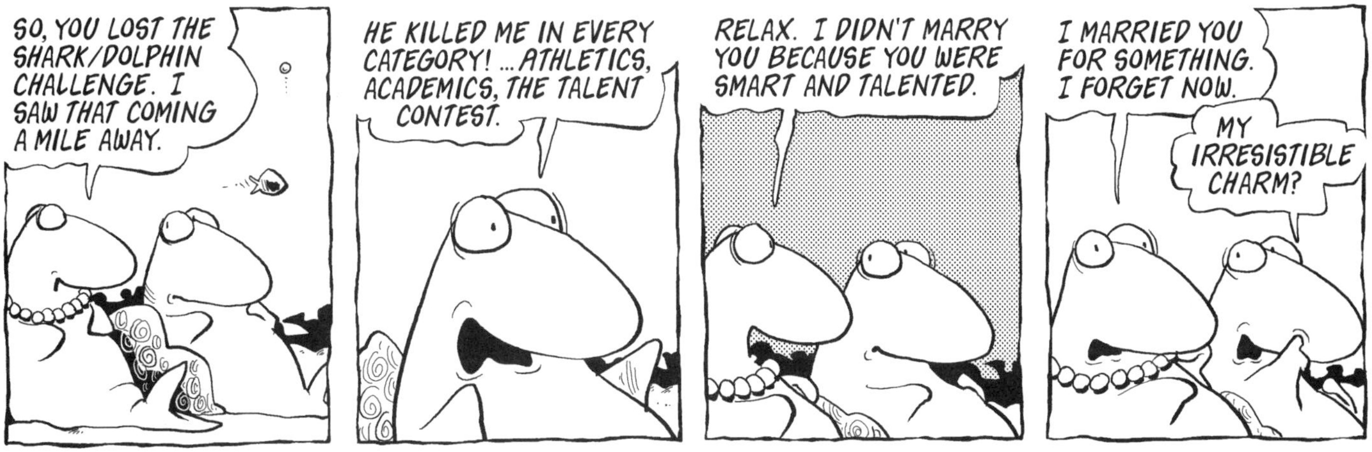
SO, YOU LOST THE SHARK/DOLPHIN CHALLENGE. I SAW THAT COMING A MILE AWAY.
HE KILLED ME IN EVERY CATEGORY! ...ATHLETICS, ACADEMICS, THE TALENT CONTEST.
RELAX. I DIDN'T MARRY YOU BECAUSE YOU WERE SMART AND TALENTED.
I MARRIED YOU FOR SOMETHING. I FORGET NOW.
MY IRRESISTIBLE CHARM?

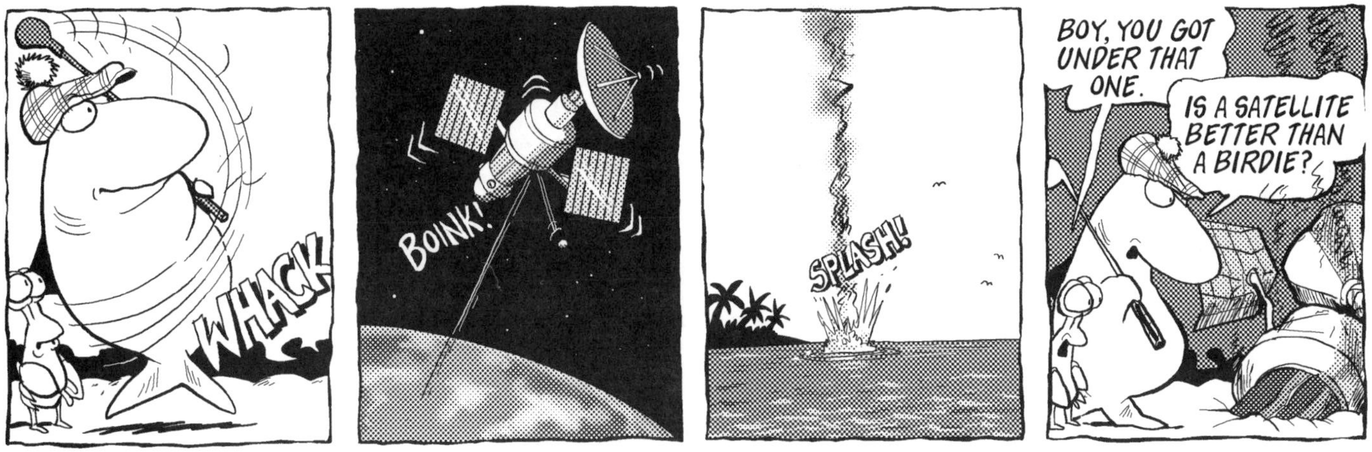
WHACK
BOINK!
SPLASH!
BOY, YOU GOT UNDER THAT ONE.
IS A SATELLITE BETTER THAN A BIRDIE?

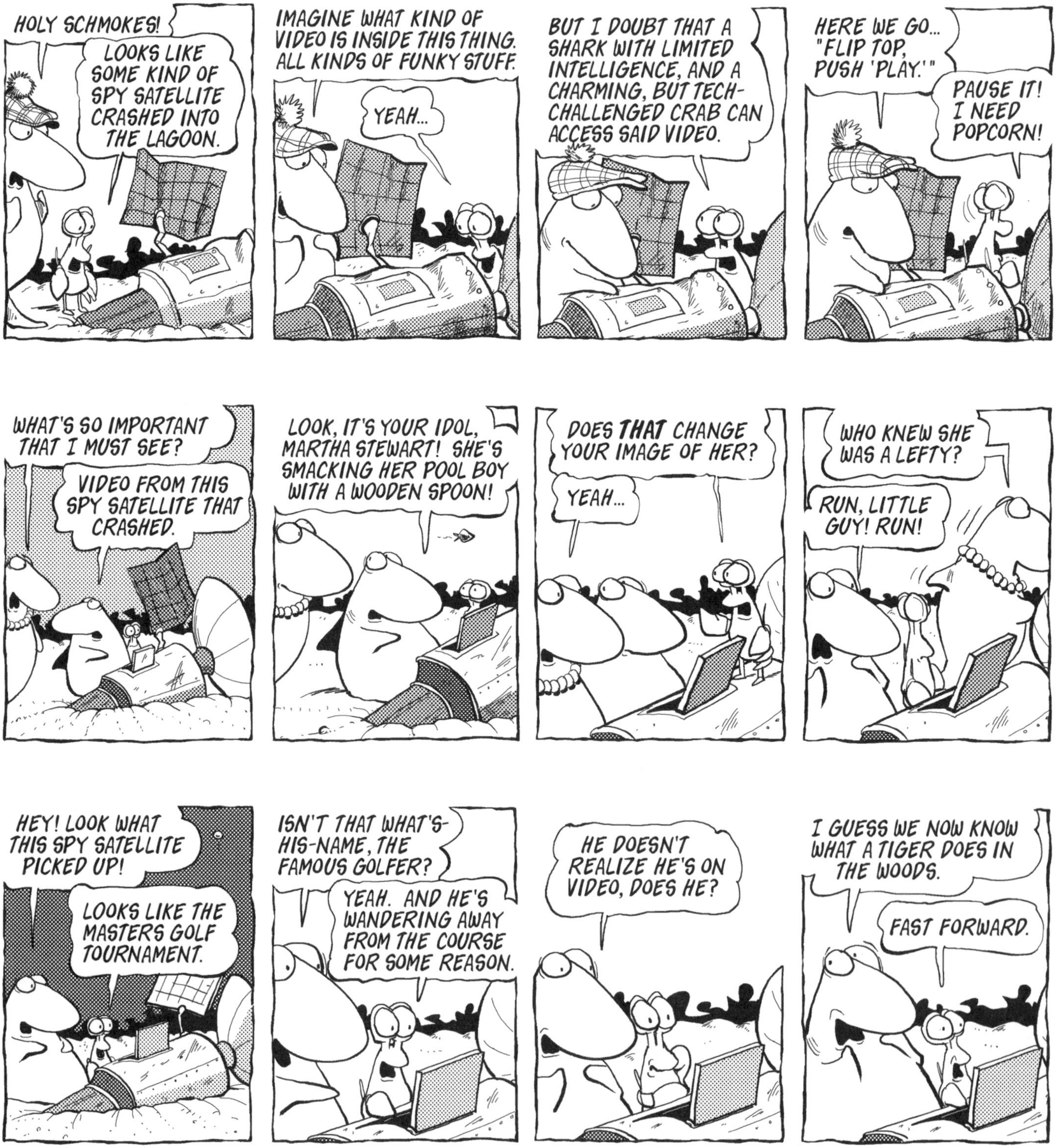
HOLY SCHMOKES!
LOOKS LIKE SOME KIND OF SPY SATELLITE CRASHED INTO THE LAGOON.
IMAGINE WHAT KIND OF VIDEO IS INSIDE THIS THING. ALL KINDS OF FUNKY STUFF.
YEAH...
BUT I DOUBT THAT A SHARK WITH LIMITED INTELLIGENCE, AND A CHARMING, BUT TECH-CHALLENGED CRAB CAN ACCESS SAID VIDEO.
HERE WE GO... "FLIP TOP, PUSH 'PLAY.'"
PAUSE IT! I NEED POPCORN!
WHAT'S SO IMPORTANT THAT I MUST SEE?
VIDEO FROM THIS SPY SATELLITE THAT CRASHED.
LOOK, IT'S YOUR IDOL, MARTHA STEWART! SHE'S SMACKING HER POOL BOY WITH A WOODEN SPOON!
DOES THAT CHANGE YOUR IMAGE OF HER?
YEAH...
WHO KNEW SHE WAS A LEFTY?
RUN, LITTLE GUY! RUN!
HEY! LOOK WHAT THIS SPY SATELLITE PICKED UP!
LOOKS LIKE THE MASTERS GOLF TOURNAMENT.
ISN'T THAT WHAT'S-HIS-NAME, THE FAMOUS GOLFER?
YEAH. AND HE'S WANDERING AWAY FROM THE COURSE FOR SOME REASON.
HE DOESN'T REALIZE HE'S ON VIDEO, DOES HE?
I GUESS WE NOW KNOW WHAT A TIGER DOES IN THE WOODS.
FAST FORWARD.

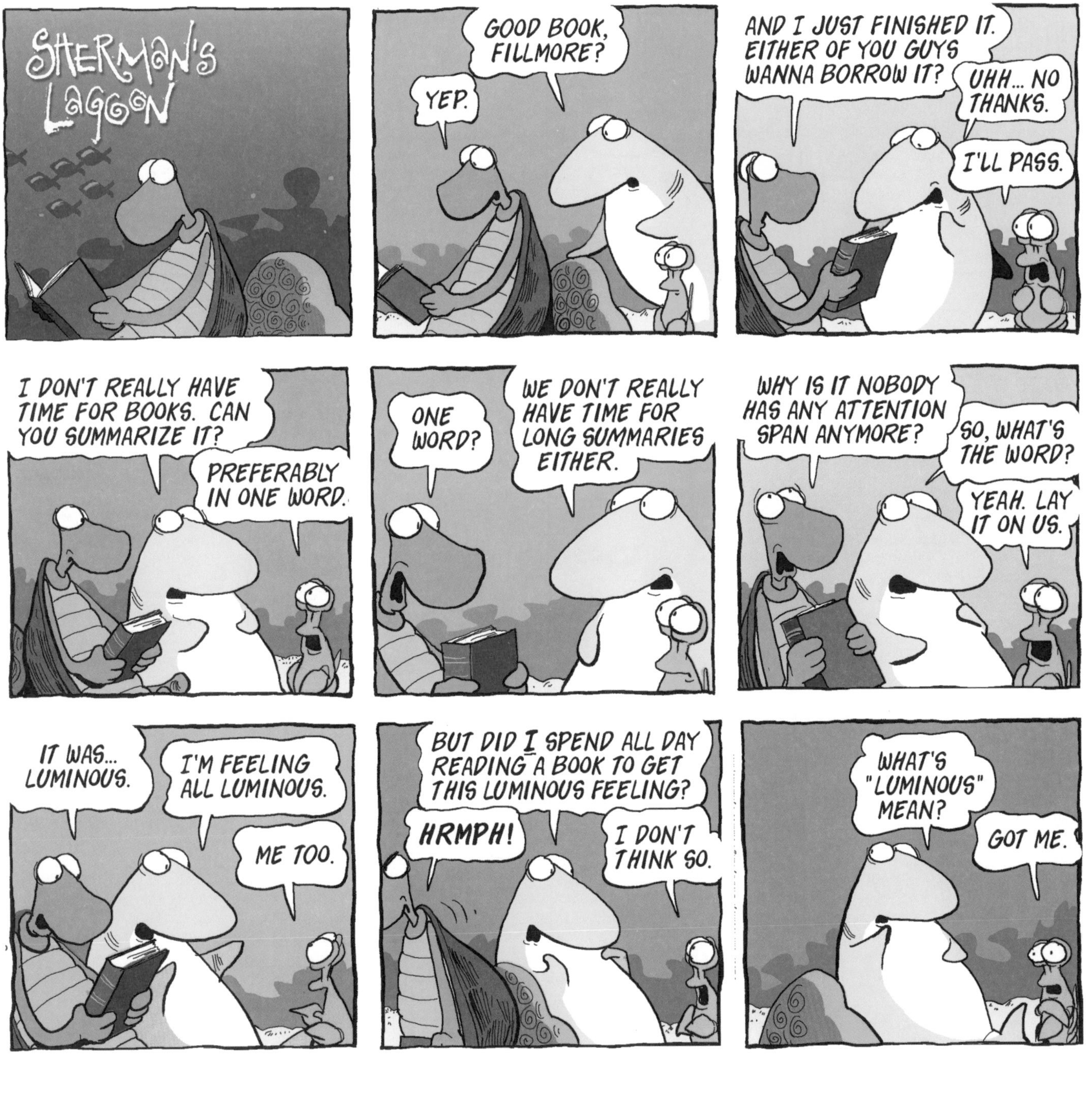
SHERMAN'S LAGOON
GOOD BOOK, FILLMORE?
YEP.
AND I JUST FINISHED IT. EITHER OF YOU GUYS WANNA BORROW IT?
UHH... NO THANKS.
I'LL PASS.
I DON'T REALLY HAVE TIME FOR BOOKS. CAN YOU SUMMARIZE IT?
PREFERABLY IN ONE WORD.
ONE WORD?
WE DON'T REALLY HAVE TIME FOR LONG SUMMARIES EITHER.
WHY IS IT NOBODY HAS ANY ATTENTION SPAN ANYMORE?
SO, WHAT'S THE WORD?
YEAH. LAY IT ON US.
IT WAS... LUMINOUS.
I'M FEELING ALL LUMINOUS.
ME TOO.
BUT DID I SPEND ALL DAY READING A BOOK TO GET THIS LUMINOUS FEELING?
HRMPH!
I DON'T THINK SO.
WHAT'S "LUMINOUS" MEAN?
GOT ME.

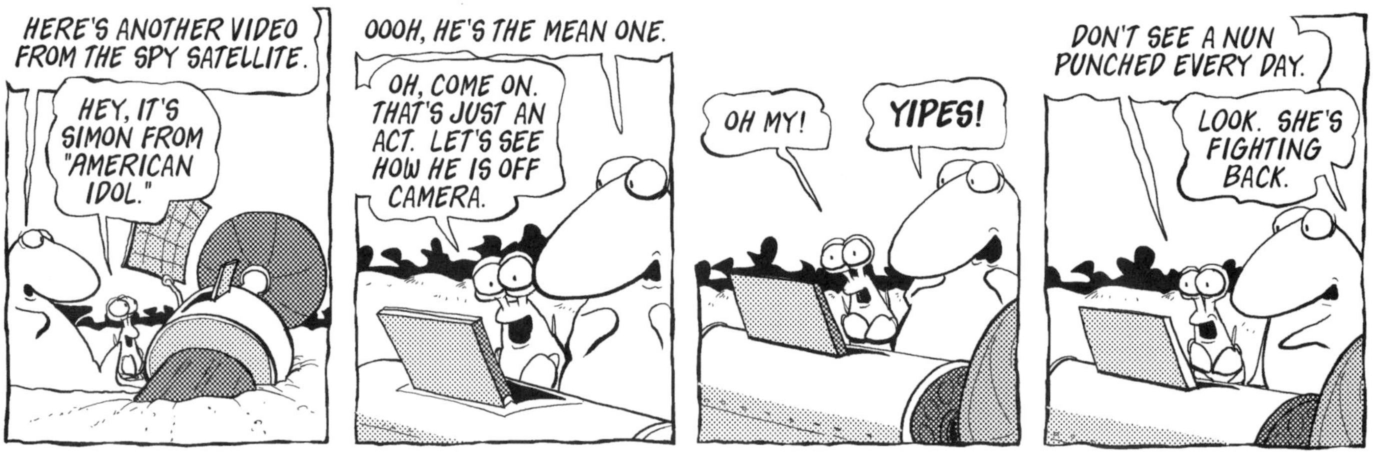
HERE'S ANOTHER VIDEO FROM THE SPY SATELLITE.
HEY, IT'S SIMON FROM "AMERICAN IDOL."
OOOH, HE'S THE MEAN ONE.
OH, COME ON. THAT'S JUST AN ACT. LET'S SEE HOW HE IS OFF CAMERA.
OH MY!
YIPES!
DON'T SEE A NUN PUNCHED EVERY DAY.
LOOK. SHE'S FIGHTING BACK.

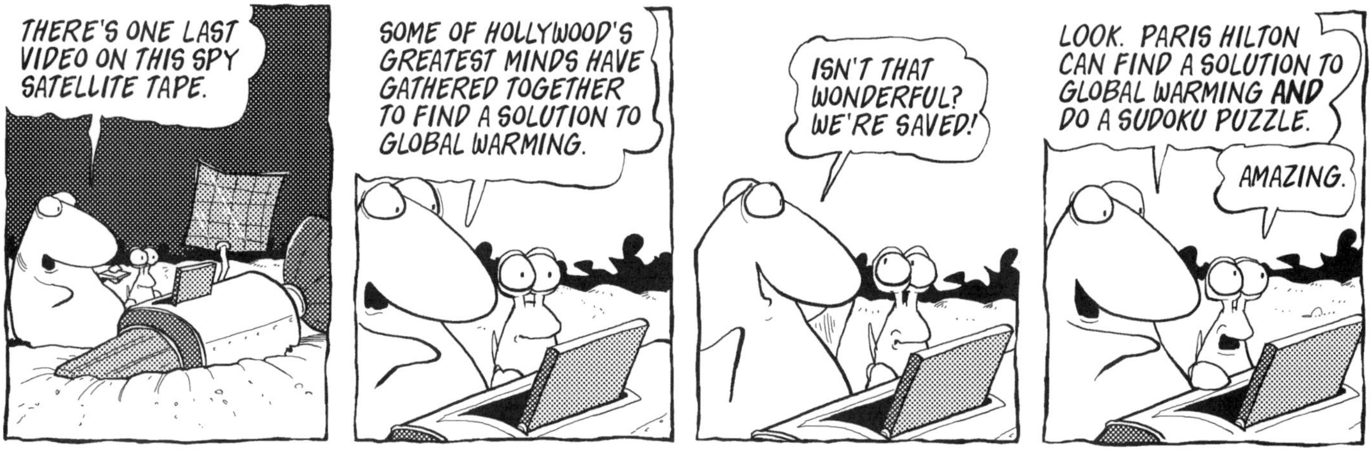
THERE'S ONE LAST VIDEO ON THIS SPY SATELLITE TAPE.
SOME OF HOLLYWOOD'S GREATEST MINDS HAVE GATHERED TOGETHER TO FIND A SOLUTION TO GLOBAL WARMING.
ISN'T THAT WONDERFUL? WE'RE SAVED!
LOOK. PARIS HILTON CAN FIND A SOLUTION TO GLOBAL WARMING AND DO A SUDOKU PUZZLE.
AMAZING.

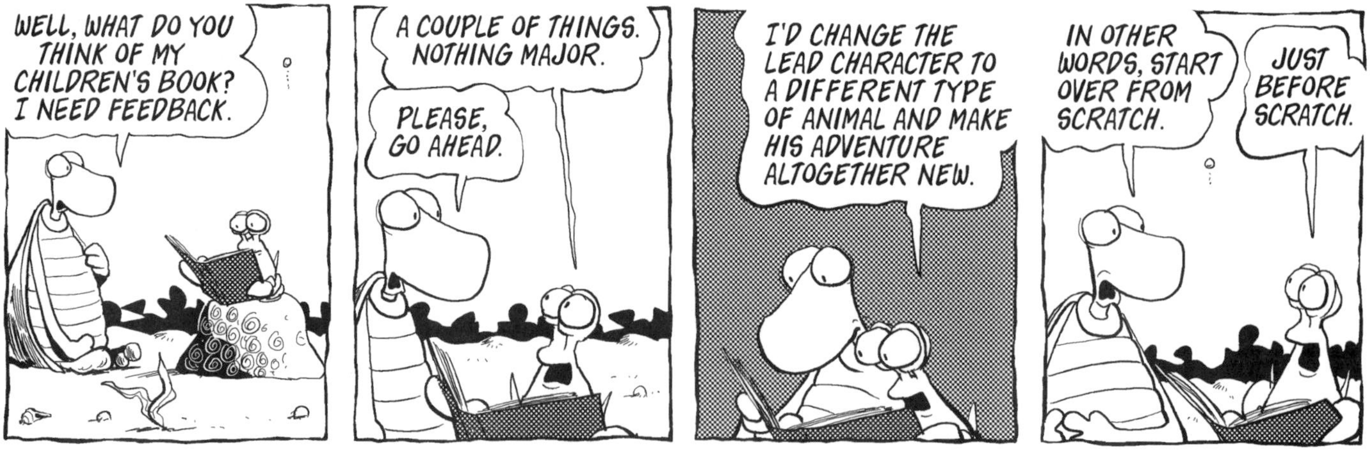
WELL, WHAT DO YOU THINK OF MY CHILDREN'S BOOK? I NEED FEEDBACK.
A COUPLE OF THINGS. NOTHING MAJOR.
PLEASE, GO AHEAD.
I'D CHANGE THE LEAD CHARACTER TO A DIFFERENT TYPE OF ANIMAL AND MAKE HIS ADVENTURE ALTOGETHER NEW.
IN OTHER WORDS, START OVER FROM SCRATCH.
JUST BEFORE SCRATCH.

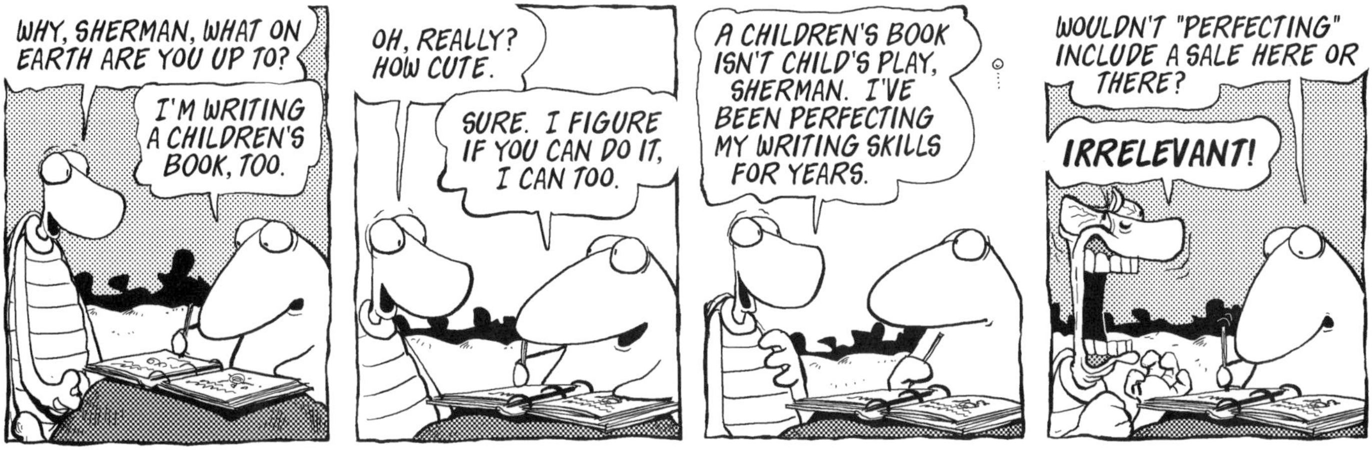
WHY, SHERMAN, WHAT ON EARTH ARE YOU UP TO?
I'M WRITING A CHILDREN'S BOOK, TOO.
OH, REALLY? HOW CUTE.
SURE. I FIGURE IF YOU CAN DO IT, I CAN TOO.
A CHILDREN'S BOOK ISN'T CHILD'S PLAY, SHERMAN. I'VE BEEN PERFECTING MY WRITING SKILLS FOR YEARS.
WOULDN'T "PERFECTING" INCLUDE A SALE HERE OR THERE?
IRRELEVANT!

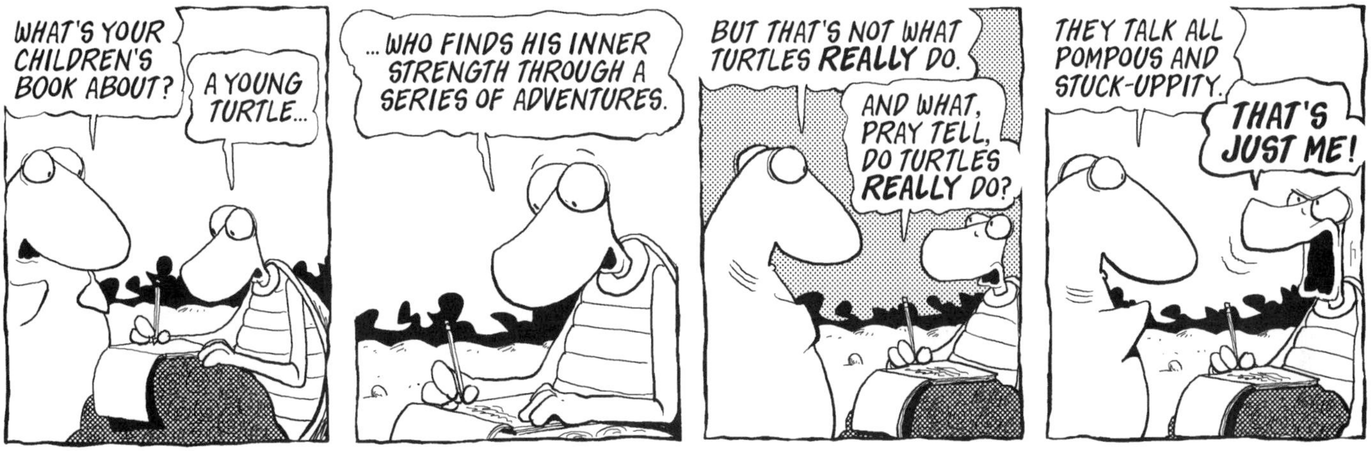
WHAT'S YOUR CHILDREN'S BOOK ABOUT?
A YOUNG TURTLE...
...WHO FINDS HIS INNER STRENGTH THROUGH A SERIES OF ADVENTURES.
BUT THAT'S NOT WHAT TURTLES **REALLY** DO.
AND WHAT, PRAY TELL, DO TURTLES **REALLY** DO?
THEY TALK ALL POMPOUS AND STUCK-UPPITY.
THAT'S JUST ME!

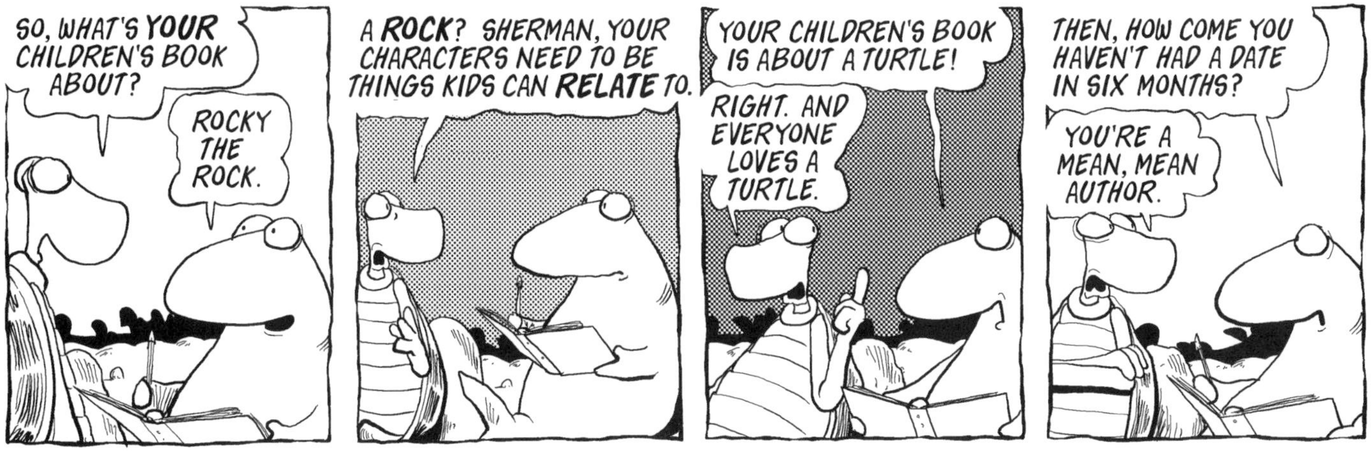
SO, WHAT'S **YOUR** CHILDREN'S BOOK ABOUT?
ROCKY THE ROCK.
A **ROCK**? SHERMAN, YOUR CHARACTERS NEED TO BE THINGS KIDS CAN **RELATE** TO.
YOUR CHILDREN'S BOOK IS ABOUT A TURTLE!
RIGHT. AND EVERYONE LOVES A TURTLE.
THEN, HOW COME YOU HAVEN'T HAD A DATE IN SIX MONTHS?
YOU'RE A MEAN, MEAN AUTHOR.

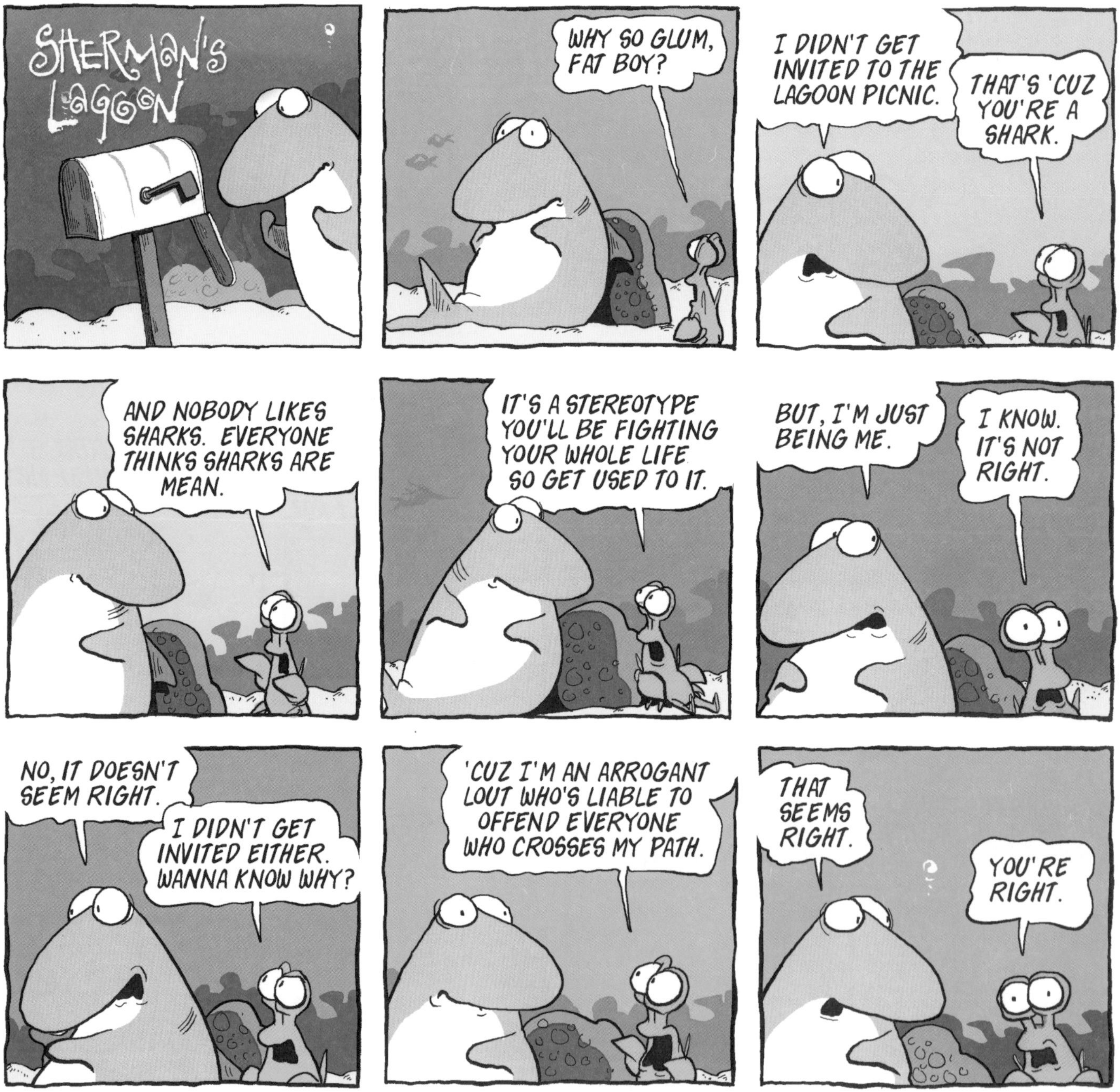
SHERMAN'S LAGOON
WHY SO GLUM, FAT BOY?
I DIDN'T GET INVITED TO THE LAGOON PICNIC.
THAT'S 'CUZ YOU'RE A SHARK.
AND NOBODY LIKES SHARKS. EVERYONE THINKS SHARKS ARE MEAN.
IT'S A STEREOTYPE YOU'LL BE FIGHTING YOUR WHOLE LIFE SO GET USED TO IT.
BUT, I'M JUST BEING ME.
I KNOW. IT'S NOT RIGHT.
NO, IT DOESN'T SEEM RIGHT.
I DIDN'T GET INVITED EITHER. WANNA KNOW WHY?
'CUZ I'M AN ARROGANT LOUT WHO'S LIABLE TO OFFEND EVERYONE WHO CROSSES MY PATH.
THAT SEEMS RIGHT.
YOU'RE RIGHT.

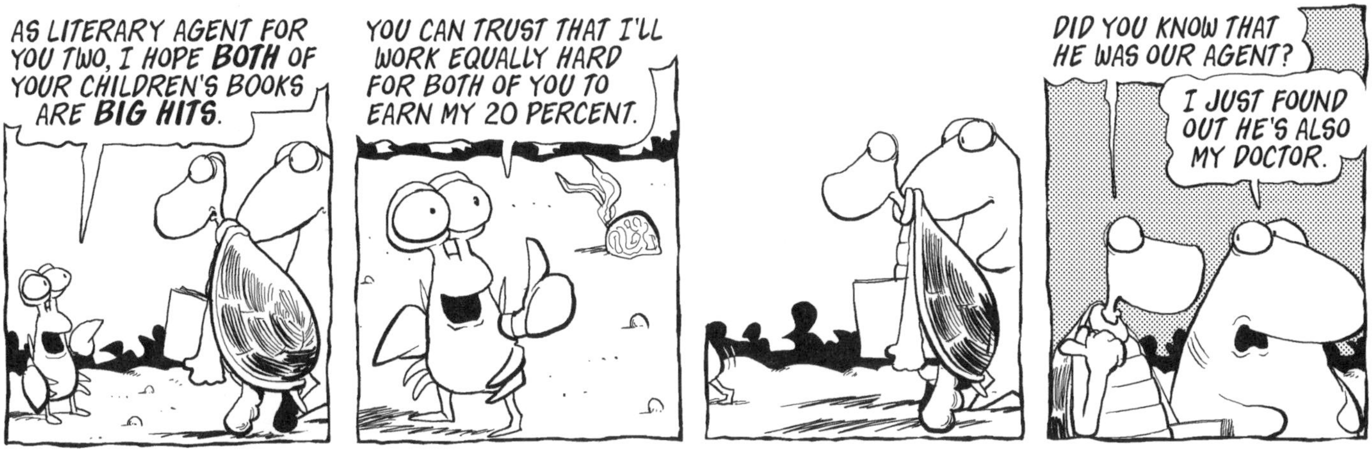
AS LITERARY AGENT FOR YOU TWO, I HOPE **BOTH** OF YOUR CHILDREN'S BOOKS ARE **BIG HITS**.
YOU CAN TRUST THAT I'LL WORK EQUALLY HARD FOR BOTH OF YOU TO EARN MY 20 PERCENT.
DID YOU KNOW THAT HE WAS OUR AGENT?
I JUST FOUND OUT HE'S ALSO MY DOCTOR.

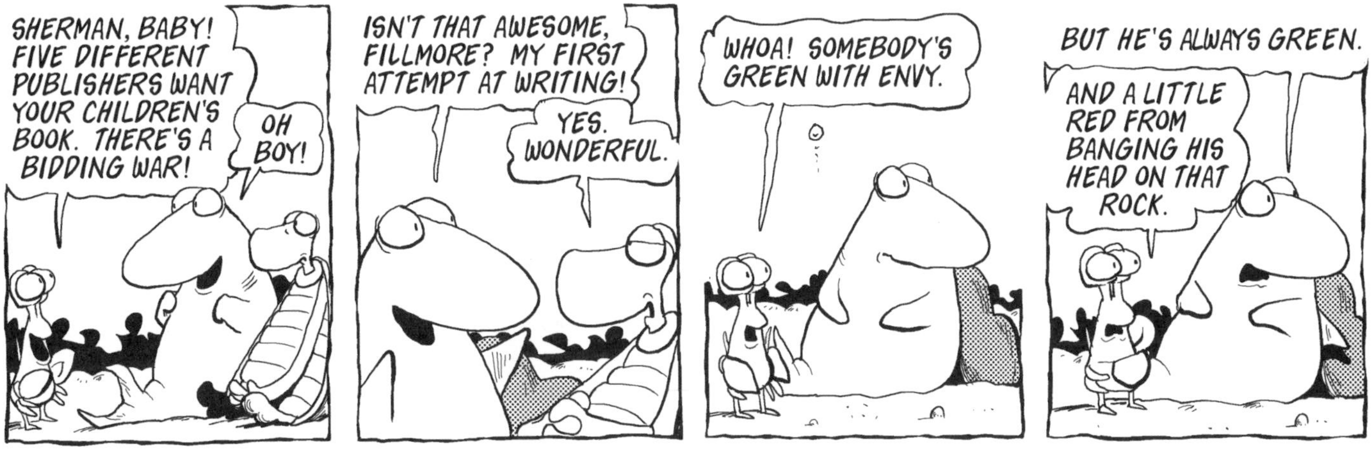
SHERMAN, BABY! FIVE DIFFERENT PUBLISHERS WANT YOUR CHILDREN'S BOOK. THERE'S A BIDDING WAR!
OH BOY!
ISN'T THAT AWESOME, FILLMORE? MY FIRST ATTEMPT AT WRITING!
YES. WONDERFUL.
WHOA! SOMEBODY'S GREEN WITH ENVY.
BUT HE'S ALWAYS GREEN.
AND A LITTLE RED FROM BANGING HIS HEAD ON THAT ROCK.

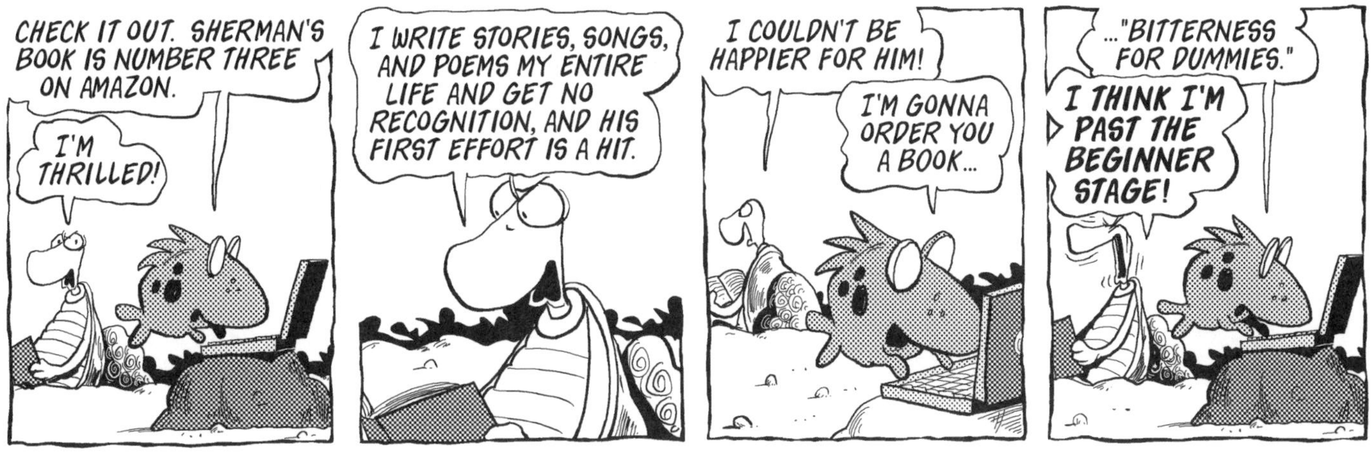
CHECK IT OUT. SHERMAN'S BOOK IS NUMBER THREE ON AMAZON.
I'M THRILLED!
I WRITE STORIES, SONGS, AND POEMS MY ENTIRE LIFE AND GET NO RECOGNITION, AND HIS FIRST EFFORT IS A HIT.
I COULDN'T BE HAPPIER FOR HIM!
I'M GONNA ORDER YOU A BOOK...
..."BITTERNESS FOR DUMMIES."
I THINK I'M PAST THE BEGINNER STAGE!

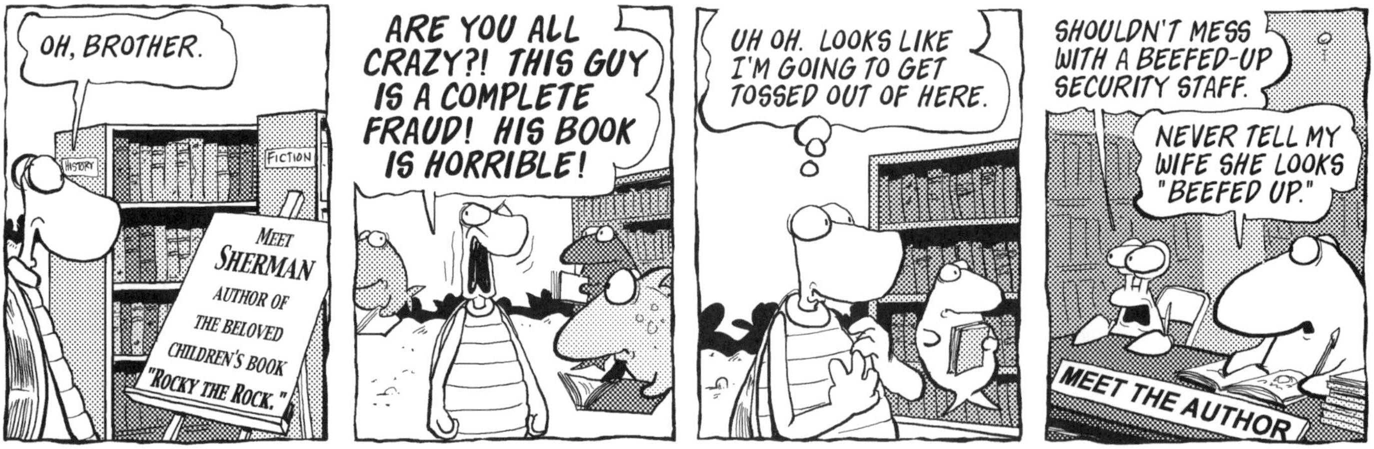
OH, BROTHER.
HISTORY
FICTION
MEET SHERMAN AUTHOR OF THE BELOVED CHILDREN'S BOOK "ROCKY THE ROCK."
ARE YOU ALL CRAZY?! THIS GUY IS A COMPLETE FRAUD! HIS BOOK IS HORRIBLE!
UH OH. LOOKS LIKE I'M GOING TO GET TOSSED OUT OF HERE.
SHOULDN'T MESS WITH A BEEFED-UP SECURITY STAFF.
NEVER TELL MY WIFE SHE LOOKS "BEEFED UP."
MEET THE AUTHOR

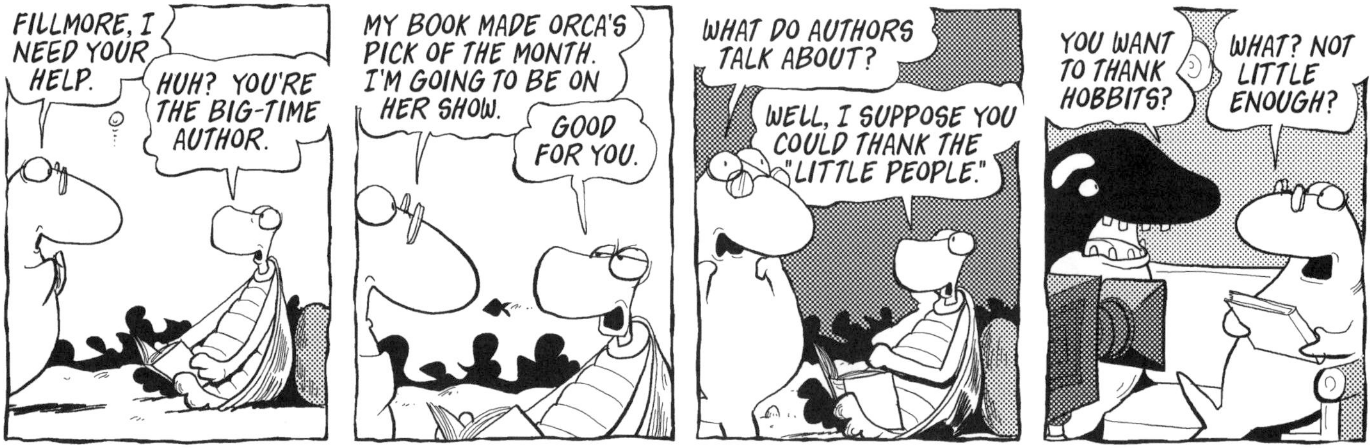
FILLMORE, I NEED YOUR HELP.
HUH? YOU'RE THE BIG-TIME AUTHOR.
MY BOOK MADE ORCA'S PICK OF THE MONTH. I'M GOING TO BE ON HER SHOW.
GOOD FOR YOU.
WHAT DO AUTHORS TALK ABOUT?
WELL, I SUPPOSE YOU COULD THANK THE "LITTLE PEOPLE."
YOU WANT TO THANK HOBBITS?
WHAT? NOT LITTLE ENOUGH?

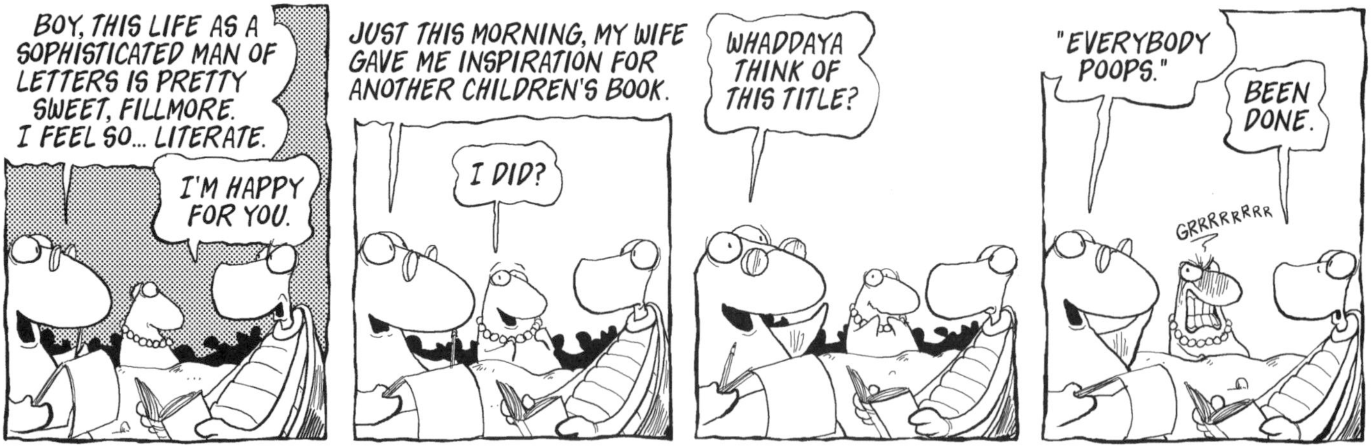
BOY, THIS LIFE AS A SOPHISTICATED MAN OF LETTERS IS PRETTY SWEET, FILLMORE. I FEEL SO... LITERATE.
I'M HAPPY FOR YOU.
JUST THIS MORNING, MY WIFE GAVE ME INSPIRATION FOR ANOTHER CHILDREN'S BOOK.
I DID?
WHADDAYA THINK OF THIS TITLE?
"EVERYBODY POOPS."
BEEN DONE.
GRRRRRRRR

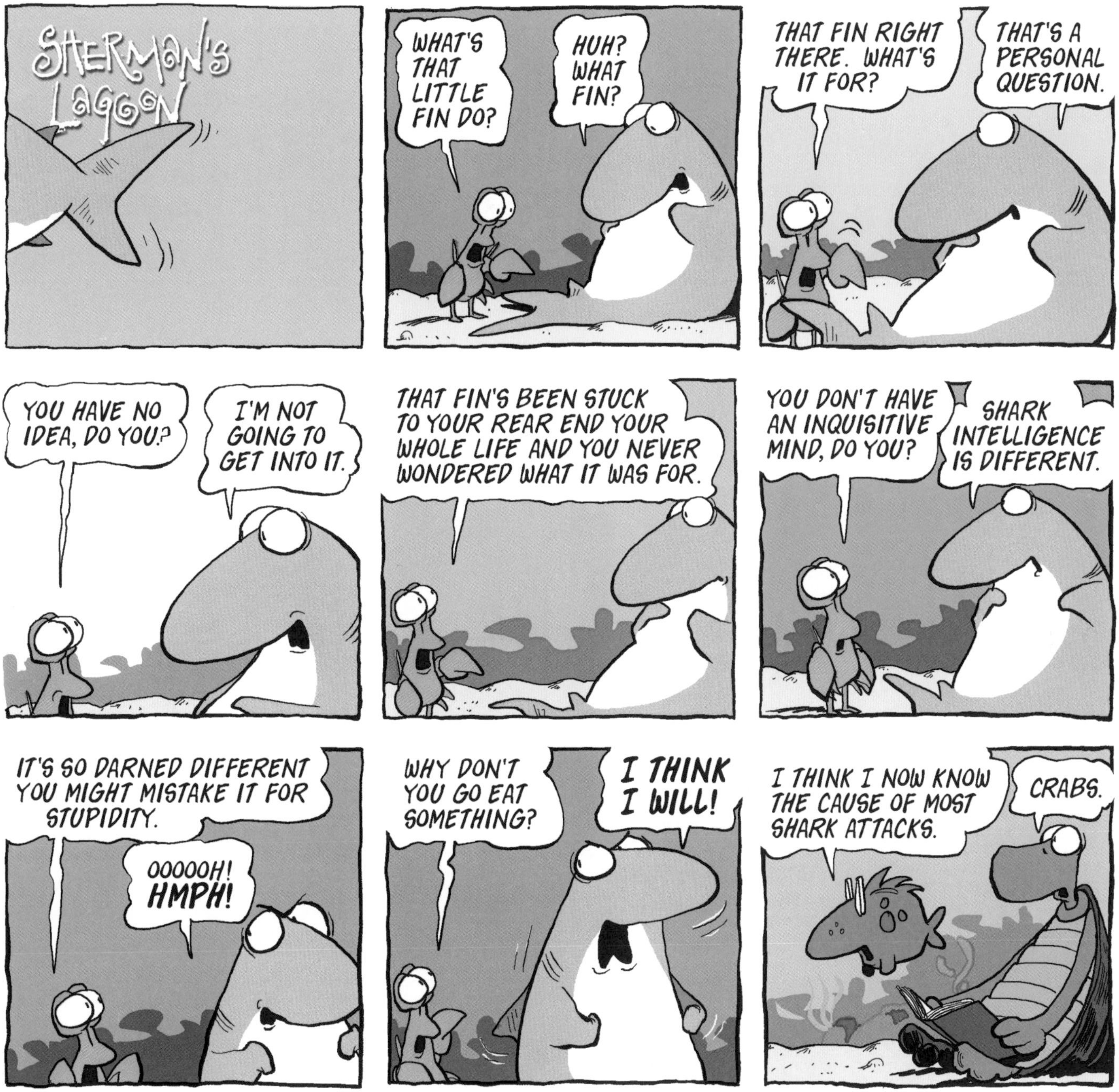
SHERMAN'S LAGOON
WHAT'S THAT LITTLE FIN DO?
HUH? WHAT FIN?
THAT FIN RIGHT THERE. WHAT'S IT FOR?
THAT'S A PERSONAL QUESTION.
YOU HAVE NO IDEA, DO YOU?
I'M NOT GOING TO GET INTO IT.
THAT FIN'S BEEN STUCK TO YOUR REAR END YOUR WHOLE LIFE AND YOU NEVER WONDERED WHAT IT WAS FOR.
YOU DON'T HAVE AN INQUISITIVE MIND, DO YOU?
SHARK INTELLIGENCE IS DIFFERENT.
IT'S SO DARNED DIFFERENT YOU MIGHT MISTAKE IT FOR STUPIDITY.
OOOOOH! HMPH!
WHY DON'T YOU GO EAT SOMETHING?
I THINK I WILL!
I THINK I NOW KNOW THE CAUSE OF MOST SHARK ATTACKS.
CRABS.

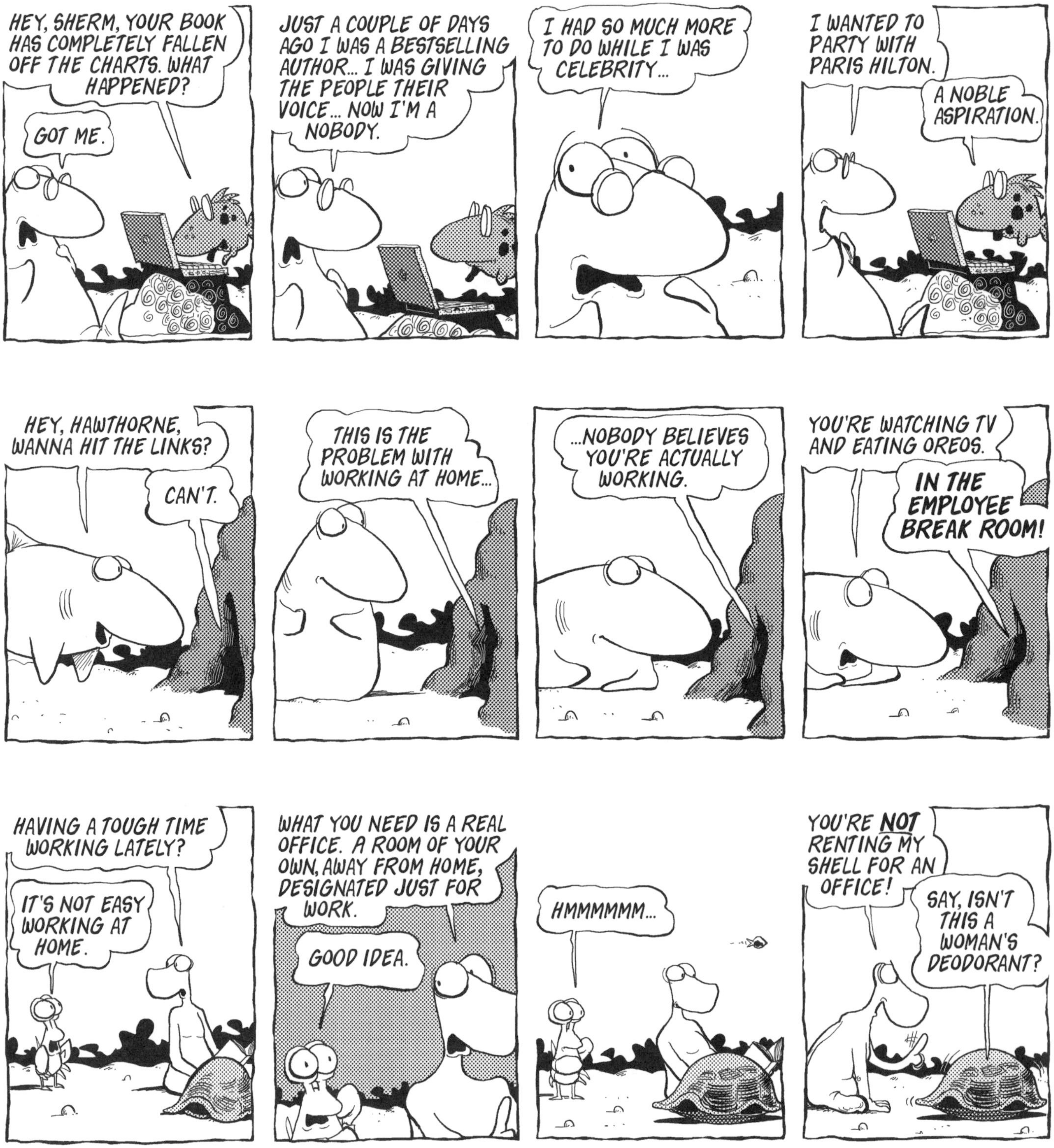
HEY, SHERM, YOUR BOOK HAS COMPLETELY FALLEN OFF THE CHARTS. WHAT HAPPENED?
GOT ME.
JUST A COUPLE OF DAYS AGO I WAS A BESTSELLING AUTHOR... I WAS GIVING THE PEOPLE THEIR VOICE... NOW I'M A NOBODY.
I HAD SO MUCH MORE TO DO WHILE I WAS CELEBRITY...
I WANTED TO PARTY WITH PARIS HILTON.
A NOBLE ASPIRATION.
HEY, HAWTHORNE, WANNA HIT THE LINKS?
CAN'T.
THIS IS THE PROBLEM WITH WORKING AT HOME...
...NOBODY BELIEVES YOU'RE ACTUALLY WORKING.
YOU'RE WATCHING TV AND EATING OREOS.
IN THE EMPLOYEE BREAK ROOM!
HAVING A TOUGH TIME WORKING LATELY?
IT'S NOT EASY WORKING AT HOME.
WHAT YOU NEED IS A REAL OFFICE. A ROOM OF YOUR OWN, AWAY FROM HOME, DESIGNATED JUST FOR WORK.
GOOD IDEA.
HMMMMMM...
YOU'RE NOT RENTING MY SHELL FOR AN OFFICE!
SAY, ISN'T THIS A WOMAN'S DEODORANT?

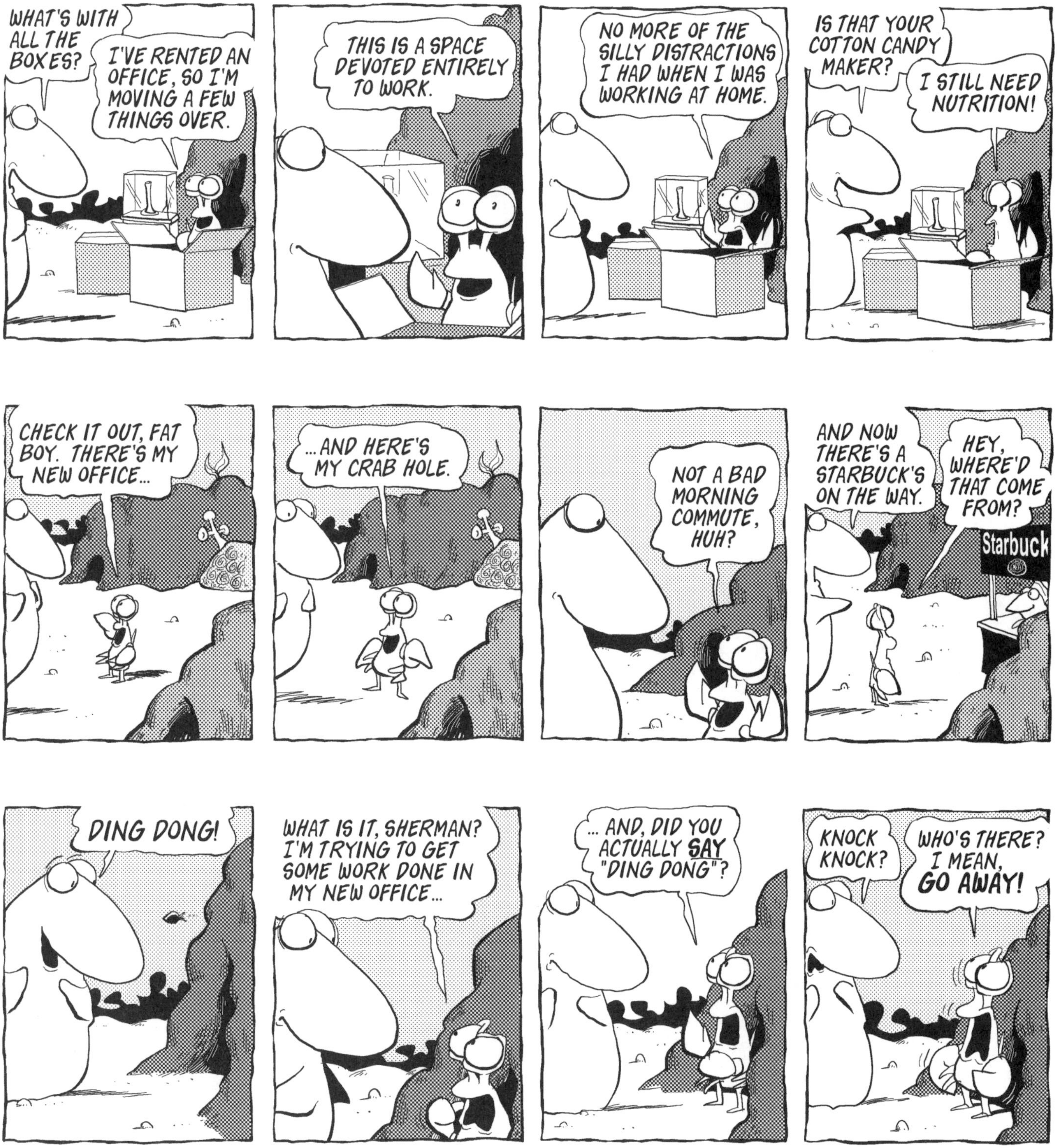
WHAT'S WITH ALL THE BOXES?
I'VE RENTED AN OFFICE, SO I'M MOVING A FEW THINGS OVER.
THIS IS A SPACE DEVOTED ENTIRELY TO WORK.
NO MORE OF THE SILLY DISTRACTIONS I HAD WHEN I WAS WORKING AT HOME.
IS THAT YOUR COTTON CANDY MAKER?
I STILL NEED NUTRITION!
CHECK IT OUT, FAT BOY. THERE'S MY NEW OFFICE...
...AND HERE'S MY CRAB HOLE.
NOT A BAD MORNING COMMUTE, HUH?
AND NOW THERE'S A STARBUCK'S ON THE WAY.
HEY, WHERE'D THAT COME FROM?
Starbuck
DING DONG!
WHAT IS IT, SHERMAN? I'M TRYING TO GET SOME WORK DONE IN MY NEW OFFICE...
... AND, DID YOU ACTUALLY SAY "DING DONG"?
KNOCK KNOCK?
WHO'S THERE? I MEAN, GO AWAY!

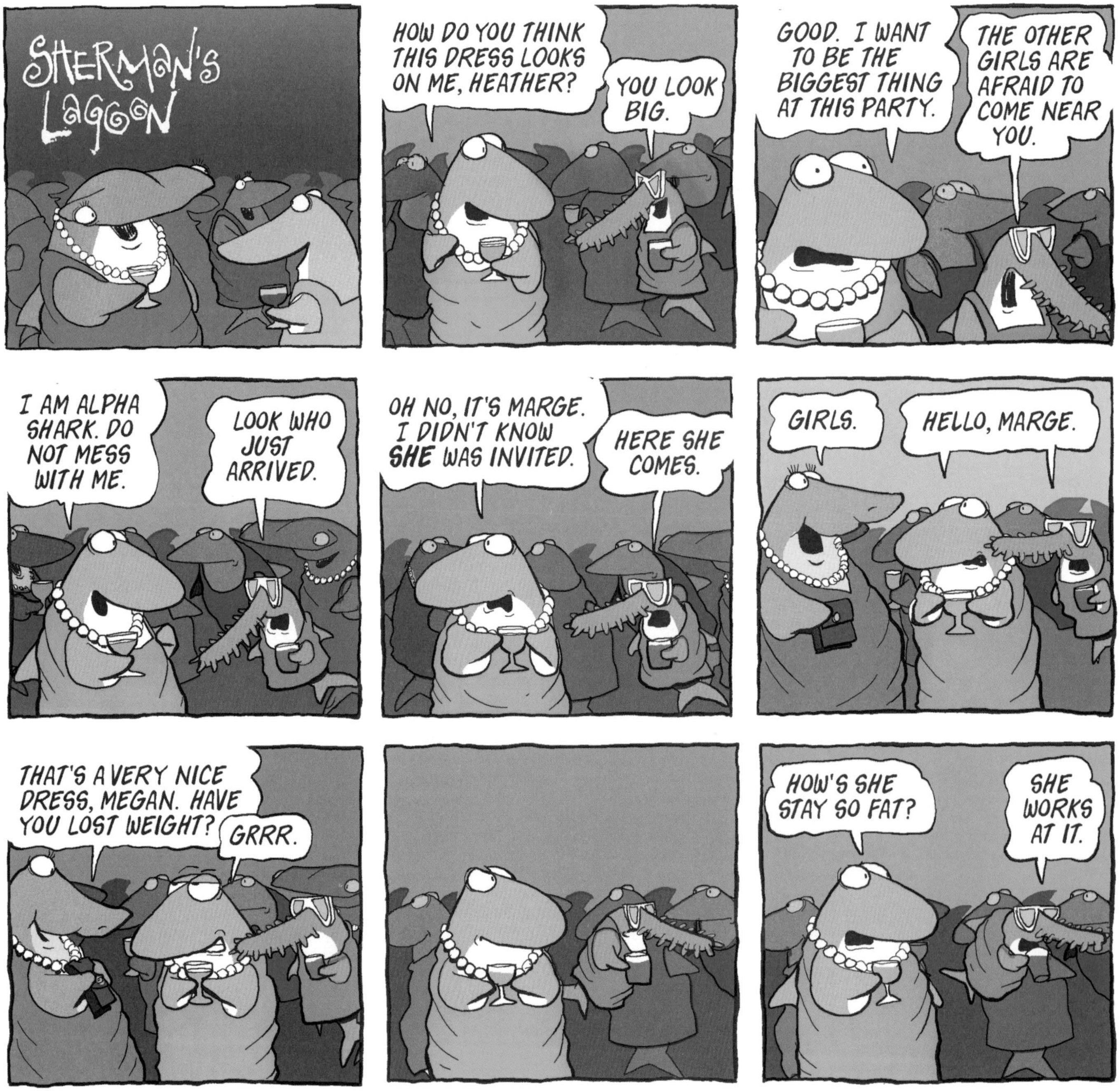
SHERMAN'S LAGOON
HOW DO YOU THINK THIS DRESS LOOKS ON ME, HEATHER?
YOU LOOK BIG.
GOOD. I WANT TO BE THE BIGGEST THING AT THIS PARTY.
THE OTHER GIRLS ARE AFRAID TO COME NEAR YOU.
I AM ALPHA SHARK. DO NOT MESS WITH ME.
LOOK WHO JUST ARRIVED.
OH NO, IT'S MARGE. I DIDN'T KNOW SHE WAS INVITED.
HERE SHE COMES.
GIRLS.
HELLO, MARGE.
THAT'S A VERY NICE DRESS, MEGAN. HAVE YOU LOST WEIGHT?
GRRR.
HOW'S SHE STAY SO FAT?
SHE WORKS AT IT.

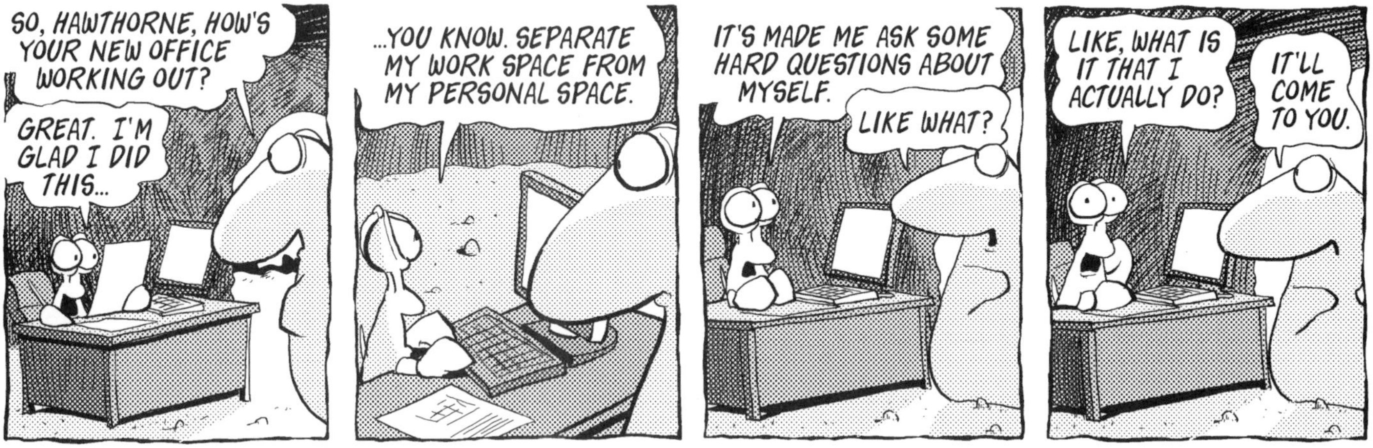
SO, HAWTHORNE, HOW'S YOUR NEW OFFICE WORKING OUT?
GREAT. I'M GLAD I DID THIS...
...YOU KNOW. SEPARATE MY WORK SPACE FROM MY PERSONAL SPACE.
IT'S MADE ME ASK SOME HARD QUESTIONS ABOUT MYSELF.
LIKE WHAT?
LIKE, WHAT IS IT THAT I ACTUALLY DO?
IT'LL COME TO YOU.

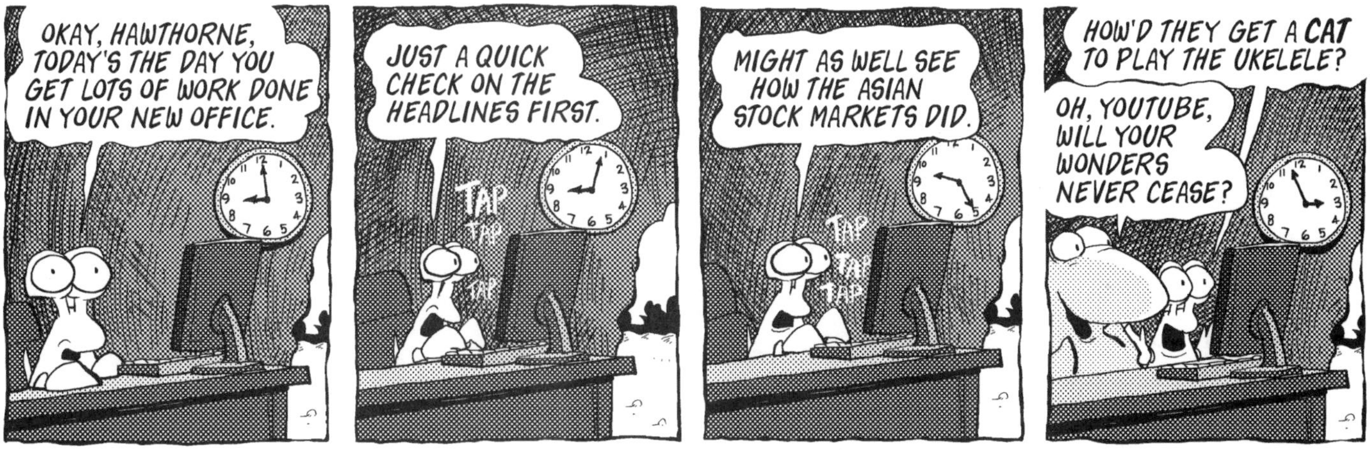
OKAY, HAWTHORNE, TODAY'S THE DAY YOU GET LOTS OF WORK DONE IN YOUR NEW OFFICE.
JUST A QUICK CHECK ON THE HEADLINES FIRST.
TAP TAP TAP
MIGHT AS WELL SEE HOW THE ASIAN STOCK MARKETS DID.
TAP TAP TAP
HOW'D THEY GET A **CAT** TO PLAY THE UKELELE?
OH, YOUTUBE, WILL YOUR WONDERS NEVER CEASE?

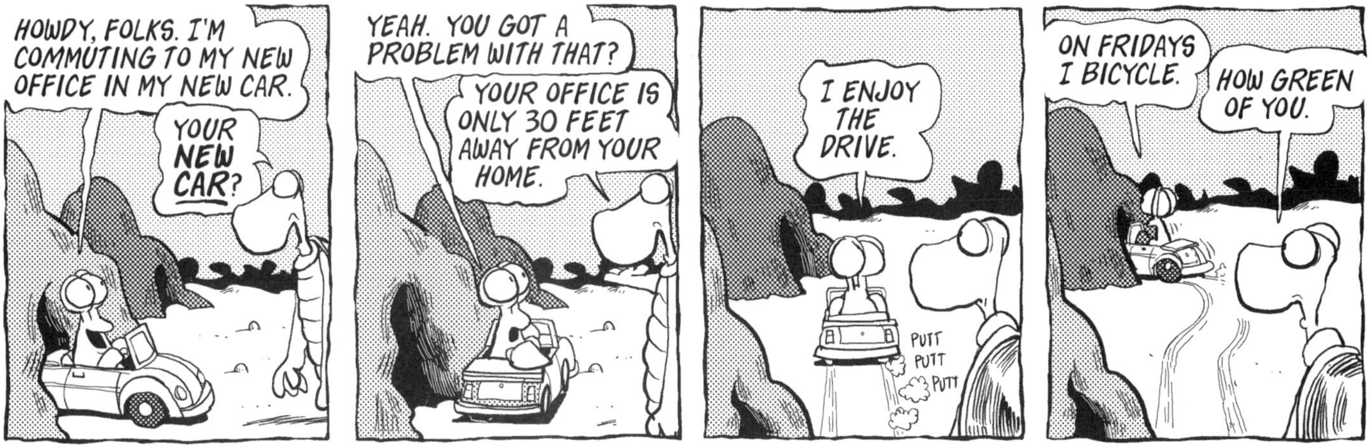
HOWDY, FOLKS. I'M COMMUTING TO MY NEW OFFICE IN MY NEW CAR.
YOUR **NEW CAR**?
YEAH. YOU GOT A PROBLEM WITH THAT?
YOUR OFFICE IS ONLY 30 FEET AWAY FROM YOUR HOME.
I ENJOY THE DRIVE.
PUTT PUTT PUTT
ON FRIDAYS I BICYCLE.
HOW GREEN OF YOU.

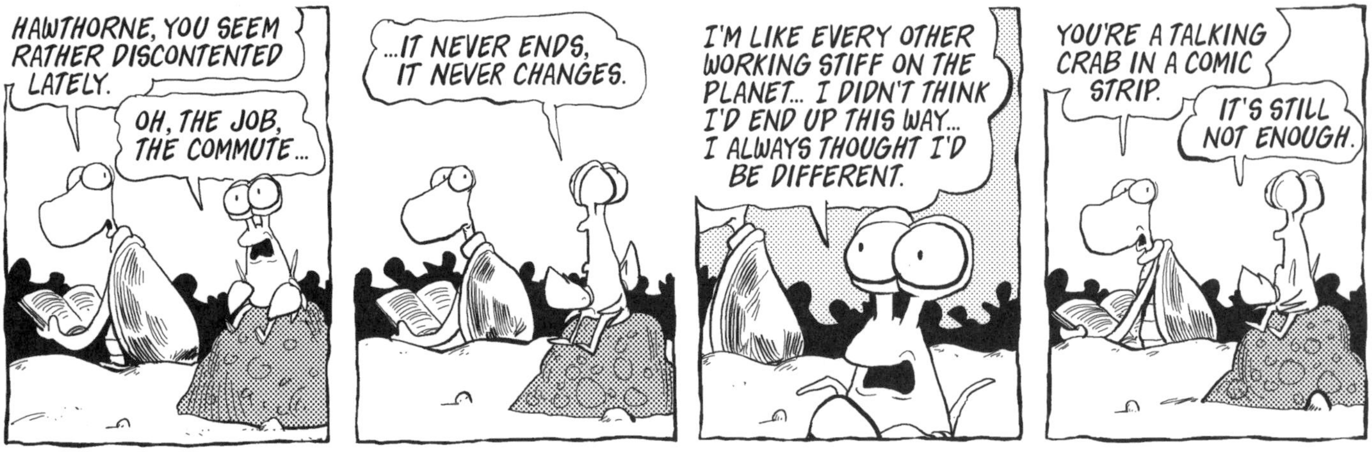
HAWTHORNE, YOU SEEM RATHER DISCONTENTED LATELY.
OH, THE JOB, THE COMMUTE...
...IT NEVER ENDS, IT NEVER CHANGES.
I'M LIKE EVERY OTHER WORKING STIFF ON THE PLANET... I DIDN'T THINK I'D END UP THIS WAY... I ALWAYS THOUGHT I'D BE DIFFERENT.
YOU'RE A TALKING CRAB IN A COMIC STRIP.
IT'S STILL NOT ENOUGH.

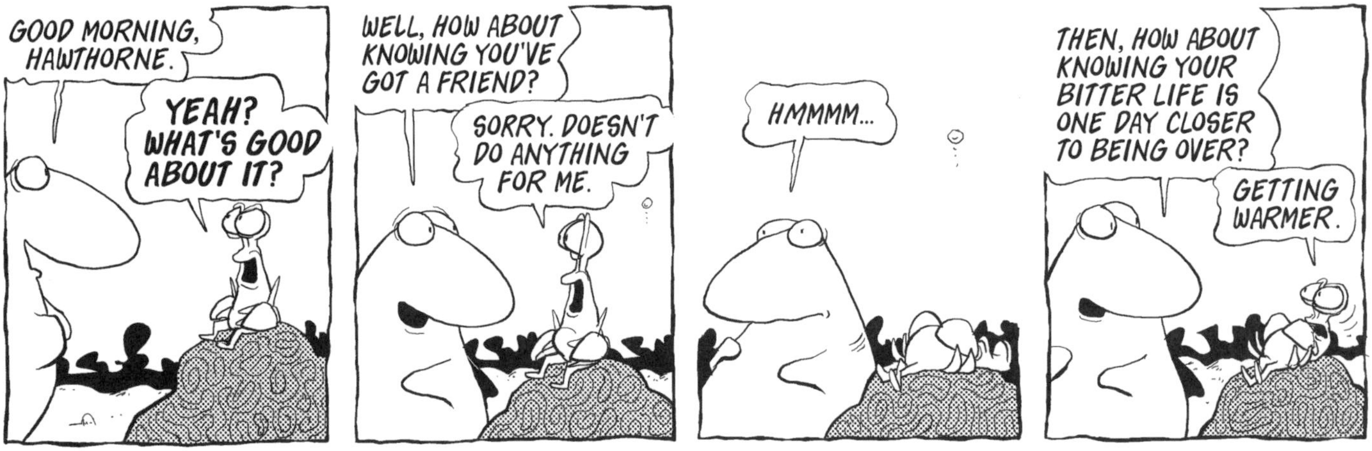
GOOD MORNING, HAWTHORNE.
YEAH? WHAT'S GOOD ABOUT IT?
WELL, HOW ABOUT KNOWING YOU'VE GOT A FRIEND?
SORRY. DOESN'T DO ANYTHING FOR ME.
HMMMM...
THEN, HOW ABOUT KNOWING YOUR BITTER LIFE IS ONE DAY CLOSER TO BEING OVER?
GETTING WARMER.

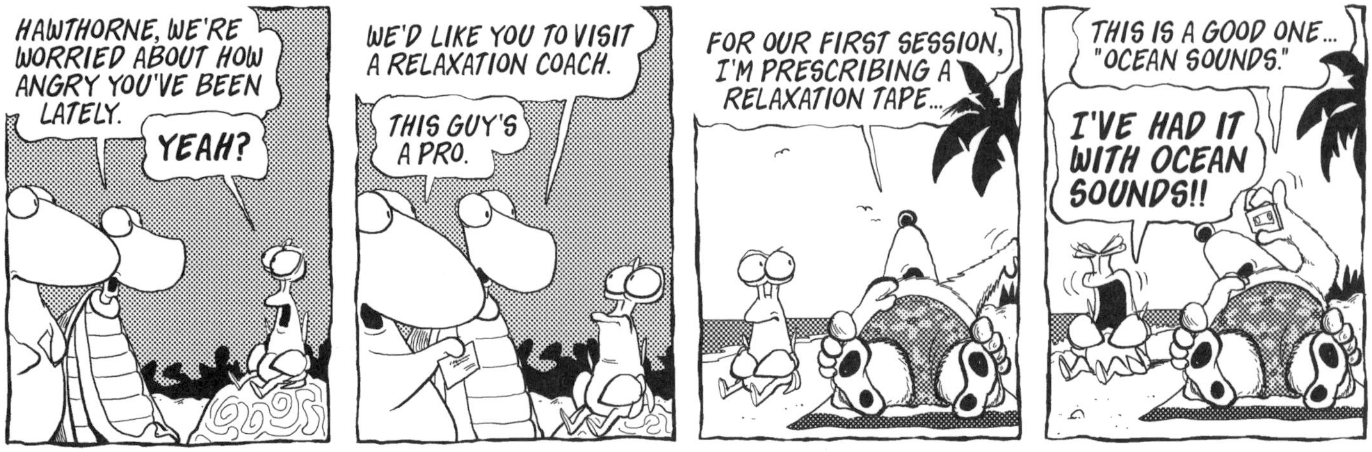
HAWTHORNE, WE'RE WORRIED ABOUT HOW ANGRY YOU'VE BEEN LATELY.
YEAH?
WE'D LIKE YOU TO VISIT A RELAXATION COACH.
THIS GUY'S A PRO.
FOR OUR FIRST SESSION, I'M PRESCRIBING A RELAXATION TAPE...
THIS IS A GOOD ONE... "OCEAN SOUNDS."
I'VE HAD IT WITH OCEAN SOUNDS!!

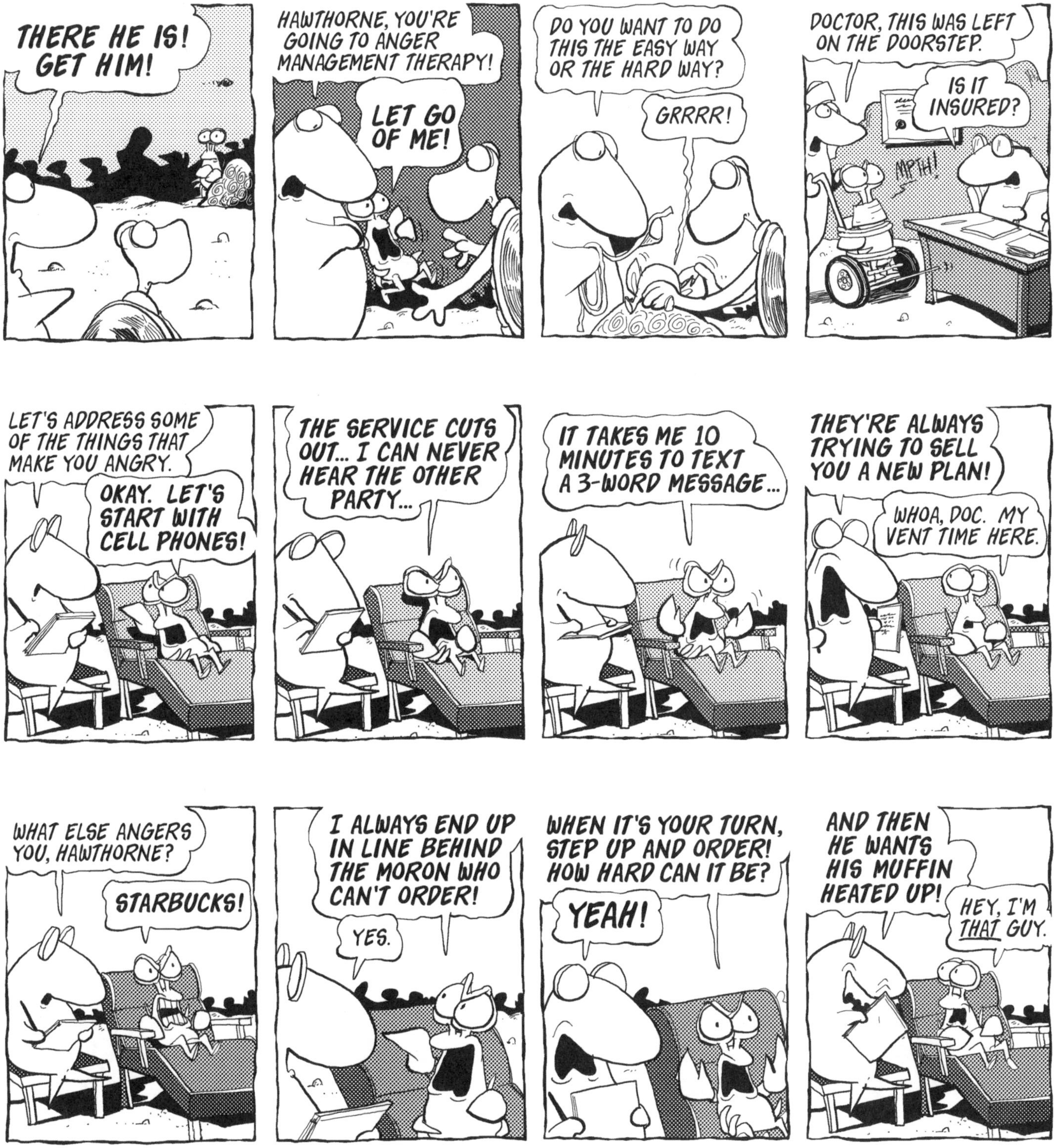
THERE HE IS! GET HIM!
HAWTHORNE, YOU'RE GOING TO ANGER MANAGEMENT THERAPY!
LET GO OF ME!
DO YOU WANT TO DO THIS THE EASY WAY OR THE HARD WAY?
GRRRR!
DOCTOR, THIS WAS LEFT ON THE DOORSTEP.
IS IT INSURED?
MPTH!
LET'S ADDRESS SOME OF THE THINGS THAT MAKE YOU ANGRY.
OKAY. LET'S START WITH CELL PHONES!
THE SERVICE CUTS OUT... I CAN NEVER HEAR THE OTHER PARTY...
IT TAKES ME 10 MINUTES TO TEXT A 3-WORD MESSAGE...
THEY'RE ALWAYS TRYING TO SELL YOU A NEW PLAN!
WHOA, DOC. MY VENT TIME HERE.
WHAT ELSE ANGERS YOU, HAWTHORNE?
STARBUCKS!
I ALWAYS END UP IN LINE BEHIND THE MORON WHO CAN'T ORDER!
YES.
WHEN IT'S YOUR TURN, STEP UP AND ORDER! HOW HARD CAN IT BE?
YEAH!
AND THEN HE WANTS HIS MUFFIN HEATED UP!
HEY, I'M THAT GUY.

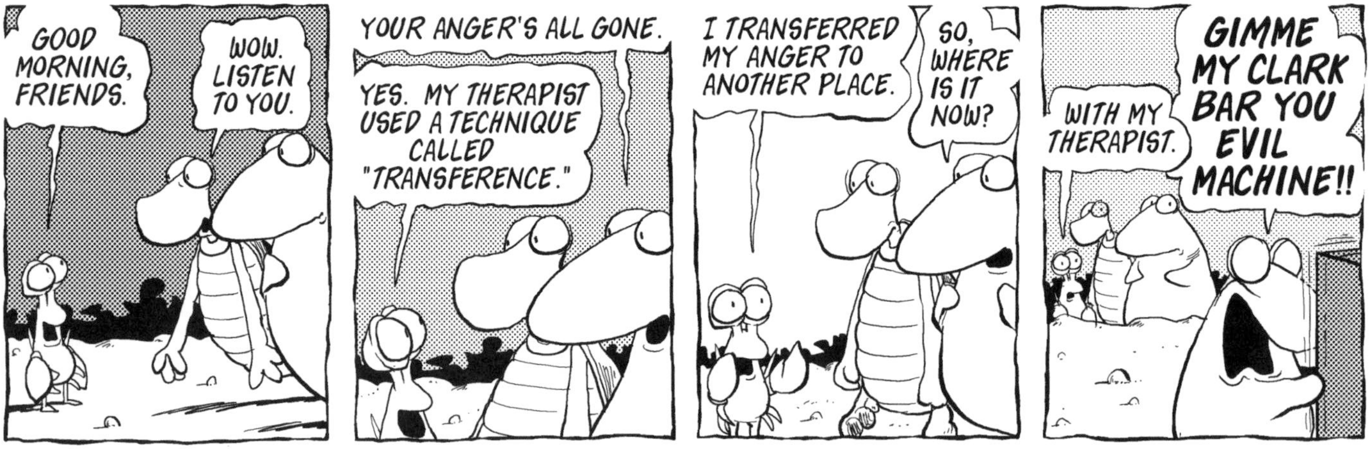
GOOD MORNING, FRIENDS.
WOW. LISTEN TO YOU.
YOUR ANGER'S ALL GONE.
YES. MY THERAPIST USED A TECHNIQUE CALLED "TRANSFERENCE."
I TRANSFERRED MY ANGER TO ANOTHER PLACE.
SO, WHERE IS IT NOW?
WITH MY THERAPIST.
GIMME MY CLARK BAR YOU EVIL MACHINE!!

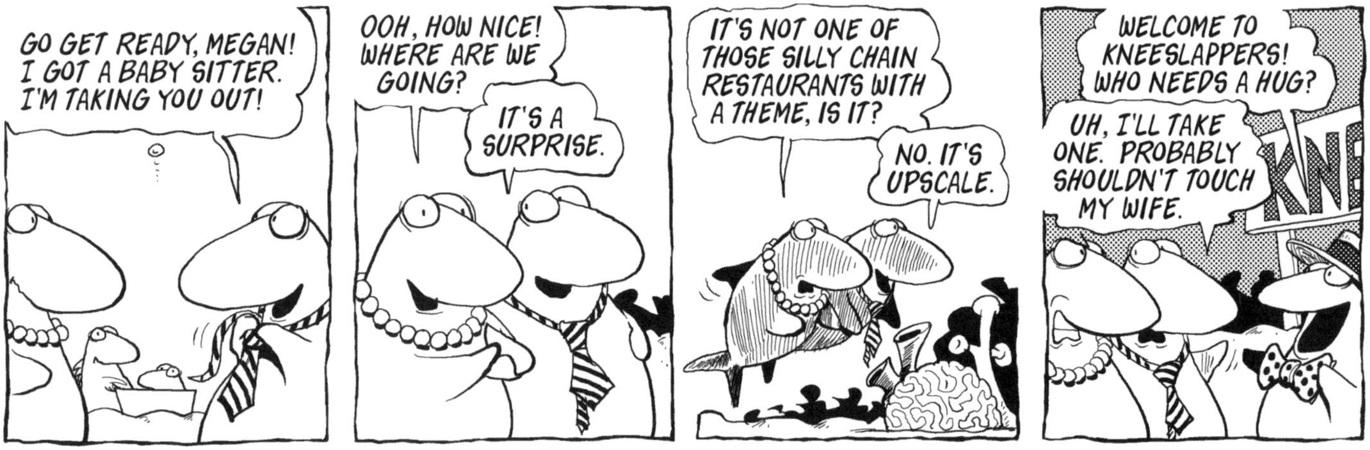
GO GET READY, MEGAN! I GOT A BABY SITTER. I'M TAKING YOU OUT!
OOH, HOW NICE! WHERE ARE WE GOING?
IT'S A SURPRISE.
IT'S NOT ONE OF THOSE SILLY CHAIN RESTAURANTS WITH A THEME, IS IT?
NO. IT'S UPSCALE.
WELCOME TO KNEESLAPPERS! WHO NEEDS A HUG?
UH, I'LL TAKE ONE. PROBABLY SHOULDN'T TOUCH MY WIFE.

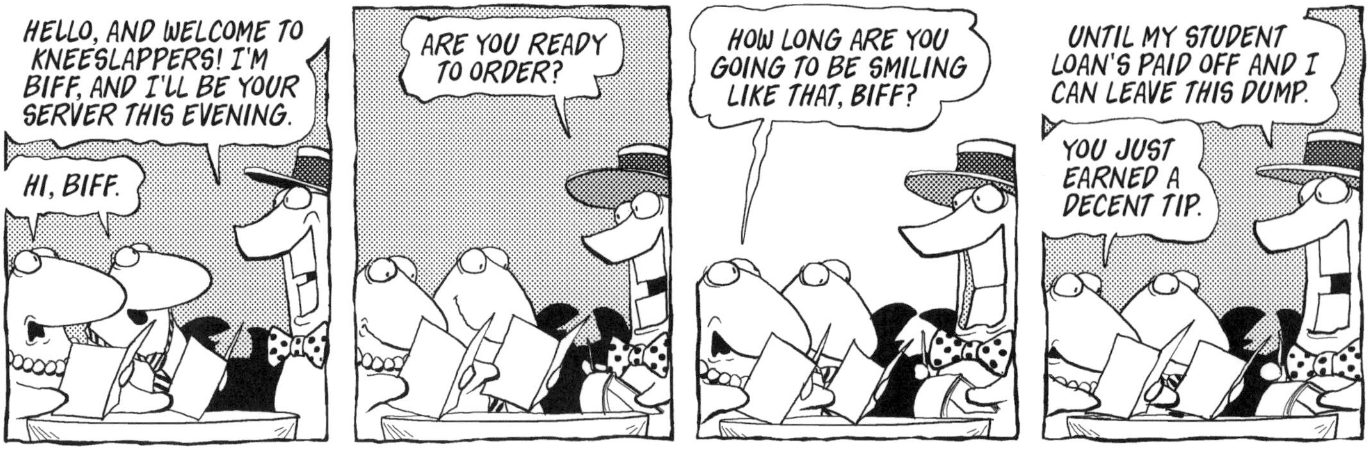
HELLO, AND WELCOME TO KNEESLAPPERS! I'M BIFF, AND I'LL BE YOUR SERVER THIS EVENING.
HI, BIFF.
ARE YOU READY TO ORDER?
HOW LONG ARE YOU GOING TO BE SMILING LIKE THAT, BIFF?
UNTIL MY STUDENT LOAN'S PAID OFF AND I CAN LEAVE THIS DUMP.
YOU JUST EARNED A DECENT TIP.

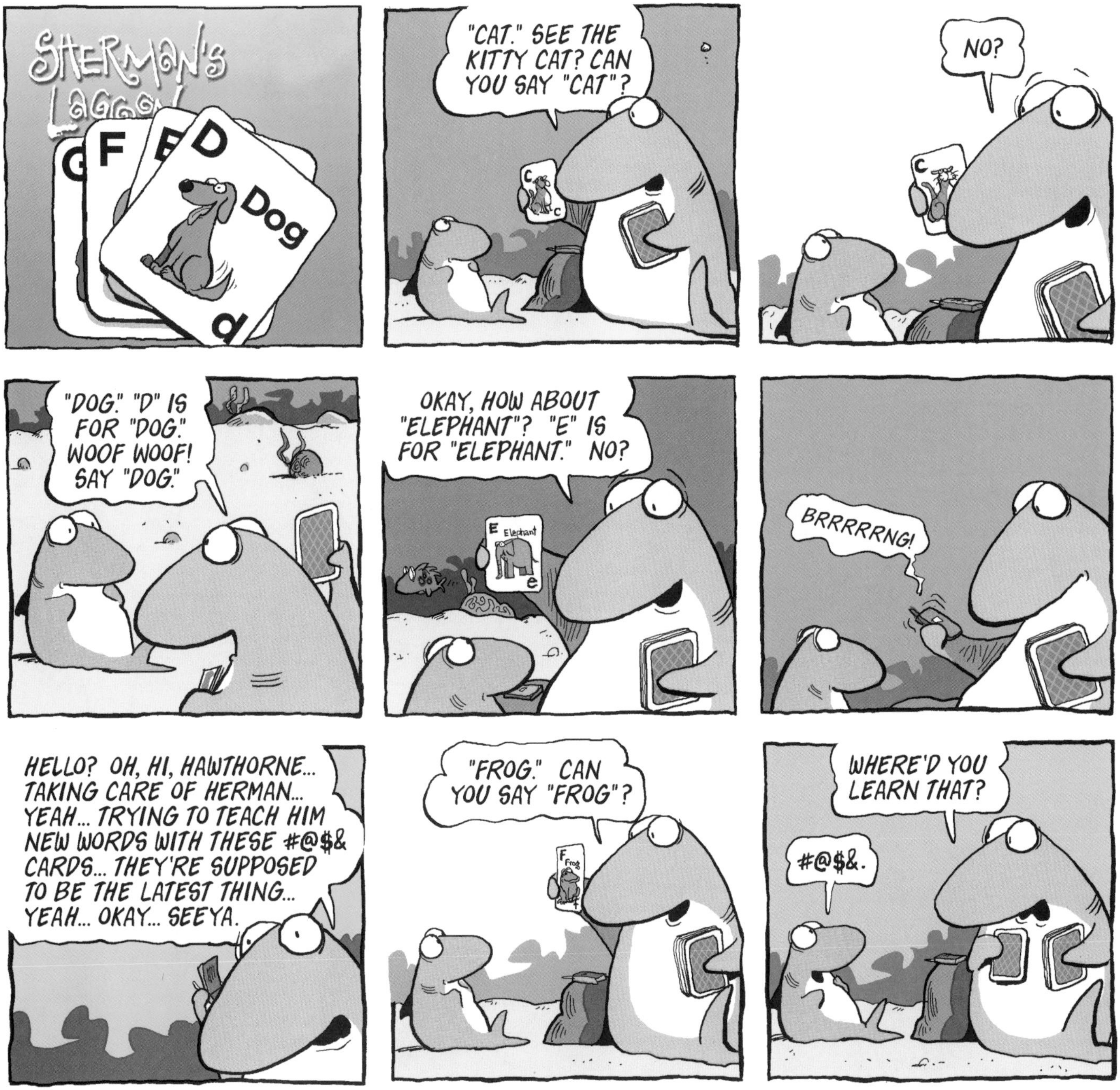
SHERMAN'S LAGOON
G
F
E
D
Dog
d
"CAT." SEE THE KITTY CAT? CAN YOU SAY "CAT"?
NO?
"DOG." "D" IS FOR "DOG." WOOF WOOF! SAY "DOG."
OKAY, HOW ABOUT "ELEPHANT"? "E" IS FOR "ELEPHANT." NO?
BRRRRRNG!
HELLO? OH, HI, HAWTHORNE... TAKING CARE OF HERMAN... YEAH... TRYING TO TEACH HIM NEW WORDS WITH THESE #@$& CARDS... THEY'RE SUPPOSED TO BE THE LATEST THING... YEAH... OKAY... SEEYA.
"FROG." CAN YOU SAY "FROG"?
WHERE'D YOU LEARN THAT?
#@$&.

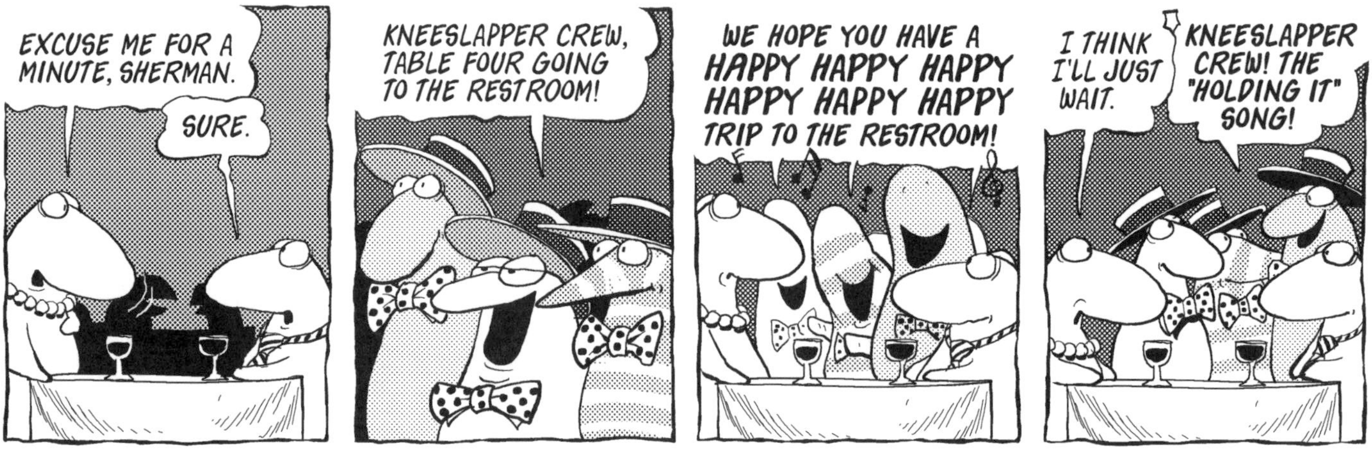
EXCUSE ME FOR A MINUTE, SHERMAN.
SURE.
KNEESLAPPER CREW, TABLE FOUR GOING TO THE RESTROOM!
WE HOPE YOU HAVE A HAPPY HAPPY HAPPY HAPPY HAPPY HAPPY TRIP TO THE RESTROOM!
I THINK I'LL JUST WAIT.
KNEESLAPPER CREW! THE "HOLDING IT" SONG!

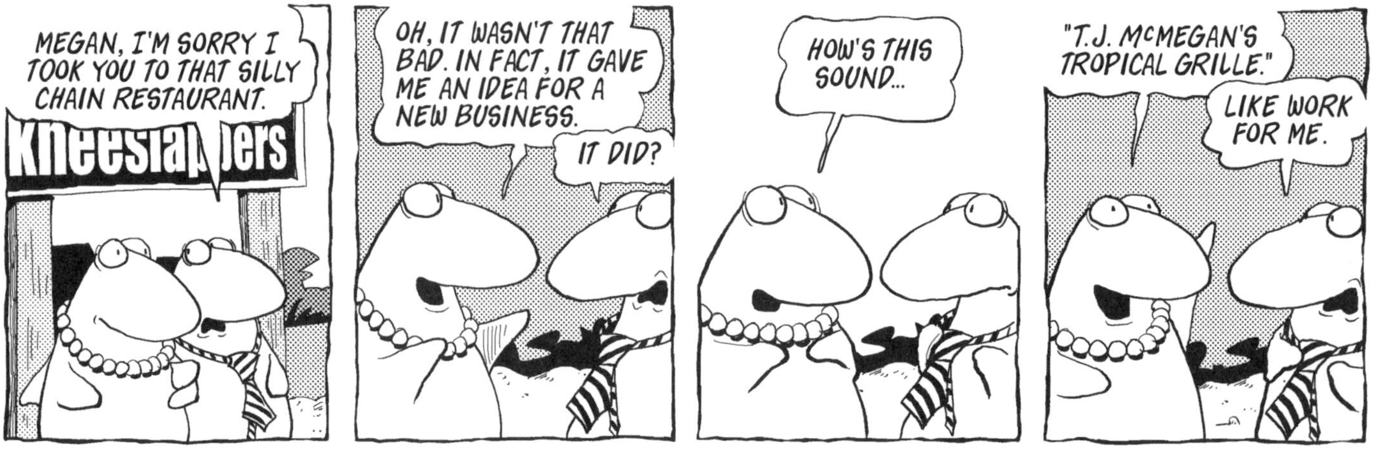
MEGAN, I'M SORRY I TOOK YOU TO THAT SILLY CHAIN RESTAURANT.
Kneeslap ers
OH, IT WASN'T THAT BAD. IN FACT, IT GAVE ME AN IDEA FOR A NEW BUSINESS.
IT DID?
HOW'S THIS SOUND...
"T.J. McMEGAN'S TROPICAL GRILLE."
LIKE WORK FOR ME.

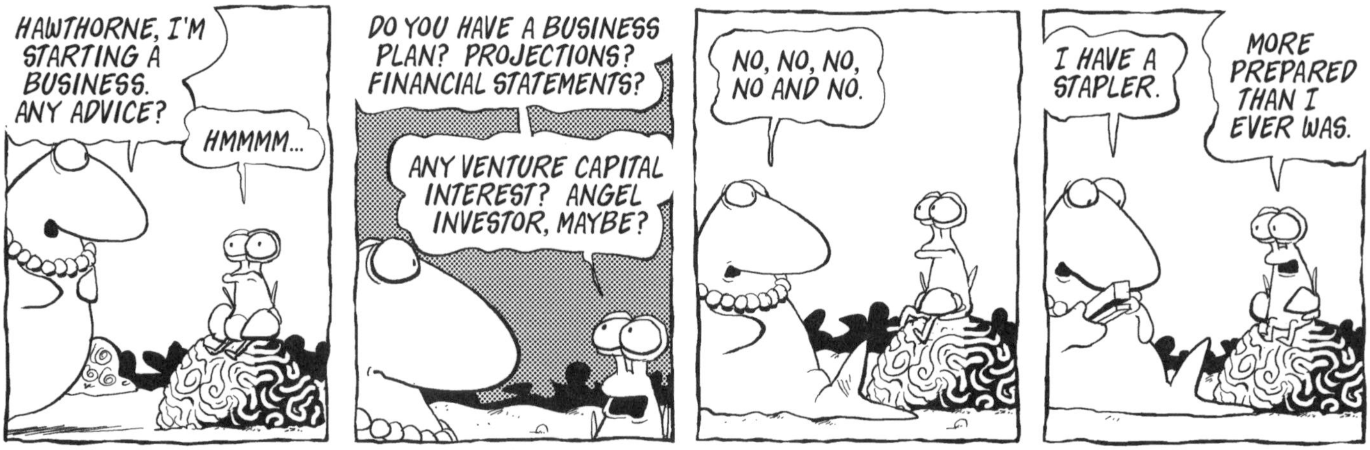
HAWTHORNE, I'M STARTING A BUSINESS. ANY ADVICE?
HMMMM...
DO YOU HAVE A BUSINESS PLAN? PROJECTIONS? FINANCIAL STATEMENTS?
ANY VENTURE CAPITAL INTEREST? ANGEL INVESTOR, MAYBE?
NO, NO, NO, NO AND NO.
I HAVE A STAPLER.
MORE PREPARED THAN I EVER WAS.

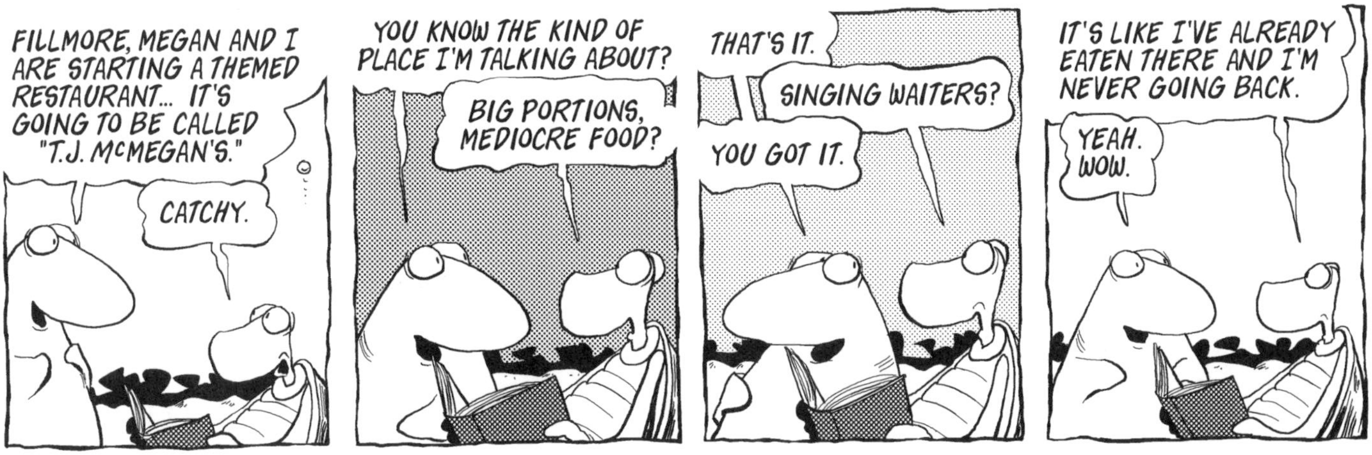
FILLMORE, MEGAN AND I ARE STARTING A THEMED RESTAURANT... IT'S GOING TO BE CALLED "T.J. McMEGAN'S."
CATCHY.
YOU KNOW THE KIND OF PLACE I'M TALKING ABOUT?
BIG PORTIONS, MEDIOCRE FOOD?
THAT'S IT.
SINGING WAITERS?
YOU GOT IT.
IT'S LIKE I'VE ALREADY EATEN THERE AND I'M NEVER GOING BACK.
YEAH. WOW.

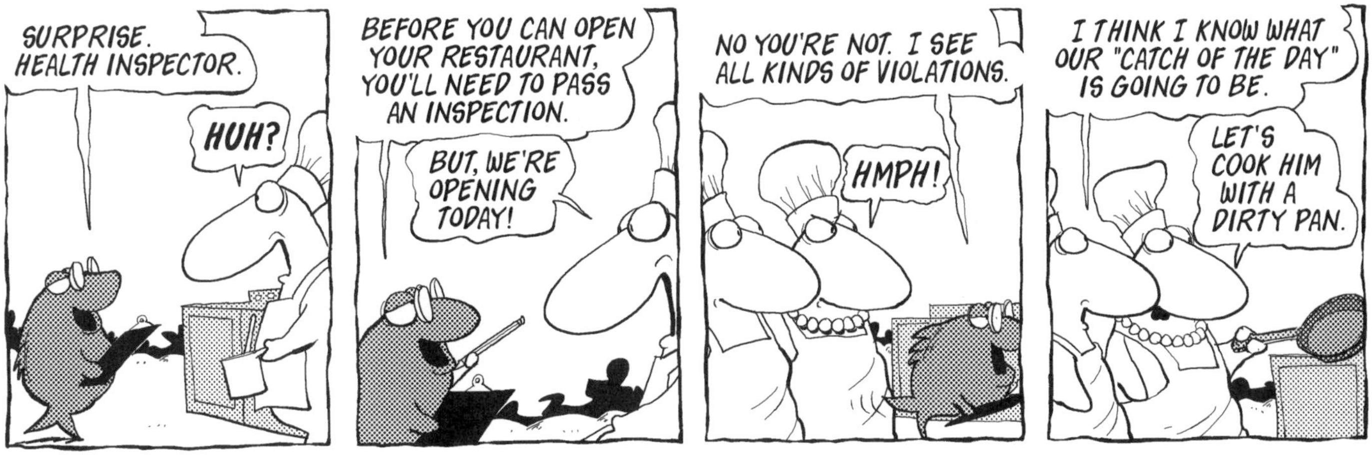
SURPRISE. HEALTH INSPECTOR.
HUH?
BEFORE YOU CAN OPEN YOUR RESTAURANT, YOU'LL NEED TO PASS AN INSPECTION.
BUT, WE'RE OPENING TODAY!
NO YOU'RE NOT. I SEE ALL KINDS OF VIOLATIONS.
HMPH!
I THINK I KNOW WHAT OUR "CATCH OF THE DAY" IS GOING TO BE.
LET'S COOK HIM WITH A DIRTY PAN.

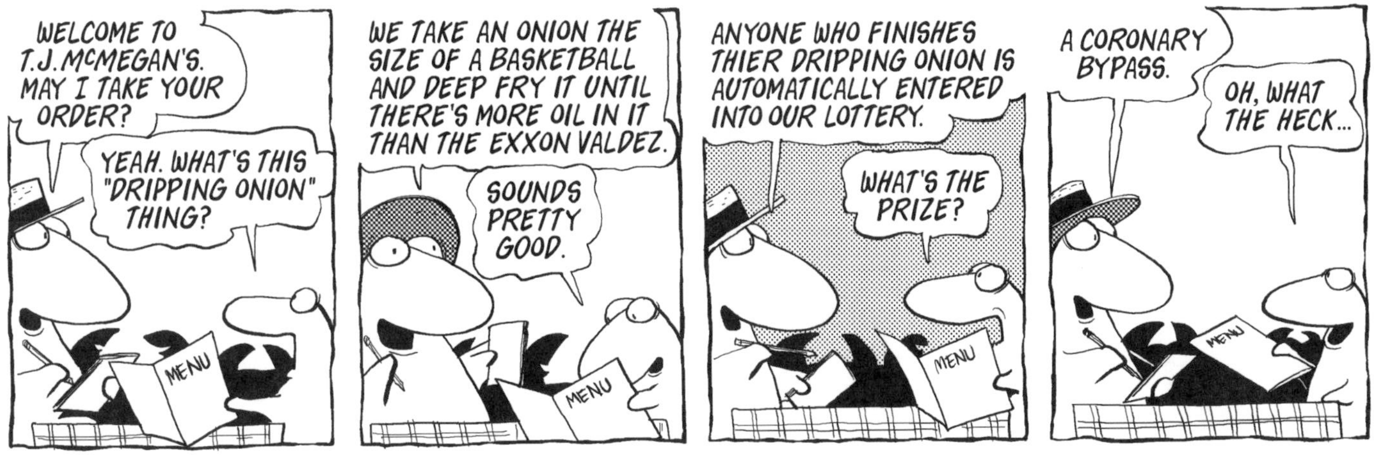
WELCOME TO T.J. McMEGAN'S. MAY I TAKE YOUR ORDER?
YEAH. WHAT'S THIS "DRIPPING ONION" THING?
MENU
WE TAKE AN ONION THE SIZE OF A BASKETBALL AND DEEP FRY IT UNTIL THERE'S MORE OIL IN IT THAN THE EXXON VALDEZ.
SOUNDS PRETTY GOOD.
MENU
ANYONE WHO FINISHES THIER DRIPPING ONION IS AUTOMATICALLY ENTERED INTO OUR LOTTERY.
WHAT'S THE PRIZE?
MENU
A CORONARY BYPASS.
OH, WHAT THE HECK...
MENU

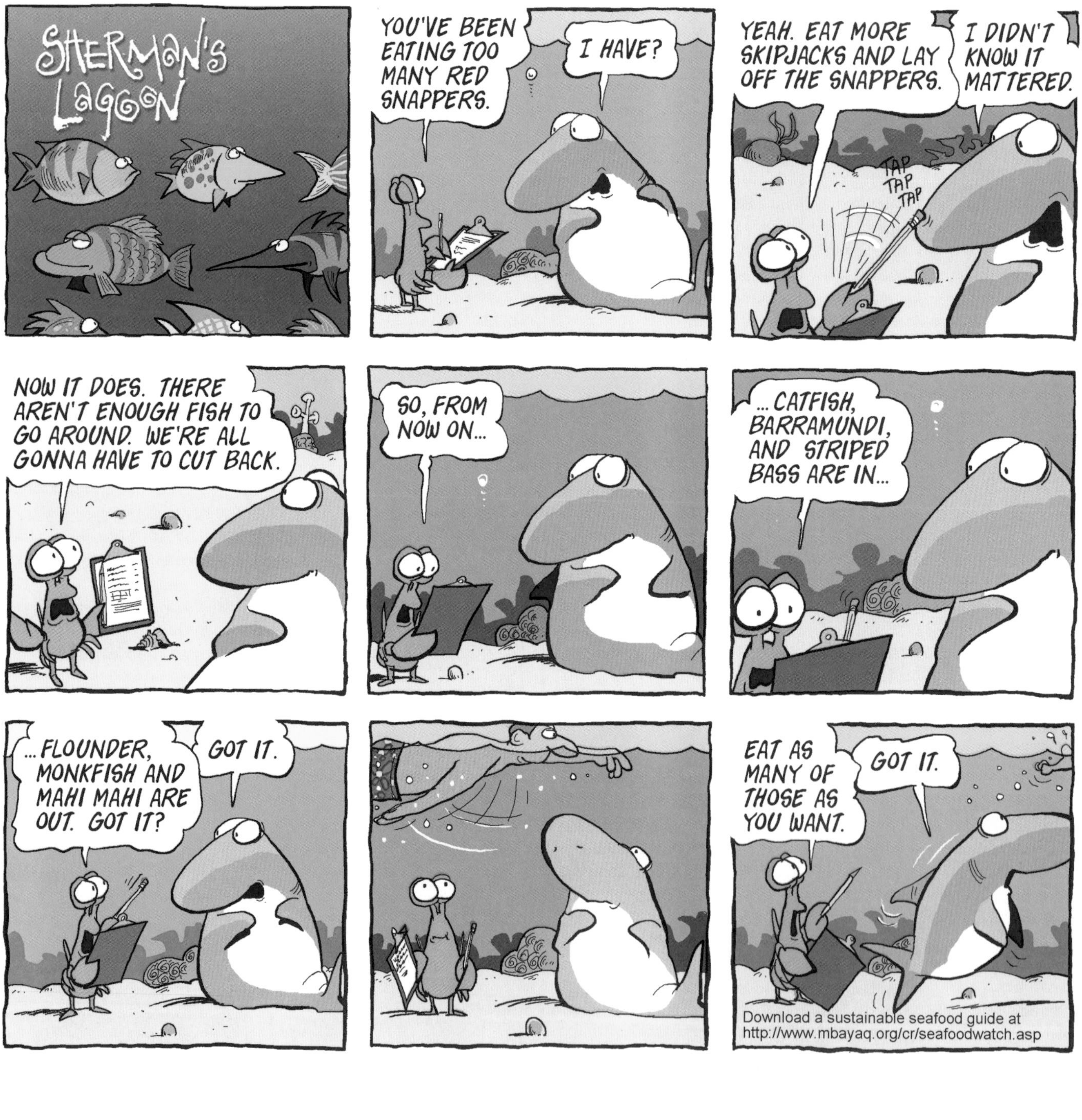
SHERMAN'S LAGOON
YOU'VE BEEN EATING TOO MANY RED SNAPPERS.
I HAVE?
YEAH. EAT MORE SKIPJACKS AND LAY OFF THE SNAPPERS.
I DIDN'T KNOW IT MATTERED.
TAP TAP TAP
NOW IT DOES. THERE AREN'T ENOUGH FISH TO GO AROUND. WE'RE ALL GONNA HAVE TO CUT BACK.
SO, FROM NOW ON...
... CATFISH, BARRAMUNDI, AND STRIPED BASS ARE IN...
... FLOUNDER, MONKFISH AND MAHI MAHI ARE OUT. GOT IT?
GOT IT.
EAT AS MANY OF THOSE AS YOU WANT.
GOT IT.
Download a sustainable seafood guide at
http://www.mbayaq.org/cr/seafoodwatch.asp

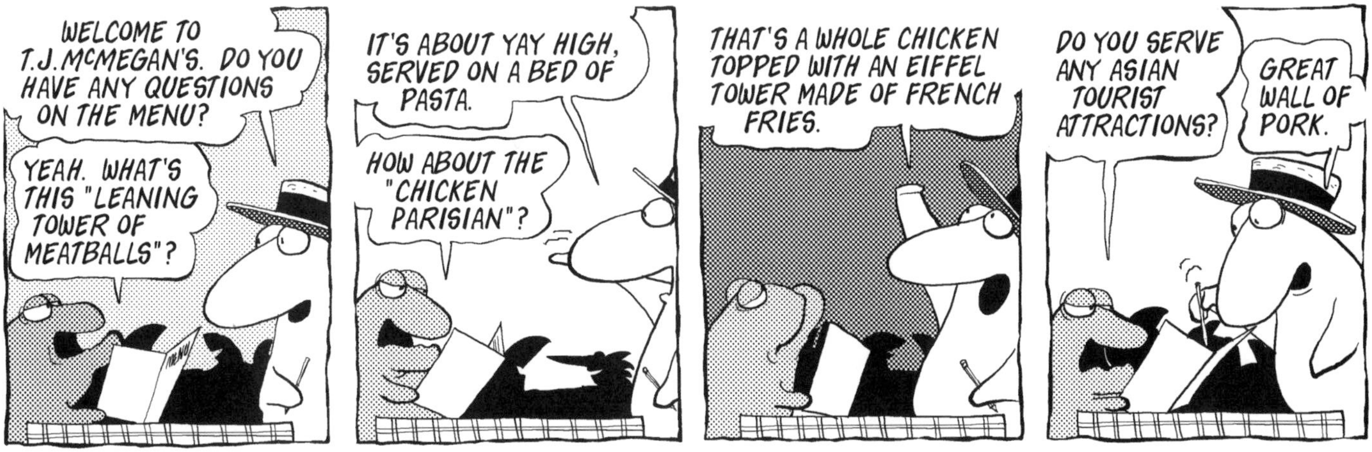
WELCOME TO T.J. McMEGAN'S. DO YOU HAVE ANY QUESTIONS ON THE MENU?
YEAH. WHAT'S THIS "LEANING TOWER OF MEATBALLS"?
MENU
IT'S ABOUT YAY HIGH, SERVED ON A BED OF PASTA.
HOW ABOUT THE "CHICKEN PARISIAN"?
THAT'S A WHOLE CHICKEN TOPPED WITH AN EIFFEL TOWER MADE OF FRENCH FRIES.
DO YOU SERVE ANY ASIAN TOURIST ATTRACTIONS?
GREAT WALL OF PORK.

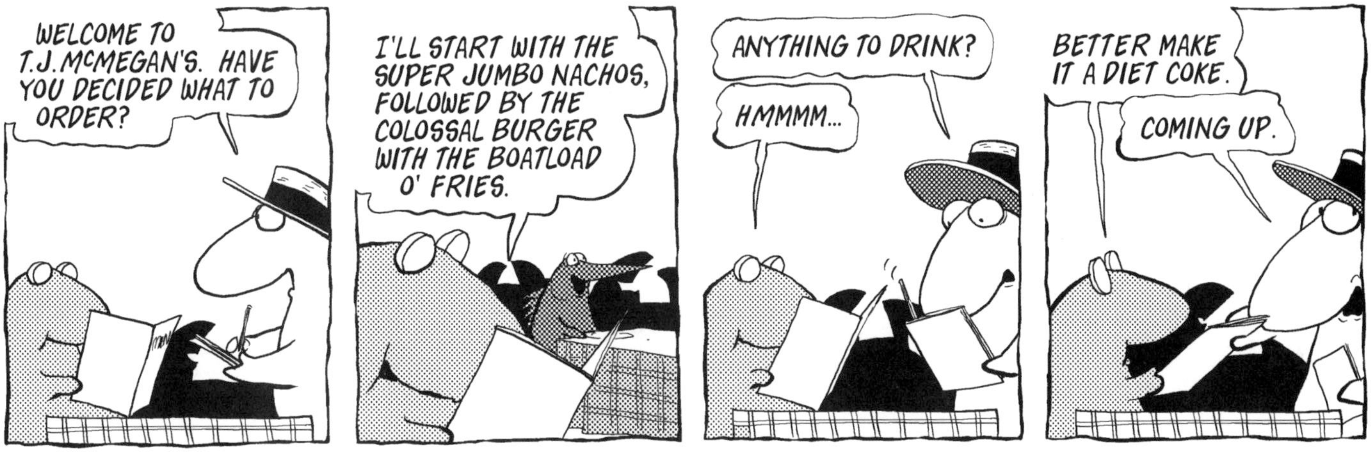
WELCOME TO T.J. McMEGAN'S. HAVE YOU DECIDED WHAT TO ORDER?
MENU
I'LL START WITH THE SUPER JUMBO NACHOS, FOLLOWED BY THE COLOSSAL BURGER WITH THE BOATLOAD O' FRIES.
ANYTHING TO DRINK?
HMMMM...
BETTER MAKE IT A DIET COKE.
COMING UP.

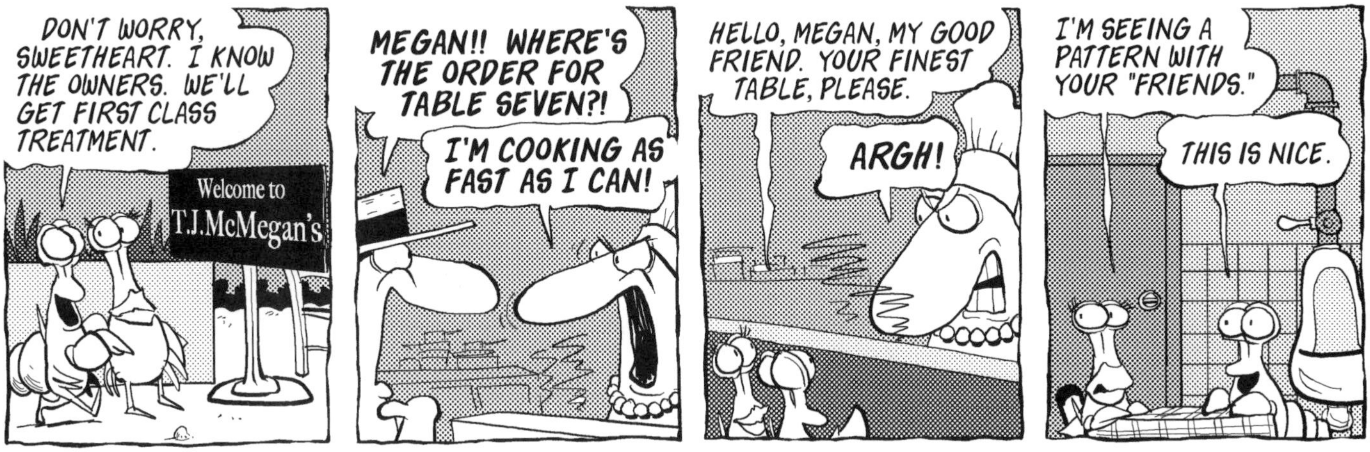
DON'T WORRY, SWEETHEART. I KNOW THE OWNERS. WE'LL GET FIRST CLASS TREATMENT.
Welcome to T.J.McMegan's
MEGAN!! WHERE'S THE ORDER FOR TABLE SEVEN?!
I'M COOKING AS FAST AS I CAN!
HELLO, MEGAN, MY GOOD FRIEND. YOUR FINEST TABLE, PLEASE.
ARGH!
I'M SEEING A PATTERN WITH YOUR "FRIENDS."
THIS IS NICE.

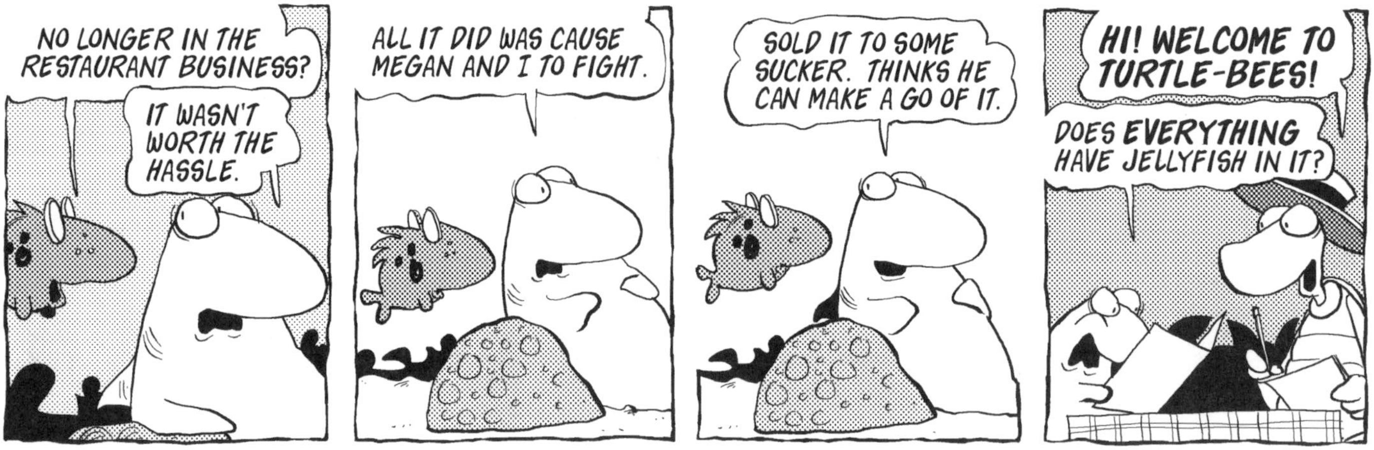
NO LONGER IN THE RESTAURANT BUSINESS?
IT WASN'T WORTH THE HASSLE.
ALL IT DID WAS CAUSE MEGAN AND I TO FIGHT.
SOLD IT TO SOME SUCKER. THINKS HE CAN MAKE A GO OF IT.
HI! WELCOME TO TURTLE-BEES!
DOES EVERYTHING HAVE JELLYFISH IN IT?

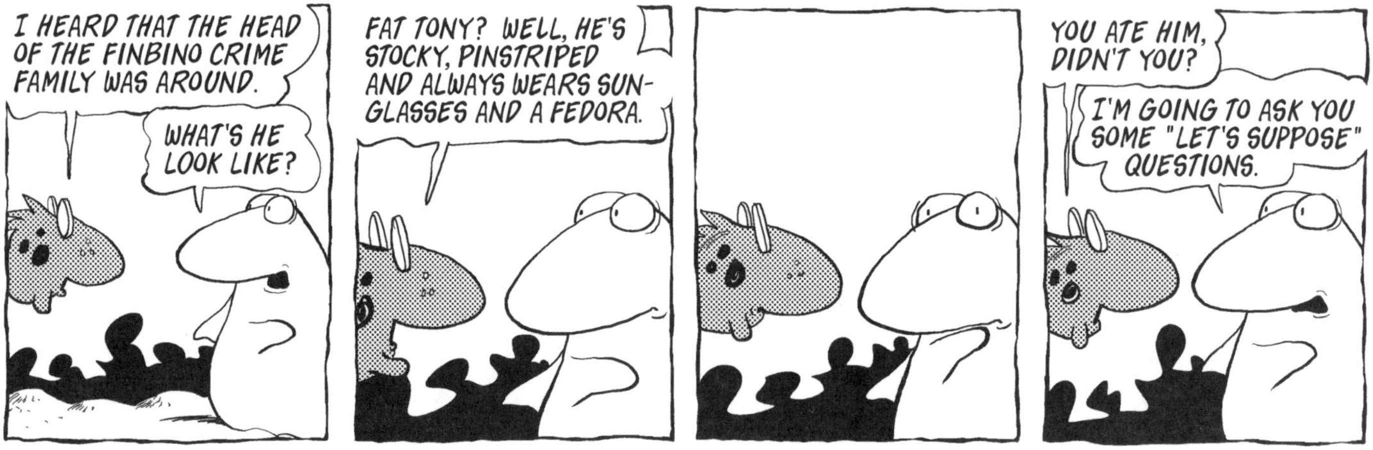
I HEARD THAT THE HEAD OF THE FINBINO CRIME FAMILY WAS AROUND.
WHAT'S HE LOOK LIKE?
FAT TONY? WELL, HE'S STOCKY, PINSTRIPED AND ALWAYS WEARS SUN-GLASSES AND A FEDORA.
YOU ATE HIM, DIDN'T YOU?
I'M GOING TO ASK YOU SOME "LET'S SUPPOSE" QUESTIONS.

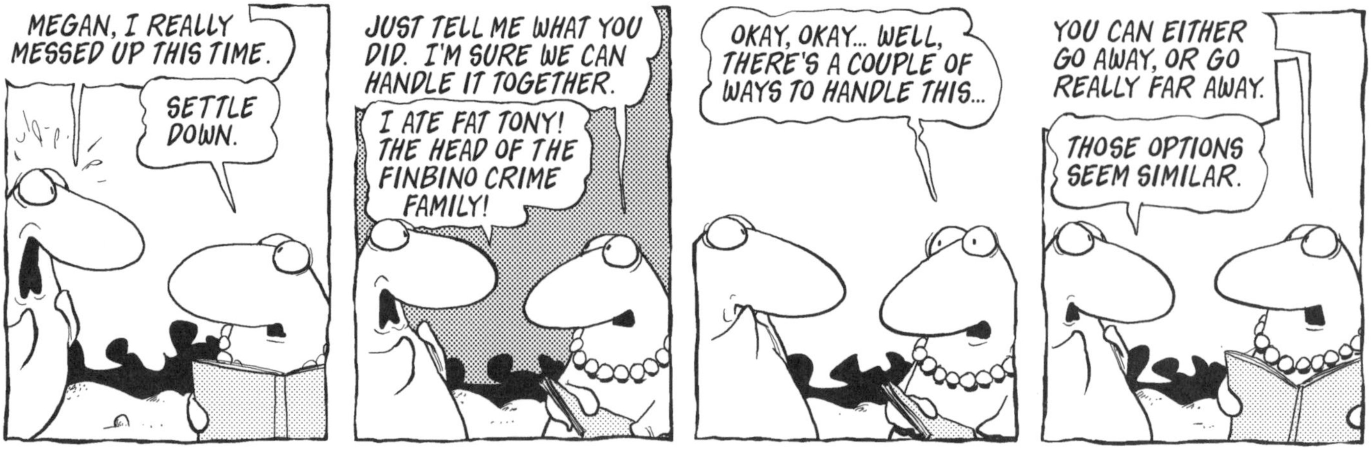
MEGAN, I REALLY MESSED UP THIS TIME.
SETTLE DOWN.
JUST TELL ME WHAT YOU DID. I'M SURE WE CAN HANDLE IT TOGETHER.
I ATE FAT TONY! THE HEAD OF THE FINBINO CRIME FAMILY!
OKAY, OKAY... WELL, THERE'S A COUPLE OF WAYS TO HANDLE THIS...
YOU CAN EITHER GO AWAY, OR GO REALLY FAR AWAY.
THOSE OPTIONS SEEM SIMILAR.

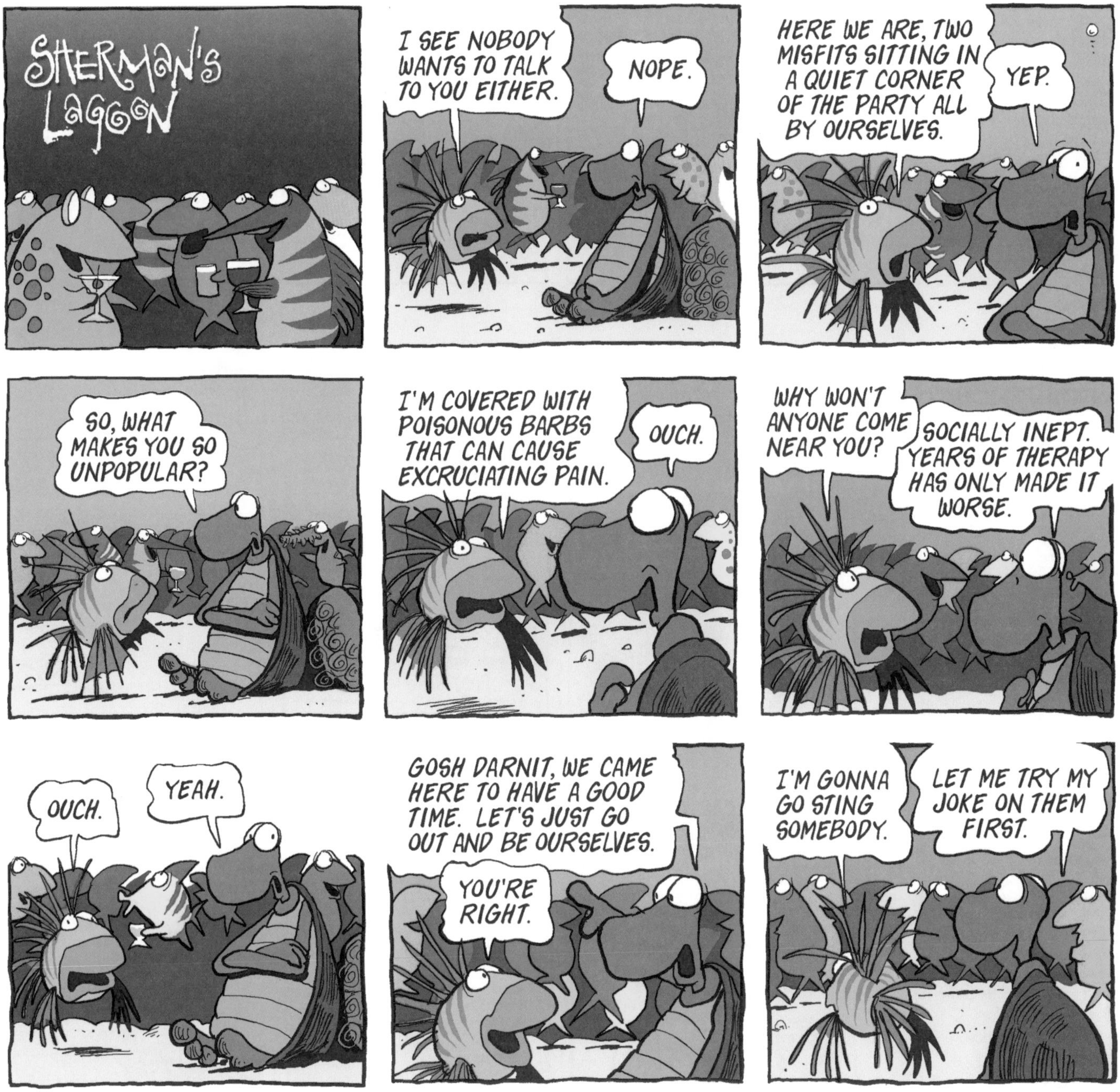
SHERMAN'S LAGOON
I SEE NOBODY WANTS TO TALK TO YOU EITHER.
NOPE.
HERE WE ARE, TWO MISFITS SITTING IN A QUIET CORNER OF THE PARTY ALL BY OURSELVES.
YEP.
SO, WHAT MAKES YOU SO UNPOPULAR?
I'M COVERED WITH POISONOUS BARBS THAT CAN CAUSE EXCRUCIATING PAIN.
OUCH.
WHY WON'T ANYONE COME NEAR YOU?
SOCIALLY INEPT. YEARS OF THERAPY HAS ONLY MADE IT WORSE.
OUCH.
YEAH.
GOSH DARNIT, WE CAME HERE TO HAVE A GOOD TIME. LET'S JUST GO OUT AND BE OURSELVES.
YOU'RE RIGHT.
I'M GONNA GO STING SOMEBODY.
LET ME TRY MY JOKE ON THEM FIRST.

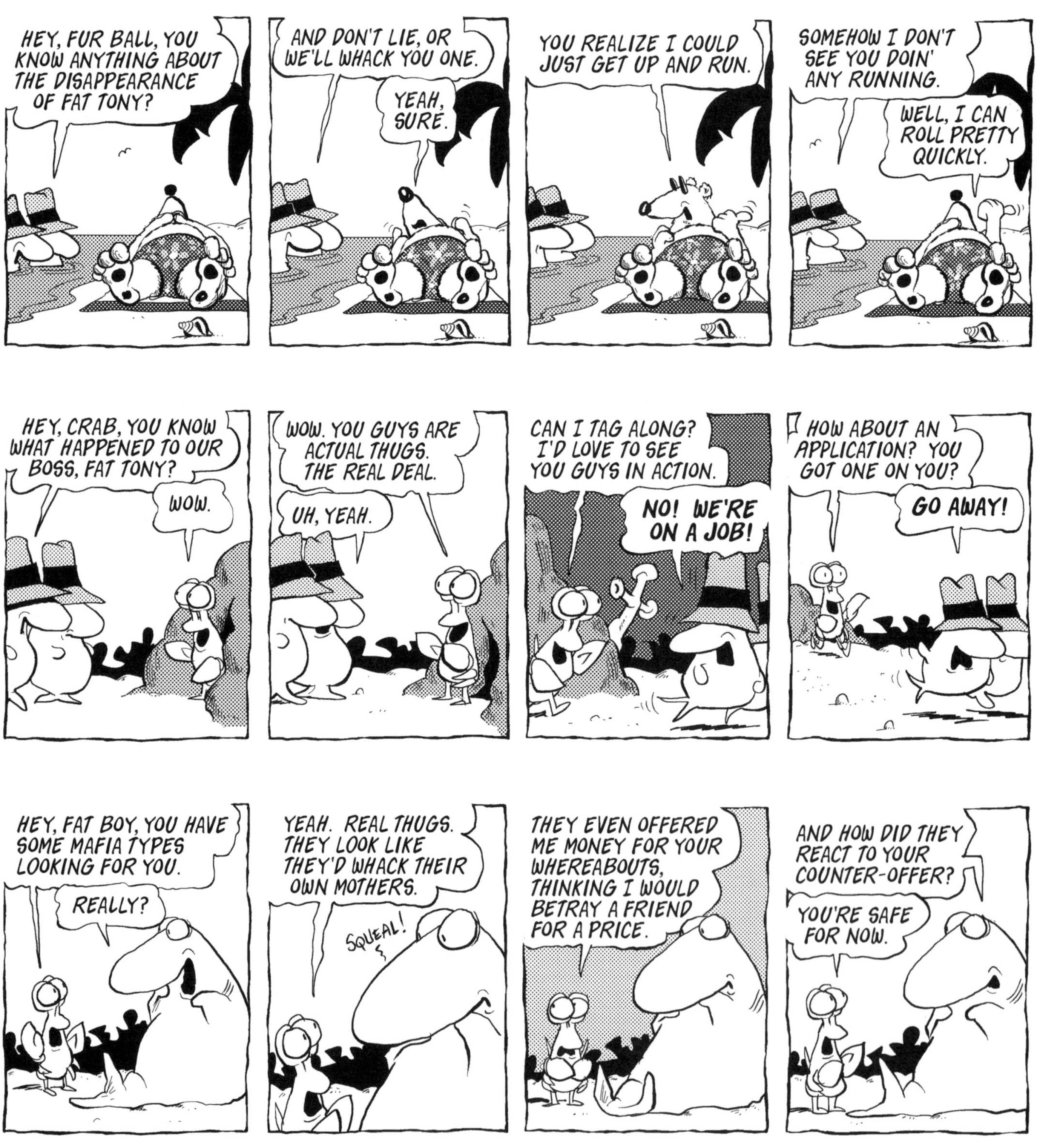
HEY, FUR BALL, YOU KNOW ANYTHING ABOUT THE DISAPPEARANCE OF FAT TONY?
AND DON'T LIE, OR WE'LL WHACK YOU ONE.
YEAH, SURE.
YOU REALIZE I COULD JUST GET UP AND RUN.
SOMEHOW I DON'T SEE YOU DOIN' ANY RUNNING.
WELL, I CAN ROLL PRETTY QUICKLY.
HEY, CRAB, YOU KNOW WHAT HAPPENED TO OUR BOSS, FAT TONY?
WOW.
WOW. YOU GUYS ARE ACTUAL THUGS. THE REAL DEAL.
UH, YEAH.
CAN I TAG ALONG? I'D LOVE TO SEE YOU GUYS IN ACTION.
NO! WE'RE ON A JOB!
HOW ABOUT AN APPLICATION? YOU GOT ONE ON YOU?
GO AWAY!
HEY, FAT BOY, YOU HAVE SOME MAFIA TYPES LOOKING FOR YOU.
REALLY?
YEAH. REAL THUGS. THEY LOOK LIKE THEY'D WHACK THEIR OWN MOTHERS.
SQUEAL!
THEY EVEN OFFERED ME MONEY FOR YOUR WHEREABOUTS, THINKING I WOULD BETRAY A FRIEND FOR A PRICE.
AND HOW DID THEY REACT TO YOUR COUNTER-OFFER?
YOU'RE SAFE FOR NOW.

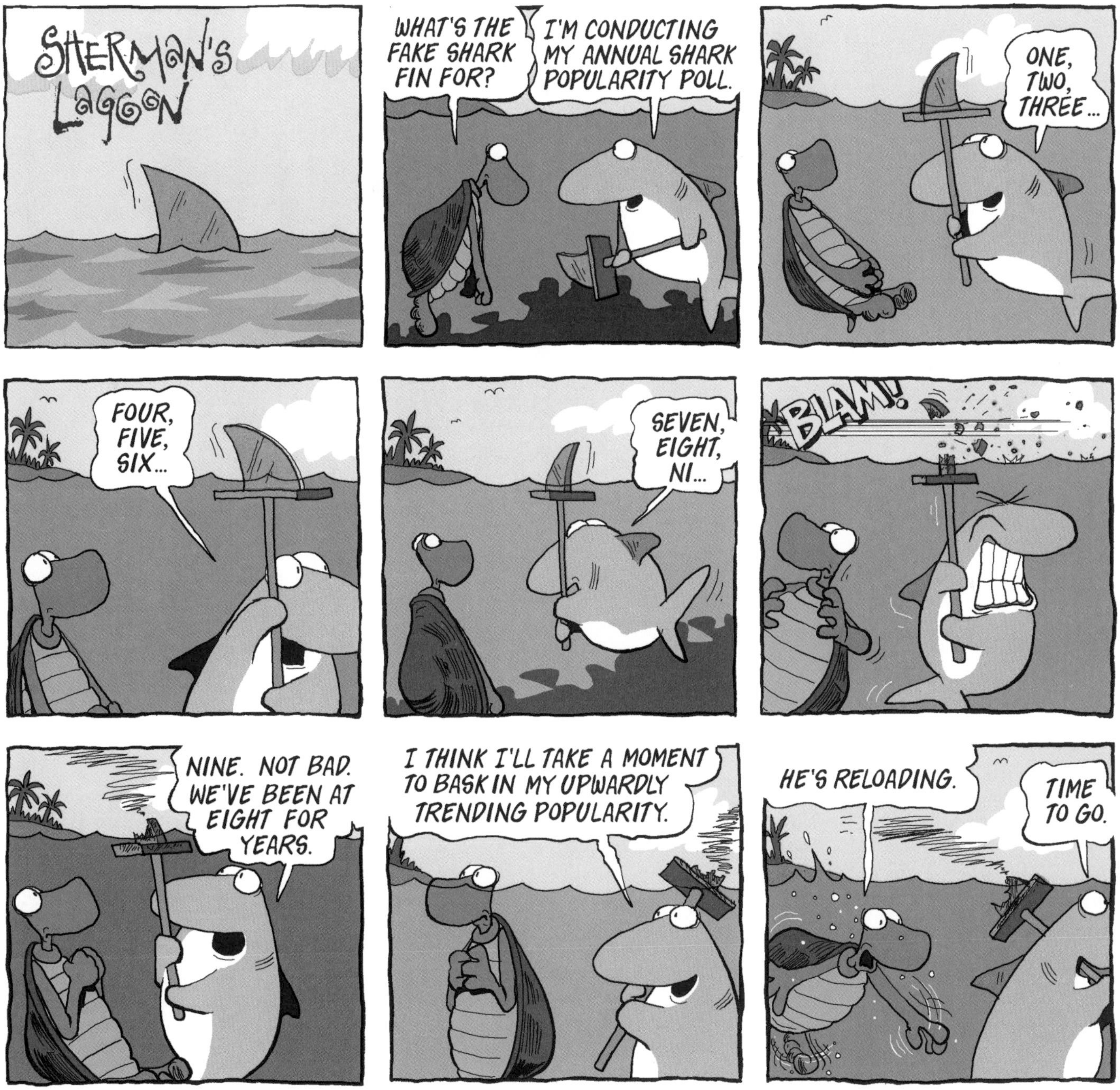
SHERMAN'S LAGOON
WHAT'S THE FAKE SHARK FIN FOR?
I'M CONDUCTING MY ANNUAL SHARK POPULARITY POLL.
ONE, TWO, THREE...
FOUR, FIVE, SIX...
SEVEN, EIGHT, NI...
BLAM!
NINE. NOT BAD. WE'VE BEEN AT EIGHT FOR YEARS.
I THINK I'LL TAKE A MOMENT TO BASK IN MY UPWARDLY TRENDING POPULARITY.
HE'S RELOADING.
TIME TO GO.

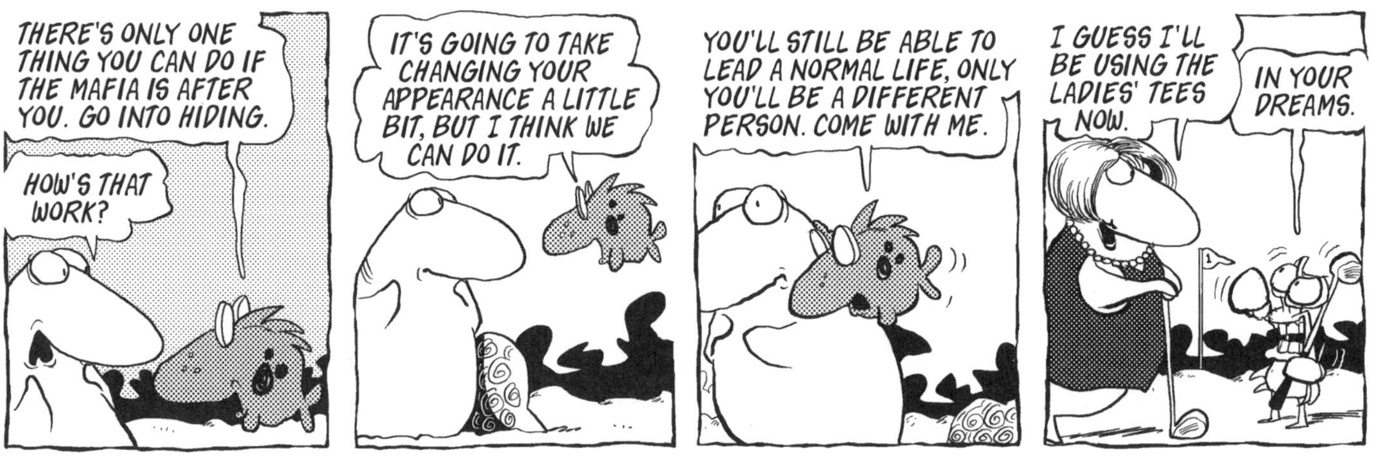
THERE'S ONLY ONE THING YOU CAN DO IF THE MAFIA IS AFTER YOU. GO INTO HIDING.
HOW'S THAT WORK?
IT'S GOING TO TAKE CHANGING YOUR APPEARANCE A LITTLE BIT, BUT I THINK WE CAN DO IT.
YOU'LL STILL BE ABLE TO LEAD A NORMAL LIFE, ONLY YOU'LL BE A DIFFERENT PERSON. COME WITH ME.
I GUESS I'LL BE USING THE LADIES' TEES NOW.
IN YOUR DREAMS.

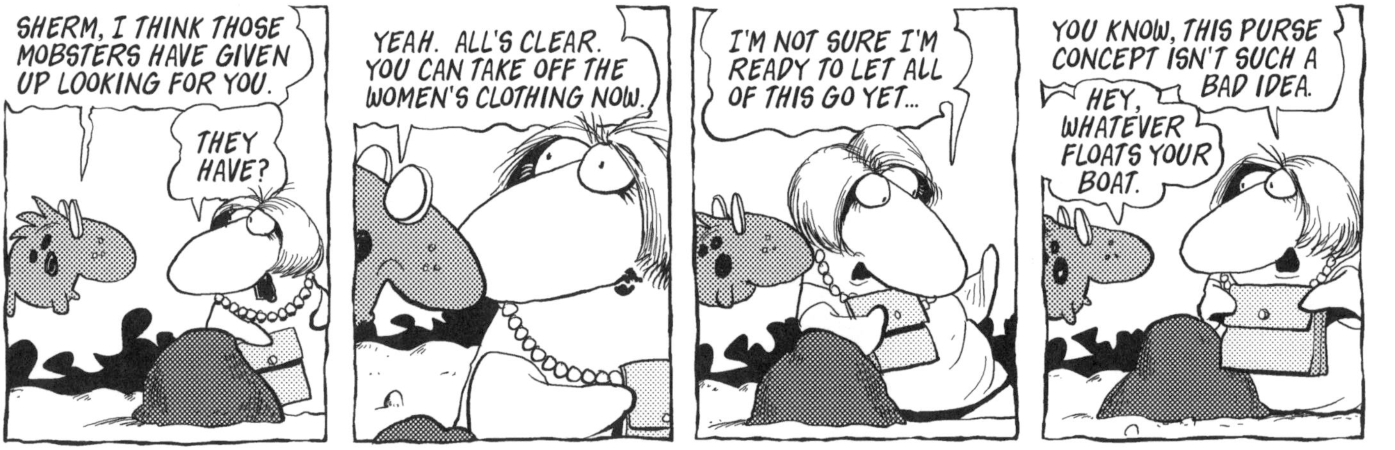
SHERM, I THINK THOSE MOBSTERS HAVE GIVEN UP LOOKING FOR YOU.
THEY HAVE?
YEAH. ALL'S CLEAR. YOU CAN TAKE OFF THE WOMEN'S CLOTHING NOW.
I'M NOT SURE I'M READY TO LET ALL OF THIS GO YET...
YOU KNOW, THIS PURSE CONCEPT ISN'T SUCH A BAD IDEA.
HEY, WHATEVER FLOATS YOUR BOAT.

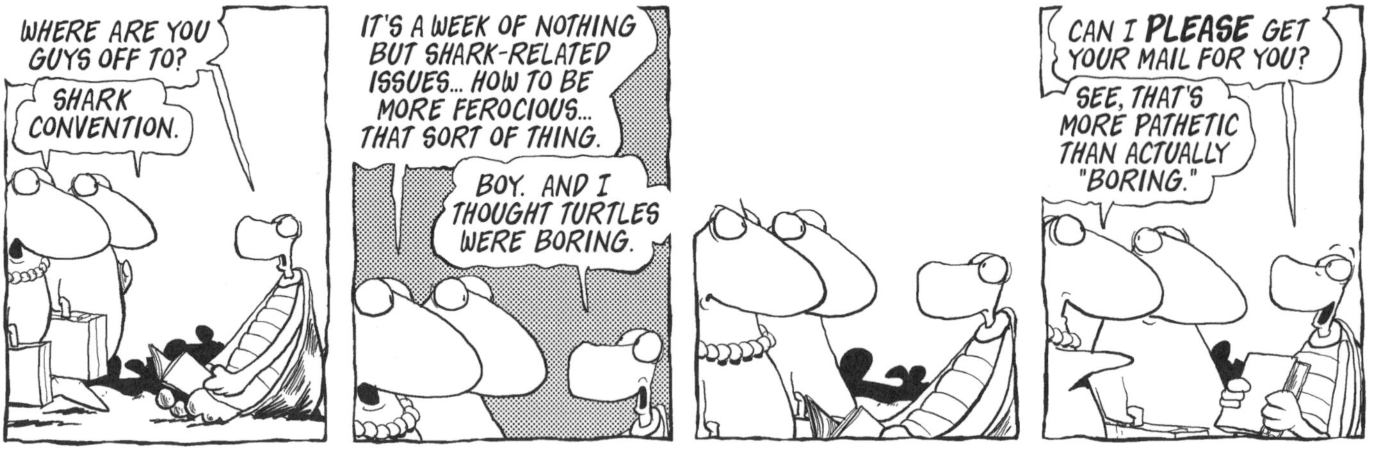
WHERE ARE YOU GUYS OFF TO?
SHARK CONVENTION.
IT'S A WEEK OF NOTHING BUT SHARK-RELATED ISSUES... HOW TO BE MORE FEROCIOUS... THAT SORT OF THING.
BOY. AND I THOUGHT TURTLES WERE BORING.
CAN I **PLEASE** GET YOUR MAIL FOR YOU?
SEE, THAT'S MORE PATHETIC THAN ACTUALLY "BORING."

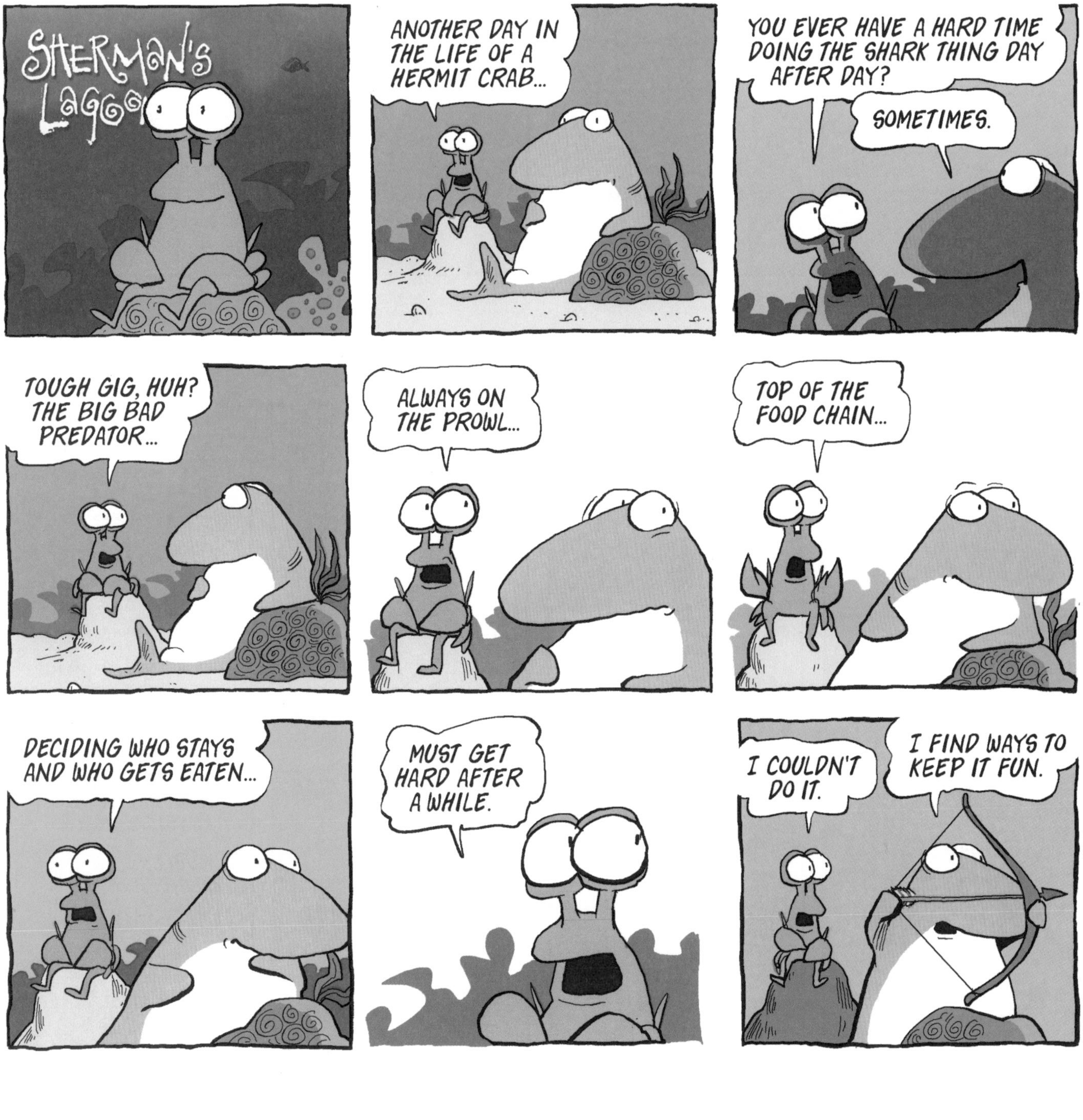
SHERMAN'S LAGOON
ANOTHER DAY IN THE LIFE OF A HERMIT CRAB...
YOU EVER HAVE A HARD TIME DOING THE SHARK THING DAY AFTER DAY?
SOMETIMES.
TOUGH GIG, HUH? THE BIG BAD PREDATOR...
ALWAYS ON THE PROWL...
TOP OF THE FOOD CHAIN...
DECIDING WHO STAYS AND WHO GETS EATEN...
MUST GET HARD AFTER A WHILE.
I COULDN'T DO IT.
I FIND WAYS TO KEEP IT FUN.

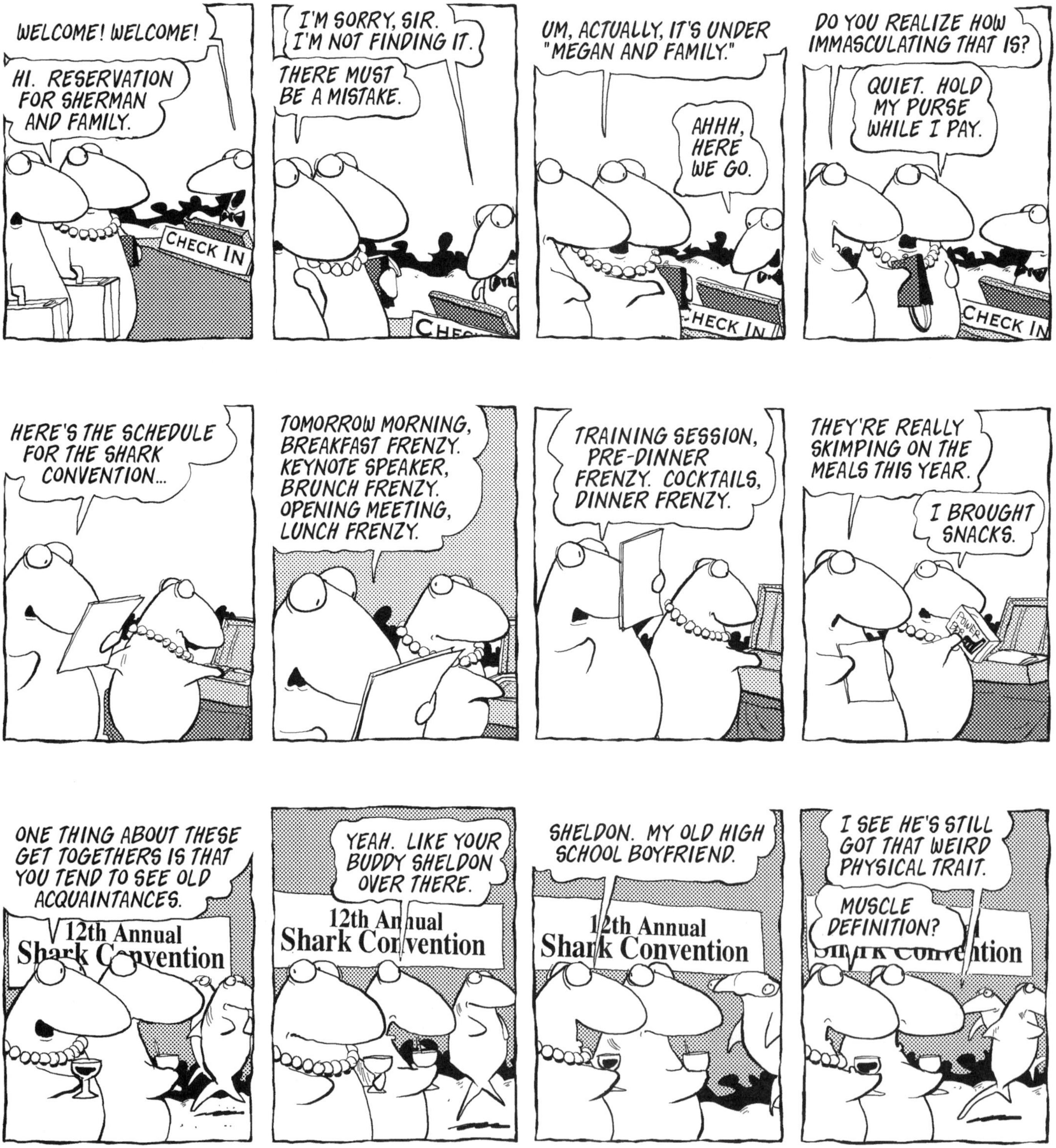
WELCOME! WELCOME!
HI. RESERVATION FOR SHERMAN AND FAMILY.
CHECK IN
I'M SORRY, SIR. I'M NOT FINDING IT.
THERE MUST BE A MISTAKE.
UM, ACTUALLY, IT'S UNDER "MEGAN AND FAMILY."
AHHH, HERE WE GO.
DO YOU REALIZE HOW IMMASCULATING THAT IS?
QUIET. HOLD MY PURSE WHILE I PAY.
CHECK IN
HERE'S THE SCHEDULE FOR THE SHARK CONVENTION...
TOMORROW MORNING, BREAKFAST FRENZY. KEYNOTE SPEAKER, BRUNCH FRENZY. OPENING MEETING, LUNCH FRENZY.
TRAINING SESSION, PRE-DINNER FRENZY. COCKTAILS, DINNER FRENZY.
THEY'RE REALLY SKIMPING ON THE MEALS THIS YEAR.
I BROUGHT SNACKS.
ONE THING ABOUT THESE GET TOGETHERS IS THAT YOU TEND TO SEE OLD ACQUAINTANCES.
12th Annual Shark Convention
YEAH. LIKE YOUR BUDDY SHELDON OVER THERE.
SHELDON. MY OLD HIGH SCHOOL BOYFRIEND.
I SEE HE'S STILL GOT THAT WEIRD PHYSICAL TRAIT.
MUSCLE DEFINITION?

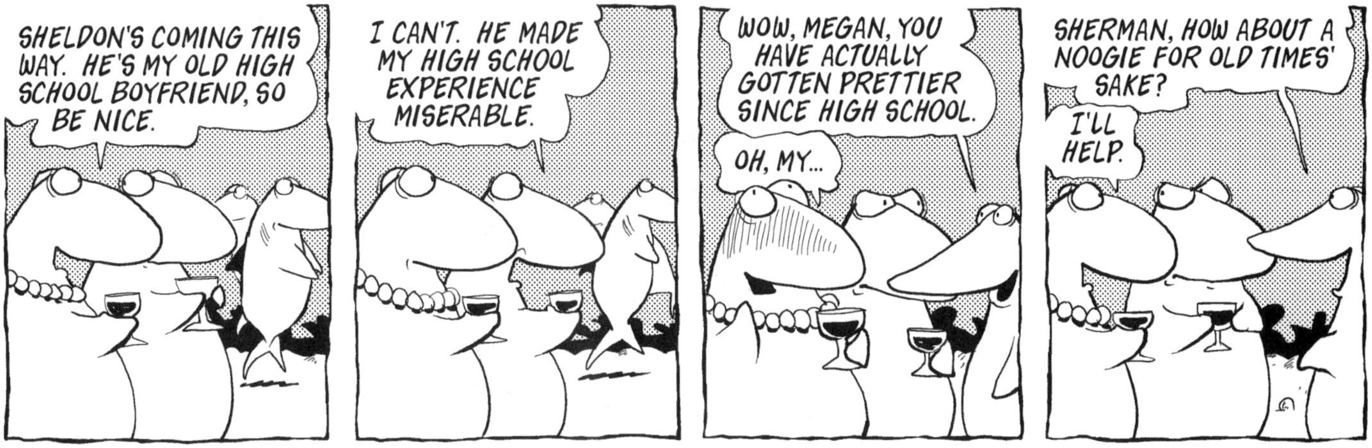

SHELDON'S COMING THIS WAY. HE'S MY OLD HIGH SCHOOL BOYFRIEND, SO BE NICE.
I CAN'T. HE MADE MY HIGH SCHOOL EXPERIENCE MISERABLE.
WOW, MEGAN, YOU HAVE ACTUALLY GOTTEN PRETTIER SINCE HIGH SCHOOL.
OH, MY...
SHERMAN, HOW ABOUT A NOOGIE FOR OLD TIMES' SAKE?
I'LL HELP.

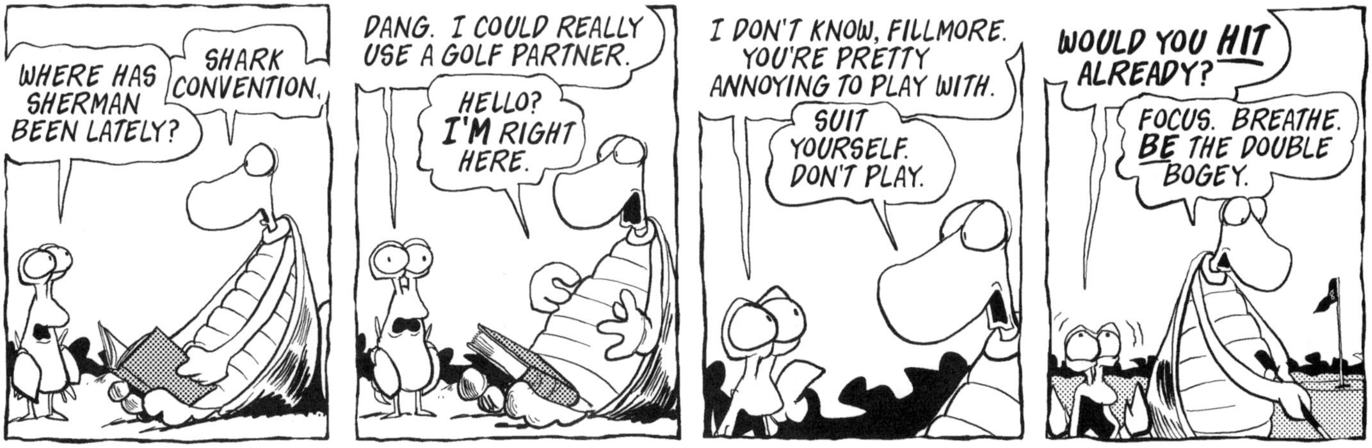

WHERE HAS SHERMAN BEEN LATELY?
SHARK CONVENTION.
DANG. I COULD REALLY USE A GOLF PARTNER.
HELLO? I'M RIGHT HERE.
I DON'T KNOW, FILLMORE. YOU'RE PRETTY ANNOYING TO PLAY WITH.
SUIT YOURSELF. DON'T PLAY.
WOULD YOU HIT ALREADY?
FOCUS. BREATHE. BE THE DOUBLE BOGEY.

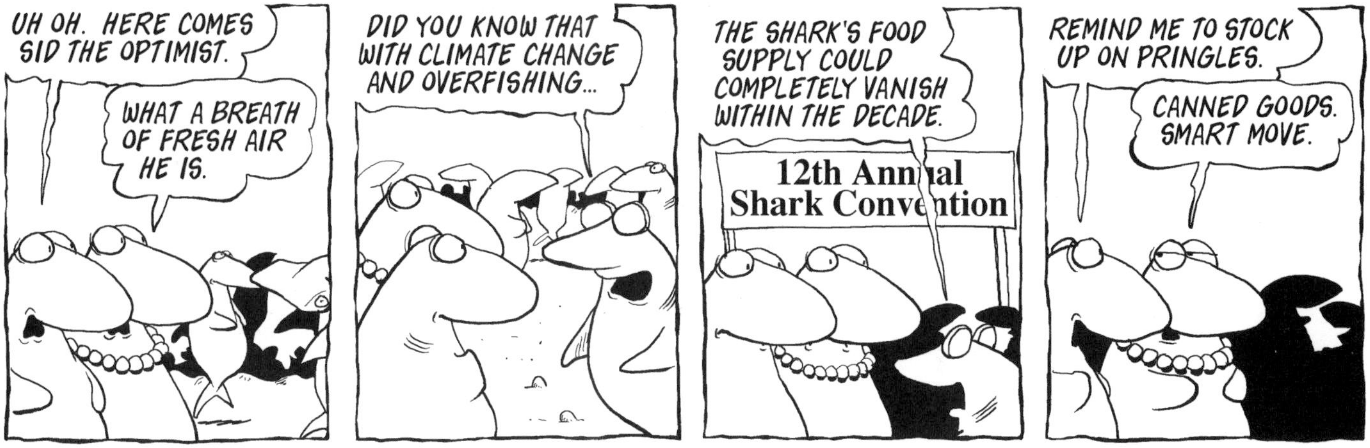

UH OH. HERE COMES SID THE OPTIMIST.
WHAT A BREATH OF FRESH AIR HE IS.
DID YOU KNOW THAT WITH CLIMATE CHANGE AND OVERFISHING...
THE SHARK'S FOOD SUPPLY COULD COMPLETELY VANISH WITHIN THE DECADE.
12th Annual Shark Convention
REMIND ME TO STOCK UP ON PRINGLES.
CANNED GOODS. SMART MOVE.

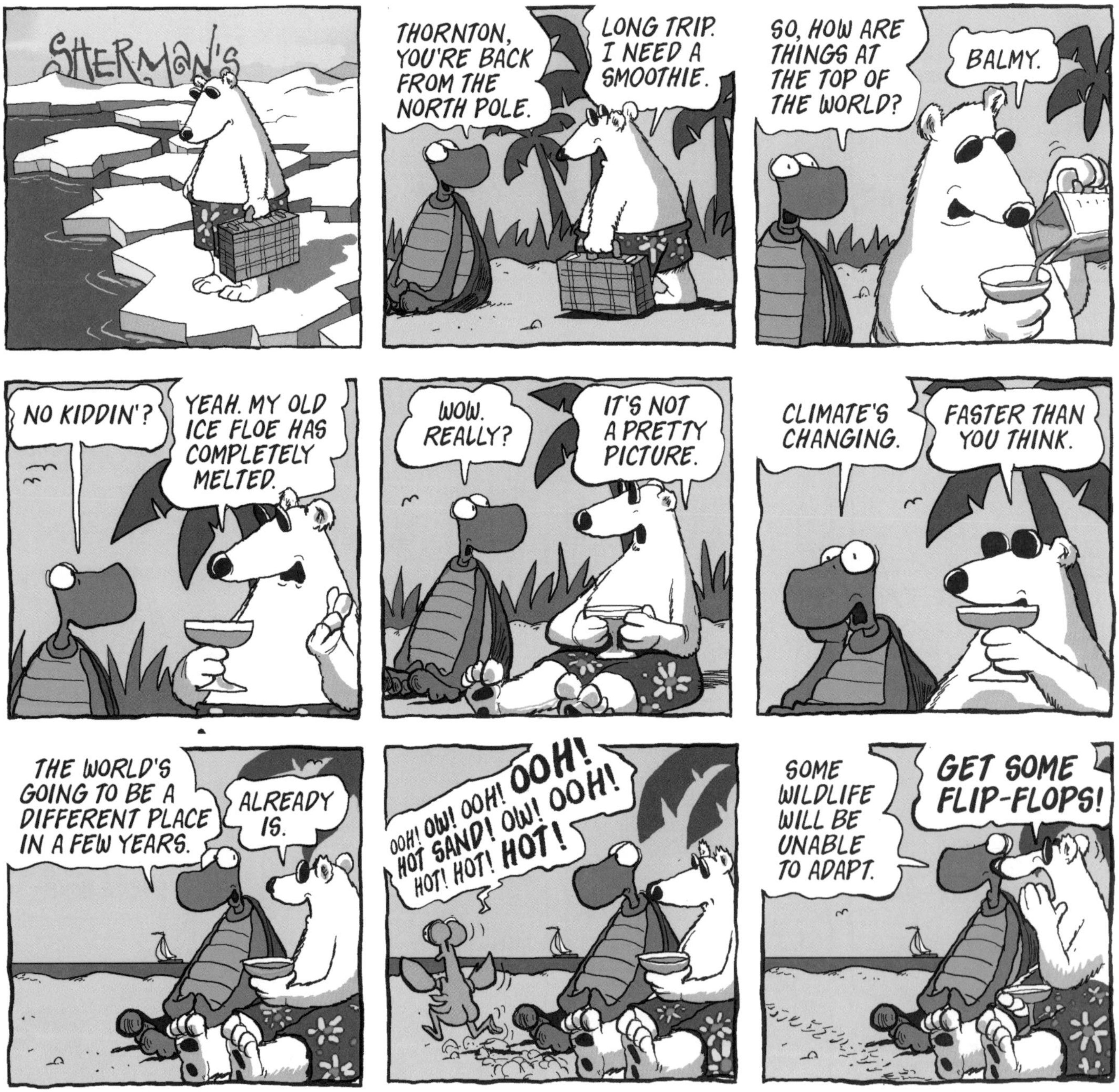
SHERMAN'S
THORNTON, YOU'RE BACK FROM THE NORTH POLE.
LONG TRIP. I NEED A SMOOTHIE.
SO, HOW ARE THINGS AT THE TOP OF THE WORLD?
BALMY.
NO KIDDIN'?
YEAH. MY OLD ICE FLOE HAS COMPLETELY MELTED.
WOW. REALLY?
IT'S NOT A PRETTY PICTURE.
CLIMATE'S CHANGING.
FASTER THAN YOU THINK.
THE WORLD'S GOING TO BE A DIFFERENT PLACE IN A FEW YEARS.
ALREADY IS.
OOH! OW! OOH! OOH! HOT SAND! OW! OOH! HOT! HOT! HOT!
SOME WILDLIFE WILL BE UNABLE TO ADAPT.
GET SOME FLIP-FLOPS!

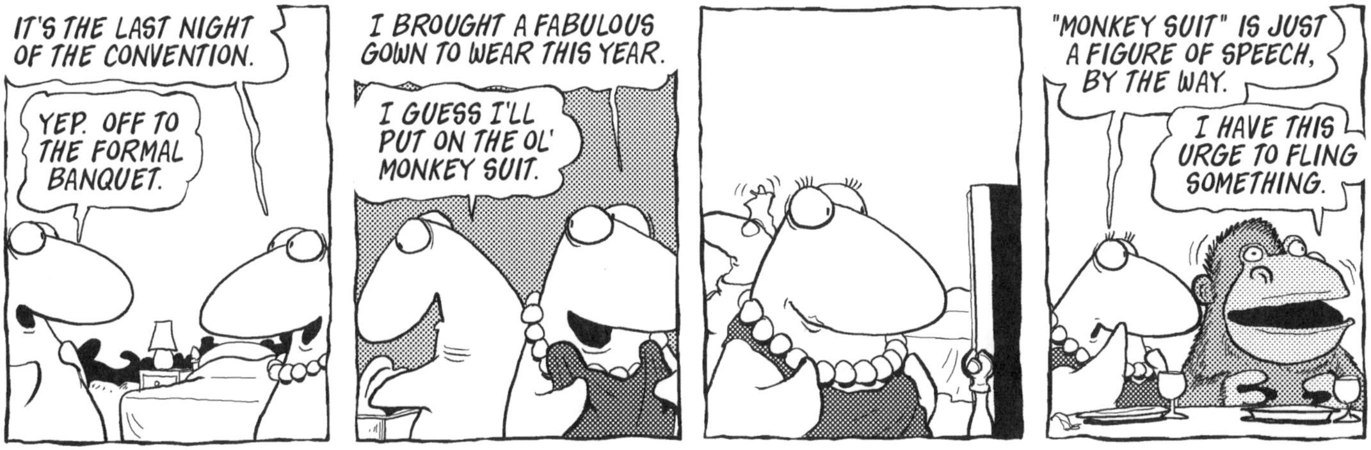
IT'S THE LAST NIGHT OF THE CONVENTION.
YEP. OFF TO THE FORMAL BANQUET.
I BROUGHT A FABULOUS GOWN TO WEAR THIS YEAR.
I GUESS I'LL PUT ON THE OL' MONKEY SUIT.
"MONKEY SUIT" IS JUST A FIGURE OF SPEECH, BY THE WAY.
I HAVE THIS URGE TO FLING SOMETHING.

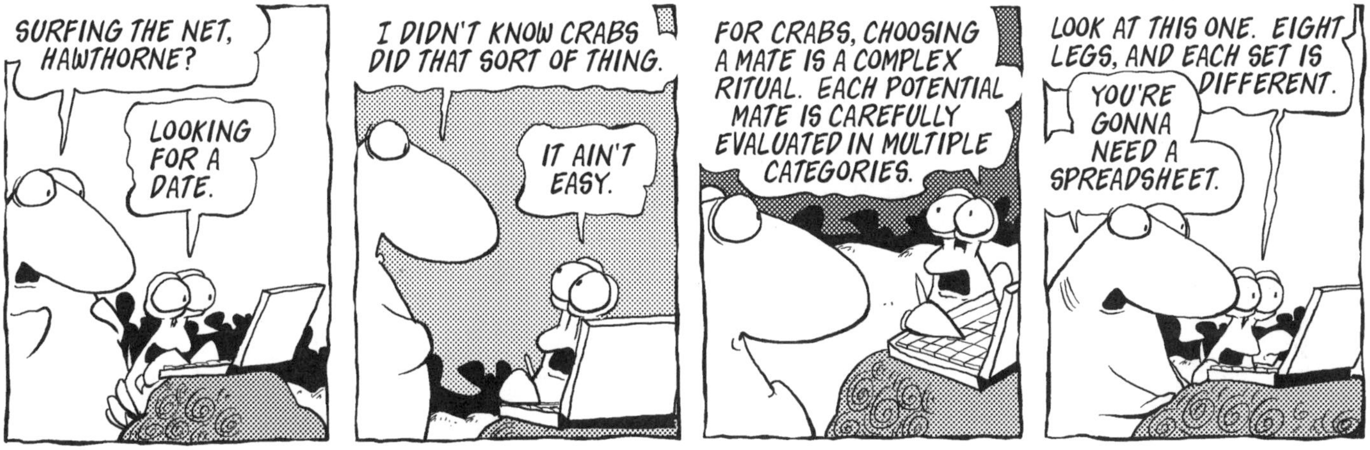
SURFING THE NET, HAWTHORNE?
LOOKING FOR A DATE.
I DIDN'T KNOW CRABS DID THAT SORT OF THING.
IT AIN'T EASY.
FOR CRABS, CHOOSING A MATE IS A COMPLEX RITUAL. EACH POTENTIAL MATE IS CAREFULLY EVALUATED IN MULTIPLE CATEGORIES.
LOOK AT THIS ONE. EIGHT LEGS, AND EACH SET IS DIFFERENT.
YOU'RE GONNA NEED A SPREADSHEET.

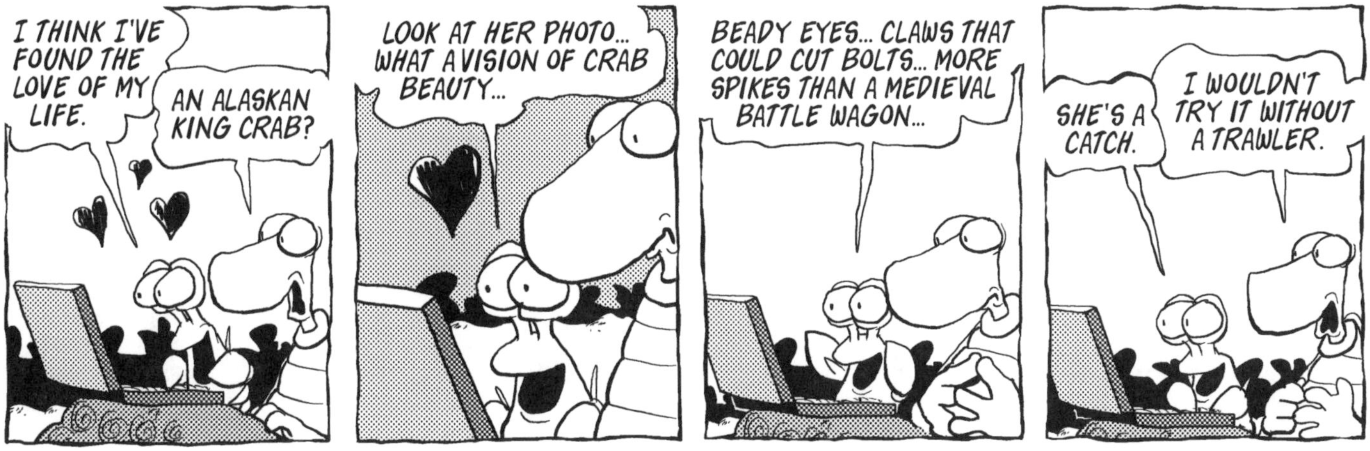
I THINK I'VE FOUND THE LOVE OF MY LIFE.
AN ALASKAN KING CRAB?
LOOK AT HER PHOTO... WHAT A VISION OF CRAB BEAUTY...
BEADY EYES... CLAWS THAT COULD CUT BOLTS... MORE SPIKES THAN A MEDIEVAL BATTLE WAGON...
SHE'S A CATCH.
I WOULDN'T TRY IT WITHOUT A TRAWLER.

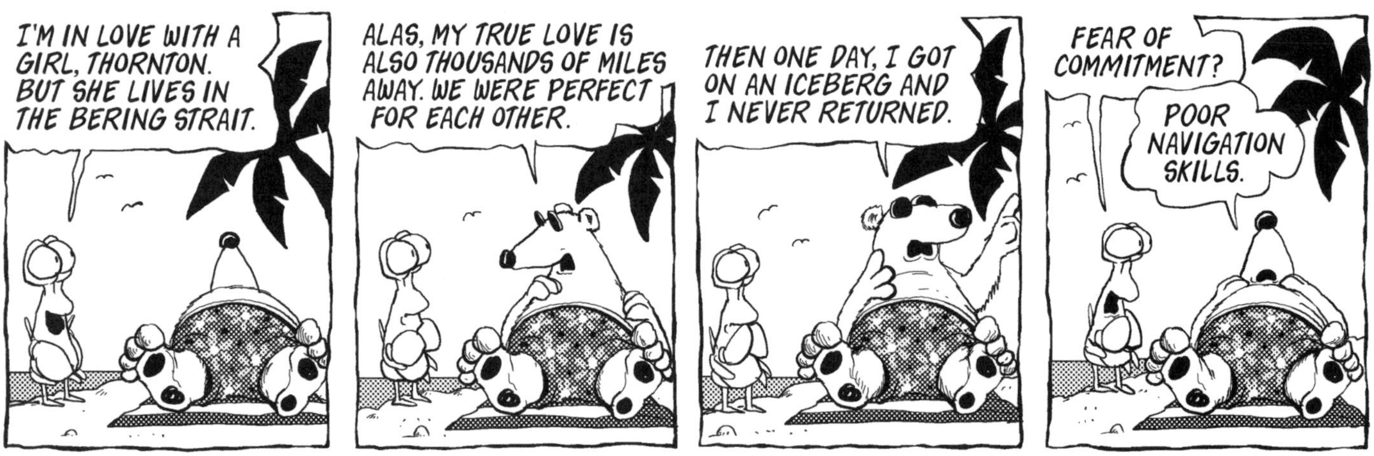
I'M IN LOVE WITH A GIRL, THORNTON. BUT SHE LIVES IN THE BERING STRAIT.
ALAS, MY TRUE LOVE IS ALSO THOUSANDS OF MILES AWAY. WE WERE PERFECT FOR EACH OTHER.
THEN ONE DAY, I GOT ON AN ICEBERG AND I NEVER RETURNED.
FEAR OF COMMITMENT?
POOR NAVIGATION SKILLS.

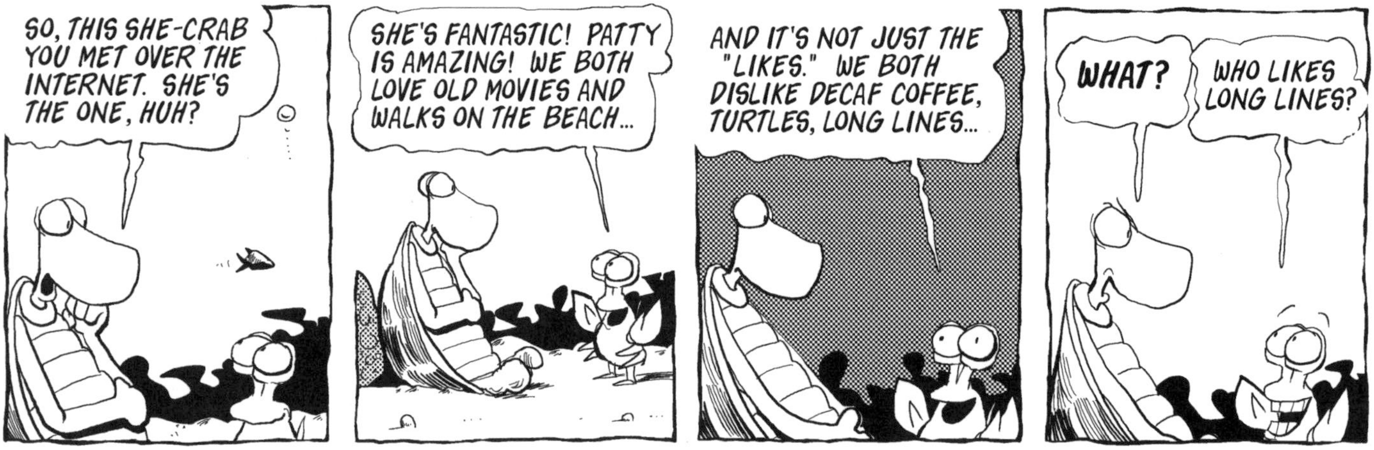
SO, THIS SHE-CRAB YOU MET OVER THE INTERNET. SHE'S THE ONE, HUH?
SHE'S FANTASTIC! PATTY IS AMAZING! WE BOTH LOVE OLD MOVIES AND WALKS ON THE BEACH...
AND IT'S NOT JUST THE "LIKES." WE BOTH DISLIKE DECAF COFFEE, TURTLES, LONG LINES...
WHAT?
WHO LIKES LONG LINES?

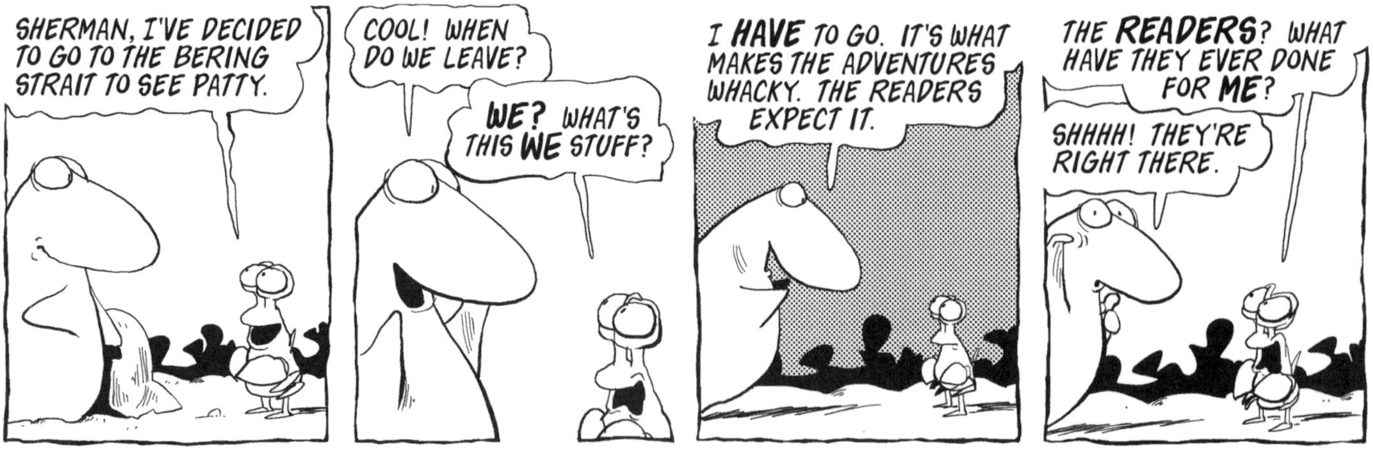
SHERMAN, I'VE DECIDED TO GO TO THE BERING STRAIT TO SEE PATTY.
COOL! WHEN DO WE LEAVE?
WE? WHAT'S THIS WE STUFF?
I HAVE TO GO. IT'S WHAT MAKES THE ADVENTURES WHACKY. THE READERS EXPECT IT.
THE READERS? WHAT HAVE THEY EVER DONE FOR ME?
SHHHH! THEY'RE RIGHT THERE.

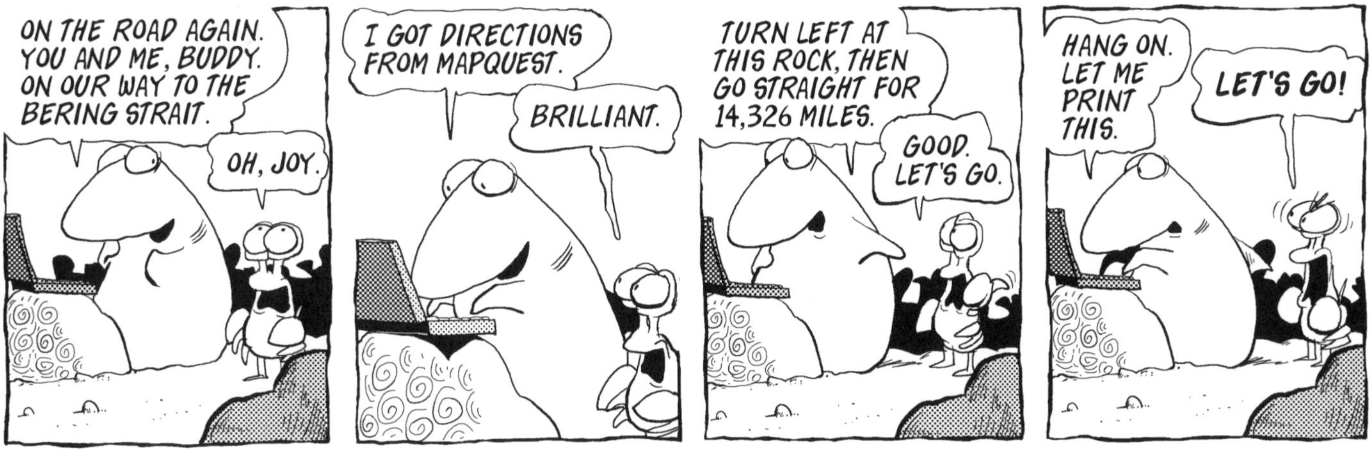
ON THE ROAD AGAIN. YOU AND ME, BUDDY. ON OUR WAY TO THE BERING STRAIT.
OH, JOY.
I GOT DIRECTIONS FROM MAPQUEST.
BRILLIANT.
TURN LEFT AT THIS ROCK, THEN GO STRAIGHT FOR 14,326 MILES.
GOOD. LET'S GO.
HANG ON. LET ME PRINT THIS.
LET'S GO!

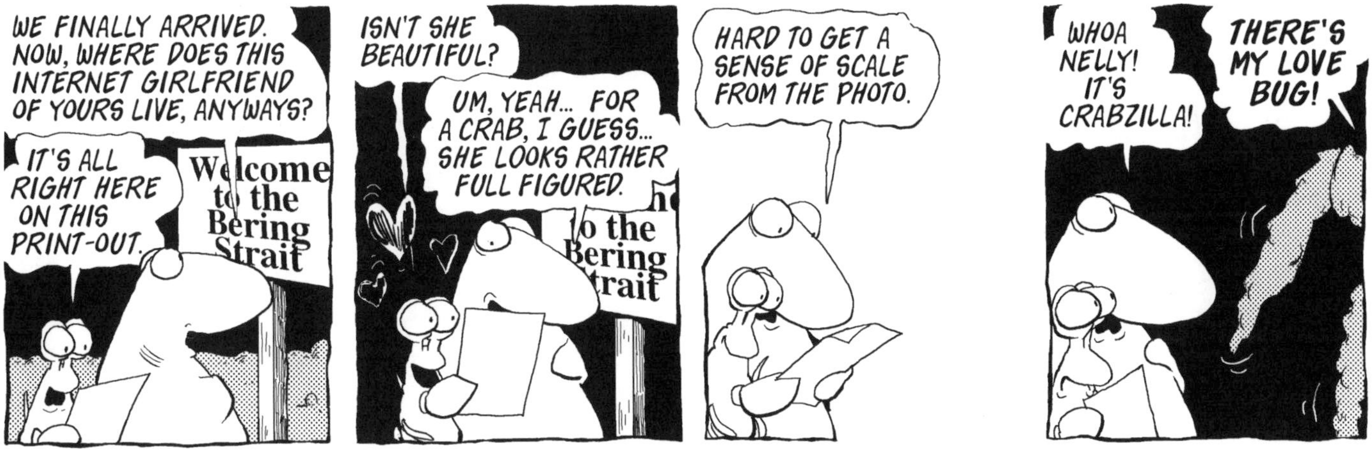
WE FINALLY ARRIVED. NOW, WHERE DOES THIS INTERNET GIRLFRIEND OF YOURS LIVE, ANYWAYS?
IT'S ALL RIGHT HERE ON THIS PRINT-OUT.
Welcome to the Bering Strait
ISN'T SHE BEAUTIFUL?
UM, YEAH... FOR A CRAB, I GUESS... SHE LOOKS RATHER FULL FIGURED.
HARD TO GET A SENSE OF SCALE FROM THE PHOTO.
WHOA NELLY! IT'S CRABZILLA!
THERE'S MY LOVE BUG!

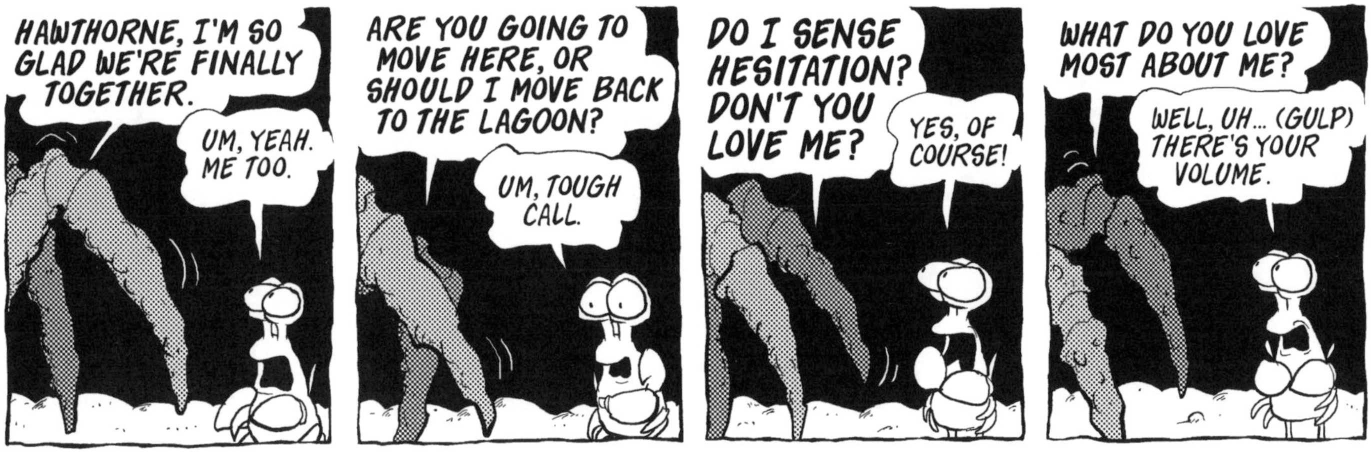
HAWTHORNE, I'M SO GLAD WE'RE FINALLY TOGETHER.
UM, YEAH. ME TOO.
ARE YOU GOING TO MOVE HERE, OR SHOULD I MOVE BACK TO THE LAGOON?
UM, TOUGH CALL.
DO I SENSE HESITATION? DON'T YOU LOVE ME?
YES, OF COURSE!
WHAT DO YOU LOVE MOST ABOUT ME?
WELL, UH... (GULP) THERE'S YOUR VOLUME.

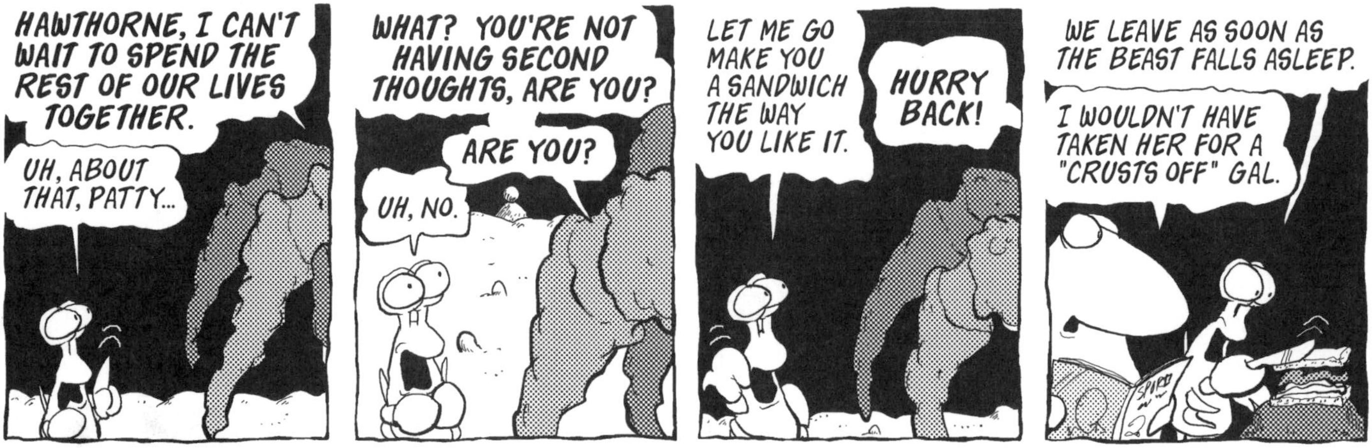
HAWTHORNE, I CAN'T WAIT TO SPEND THE REST OF OUR LIVES TOGETHER.
UH, ABOUT THAT, PATTY...
WHAT? YOU'RE NOT HAVING SECOND THOUGHTS, ARE YOU?
ARE YOU?
UH, NO.
LET ME GO MAKE YOU A SANDWICH THE WAY YOU LIKE IT.
HURRY BACK!
WE LEAVE AS SOON AS THE BEAST FALLS ASLEEP.
I WOULDN'T HAVE TAKEN HER FOR A "CRUSTS OFF" GAL.

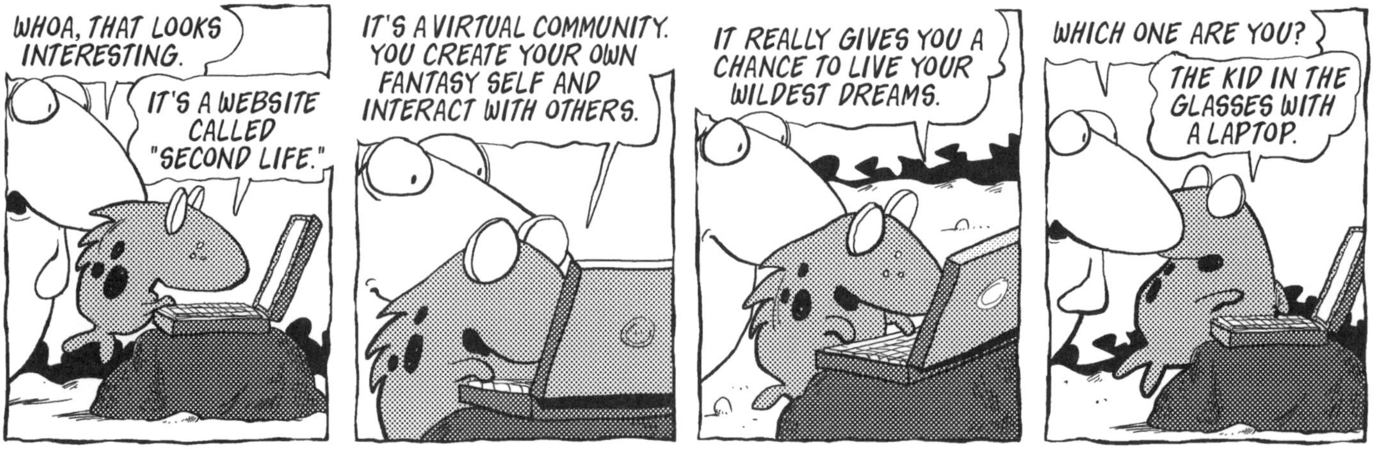
WHOA, THAT LOOKS INTERESTING.
IT'S A WEBSITE CALLED "SECOND LIFE."
IT'S A VIRTUAL COMMUNITY. YOU CREATE YOUR OWN FANTASY SELF AND INTERACT WITH OTHERS.
IT REALLY GIVES YOU A CHANCE TO LIVE YOUR WILDEST DREAMS.
WHICH ONE ARE YOU?
THE KID IN THE GLASSES WITH A LAPTOP.

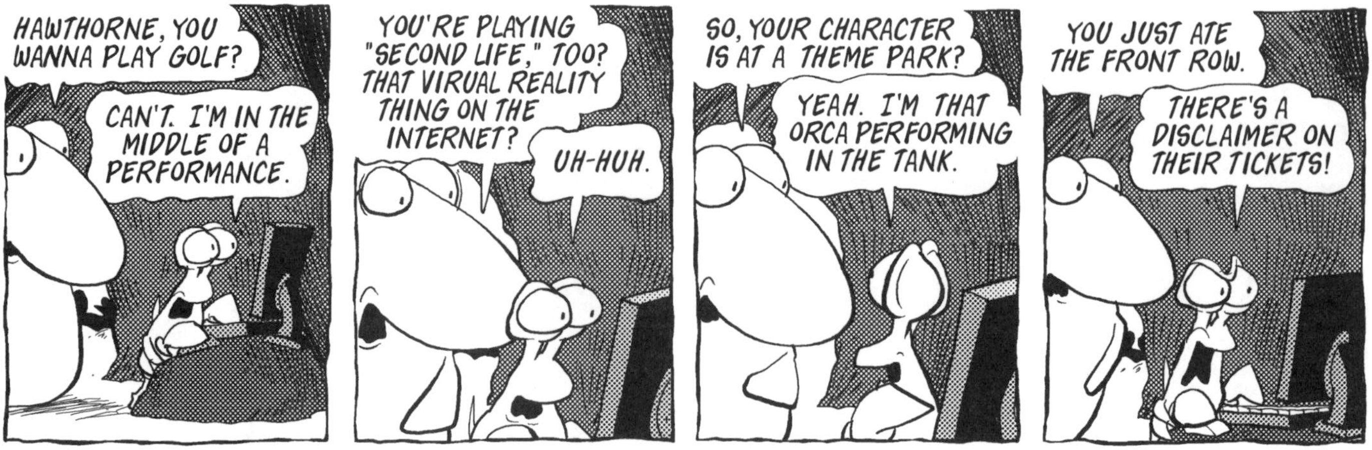
HAWTHORNE, YOU WANNA PLAY GOLF?
CAN'T. I'M IN THE MIDDLE OF A PERFORMANCE.
YOU'RE PLAYING "SECOND LIFE," TOO? THAT VIRUAL REALITY THING ON THE INTERNET?
UH-HUH.
SO, YOUR CHARACTER IS AT A THEME PARK?
YEAH. I'M THAT ORCA PERFORMING IN THE TANK.
YOU JUST ATE THE FRONT ROW.
THERE'S A DISCLAIMER ON THEIR TICKETS!

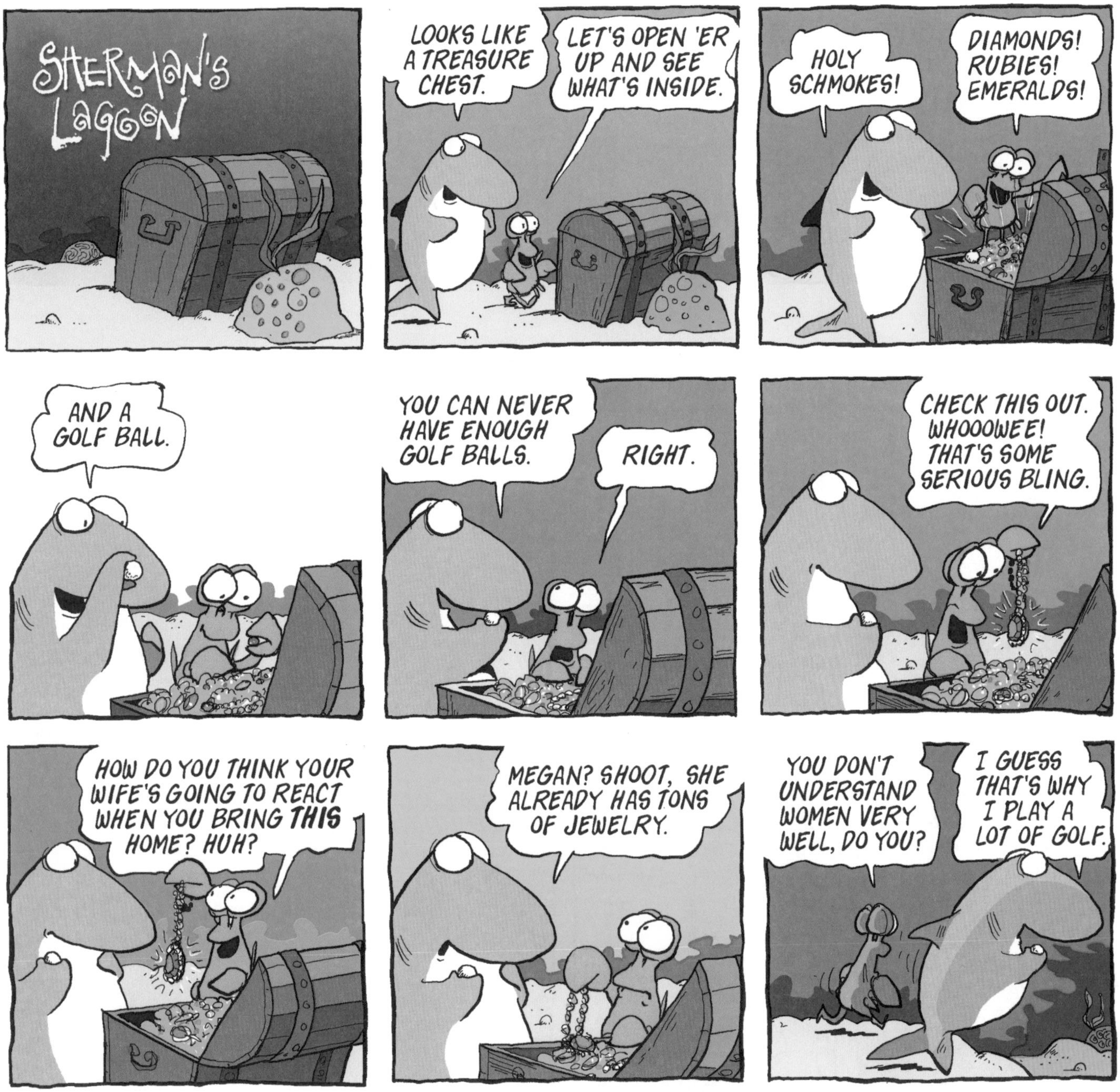
SHERMAN'S LAGOON
LOOKS LIKE A TREASURE CHEST.
LET'S OPEN 'ER UP AND SEE WHAT'S INSIDE.
HOLY SCHMOKES!
DIAMONDS! RUBIES! EMERALDS!
AND A GOLF BALL.
YOU CAN NEVER HAVE ENOUGH GOLF BALLS.
RIGHT.
CHECK THIS OUT. WHOOOWEE! THAT'S SOME SERIOUS BLING.
HOW DO YOU THINK YOUR WIFE'S GOING TO REACT WHEN YOU BRING **THIS** HOME? HUH?
MEGAN? SHOOT, SHE ALREADY HAS TONS OF JEWELRY.
YOU DON'T UNDERSTAND WOMEN VERY WELL, DO YOU?
I GUESS THAT'S WHY I PLAY A LOT OF GOLF.

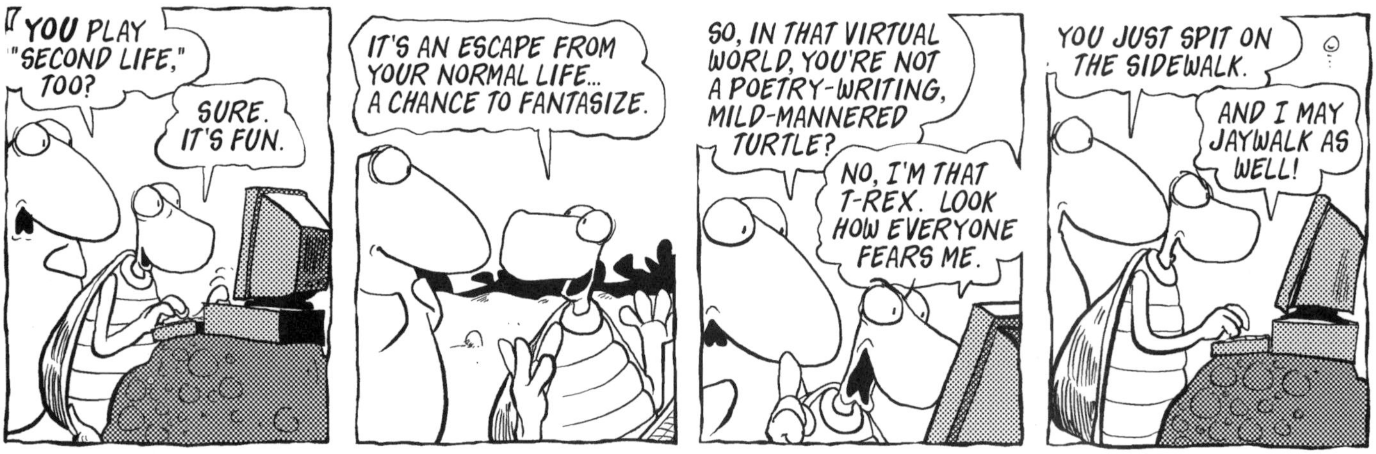
YOU PLAY "SECOND LIFE," TOO?
SURE. IT'S FUN.
IT'S AN ESCAPE FROM YOUR NORMAL LIFE... A CHANCE TO FANTASIZE.
SO, IN THAT VIRTUAL WORLD, YOU'RE NOT A POETRY-WRITING, MILD-MANNERED TURTLE?
NO, I'M THAT T-REX. LOOK HOW EVERYONE FEARS ME.
YOU JUST SPIT ON THE SIDEWALK.
AND I MAY JAYWALK AS WELL!

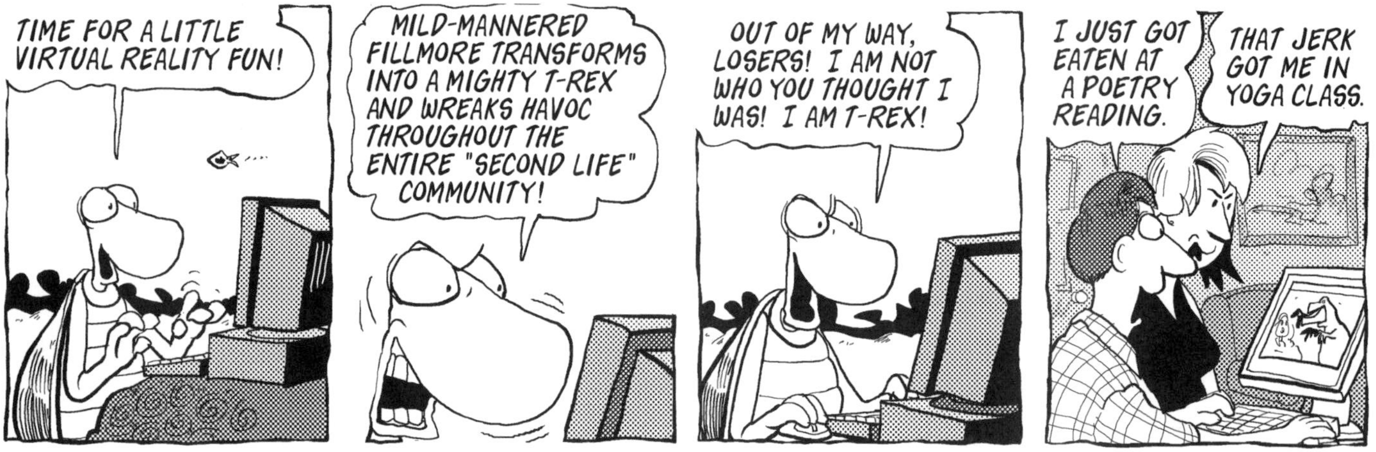
TIME FOR A LITTLE VIRTUAL REALITY FUN!
MILD-MANNERED FILLMORE TRANSFORMS INTO A MIGHTY T-REX AND WREAKS HAVOC THROUGHOUT THE ENTIRE "SECOND LIFE" COMMUNITY!
OUT OF MY WAY, LOSERS! I AM NOT WHO YOU THOUGHT I WAS! I AM T-REX!
I JUST GOT EATEN AT A POETRY READING.
THAT JERK GOT ME IN YOGA CLASS.

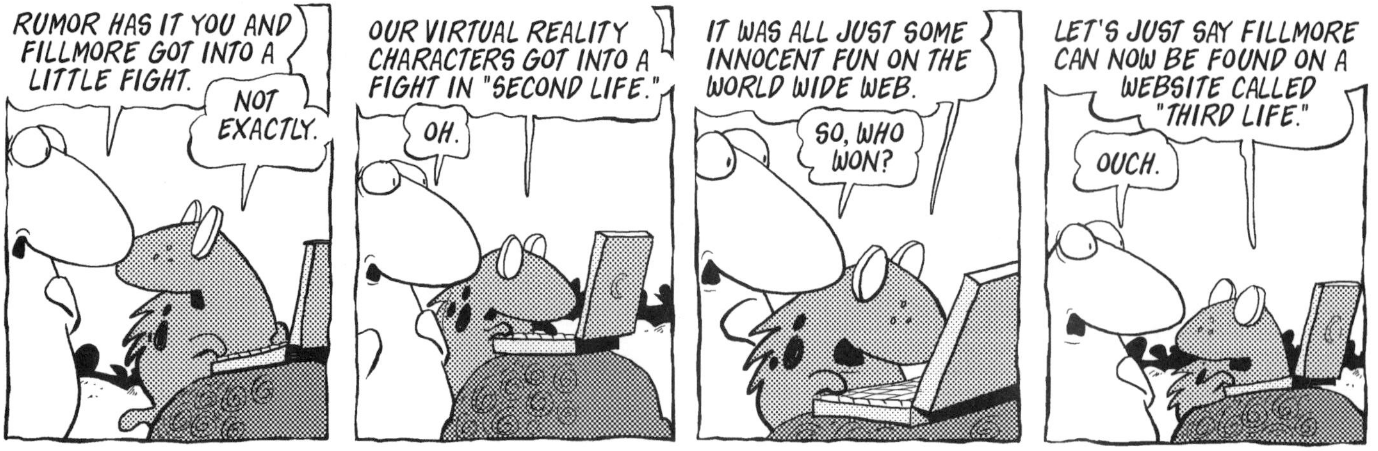
RUMOR HAS IT YOU AND FILLMORE GOT INTO A LITTLE FIGHT.
NOT EXACTLY.
OUR VIRTUAL REALITY CHARACTERS GOT INTO A FIGHT IN "SECOND LIFE."
OH.
IT WAS ALL JUST SOME INNOCENT FUN ON THE WORLD WIDE WEB.
SO, WHO WON?
LET'S JUST SAY FILLMORE CAN NOW BE FOUND ON A WEBSITE CALLED "THIRD LIFE."
OUCH.

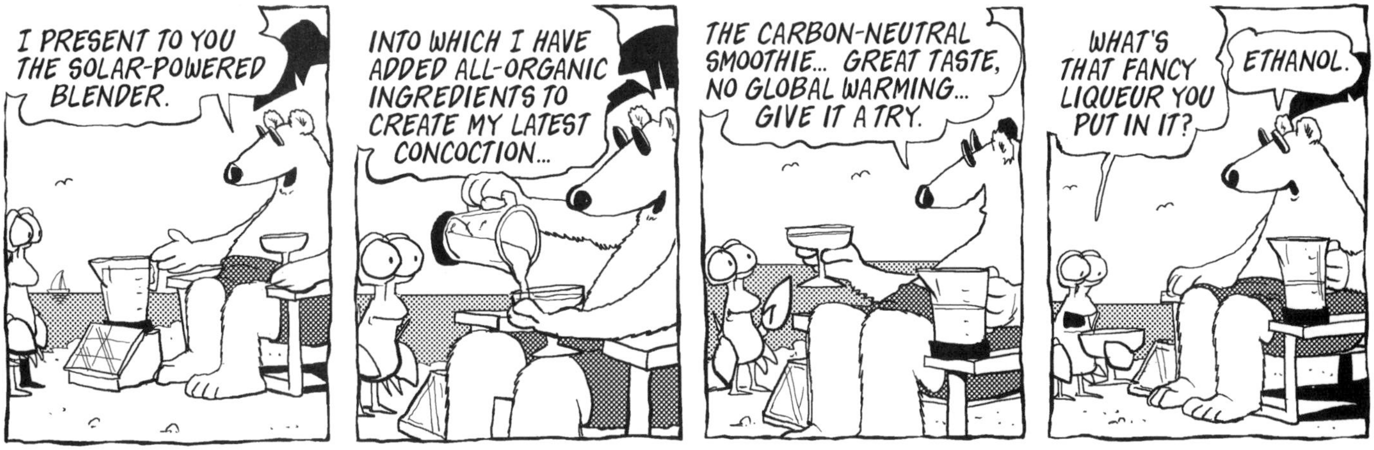
I PRESENT TO YOU THE SOLAR-POWERED BLENDER.
INTO WHICH I HAVE ADDED ALL-ORGANIC INGREDIENTS TO CREATE MY LATEST CONCOCTION...
THE CARBON-NEUTRAL SMOOTHIE... GREAT TASTE, NO GLOBAL WARMING... GIVE IT A TRY.
WHAT'S THAT FANCY LIQUEUR YOU PUT IN IT?
ETHANOL.

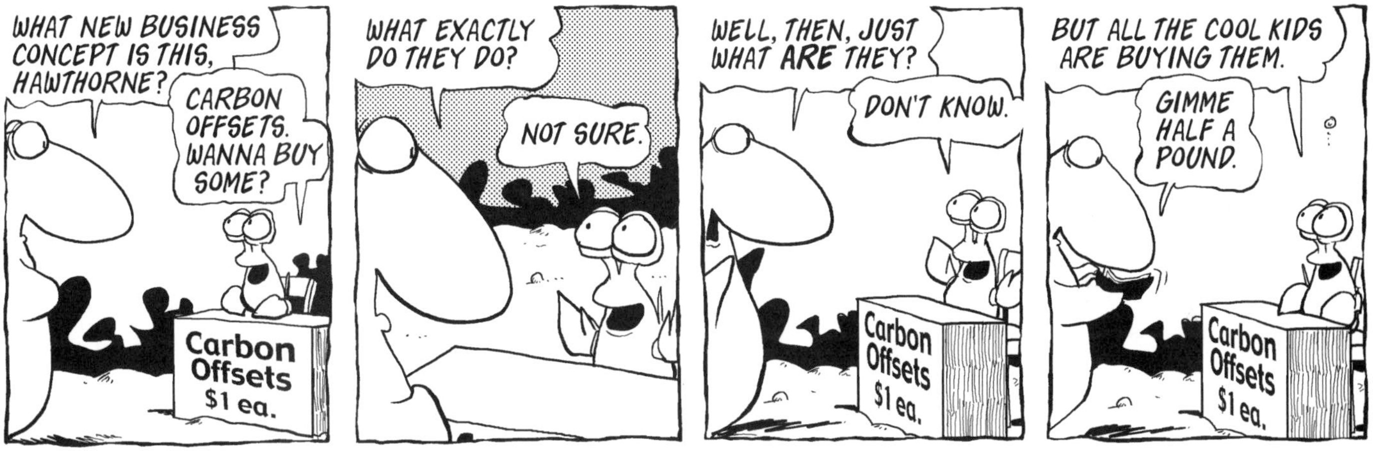
WHAT NEW BUSINESS CONCEPT IS THIS, HAWTHORNE?
CARBON OFFSETS. WANNA BUY SOME?
Carbon Offsets $1 ea.
WHAT EXACTLY DO THEY DO?
NOT SURE.
WELL, THEN, JUST WHAT **ARE** THEY?
DON'T KNOW.
Carbon Offsets $1 ea.
BUT ALL THE COOL KIDS ARE BUYING THEM.
GIMME HALF A POUND.
Carbon Offsets $1 ea.

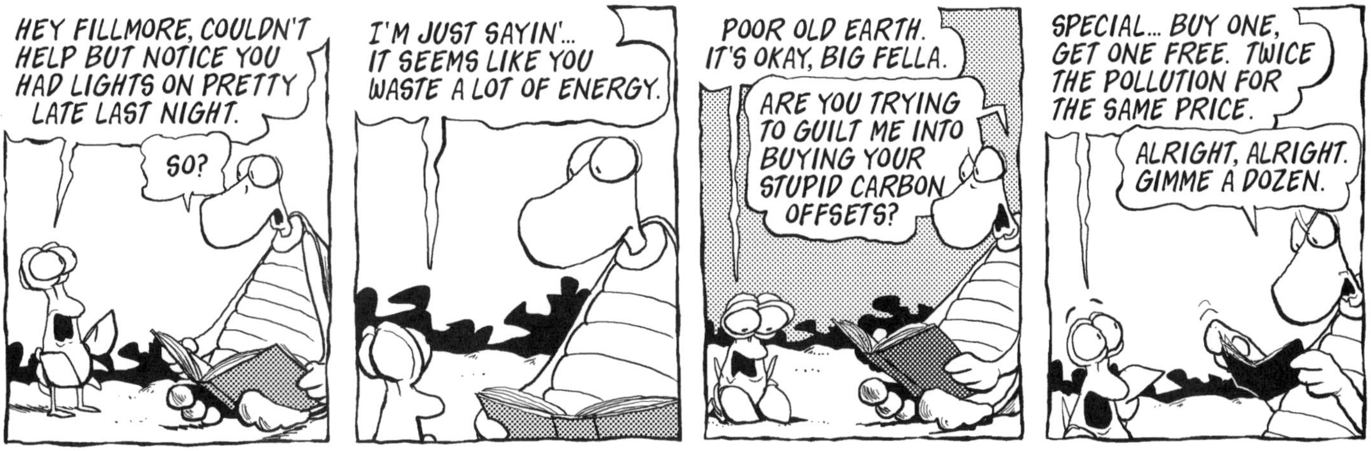
HEY FILLMORE, COULDN'T HELP BUT NOTICE YOU HAD LIGHTS ON PRETTY LATE LAST NIGHT.
SO?
I'M JUST SAYIN'... IT SEEMS LIKE YOU WASTE A LOT OF ENERGY.
POOR OLD EARTH. IT'S OKAY, BIG FELLA.
ARE YOU TRYING TO GUILT ME INTO BUYING YOUR STUPID CARBON OFFSETS?
SPECIAL... BUY ONE, GET ONE FREE. TWICE THE POLLUTION FOR THE SAME PRICE.
ALRIGHT, ALRIGHT. GIMME A DOZEN.

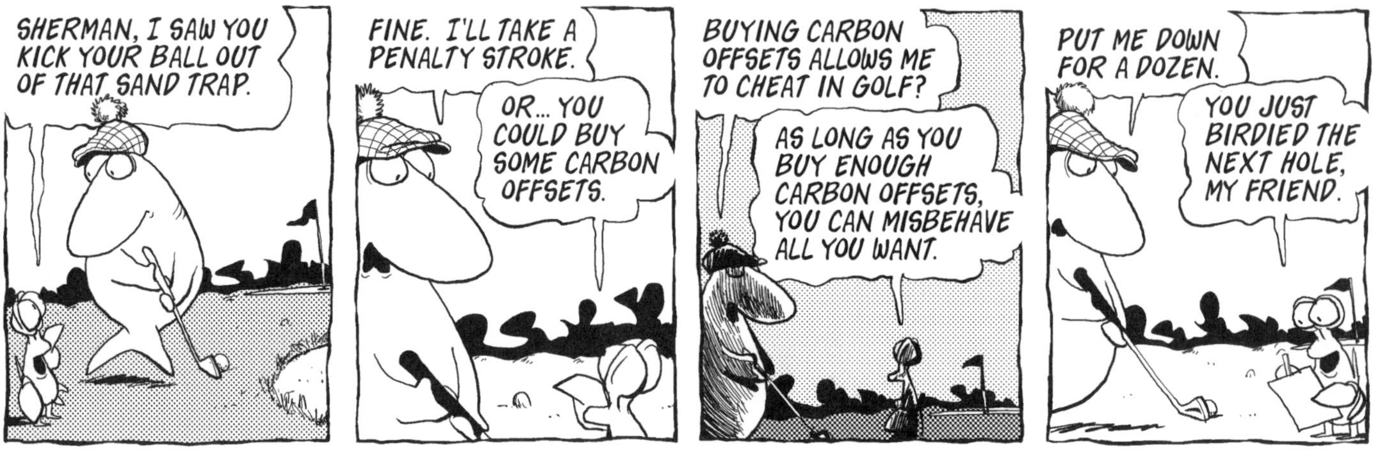
SHERMAN, I SAW YOU KICK YOUR BALL OUT OF THAT SAND TRAP.
FINE. I'LL TAKE A PENALTY STROKE.
OR... YOU COULD BUY SOME CARBON OFFSETS.
BUYING CARBON OFFSETS ALLOWS ME TO CHEAT IN GOLF?
AS LONG AS YOU BUY ENOUGH CARBON OFFSETS, YOU CAN MISBEHAVE ALL YOU WANT.
PUT ME DOWN FOR A DOZEN.
YOU JUST BIRDIED THE NEXT HOLE, MY FRIEND.

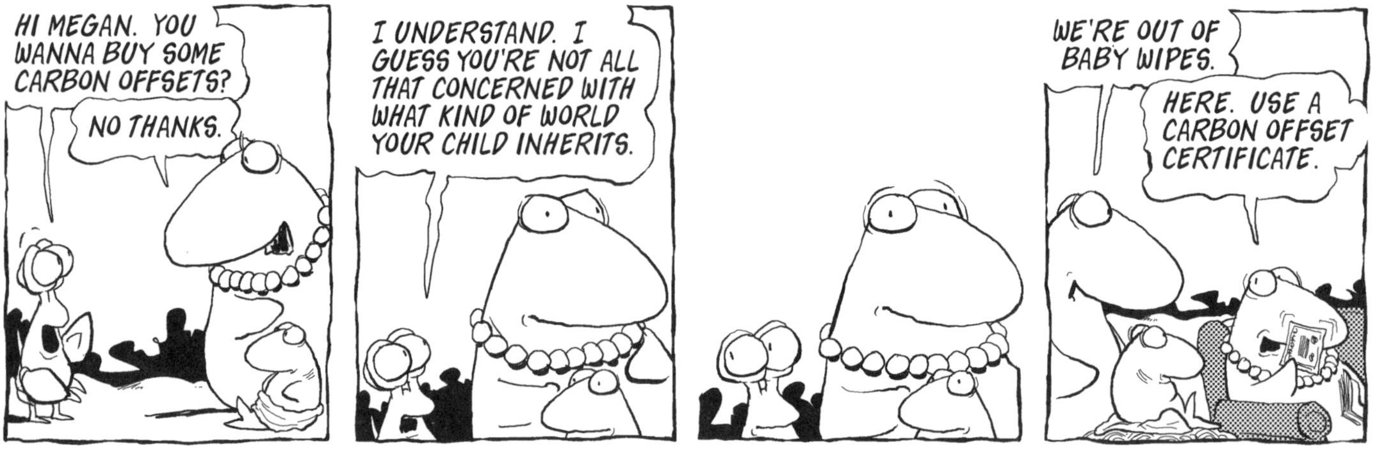
HI MEGAN. YOU WANNA BUY SOME CARBON OFFSETS?
NO THANKS.
I UNDERSTAND. I GUESS YOU'RE NOT ALL THAT CONCERNED WITH WHAT KIND OF WORLD YOUR CHILD INHERITS.
WE'RE OUT OF BABY WIPES.
HERE. USE A CARBON OFFSET CERTIFICATE.

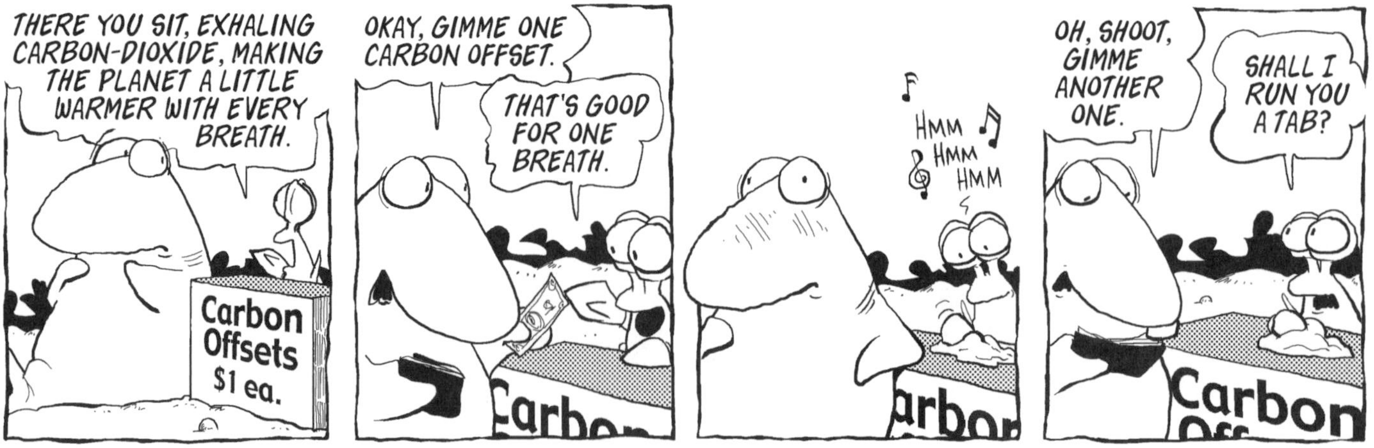
THERE YOU SIT, EXHALING CARBON-DIOXIDE, MAKING THE PLANET A LITTLE WARMER WITH EVERY BREATH.
Carbon Offsets $1 ea.
OKAY, GIMME ONE CARBON OFFSET.
THAT'S GOOD FOR ONE BREATH.
HMM HMM HMM
OH, SHOOT, GIMME ANOTHER ONE.
SHALL I RUN YOU A TAB?
Carbon

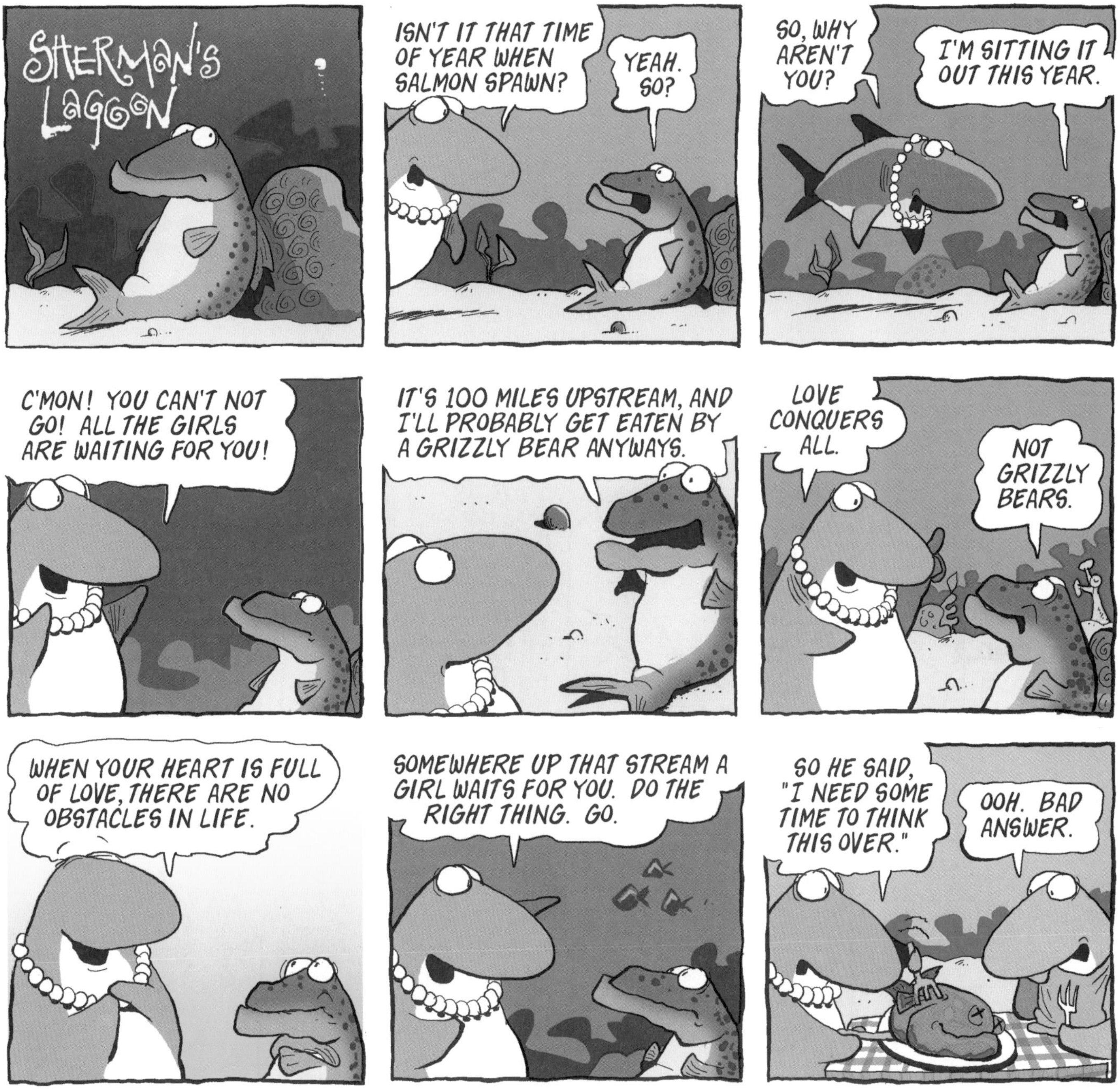
SHERMAN'S LAGOON
ISN'T IT THAT TIME OF YEAR WHEN SALMON SPAWN?
YEAH. SO?
SO, WHY AREN'T YOU?
I'M SITTING IT OUT THIS YEAR.
C'MON! YOU CAN'T NOT GO! ALL THE GIRLS ARE WAITING FOR YOU!
IT'S 100 MILES UPSTREAM, AND I'LL PROBABLY GET EATEN BY A GRIZZLY BEAR ANYWAYS.
LOVE CONQUERS ALL.
NOT GRIZZLY BEARS.
WHEN YOUR HEART IS FULL OF LOVE, THERE ARE NO OBSTACLES IN LIFE.
SOMEWHERE UP THAT STREAM A GIRL WAITS FOR YOU. DO THE RIGHT THING. GO.
SO HE SAID, "I NEED SOME TIME TO THINK THIS OVER."
OOH. BAD ANSWER.

Panel 1: HAWTHORNE, YOU'RE DISGRACEFUL! — MORE SPECIFIC, PLEASE.

Carbon Offsets $1 ea.

Panel 2: CASHING IN ON GLOBAL WARMING! YOU DON'T CARE ABOUT THIS STUFF! — HEY!

Panel 3: I'VE BEEN DOING MY RESEARCH, AND QUITE FRANKLY, I GOT SCARED!

Carb...

Panel 4: ABOUT CLIMATE CHANGE? — NO. ABOUT MY SCAMMING SKILLS. I SHOULD HAVE BEEN IN ON THIS AGES AGO.

Car...

Panel 5: HAWTHORNE, YOU CLOSED YOUR CARBON-OFFSET BUSINESS?

Carbon Offsets CLOSED

Panel 6: YEAH. I STARTED FEELING GUILTY ABOUT RIPPING EVERYONE OFF.

Carbon Offs CLOSED

Panel 7: TAKING MONEY FROM ALL YOU WELL-INTENTIONED ENVIRONMENTALISTS WAS BEYOND THE PALE. IT WAS LIKE TAKING CANDY FROM A BABY... — BY THE WAY...

Carbon Offs CLOSED

Panel 8: HERE'S ALL THE CANDY I TOOK FROM YOUR BABY. — YOU'RE THE ONE!

Car Offs CLOSED

Panel 9: SHERMAN, WE NEED TO TALK. — SURE.

Panel 10: YOU'VE BEEN EATING A LOT OF LAGOON RESIDENTS LATELY. EVERYONE'S WORRIED THEY'LL BE NEXT.

Panel 11: I CAN'T STOP BEING A SHARK. MY ONE RULE IS, IF I KNOW THEIR NAMES, I DON'T EAT THEM.

Panel 12: YOU CAN'T EAT ME! I'VE GOT A NAME TAG! — SORRY. NOT MUCH OF A READER.

CARL

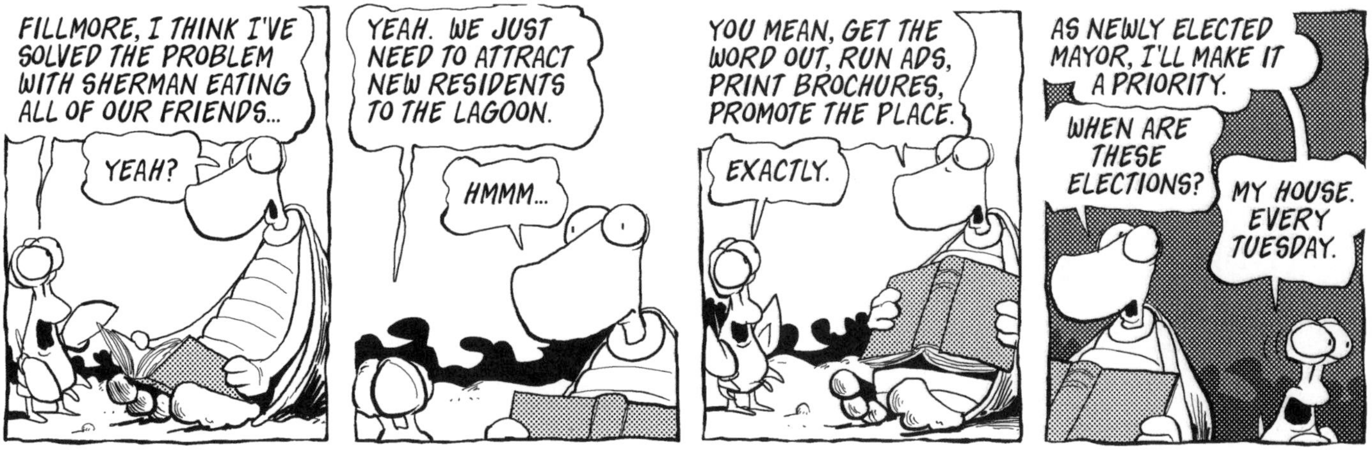
FILLMORE, I THINK I'VE SOLVED THE PROBLEM WITH SHERMAN EATING ALL OF OUR FRIENDS...
YEAH?
YEAH. WE JUST NEED TO ATTRACT NEW RESIDENTS TO THE LAGOON.
HMMM...
YOU MEAN, GET THE WORD OUT, RUN ADS, PRINT BROCHURES, PROMOTE THE PLACE.
EXACTLY.
AS NEWLY ELECTED MAYOR, I'LL MAKE IT A PRIORITY.
WHEN ARE THESE ELECTIONS?
MY HOUSE. EVERY TUESDAY.

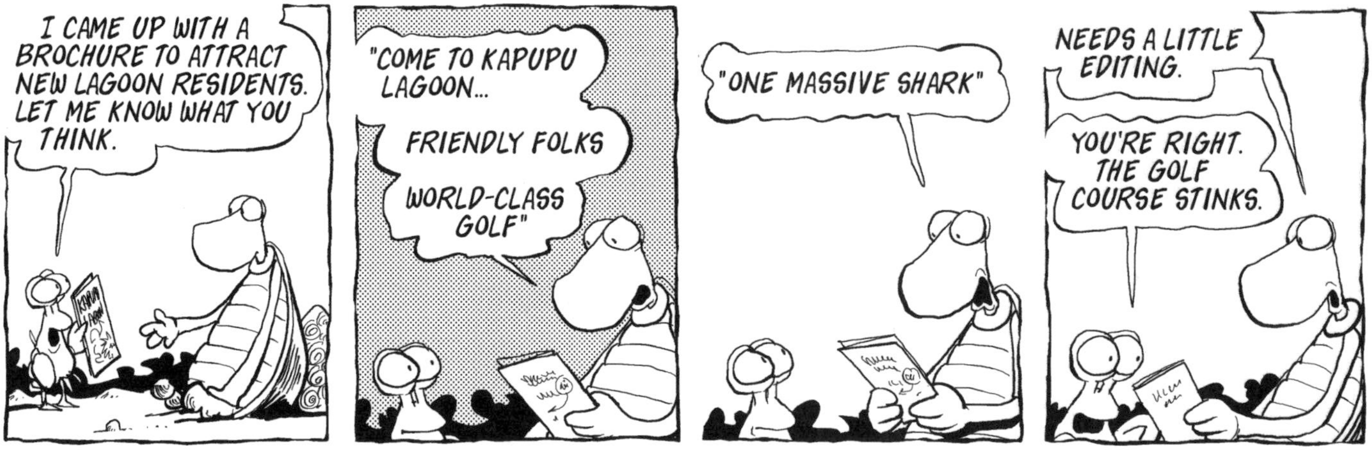
I CAME UP WITH A BROCHURE TO ATTRACT NEW LAGOON RESIDENTS. LET ME KNOW WHAT YOU THINK.
"COME TO KAPUPU LAGOON...
FRIENDLY FOLKS
WORLD-CLASS GOLF"
"ONE MASSIVE SHARK"
NEEDS A LITTLE EDITING.
YOU'RE RIGHT. THE GOLF COURSE STINKS.

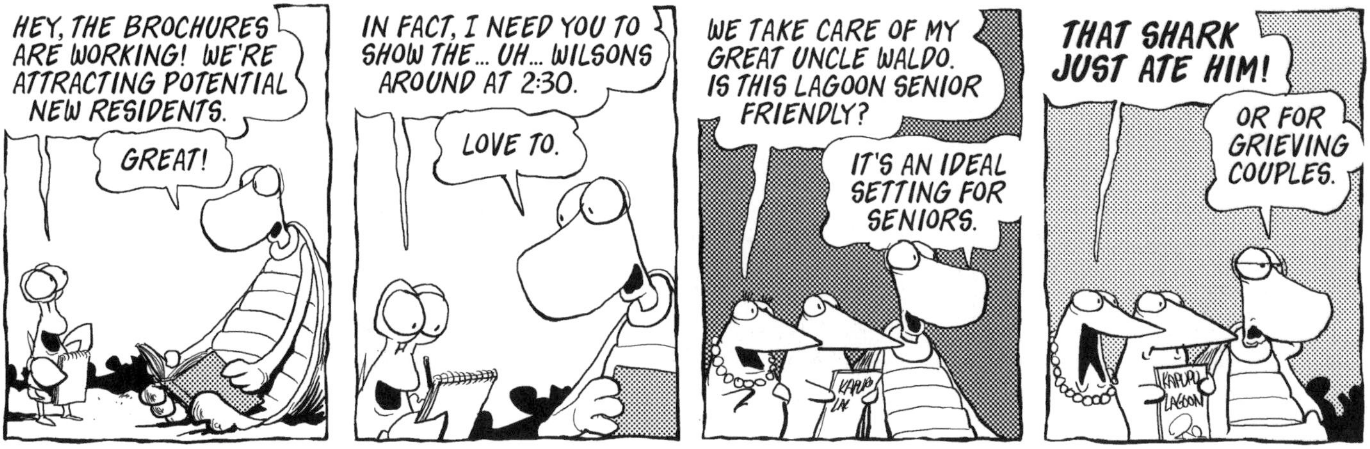
HEY, THE BROCHURES ARE WORKING! WE'RE ATTRACTING POTENTIAL NEW RESIDENTS.
GREAT!
IN FACT, I NEED YOU TO SHOW THE... UH... WILSONS AROUND AT 2:30.
LOVE TO.
WE TAKE CARE OF MY GREAT UNCLE WALDO. IS THIS LAGOON SENIOR FRIENDLY?
IT'S AN IDEAL SETTING FOR SENIORS.
THAT SHARK JUST ATE HIM!
OR FOR GRIEVING COUPLES.

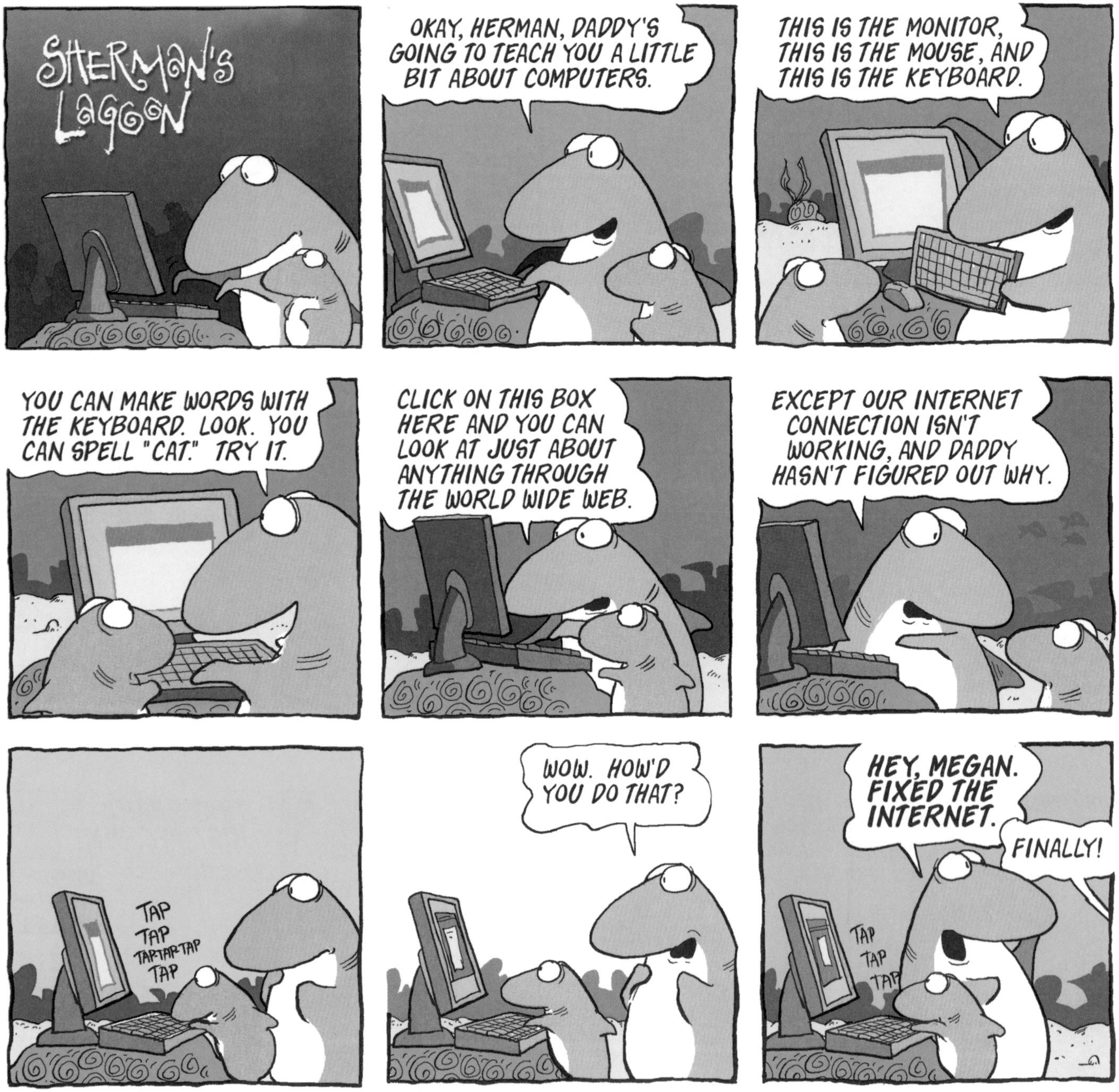
SHERMAN'S LAGOON
OKAY, HERMAN, DADDY'S GOING TO TEACH YOU A LITTLE BIT ABOUT COMPUTERS.
THIS IS THE MONITOR, THIS IS THE MOUSE, AND THIS IS THE KEYBOARD.
YOU CAN MAKE WORDS WITH THE KEYBOARD. LOOK. YOU CAN SPELL "CAT." TRY IT.
CLICK ON THIS BOX HERE AND YOU CAN LOOK AT JUST ABOUT ANYTHING THROUGH THE WORLD WIDE WEB.
EXCEPT OUR INTERNET CONNECTION ISN'T WORKING, AND DADDY HASN'T FIGURED OUT WHY.
TAP TAP TAP-TAP-TAP TAP
WOW. HOW'D YOU DO THAT?
TAP TAP TAP
HEY, MEGAN. FIXED THE INTERNET.
FINALLY!

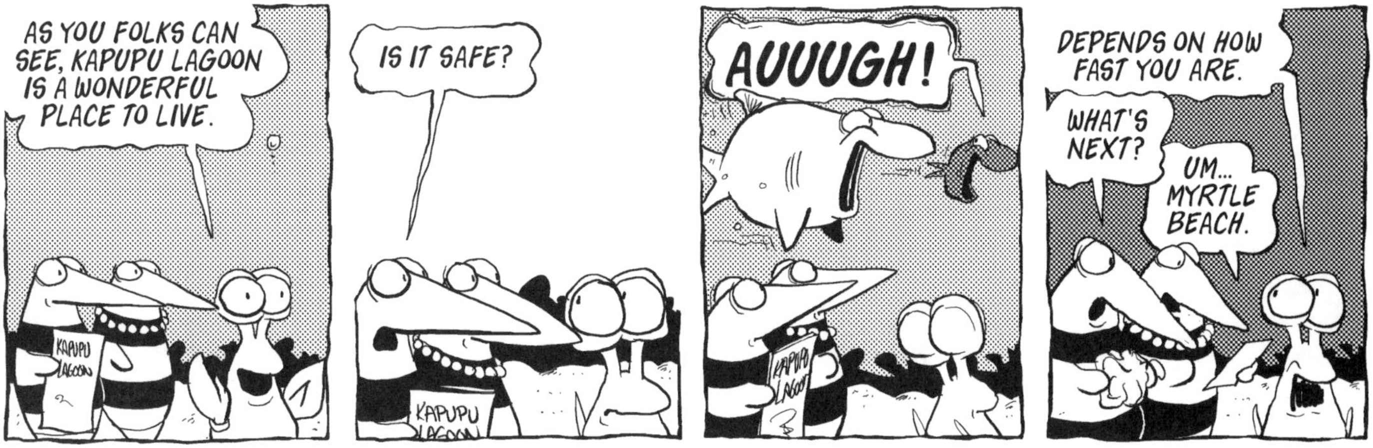
AS YOU FOLKS CAN SEE, KAPUPU LAGOON IS A WONDERFUL PLACE TO LIVE.
KAPUPU LAGOON
IS IT SAFE?
KAPUPU
AUUUGH!
DEPENDS ON HOW FAST YOU ARE.
WHAT'S NEXT?
UM... MYRTLE BEACH.

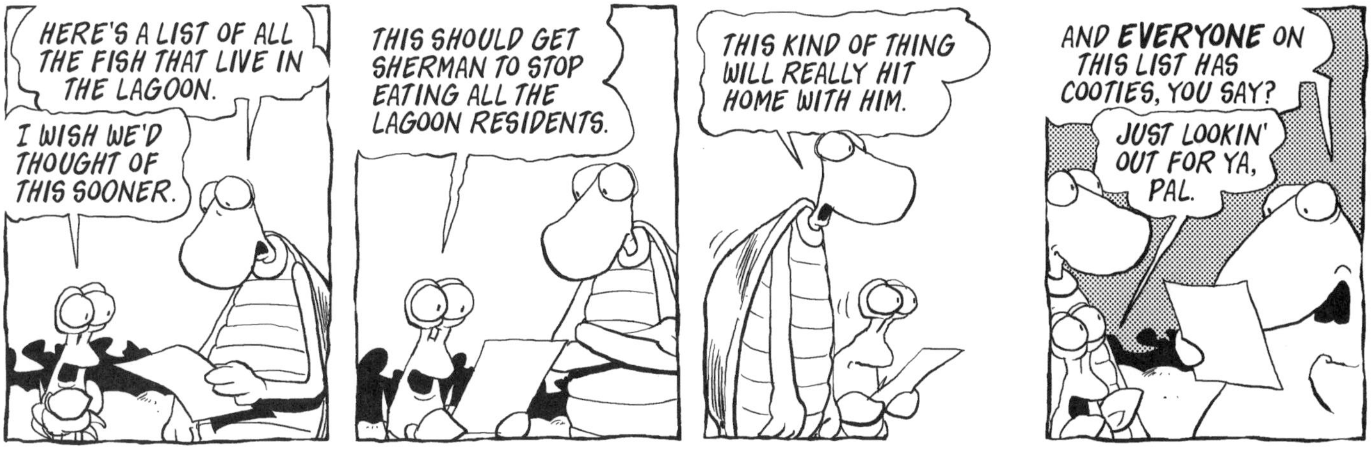
HERE'S A LIST OF ALL THE FISH THAT LIVE IN THE LAGOON.
I WISH WE'D THOUGHT OF THIS SOONER.
THIS SHOULD GET SHERMAN TO STOP EATING ALL THE LAGOON RESIDENTS.
THIS KIND OF THING WILL REALLY HIT HOME WITH HIM.
AND EVERYONE ON THIS LIST HAS COOTIES, YOU SAY?
JUST LOOKIN' OUT FOR YA, PAL.

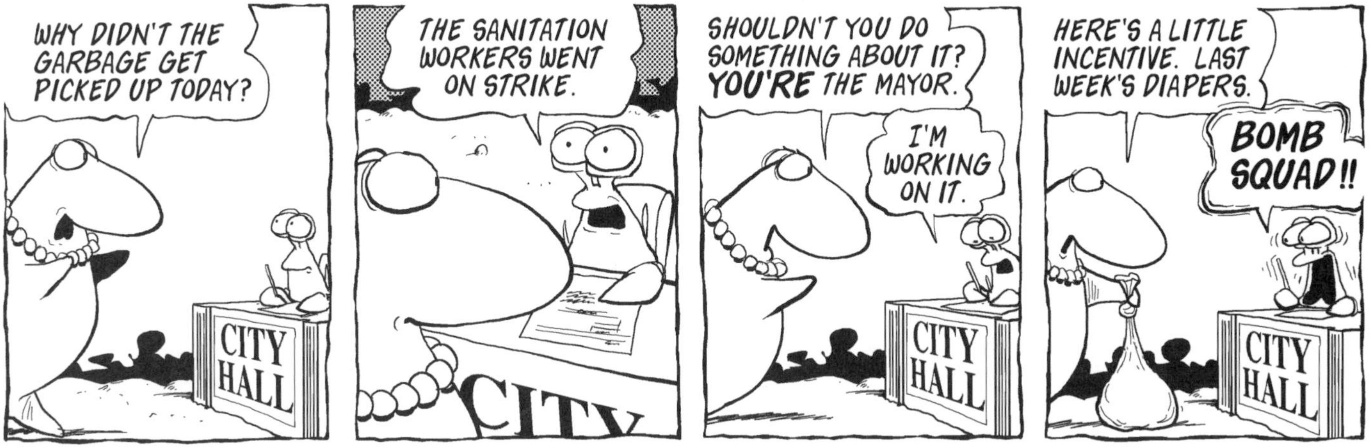
WHY DIDN'T THE GARBAGE GET PICKED UP TODAY?
CITY HALL
THE SANITATION WORKERS WENT ON STRIKE.
CITY
SHOULDN'T YOU DO SOMETHING ABOUT IT? YOU'RE THE MAYOR.
I'M WORKING ON IT.
CITY HALL
HERE'S A LITTLE INCENTIVE. LAST WEEK'S DIAPERS.
BOMB SQUAD!!
CITY HALL

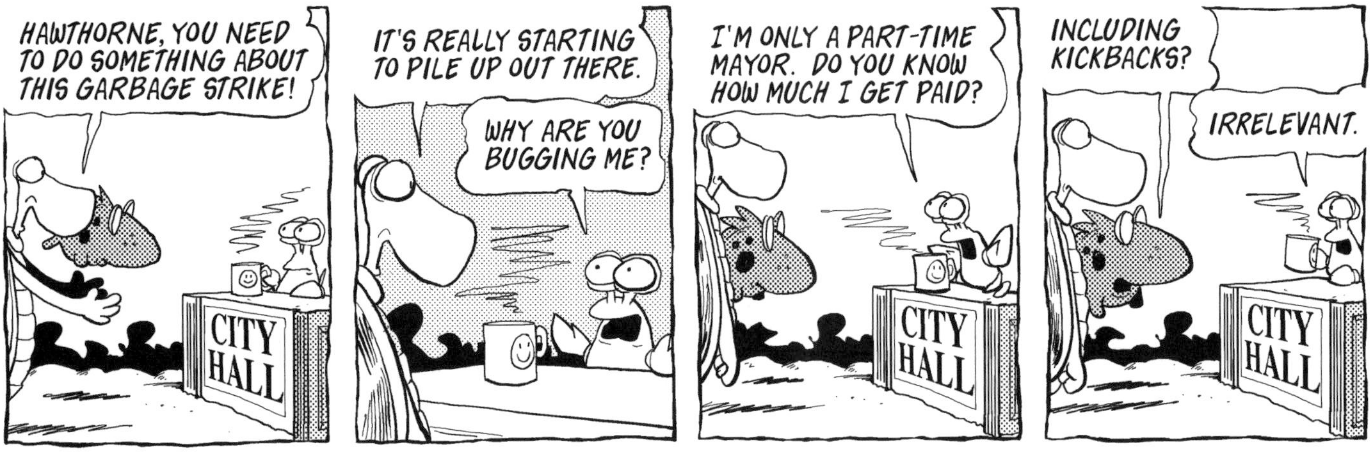
HAWTHORNE, YOU NEED TO DO SOMETHING ABOUT THIS GARBAGE STRIKE!
CITY HALL
IT'S REALLY STARTING TO PILE UP OUT THERE.
WHY ARE YOU BUGGING ME?
I'M ONLY A PART-TIME MAYOR. DO YOU KNOW HOW MUCH I GET PAID?
CITY HALL
INCLUDING KICKBACKS?
IRRELEVANT.
CITY HALL

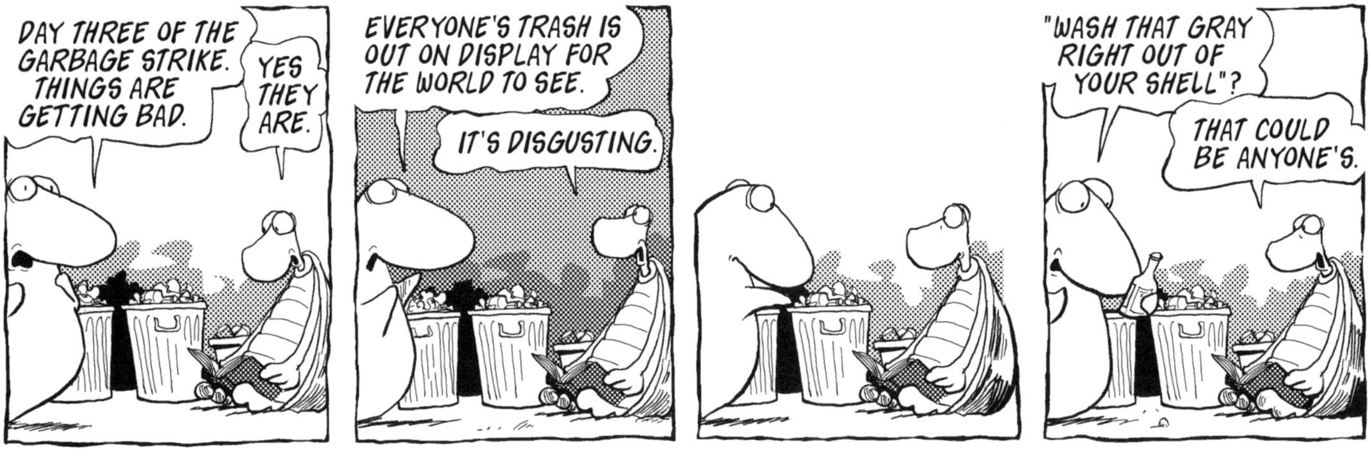
DAY THREE OF THE GARBAGE STRIKE. THINGS ARE GETTING BAD.
YES THEY ARE.
EVERYONE'S TRASH IS OUT ON DISPLAY FOR THE WORLD TO SEE.
IT'S DISGUSTING.
"WASH THAT GRAY RIGHT OUT OF YOUR SHELL"?
THAT COULD BE ANYONE'S.

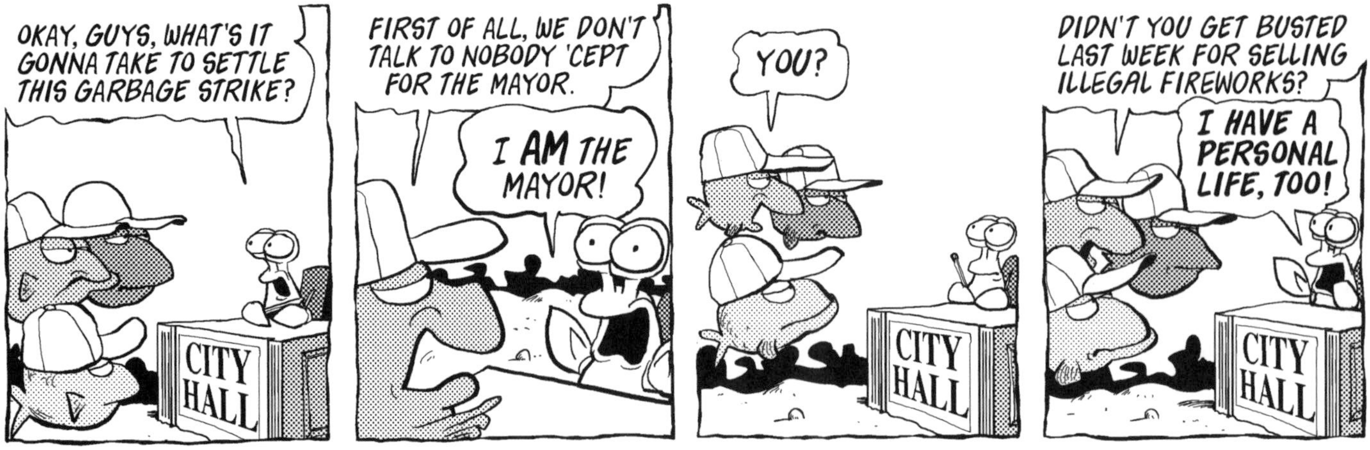
OKAY, GUYS, WHAT'S IT GONNA TAKE TO SETTLE THIS GARBAGE STRIKE?
CITY HALL
FIRST OF ALL, WE DON'T TALK TO NOBODY 'CEPT FOR THE MAYOR.
I **AM** THE MAYOR!
YOU?
CITY HALL
DIDN'T YOU GET BUSTED LAST WEEK FOR SELLING ILLEGAL FIREWORKS?
I HAVE A PERSONAL LIFE, TOO!
CITY HALL

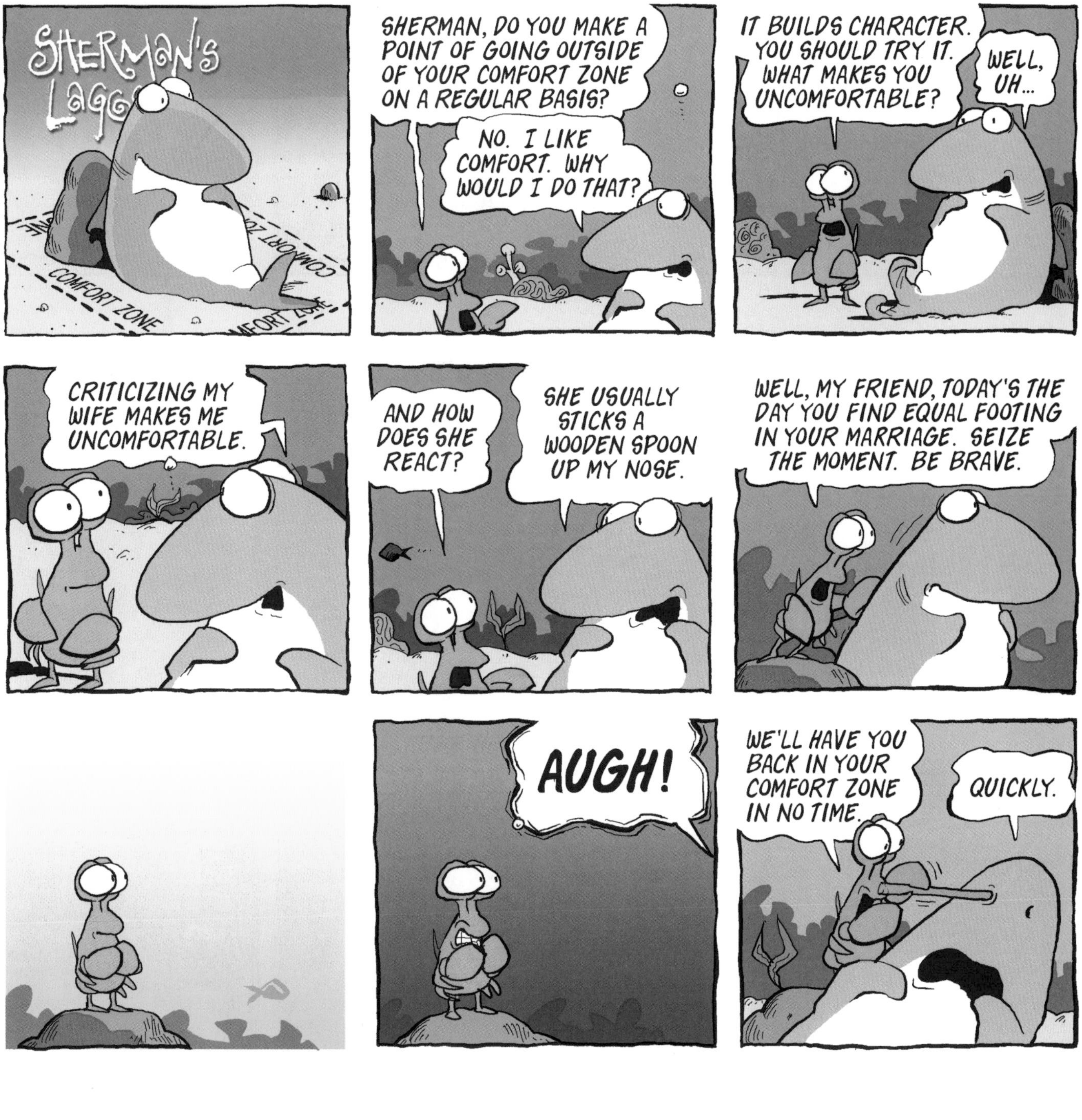
SHERMAN'S LAGOON
COMFORT ZONE
SHERMAN, DO YOU MAKE A POINT OF GOING OUTSIDE OF YOUR COMFORT ZONE ON A REGULAR BASIS?
NO. I LIKE COMFORT. WHY WOULD I DO THAT?
IT BUILDS CHARACTER. YOU SHOULD TRY IT. WHAT MAKES YOU UNCOMFORTABLE?
WELL, UH...
CRITICIZING MY WIFE MAKES ME UNCOMFORTABLE.
AND HOW DOES SHE REACT?
SHE USUALLY STICKS A WOODEN SPOON UP MY NOSE.
WELL, MY FRIEND, TODAY'S THE DAY YOU FIND EQUAL FOOTING IN YOUR MARRIAGE. SEIZE THE MOMENT. BE BRAVE.
AUGH!
WE'LL HAVE YOU BACK IN YOUR COMFORT ZONE IN NO TIME.
QUICKLY.

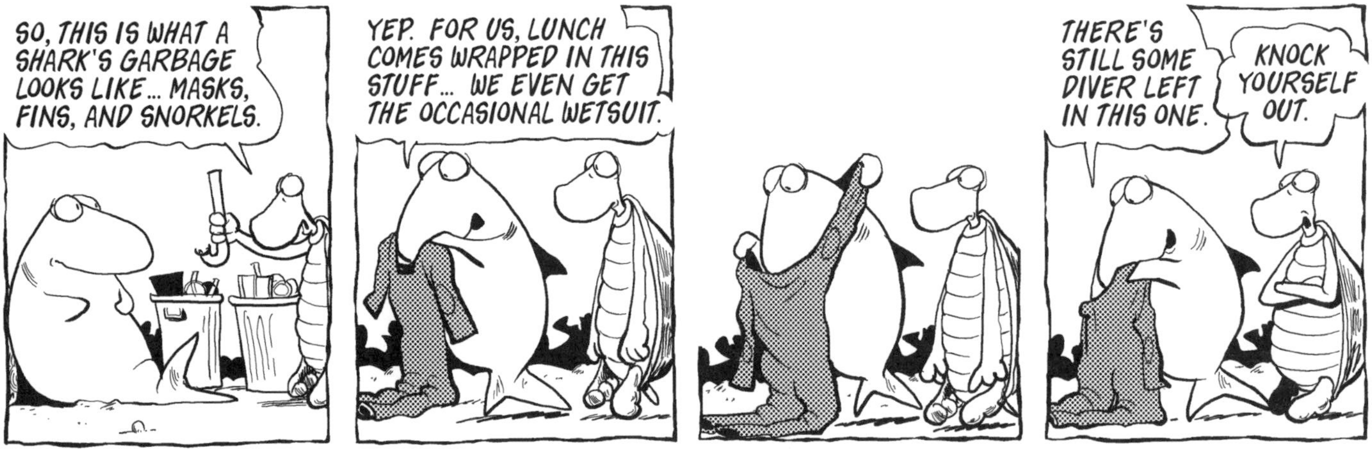
SO, THIS IS WHAT A SHARK'S GARBAGE LOOKS LIKE... MASKS, FINS, AND SNORKELS.
YEP. FOR US, LUNCH COMES WRAPPED IN THIS STUFF... WE EVEN GET THE OCCASIONAL WETSUIT.
THERE'S STILL SOME DIVER LEFT IN THIS ONE.
KNOCK YOURSELF OUT.

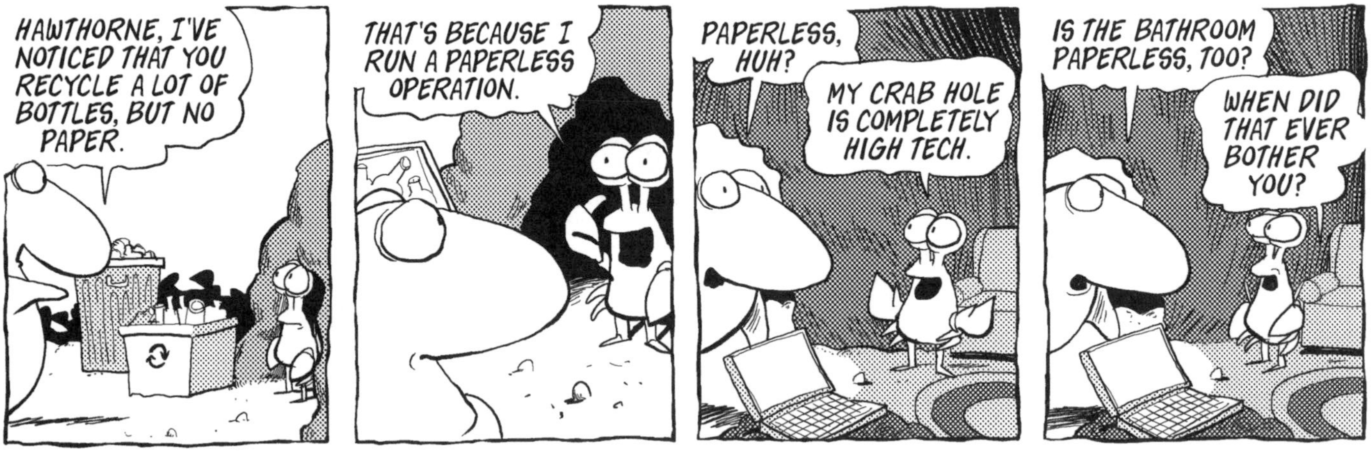
HAWTHORNE, I'VE NOTICED THAT YOU RECYCLE A LOT OF BOTTLES, BUT NO PAPER.
THAT'S BECAUSE I RUN A PAPERLESS OPERATION.
PAPERLESS, HUH?
MY CRAB HOLE IS COMPLETELY HIGH TECH.
IS THE BATHROOM PAPERLESS, TOO?
WHEN DID THAT EVER BOTHER YOU?

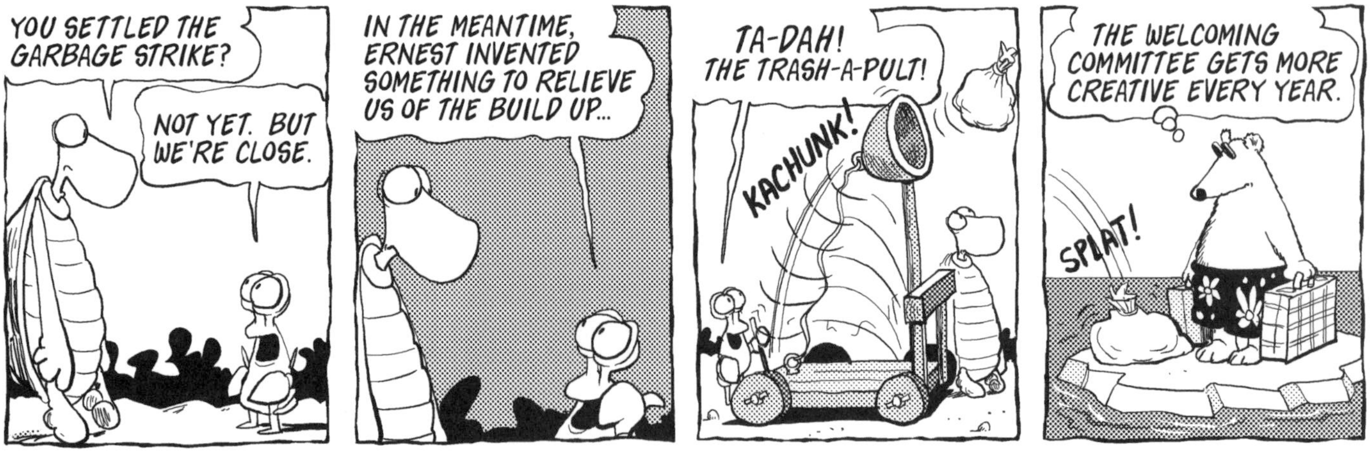
YOU SETTLED THE GARBAGE STRIKE?
NOT YET. BUT WE'RE CLOSE.
IN THE MEANTIME, ERNEST INVENTED SOMETHING TO RELIEVE US OF THE BUILD UP...
TA-DAH! THE TRASH-A-PULT!
KACHUNK!
THE WELCOMING COMMITTEE GETS MORE CREATIVE EVERY YEAR.
SPLAT!

WELCOME BACK FROM THE NORTH POLE, THORNTON.

THANKS.

YOU RODE IN ON A SMALLER ICE BERG THAN USUAL.

YEAH.

IT'S GETTING HARD TO FIND A GOOD CHUNK OF ICE UP THERE. EVERYTHING'S MELTING. CLIMATE CHANGE AND ALL THAT.

WOW. IT'S THAT BAD, HUH?

STILL ENOUGH FOR AN AWESOME DAIQUIRI.

POSITIVE THINKER.

OKAY, SHERMAN, OUR TEE TIME IS IN FIVE MINUTES. LET'S GO.

THAT'S FIVE MORE MINUTES I CAN PRACTICE.

I'VE BEEN HITTING A LOT OF SLICES LATELY.

AND YOU THINK FOUR EXTRA RANGE BALLS IS GOING TO MAKE A DIFFERENCE?

YOU HAVE NO IDEA HOW A GOLFER'S MIND WORKS.

ERNEST, YOU'RE PLAYING IN THE FUNDRAISER GOLF TOURNEY?

IT'S FOR A GOOD CAUSE.

IT'S VITALLY IMPORTANT FOR US ALL TO HELP SAVE THE WHALES.

WHACK!

THIS GETS YOU OUT OF SCHOOL, DOESN'T IT?

THEY THINK THIS THING LASTS ALL WEEK.

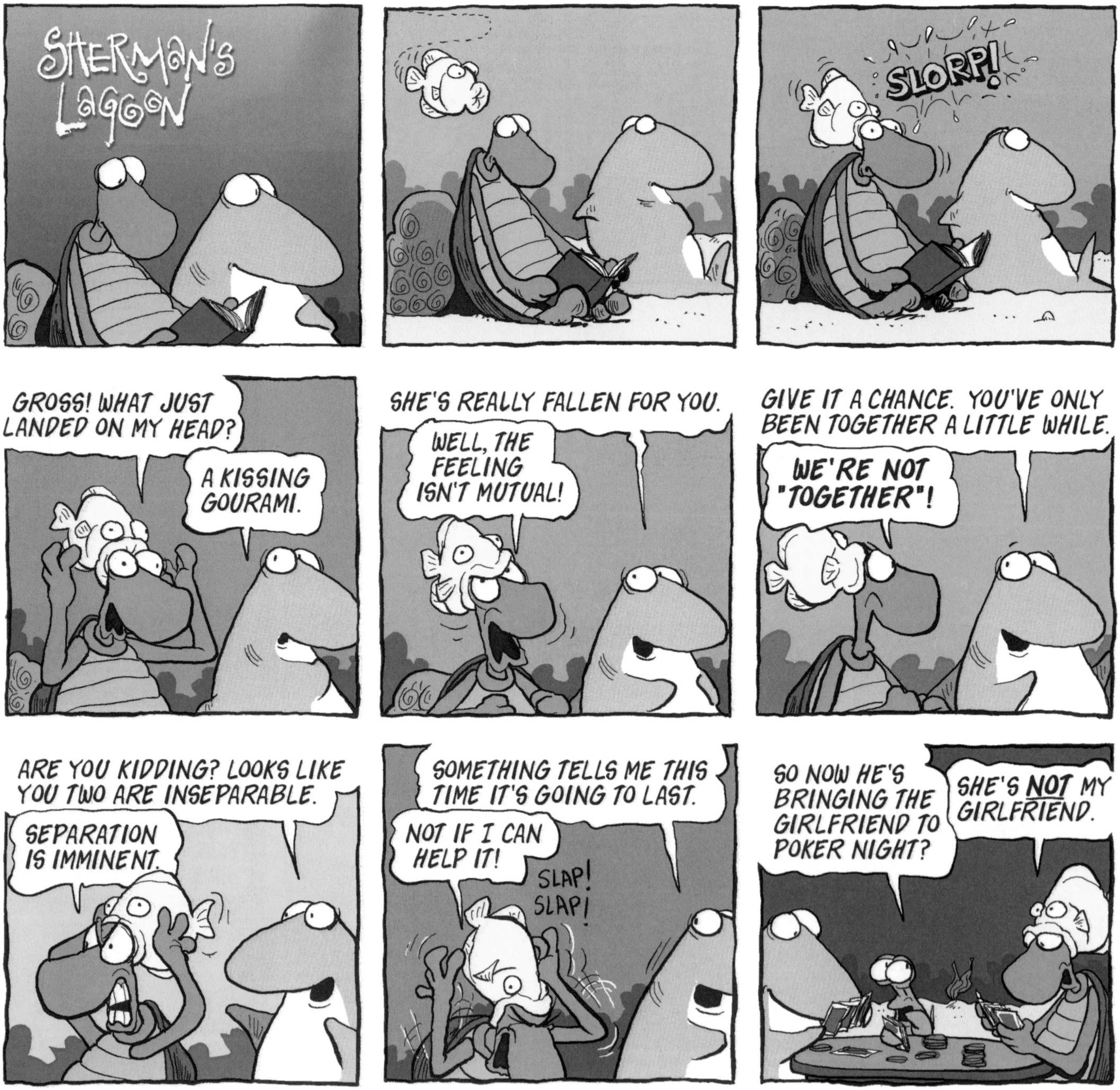
SHERMAN'S LAGOON
SLORP!
GROSS! WHAT JUST LANDED ON MY HEAD?
A KISSING GOURAMI.
SHE'S REALLY FALLEN FOR YOU.
WELL, THE FEELING ISN'T MUTUAL!
GIVE IT A CHANCE. YOU'VE ONLY BEEN TOGETHER A LITTLE WHILE.
WE'RE NOT "TOGETHER"!
ARE YOU KIDDING? LOOKS LIKE YOU TWO ARE INSEPARABLE.
SEPARATION IS IMMINENT.
SOMETHING TELLS ME THIS TIME IT'S GOING TO LAST.
NOT IF I CAN HELP IT!
SLAP! SLAP!
SO NOW HE'S BRINGING THE GIRLFRIEND TO POKER NIGHT?
SHE'S NOT MY GIRLFRIEND.

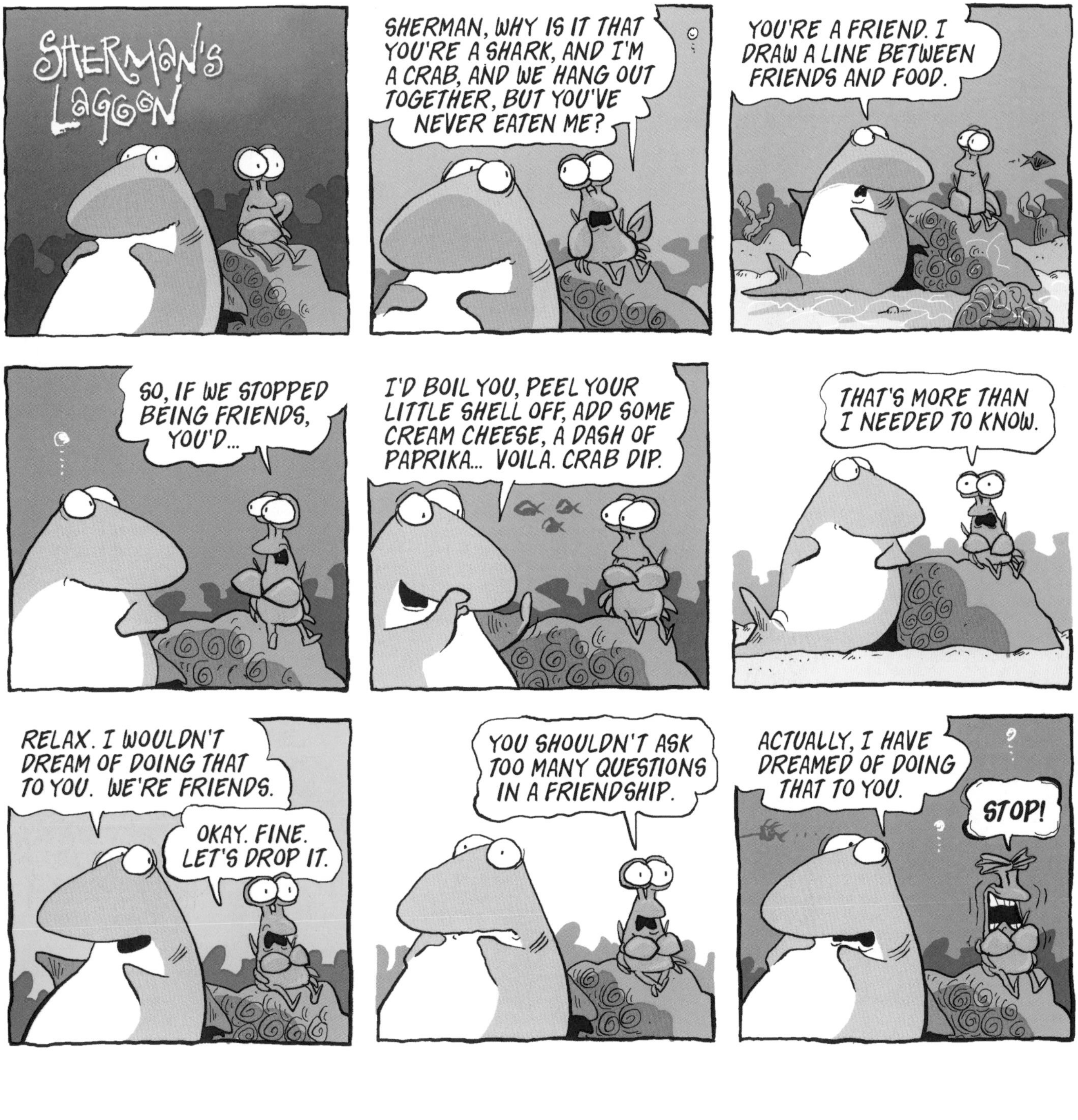
SHERMAN'S LAGOON
SHERMAN, WHY IS IT THAT YOU'RE A SHARK, AND I'M A CRAB, AND WE HANG OUT TOGETHER, BUT YOU'VE NEVER EATEN ME?
YOU'RE A FRIEND. I DRAW A LINE BETWEEN FRIENDS AND FOOD.
SO, IF WE STOPPED BEING FRIENDS, YOU'D...
I'D BOIL YOU, PEEL YOUR LITTLE SHELL OFF, ADD SOME CREAM CHEESE, A DASH OF PAPRIKA... VOILA. CRAB DIP.
THAT'S MORE THAN I NEEDED TO KNOW.
RELAX. I WOULDN'T DREAM OF DOING THAT TO YOU. WE'RE FRIENDS.
OKAY. FINE. LET'S DROP IT.
YOU SHOULDN'T ASK TOO MANY QUESTIONS IN A FRIENDSHIP.
ACTUALLY, I HAVE DREAMED OF DOING THAT TO YOU.
STOP!

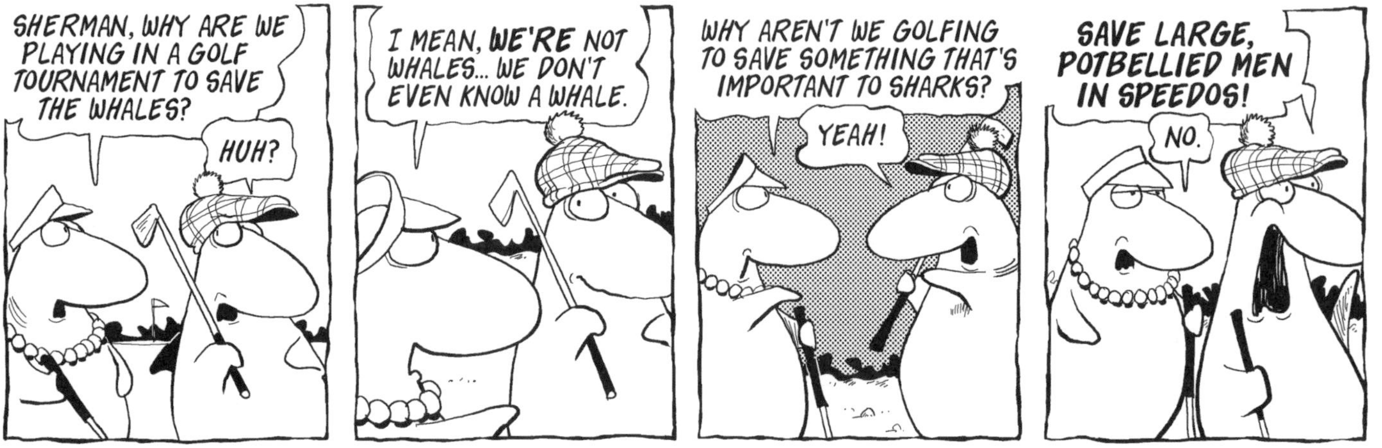
SHERMAN, WHY ARE WE PLAYING IN A GOLF TOURNAMENT TO SAVE THE WHALES?
HUH?
I MEAN, WE'RE NOT WHALES... WE DON'T EVEN KNOW A WHALE.
WHY AREN'T WE GOLFING TO SAVE SOMETHING THAT'S IMPORTANT TO SHARKS?
YEAH!
SAVE LARGE, POTBELLIED MEN IN SPEEDOS!
NO.

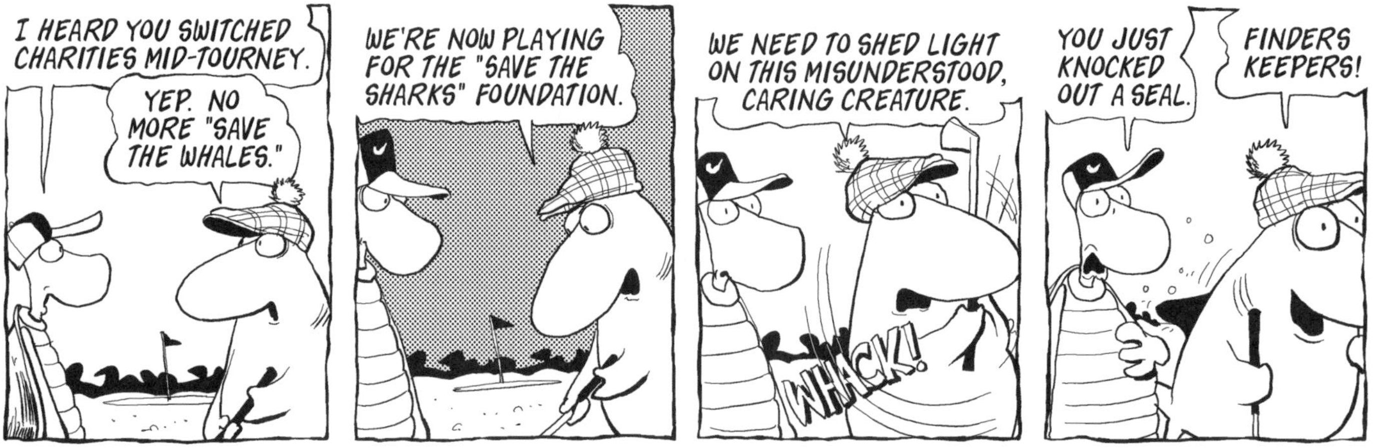
I HEARD YOU SWITCHED CHARITIES MID-TOURNEY.
YEP. NO MORE "SAVE THE WHALES."
WE'RE NOW PLAYING FOR THE "SAVE THE SHARKS" FOUNDATION.
WE NEED TO SHED LIGHT ON THIS MISUNDERSTOOD, CARING CREATURE.
WHACK!
YOU JUST KNOCKED OUT A SEAL.
FINDERS KEEPERS!

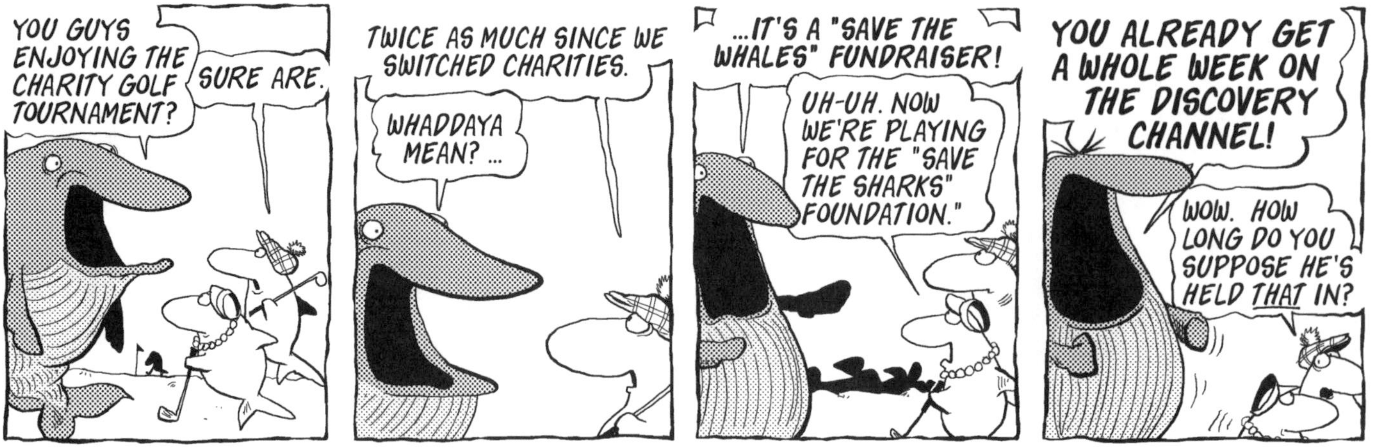
YOU GUYS ENJOYING THE CHARITY GOLF TOURNAMENT?
SURE ARE.
TWICE AS MUCH SINCE WE SWITCHED CHARITIES.
WHADDAYA MEAN? ...
...IT'S A "SAVE THE WHALES" FUNDRAISER!
UH-UH. NOW WE'RE PLAYING FOR THE "SAVE THE SHARKS" FOUNDATION."
YOU ALREADY GET A WHOLE WEEK ON THE DISCOVERY CHANNEL!
WOW. HOW LONG DO YOU SUPPOSE HE'S HELD THAT IN?

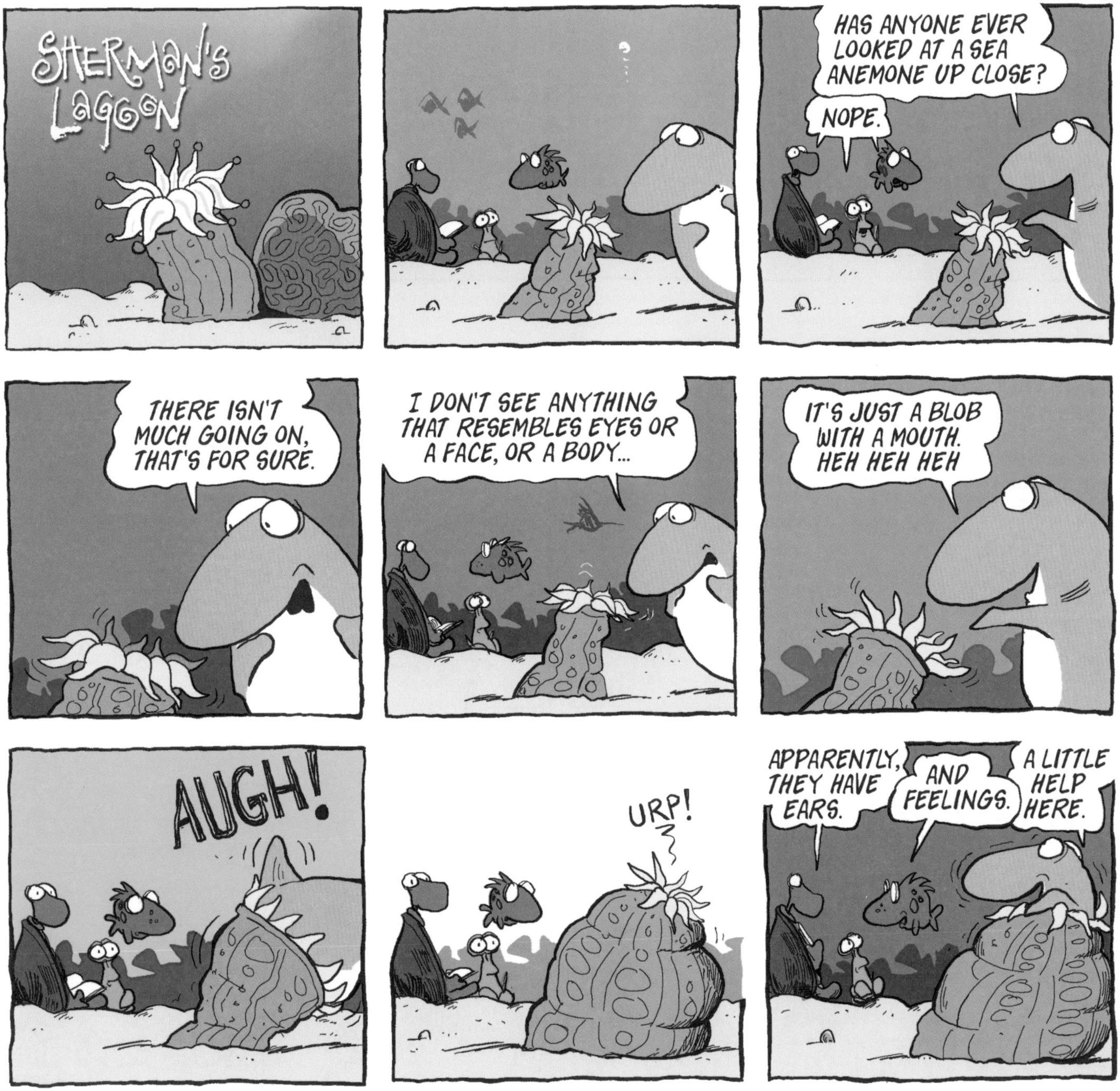
SHERMAN'S LAGOON
HAS ANYONE EVER LOOKED AT A SEA ANEMONE UP CLOSE?
NOPE.
THERE ISN'T MUCH GOING ON, THAT'S FOR SURE.
I DON'T SEE ANYTHING THAT RESEMBLES EYES OR A FACE, OR A BODY...
IT'S JUST A BLOB WITH A MOUTH. HEH HEH HEH
AUGH!
URP!
APPARENTLY, THEY HAVE EARS.
AND FEELINGS.
A LITTLE HELP HERE.

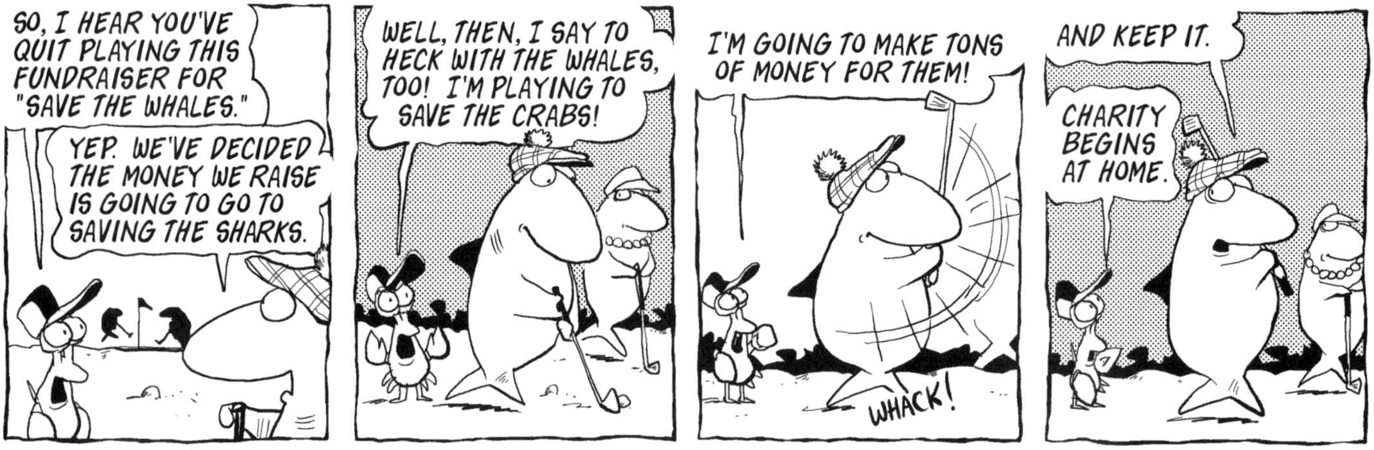
SO, I HEAR YOU'VE QUIT PLAYING THIS FUNDRAISER FOR "SAVE THE WHALES."
YEP. WE'VE DECIDED THE MONEY WE RAISE IS GOING TO GO TO SAVING THE SHARKS.
WELL, THEN, I SAY TO HECK WITH THE WHALES, TOO! I'M PLAYING TO SAVE THE CRABS!
I'M GOING TO MAKE TONS OF MONEY FOR THEM!
WHACK!
AND KEEP IT.
CHARITY BEGINS AT HOME.

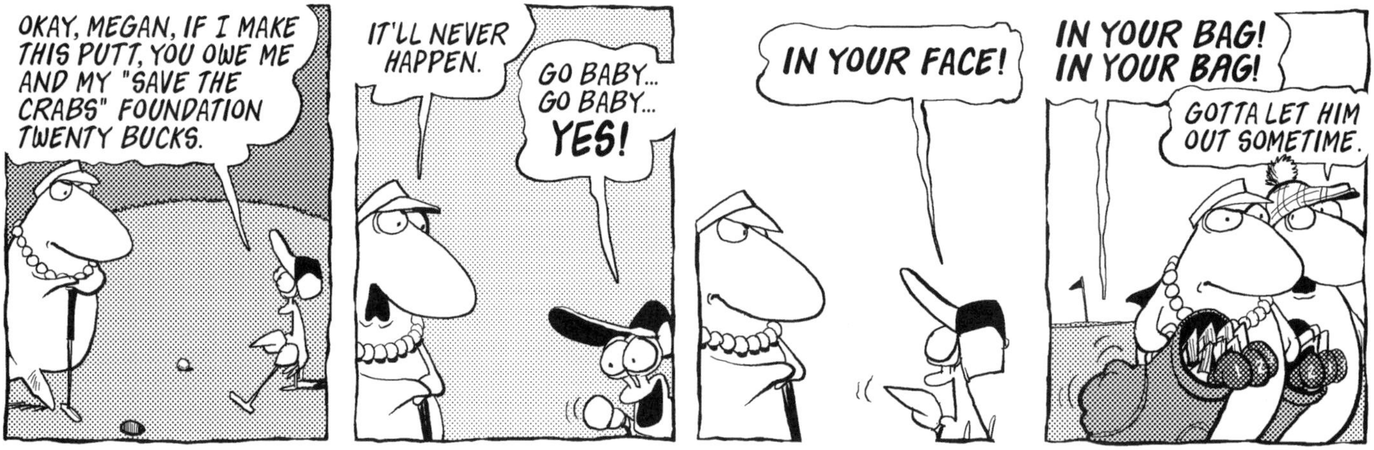
OKAY, MEGAN, IF I MAKE THIS PUTT, YOU OWE ME AND MY "SAVE THE CRABS" FOUNDATION TWENTY BUCKS.
IT'LL NEVER HAPPEN.
GO BABY... GO BABY... YES!
IN YOUR FACE!
IN YOUR BAG! IN YOUR BAG!
GOTTA LET HIM OUT SOMETIME.

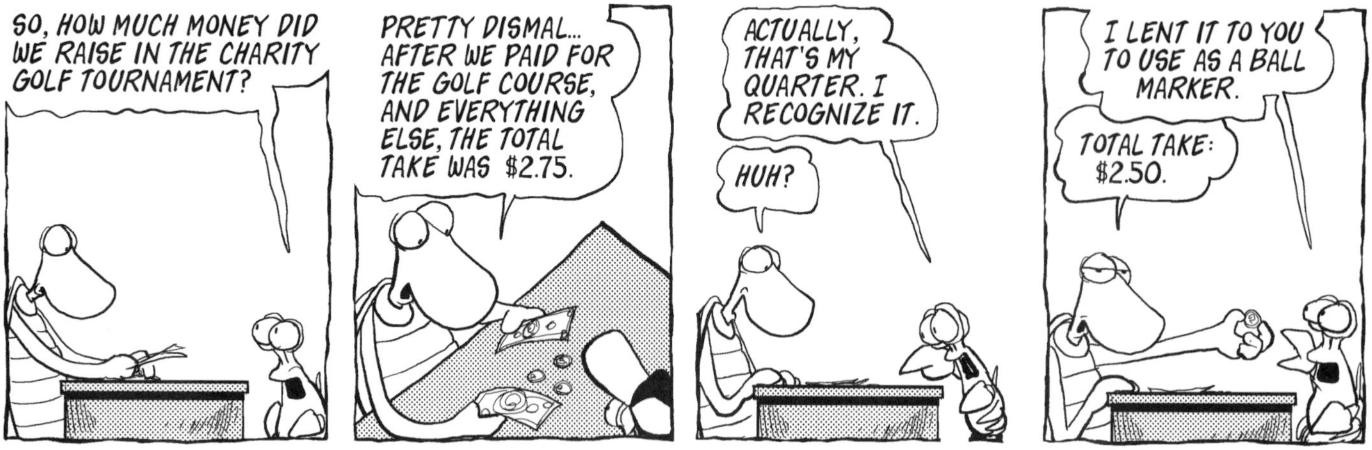
SO, HOW MUCH MONEY DID WE RAISE IN THE CHARITY GOLF TOURNAMENT?
PRETTY DISMAL... AFTER WE PAID FOR THE GOLF COURSE, AND EVERYTHING ELSE, THE TOTAL TAKE WAS $2.75.
ACTUALLY, THAT'S MY QUARTER. I RECOGNIZE IT.
HUH?
I LENT IT TO YOU TO USE AS A BALL MARKER.
TOTAL TAKE: $2.50.

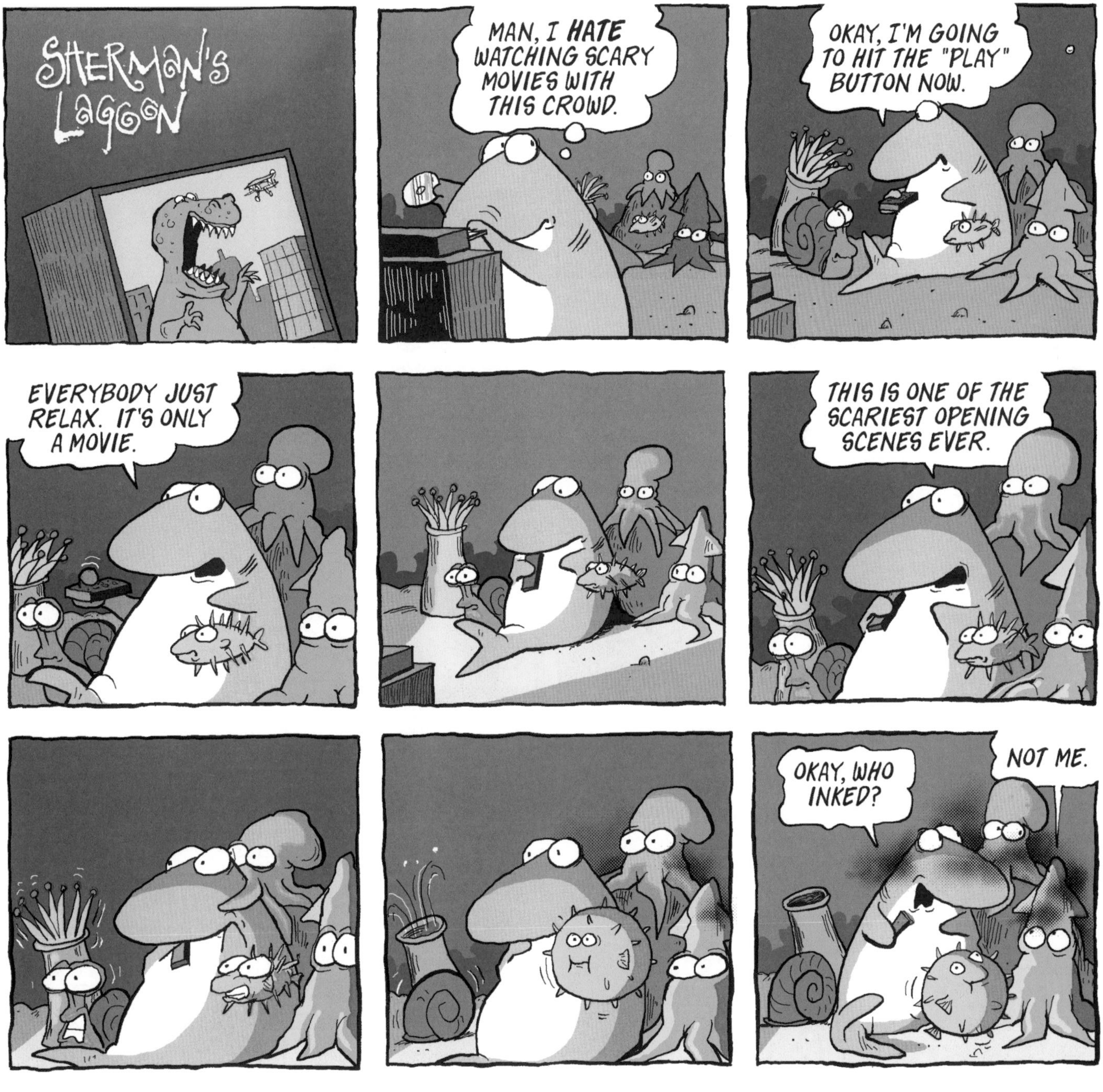
SHERMAN'S LAGOON
MAN, I HATE WATCHING SCARY MOVIES WITH THIS CROWD.
OKAY, I'M GOING TO HIT THE "PLAY" BUTTON NOW.
EVERYBODY JUST RELAX. IT'S ONLY A MOVIE.
THIS IS ONE OF THE SCARIEST OPENING SCENES EVER.
OKAY, WHO INKED?
NOT ME.

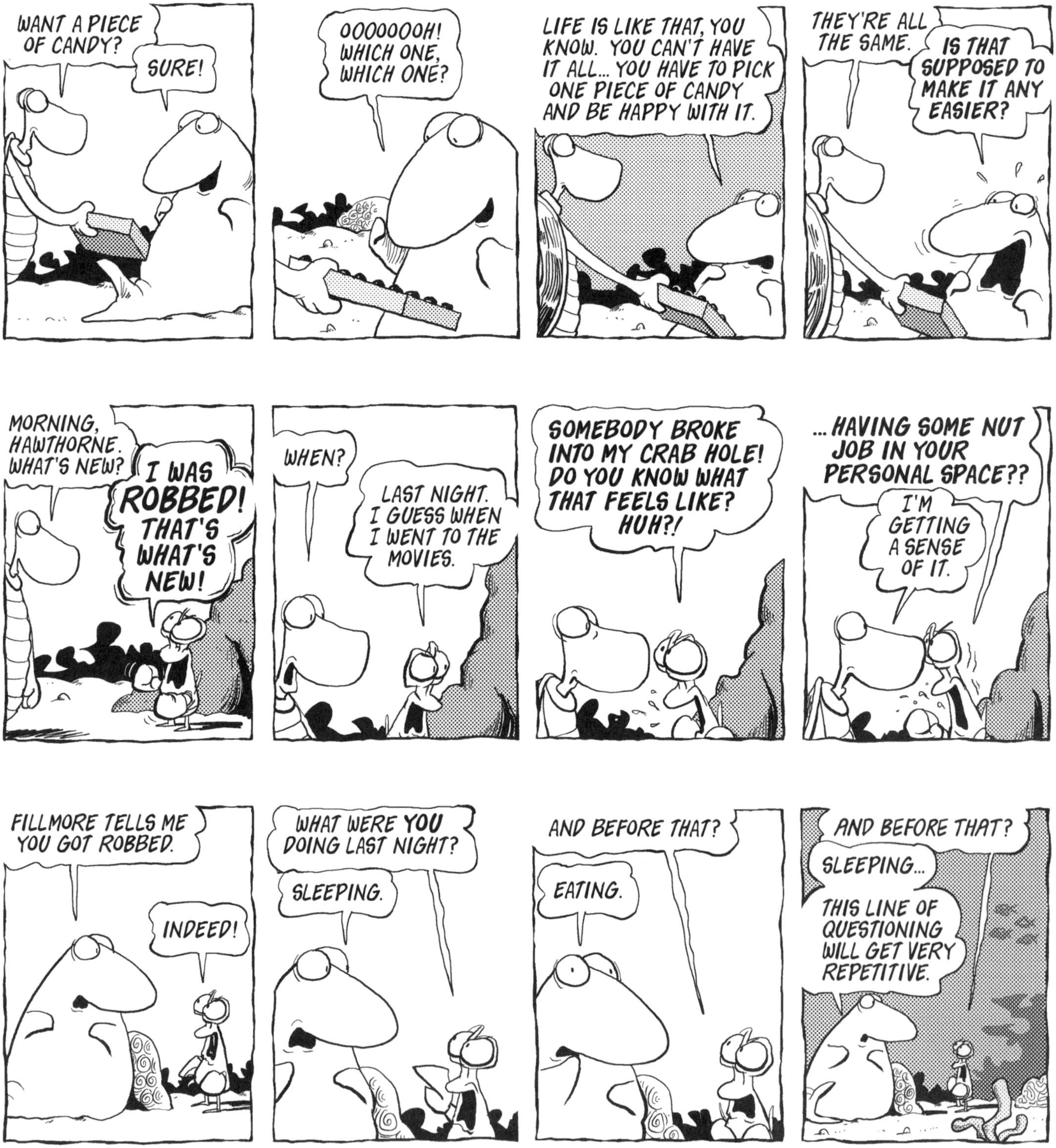
WANT A PIECE OF CANDY?
SURE!
OOOOOOOH! WHICH ONE, WHICH ONE?
LIFE IS LIKE THAT, YOU KNOW. YOU CAN'T HAVE IT ALL... YOU HAVE TO PICK ONE PIECE OF CANDY AND BE HAPPY WITH IT.
THEY'RE ALL THE SAME.
IS THAT SUPPOSED TO MAKE IT ANY EASIER?
MORNING, HAWTHORNE. WHAT'S NEW?
I WAS ROBBED! THAT'S WHAT'S NEW!
WHEN?
LAST NIGHT. I GUESS WHEN I WENT TO THE MOVIES.
SOMEBODY BROKE INTO MY CRAB HOLE! DO YOU KNOW WHAT THAT FEELS LIKE? HUH?!
...HAVING SOME NUT JOB IN YOUR PERSONAL SPACE??
I'M GETTING A SENSE OF IT.
FILLMORE TELLS ME YOU GOT ROBBED.
INDEED!
WHAT WERE YOU DOING LAST NIGHT?
SLEEPING.
AND BEFORE THAT?
EATING.
AND BEFORE THAT?
SLEEPING...
THIS LINE OF QUESTIONING WILL GET VERY REPETITIVE.

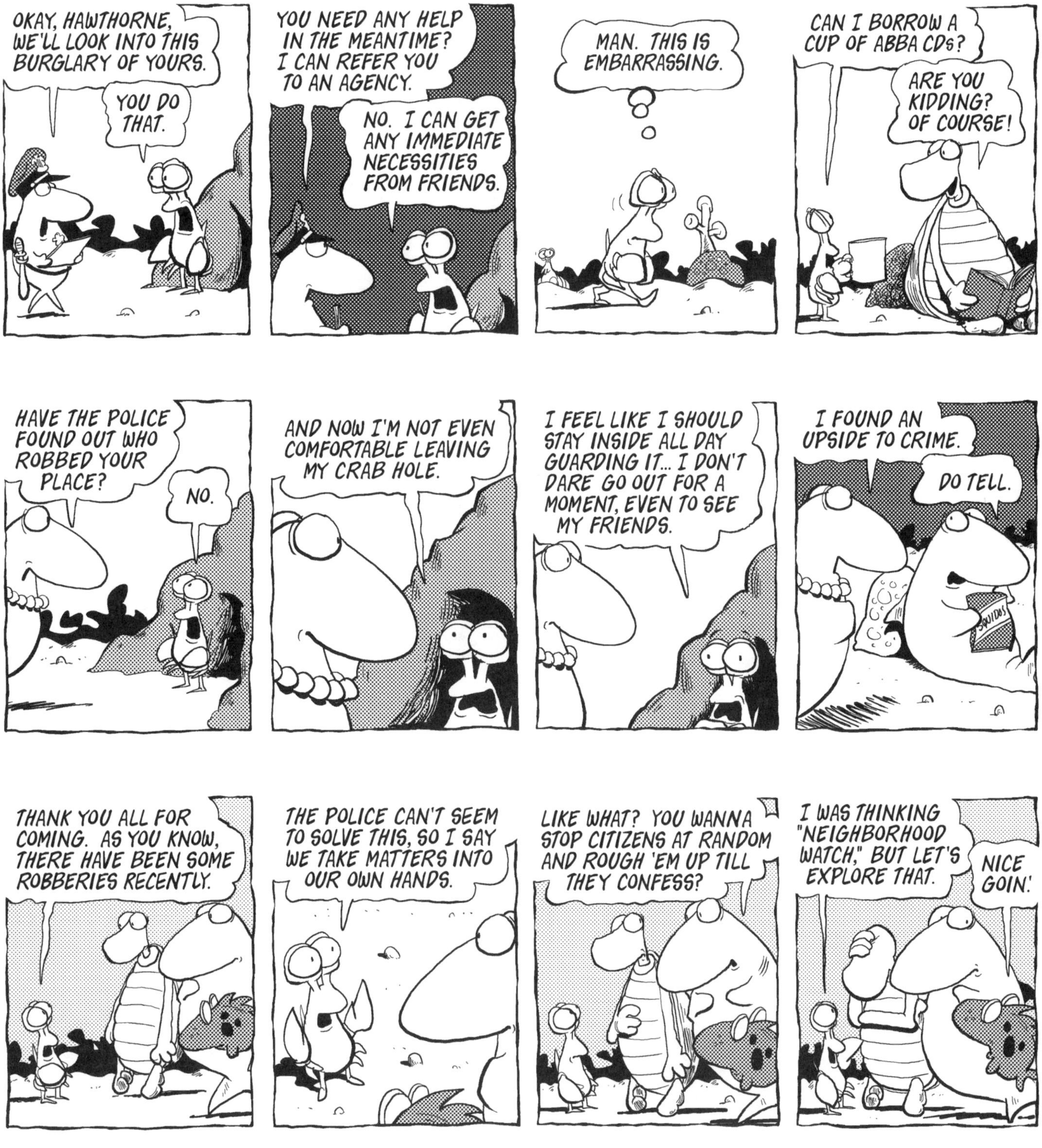
OKAY, HAWTHORNE, WE'LL LOOK INTO THIS BURGLARY OF YOURS.
YOU DO THAT.
YOU NEED ANY HELP IN THE MEANTIME? I CAN REFER YOU TO AN AGENCY.
NO. I CAN GET ANY IMMEDIATE NECESSITIES FROM FRIENDS.
MAN. THIS IS EMBARRASSING.
CAN I BORROW A CUP OF ABBA CDs?
ARE YOU KIDDING? OF COURSE!
HAVE THE POLICE FOUND OUT WHO ROBBED YOUR PLACE?
NO.
AND NOW I'M NOT EVEN COMFORTABLE LEAVING MY CRAB HOLE.
I FEEL LIKE I SHOULD STAY INSIDE ALL DAY GUARDING IT... I DON'T DARE GO OUT FOR A MOMENT, EVEN TO SEE MY FRIENDS.
I FOUND AN UPSIDE TO CRIME.
DO TELL.
SQUIDOS
THANK YOU ALL FOR COMING. AS YOU KNOW, THERE HAVE BEEN SOME ROBBERIES RECENTLY.
THE POLICE CAN'T SEEM TO SOLVE THIS, SO I SAY WE TAKE MATTERS INTO OUR OWN HANDS.
LIKE WHAT? YOU WANNA STOP CITIZENS AT RANDOM AND ROUGH 'EM UP TILL THEY CONFESS?
I WAS THINKING "NEIGHBORHOOD WATCH," BUT LET'S EXPLORE THAT.
NICE GOIN'.

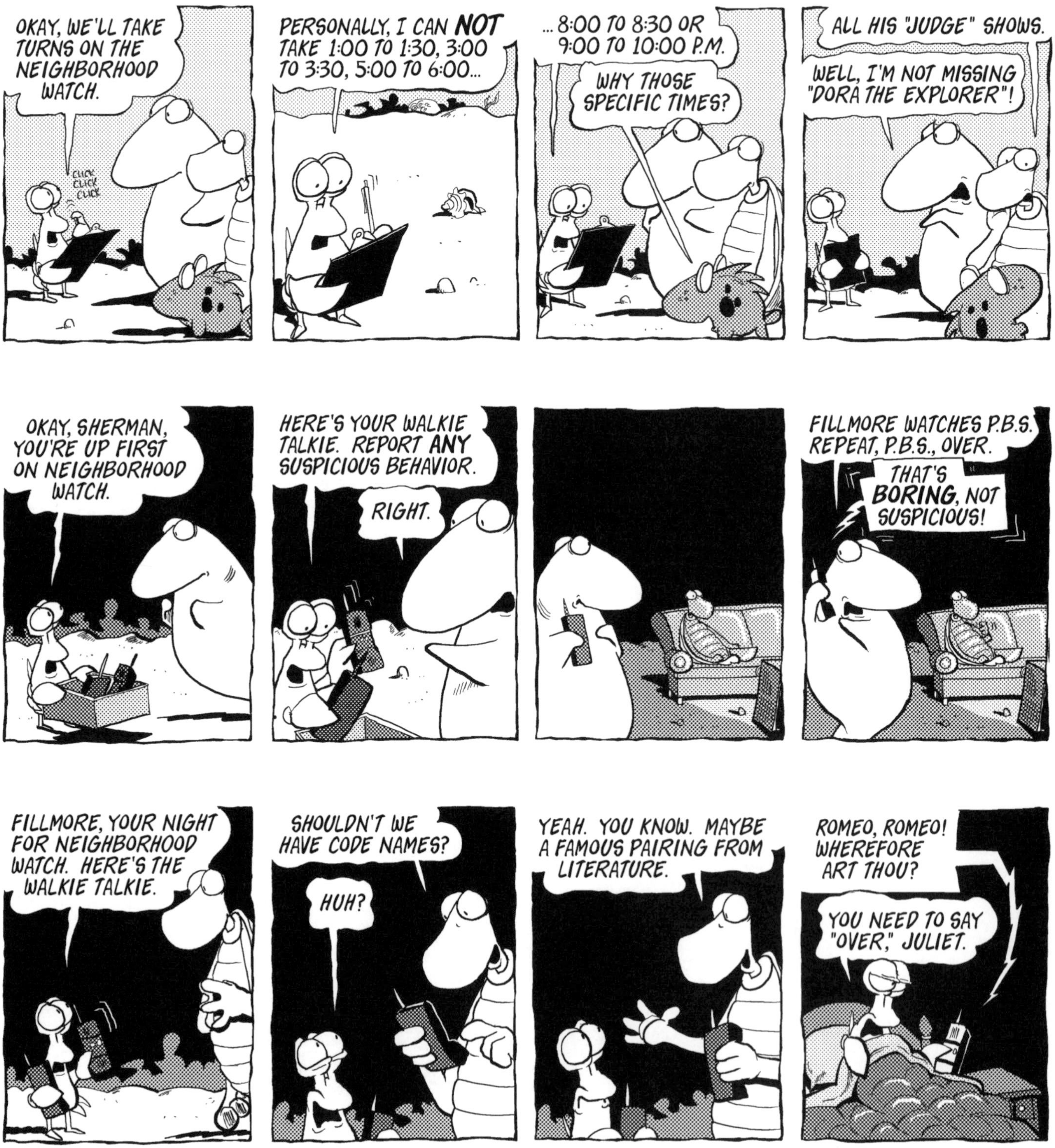
OKAY, WE'LL TAKE TURNS ON THE NEIGHBORHOOD WATCH.
CLICK CLICK CLICK
PERSONALLY, I CAN **NOT** TAKE 1:00 TO 1:30, 3:00 TO 3:30, 5:00 TO 6:00...
...8:00 TO 8:30 OR 9:00 TO 10:00 P.M.
WHY THOSE SPECIFIC TIMES?
ALL HIS "JUDGE" SHOWS.
WELL, I'M NOT MISSING "DORA THE EXPLORER"!
OKAY, SHERMAN, YOU'RE UP FIRST ON NEIGHBORHOOD WATCH.
HERE'S YOUR WALKIE TALKIE. REPORT **ANY** SUSPICIOUS BEHAVIOR.
RIGHT.
FILLMORE WATCHES P.B.S. REPEAT, P.B.S., OVER.
THAT'S **BORING**, NOT SUSPICIOUS!
FILLMORE, YOUR NIGHT FOR NEIGHBORHOOD WATCH. HERE'S THE WALKIE TALKIE.
SHOULDN'T WE HAVE CODE NAMES?
HUH?
YEAH. YOU KNOW. MAYBE A FAMOUS PAIRING FROM LITERATURE.
ROMEO, ROMEO! WHEREFORE ART THOU?
YOU NEED TO SAY "OVER," JULIET.

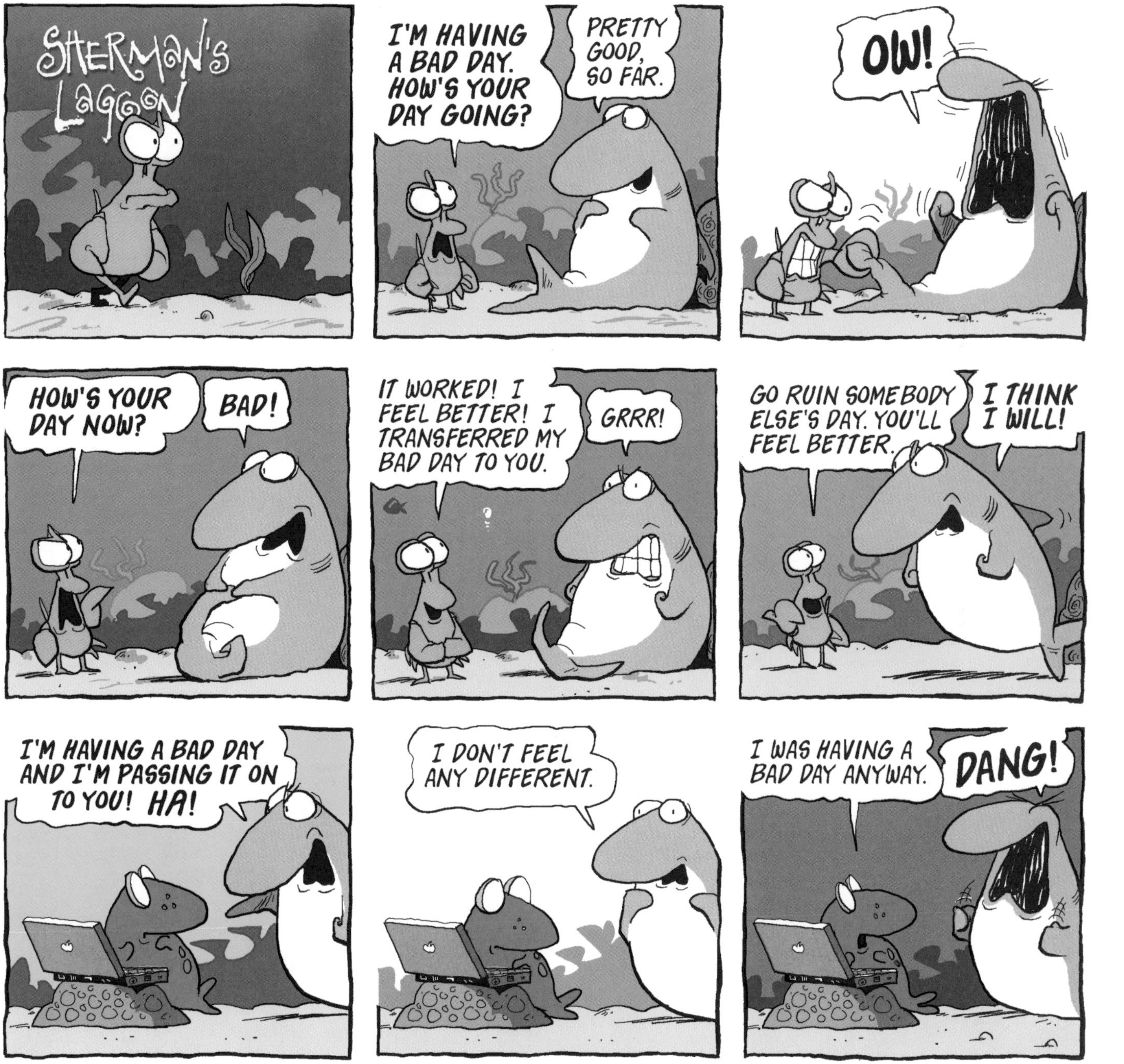
SHERMAN'S LAGOON
I'M HAVING A BAD DAY. HOW'S YOUR DAY GOING?
PRETTY GOOD, SO FAR.
OW!
HOW'S YOUR DAY NOW?
BAD!
IT WORKED! I FEEL BETTER! I TRANSFERRED MY BAD DAY TO YOU.
GRRR!
GO RUIN SOMEBODY ELSE'S DAY. YOU'LL FEEL BETTER.
I THINK I WILL!
I'M HAVING A BAD DAY AND I'M PASSING IT ON TO YOU! HA!
I DON'T FEEL ANY DIFFERENT.
I WAS HAVING A BAD DAY ANYWAY.
DANG!

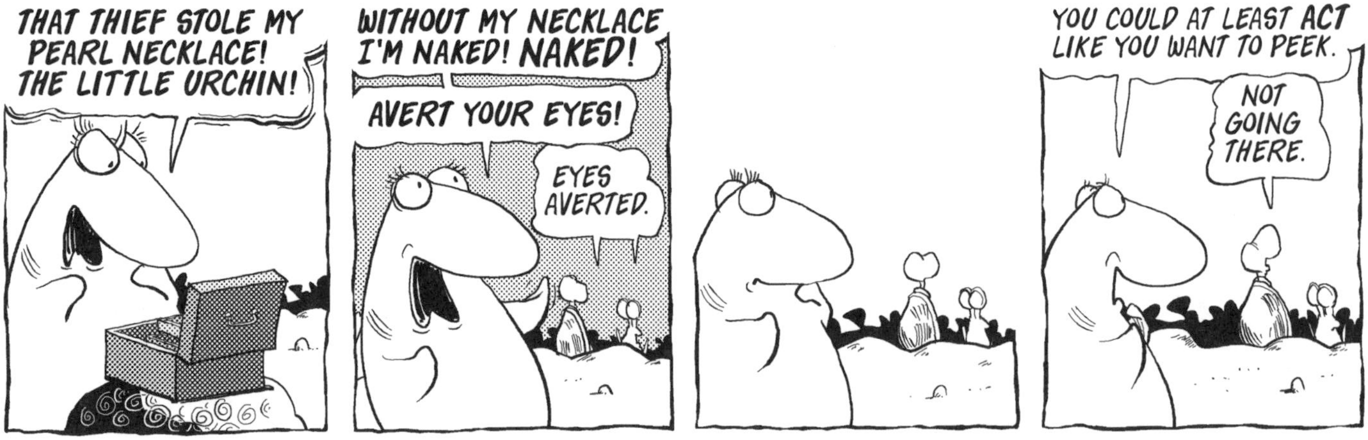
THAT THIEF STOLE MY PEARL NECKLACE! THE LITTLE URCHIN!
WITHOUT MY NECKLACE I'M NAKED! NAKED!
AVERT YOUR EYES!
EYES AVERTED.
YOU COULD AT LEAST ACT LIKE YOU WANT TO PEEK.
NOT GOING THERE.

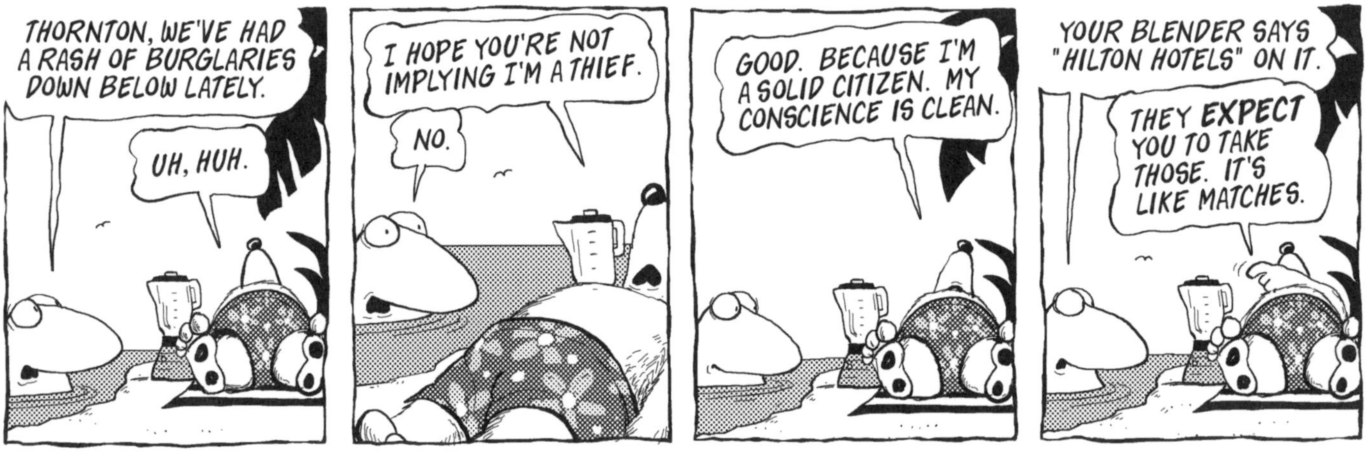
THORNTON, WE'VE HAD A RASH OF BURGLARIES DOWN BELOW LATELY.
UH, HUH.
I HOPE YOU'RE NOT IMPLYING I'M A THIEF.
NO.
GOOD. BECAUSE I'M A SOLID CITIZEN. MY CONSCIENCE IS CLEAN.
YOUR BLENDER SAYS "HILTON HOTELS" ON IT.
THEY EXPECT YOU TO TAKE THOSE. IT'S LIKE MATCHES.

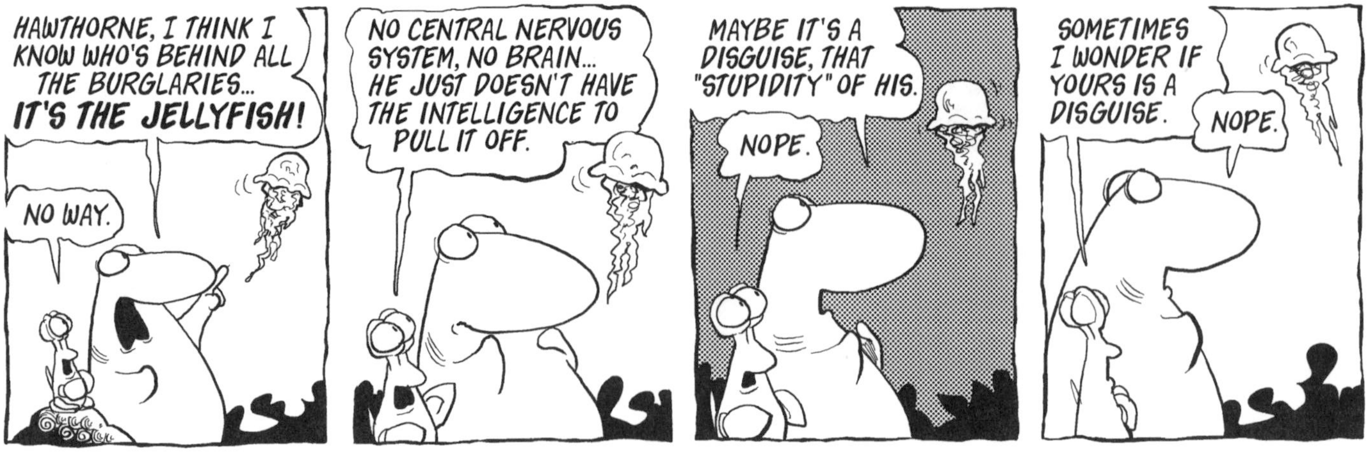
HAWTHORNE, I THINK I KNOW WHO'S BEHIND ALL THE BURGLARIES... IT'S THE JELLYFISH!
NO WAY.
NO CENTRAL NERVOUS SYSTEM, NO BRAIN... HE JUST DOESN'T HAVE THE INTELLIGENCE TO PULL IT OFF.
MAYBE IT'S A DISGUISE, THAT "STUPIDITY" OF HIS.
NOPE.
SOMETIMES I WONDER IF YOURS IS A DISGUISE.
NOPE.

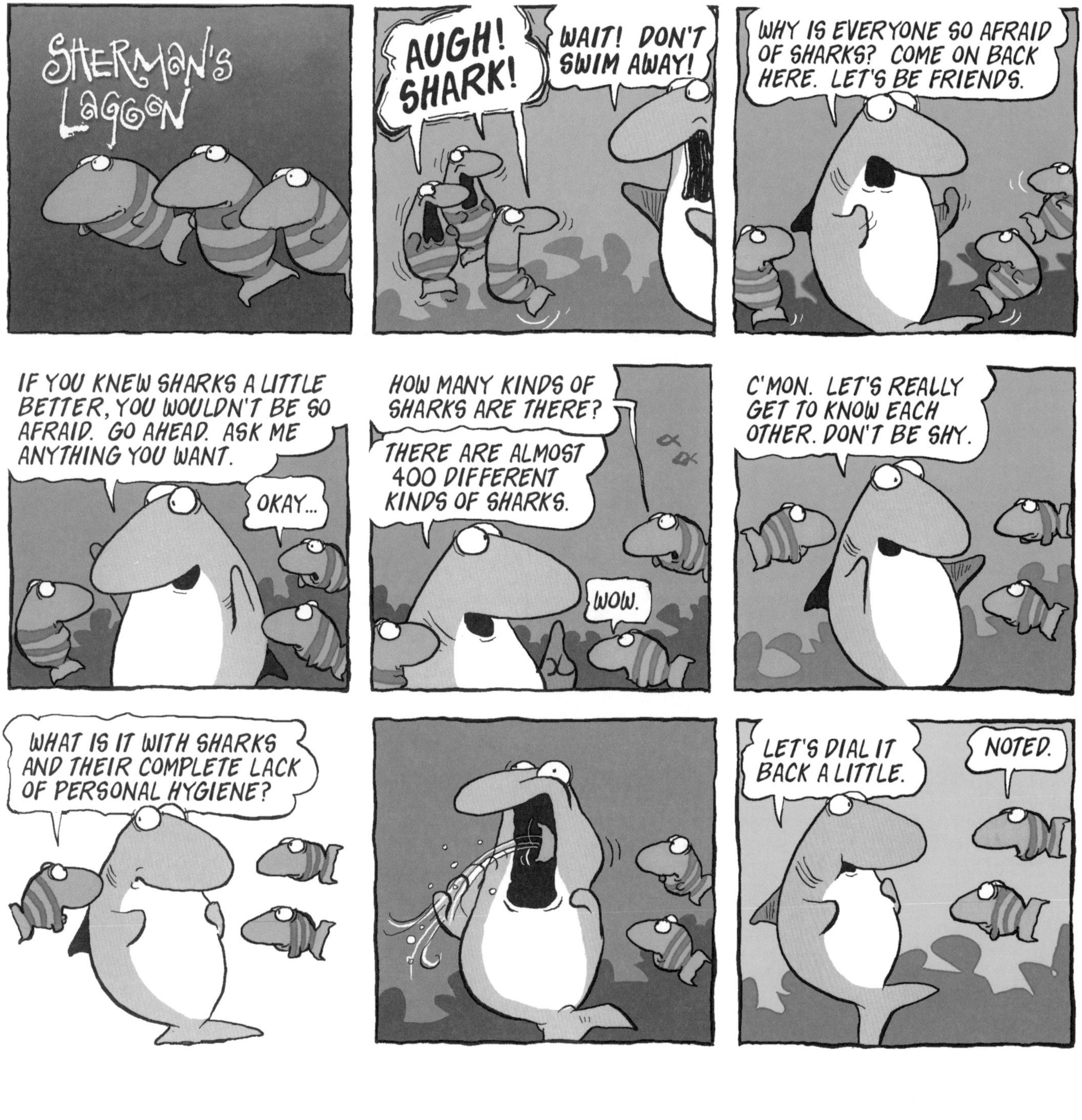
SHERMAN'S LAGOON
AUGH! SHARK!
WAIT! DON'T SWIM AWAY!
WHY IS EVERYONE SO AFRAID OF SHARKS? COME ON BACK HERE. LET'S BE FRIENDS.
IF YOU KNEW SHARKS A LITTLE BETTER, YOU WOULDN'T BE SO AFRAID. GO AHEAD. ASK ME ANYTHING YOU WANT.
OKAY...
HOW MANY KINDS OF SHARKS ARE THERE?
THERE ARE ALMOST 400 DIFFERENT KINDS OF SHARKS.
WOW.
C'MON. LET'S REALLY GET TO KNOW EACH OTHER. DON'T BE SHY.
WHAT IS IT WITH SHARKS AND THEIR COMPLETE LACK OF PERSONAL HYGIENE?
LET'S DIAL IT BACK A LITTLE.
NOTED.

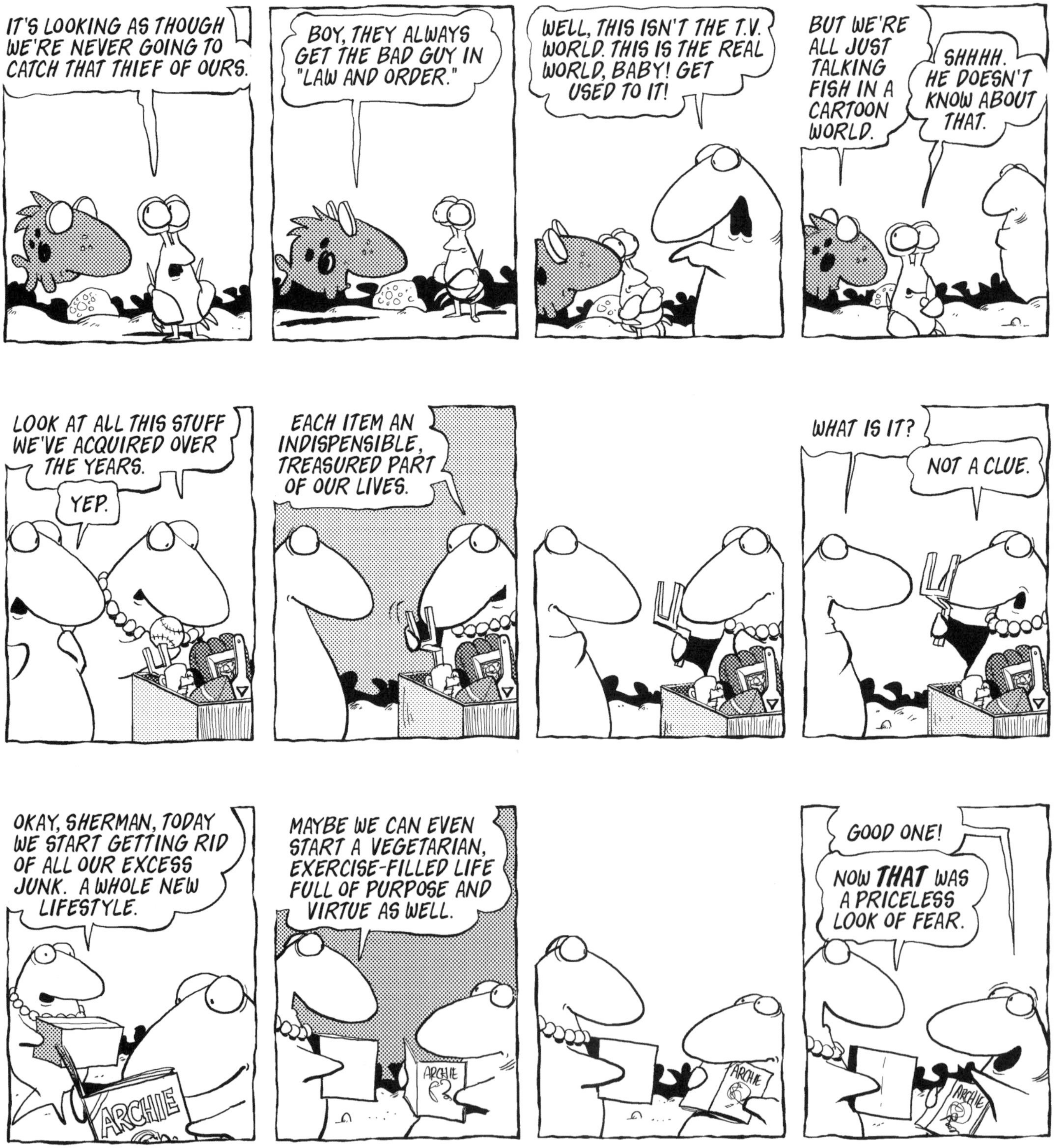
IT'S LOOKING AS THOUGH WE'RE NEVER GOING TO CATCH THAT THIEF OF OURS.
BOY, THEY ALWAYS GET THE BAD GUY IN "LAW AND ORDER."
WELL, THIS ISN'T THE T.V. WORLD. THIS IS THE REAL WORLD, BABY! GET USED TO IT!
BUT WE'RE ALL JUST TALKING FISH IN A CARTOON WORLD.
SHHHH. HE DOESN'T KNOW ABOUT THAT.
LOOK AT ALL THIS STUFF WE'VE ACQUIRED OVER THE YEARS.
YEP.
EACH ITEM AN INDISPENSIBLE, TREASURED PART OF OUR LIVES.
WHAT IS IT?
NOT A CLUE.
OKAY, SHERMAN, TODAY WE START GETTING RID OF ALL OUR EXCESS JUNK. A WHOLE NEW LIFESTYLE.
ARCHIE
MAYBE WE CAN EVEN START A VEGETARIAN, EXERCISE-FILLED LIFE FULL OF PURPOSE AND VIRTUE AS WELL.
ARCHIE
ARCHIE
GOOD ONE!
NOW THAT WAS A PRICELESS LOOK OF FEAR.
ARCHIE

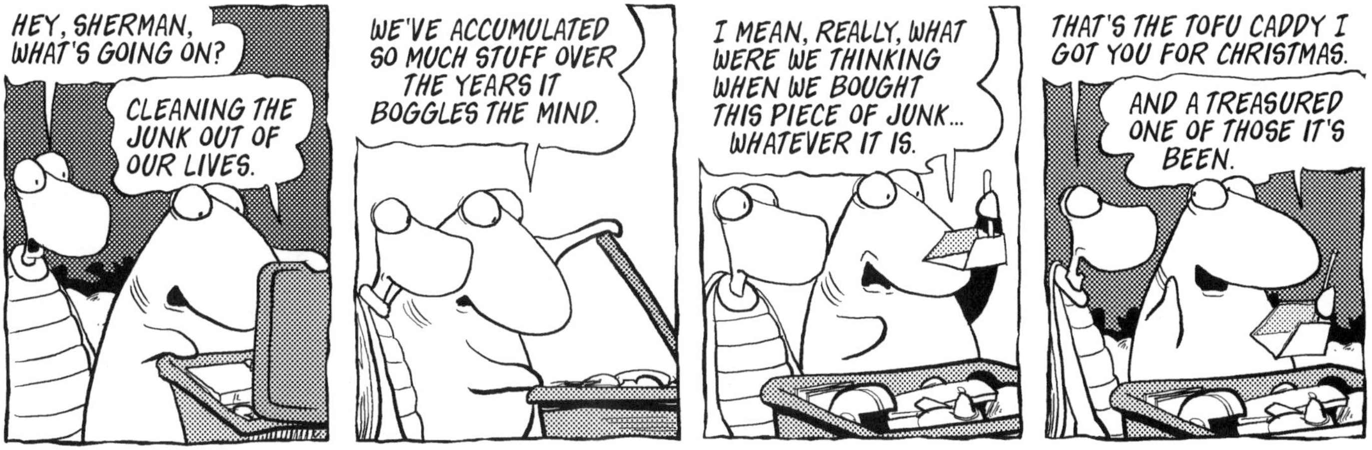
HEY, SHERMAN, WHAT'S GOING ON?
CLEANING THE JUNK OUT OF OUR LIVES.
WE'VE ACCUMULATED SO MUCH STUFF OVER THE YEARS IT BOGGLES THE MIND.
I MEAN, REALLY, WHAT WERE WE THINKING WHEN WE BOUGHT THIS PIECE OF JUNK... WHATEVER IT IS.
THAT'S THE TOFU CADDY I GOT YOU FOR CHRISTMAS.
AND A TREASURED ONE OF THOSE IT'S BEEN.

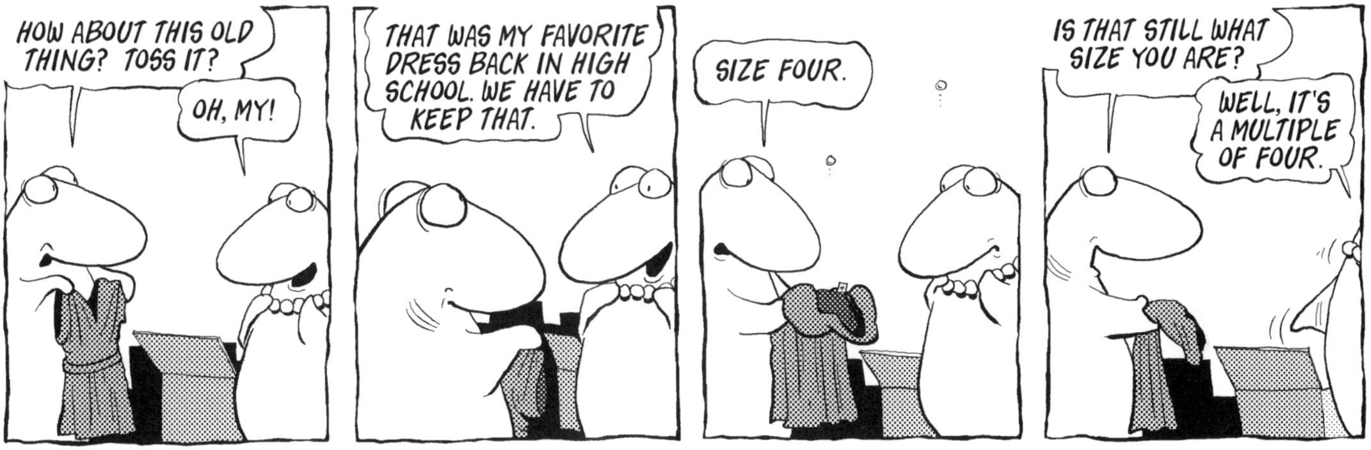
HOW ABOUT THIS OLD THING? TOSS IT?
OH, MY!
THAT WAS MY FAVORITE DRESS BACK IN HIGH SCHOOL. WE HAVE TO KEEP THAT.
SIZE FOUR.
IS THAT STILL WHAT SIZE YOU ARE?
WELL, IT'S A MULTIPLE OF FOUR.

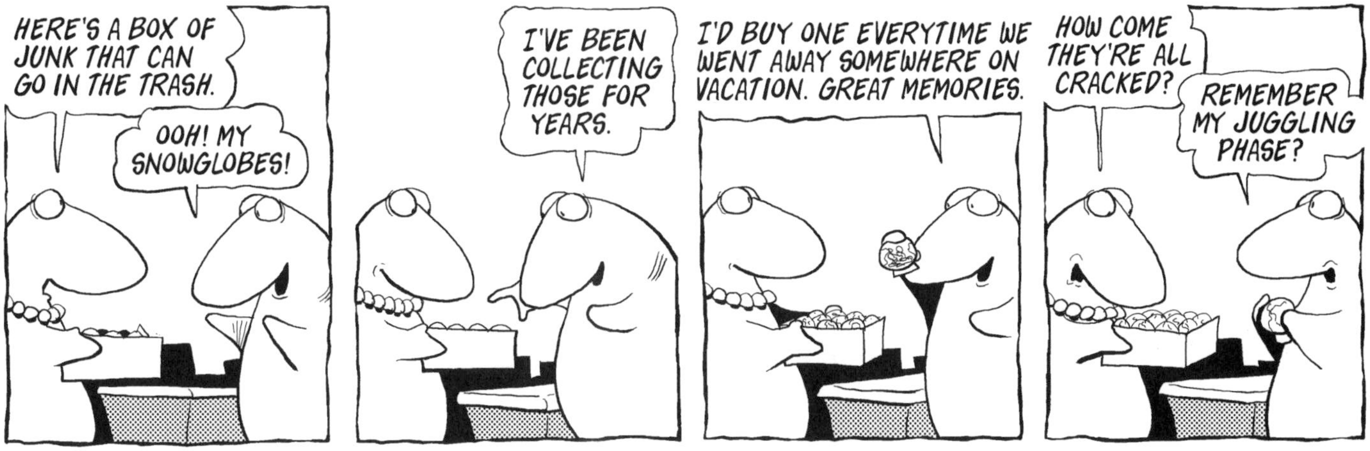
HERE'S A BOX OF JUNK THAT CAN GO IN THE TRASH.
OOH! MY SNOWGLOBES!
I'VE BEEN COLLECTING THOSE FOR YEARS.
I'D BUY ONE EVERYTIME WE WENT AWAY SOMEWHERE ON VACATION. GREAT MEMORIES.
HOW COME THEY'RE ALL CRACKED?
REMEMBER MY JUGGLING PHASE?

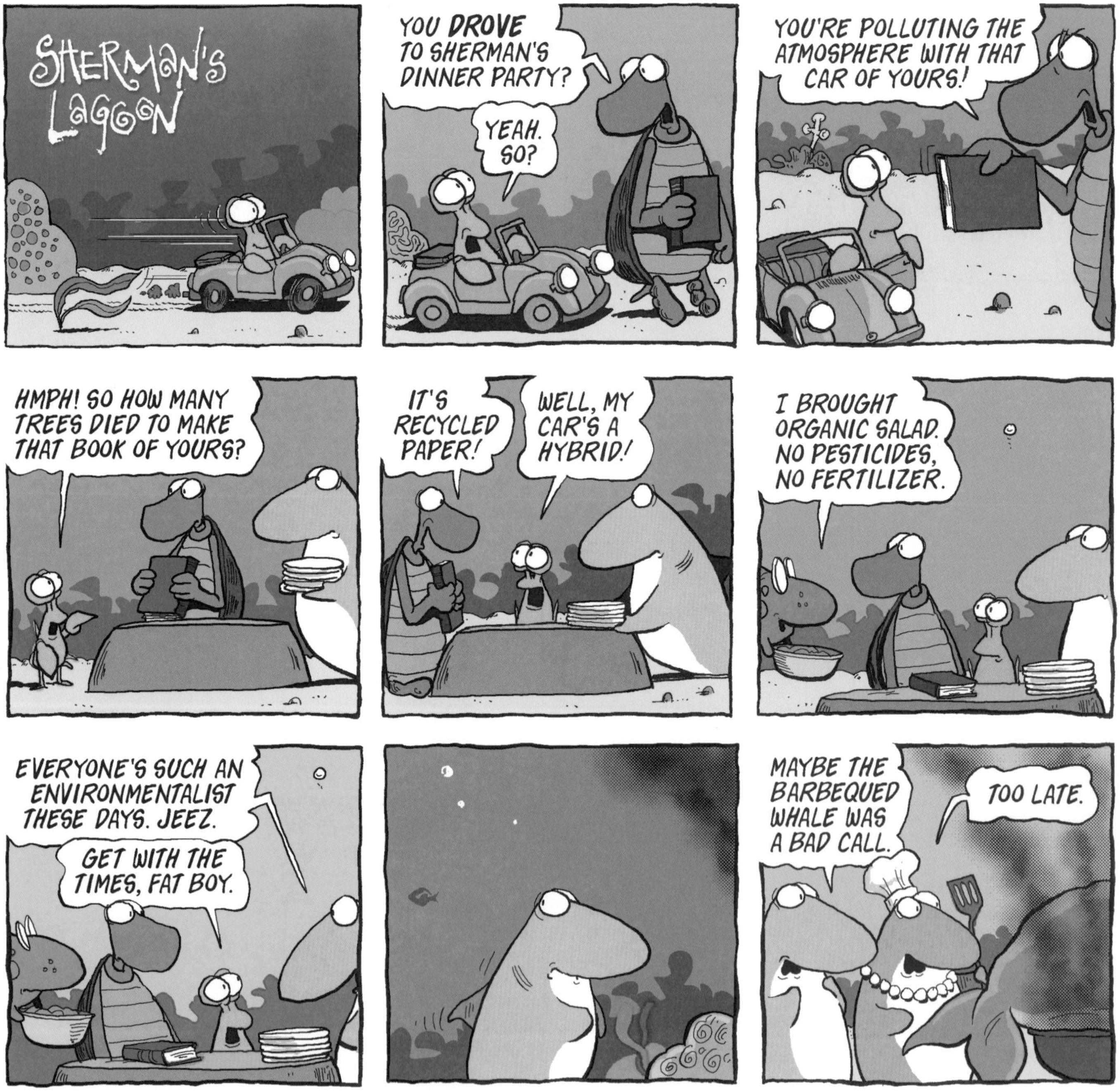
SHERMAN'S LAGOON
YOU DROVE TO SHERMAN'S DINNER PARTY?
YEAH. SO?
YOU'RE POLLUTING THE ATMOSPHERE WITH THAT CAR OF YOURS!
HMPH! SO HOW MANY TREES DIED TO MAKE THAT BOOK OF YOURS?
IT'S RECYCLED PAPER!
WELL, MY CAR'S A HYBRID!
I BROUGHT ORGANIC SALAD. NO PESTICIDES, NO FERTILIZER.
EVERYONE'S SUCH AN ENVIRONMENTALIST THESE DAYS. JEEZ.
GET WITH THE TIMES, FAT BOY.
MAYBE THE BARBEQUED WHALE WAS A BAD CALL.
TOO LATE.

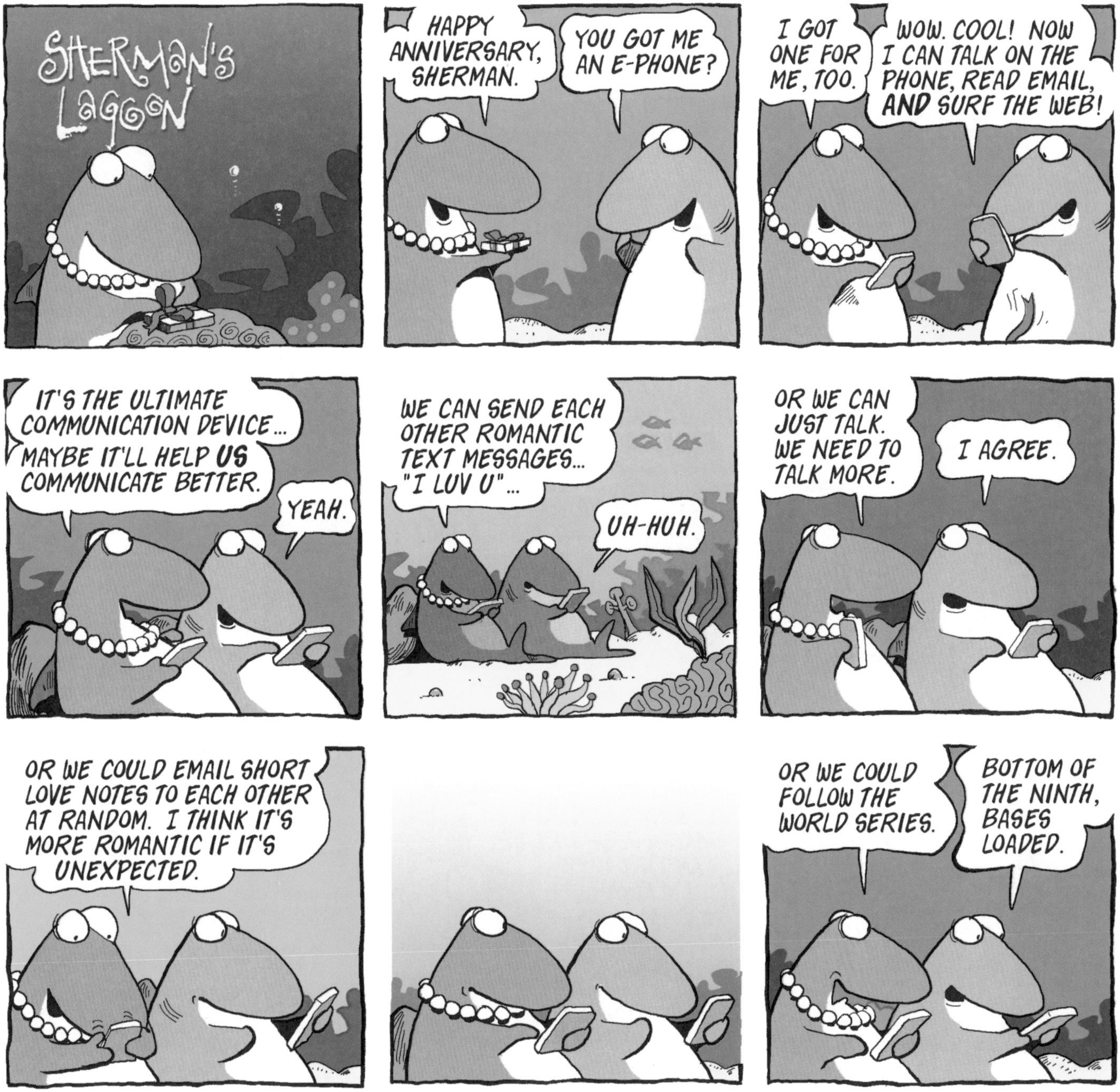
SHERMAN'S LAGOON
HAPPY ANNIVERSARY, SHERMAN.
YOU GOT ME AN E-PHONE?
I GOT ONE FOR ME, TOO.
WOW. COOL! NOW I CAN TALK ON THE PHONE, READ EMAIL, AND SURF THE WEB!
IT'S THE ULTIMATE COMMUNICATION DEVICE... MAYBE IT'LL HELP US COMMUNICATE BETTER.
YEAH.
WE CAN SEND EACH OTHER ROMANTIC TEXT MESSAGES... "I LUV U"...
UH-HUH.
OR WE CAN JUST TALK. WE NEED TO TALK MORE.
I AGREE.
OR WE COULD EMAIL SHORT LOVE NOTES TO EACH OTHER AT RANDOM. I THINK IT'S MORE ROMANTIC IF IT'S UNEXPECTED.
OR WE COULD FOLLOW THE WORLD SERIES.
BOTTOM OF THE NINTH, BASES LOADED.

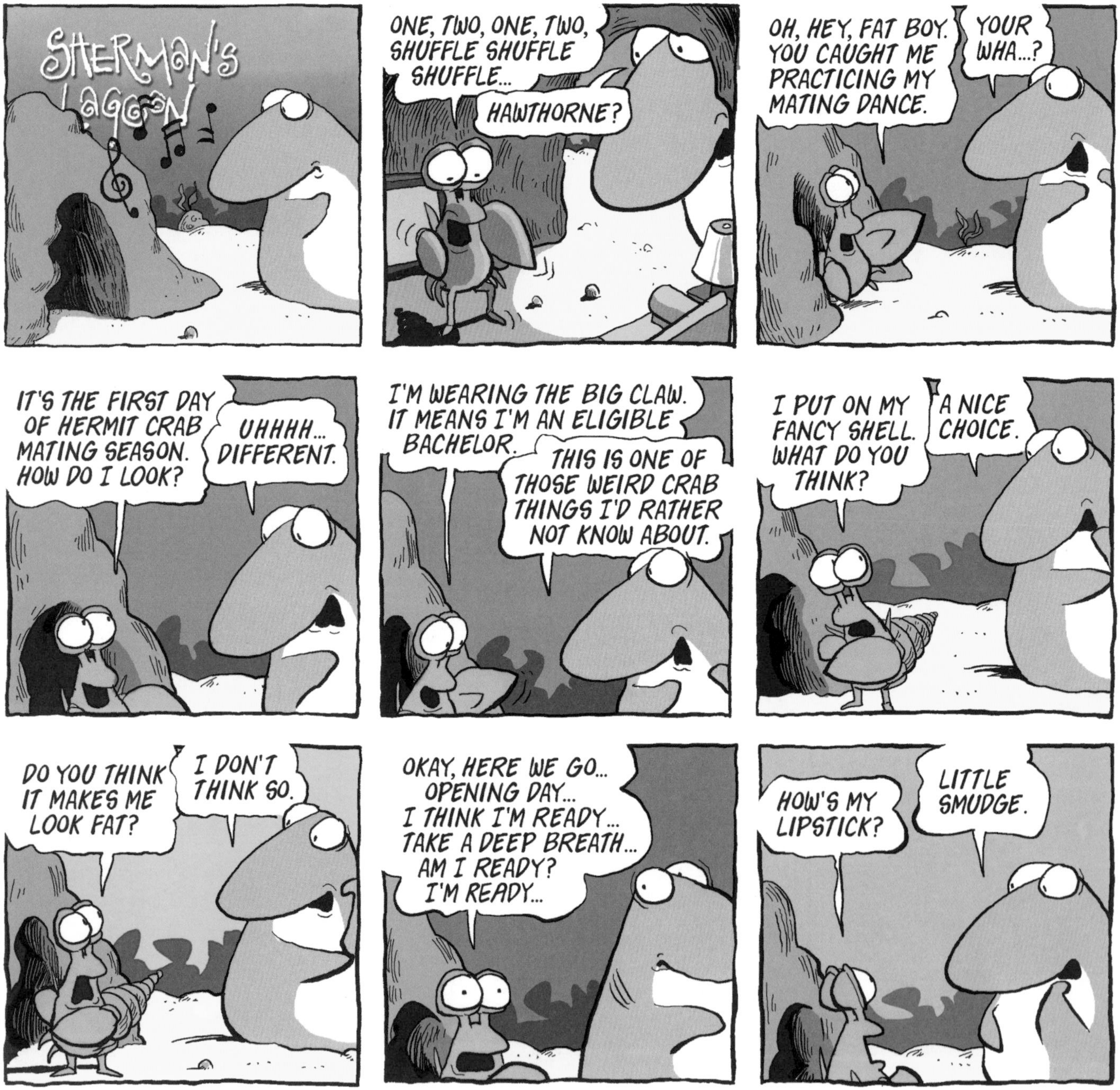
SHERMAN'S LAGOON
ONE, TWO, ONE, TWO, SHUFFLE SHUFFLE SHUFFLE...
HAWTHORNE?
OH, HEY, FAT BOY. YOU CAUGHT ME PRACTICING MY MATING DANCE.
YOUR WHA...?
IT'S THE FIRST DAY OF HERMIT CRAB MATING SEASON. HOW DO I LOOK?
UHHHH... DIFFERENT.
I'M WEARING THE BIG CLAW. IT MEANS I'M AN ELIGIBLE BACHELOR.
THIS IS ONE OF THOSE WEIRD CRAB THINGS I'D RATHER NOT KNOW ABOUT.
I PUT ON MY FANCY SHELL. WHAT DO YOU THINK?
A NICE CHOICE.
DO YOU THINK IT MAKES ME LOOK FAT?
I DON'T THINK SO.
OKAY, HERE WE GO... OPENING DAY... I THINK I'M READY... TAKE A DEEP BREATH... AM I READY? I'M READY...
HOW'S MY LIPSTICK?
LITTLE SMUDGE.

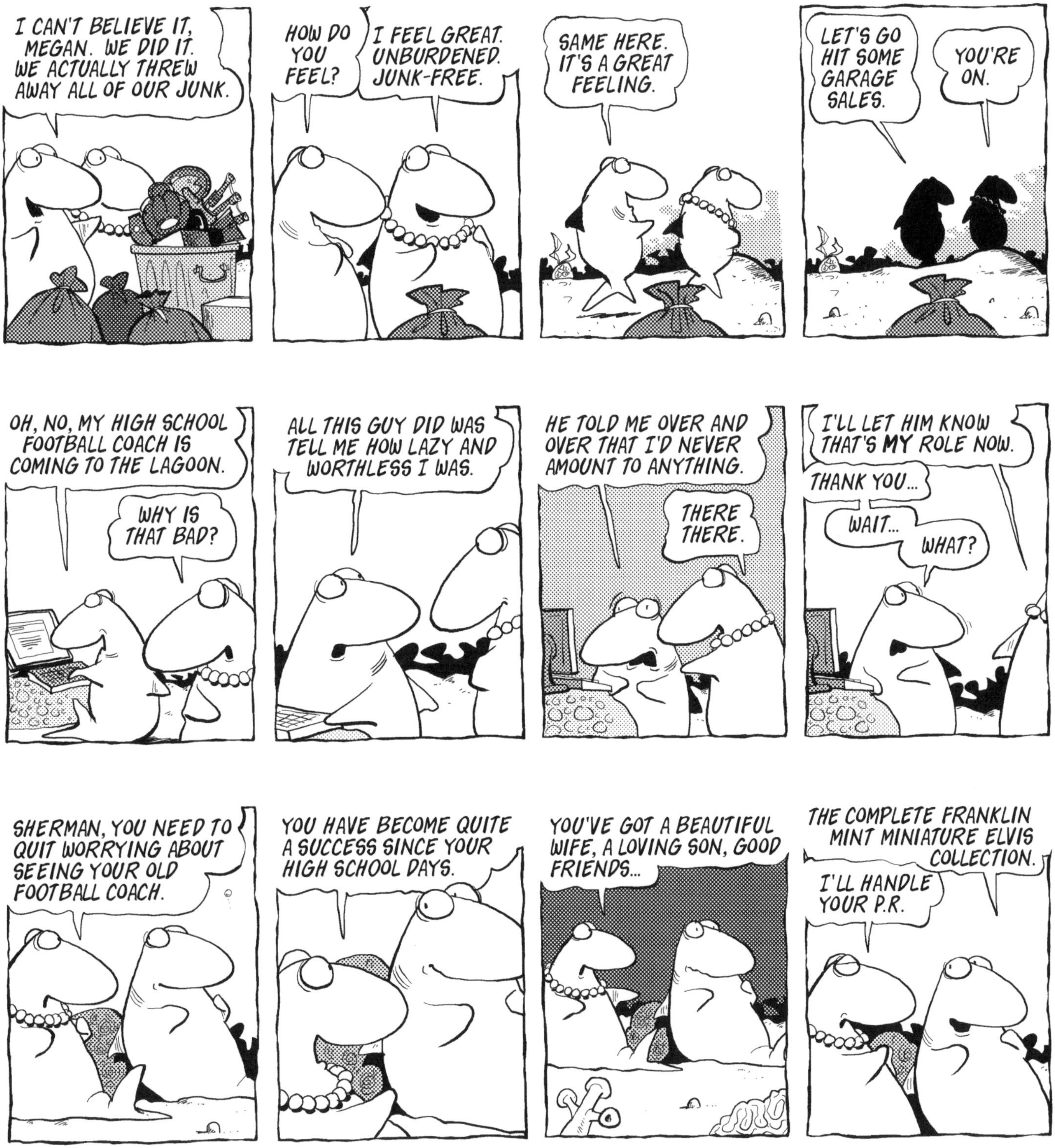
I CAN'T BELIEVE IT, MEGAN. WE DID IT. WE ACTUALLY THREW AWAY ALL OF OUR JUNK.
HOW DO YOU FEEL?
I FEEL GREAT. UNBURDENED. JUNK-FREE.
SAME HERE. IT'S A GREAT FEELING.
LET'S GO HIT SOME GARAGE SALES.
YOU'RE ON.
OH, NO, MY HIGH SCHOOL FOOTBALL COACH IS COMING TO THE LAGOON.
WHY IS THAT BAD?
ALL THIS GUY DID WAS TELL ME HOW LAZY AND WORTHLESS I WAS.
HE TOLD ME OVER AND OVER THAT I'D NEVER AMOUNT TO ANYTHING.
THERE THERE.
I'LL LET HIM KNOW THAT'S MY ROLE NOW.
THANK YOU...
WAIT...
WHAT?
SHERMAN, YOU NEED TO QUIT WORRYING ABOUT SEEING YOUR OLD FOOTBALL COACH.
YOU HAVE BECOME QUITE A SUCCESS SINCE YOUR HIGH SCHOOL DAYS.
YOU'VE GOT A BEAUTIFUL WIFE, A LOVING SON, GOOD FRIENDS...
THE COMPLETE FRANKLIN MINT MINIATURE ELVIS COLLECTION.
I'LL HANDLE YOUR P.R.

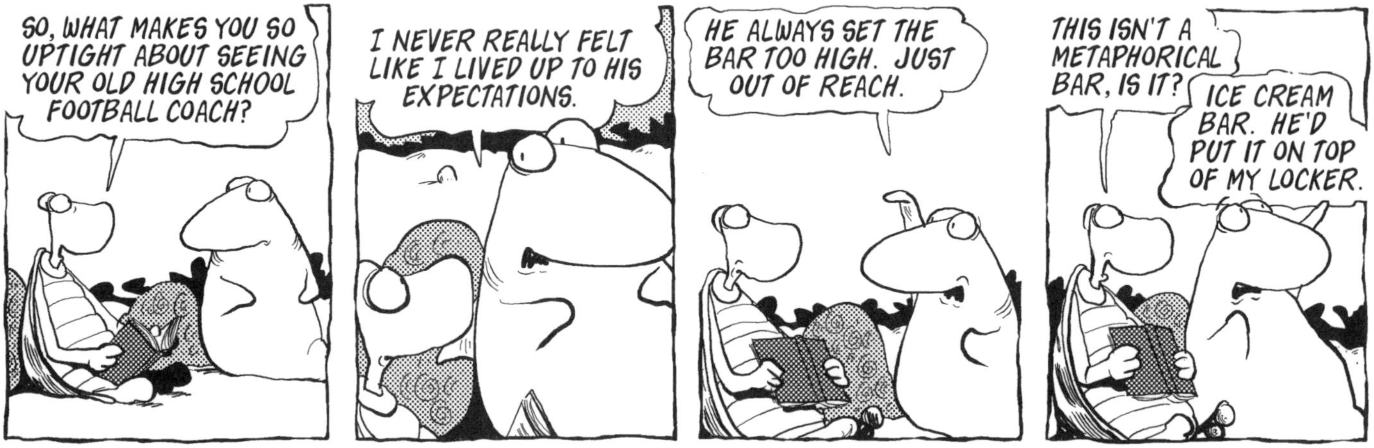
SO, WHAT MAKES YOU SO UPTIGHT ABOUT SEEING YOUR OLD HIGH SCHOOL FOOTBALL COACH?
I NEVER REALLY FELT LIKE I LIVED UP TO HIS EXPECTATIONS.
HE ALWAYS SET THE BAR TOO HIGH. JUST OUT OF REACH.
THIS ISN'T A METAPHORICAL BAR, IS IT?
ICE CREAM BAR. HE'D PUT IT ON TOP OF MY LOCKER.

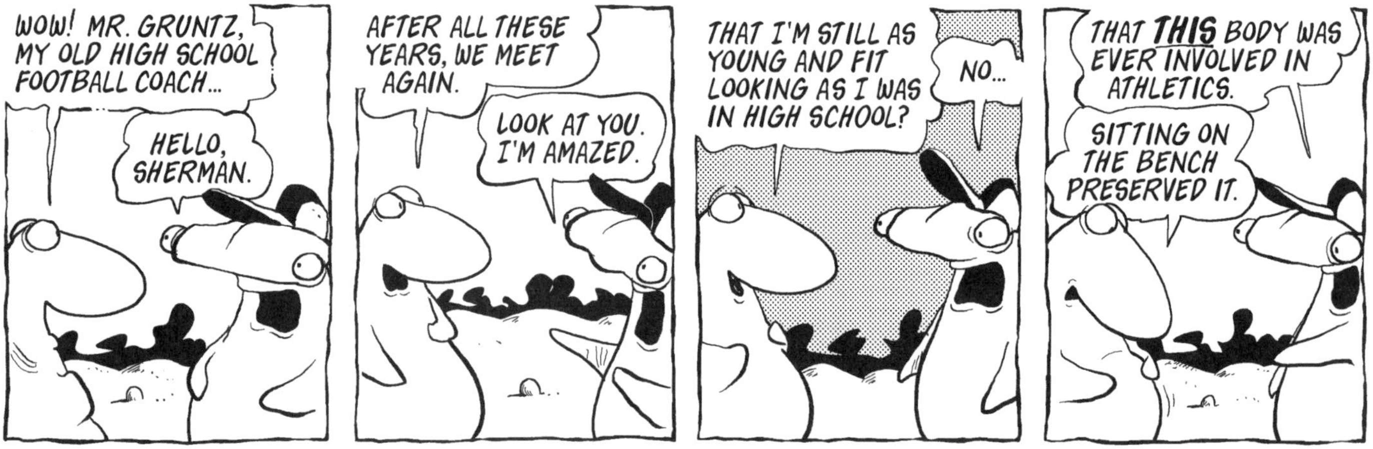
WOW! MR. GRUNTZ, MY OLD HIGH SCHOOL FOOTBALL COACH...
HELLO, SHERMAN.
AFTER ALL THESE YEARS, WE MEET AGAIN.
LOOK AT YOU. I'M AMAZED.
THAT I'M STILL AS YOUNG AND FIT LOOKING AS I WAS IN HIGH SCHOOL?
NO...
THAT **THIS** BODY WAS EVER INVOLVED IN ATHLETICS.
SITTING ON THE BENCH PRESERVED IT.

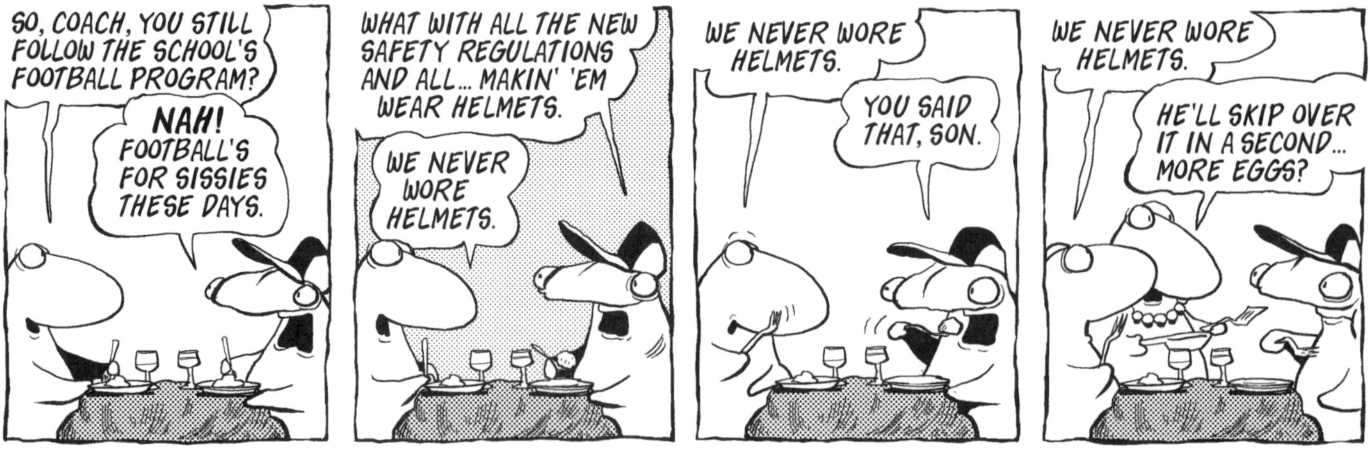
SO, COACH, YOU STILL FOLLOW THE SCHOOL'S FOOTBALL PROGRAM?
NAH! FOOTBALL'S FOR SISSIES THESE DAYS.
WHAT WITH ALL THE NEW SAFETY REGULATIONS AND ALL... MAKIN' 'EM WEAR HELMETS.
WE NEVER WORE HELMETS.
WE NEVER WORE HELMETS.
YOU SAID THAT, SON.
WE NEVER WORE HELMETS.
HE'LL SKIP OVER IT IN A SECOND... MORE EGGS?

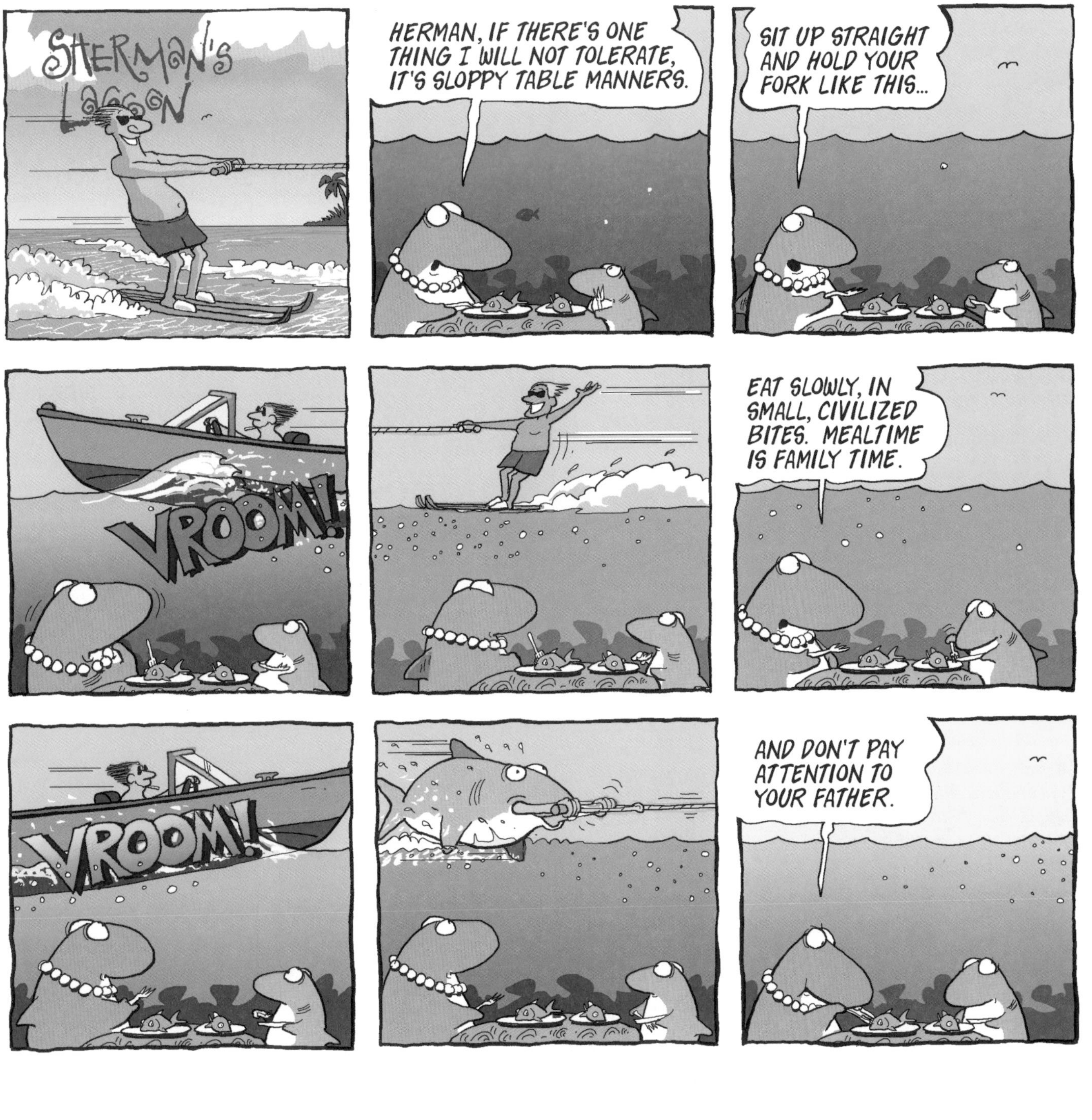
SHERMAN'S LAGOON
HERMAN, IF THERE'S ONE THING I WILL NOT TOLERATE, IT'S SLOPPY TABLE MANNERS.
SIT UP STRAIGHT AND HOLD YOUR FORK LIKE THIS...
VROOM!
EAT SLOWLY, IN SMALL, CIVILIZED BITES. MEALTIME IS FAMILY TIME.
VROOM!
AND DON'T PAY ATTENTION TO YOUR FATHER.

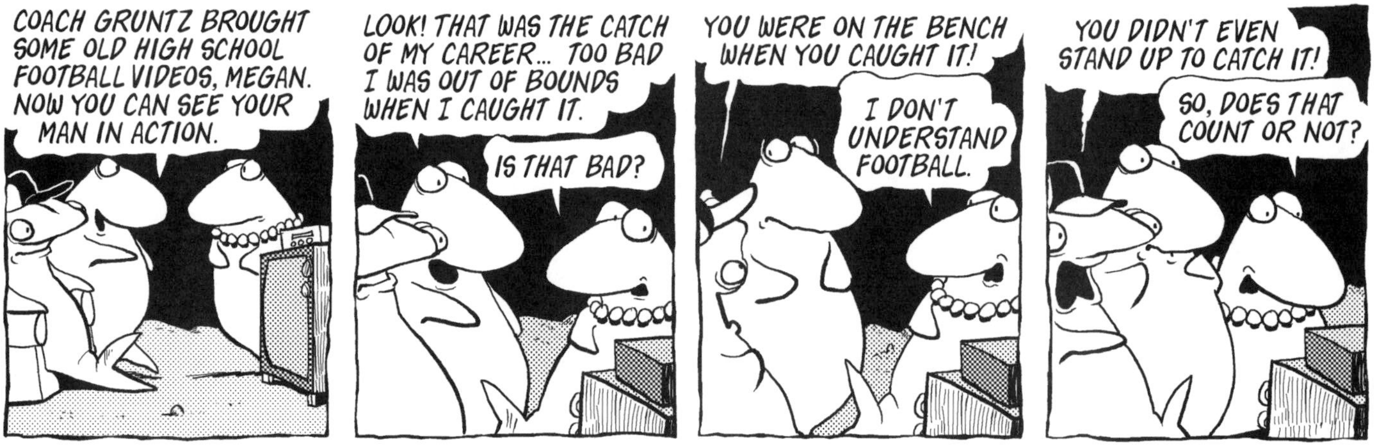
COACH GRUNTZ BROUGHT SOME OLD HIGH SCHOOL FOOTBALL VIDEOS, MEGAN. NOW YOU CAN SEE YOUR MAN IN ACTION.
LOOK! THAT WAS THE CATCH OF MY CAREER... TOO BAD I WAS OUT OF BOUNDS WHEN I CAUGHT IT.
IS THAT BAD?
YOU WERE ON THE BENCH WHEN YOU CAUGHT IT!
I DON'T UNDERSTAND FOOTBALL.
YOU DIDN'T EVEN STAND UP TO CATCH IT!
SO, DOES THAT COUNT OR NOT?

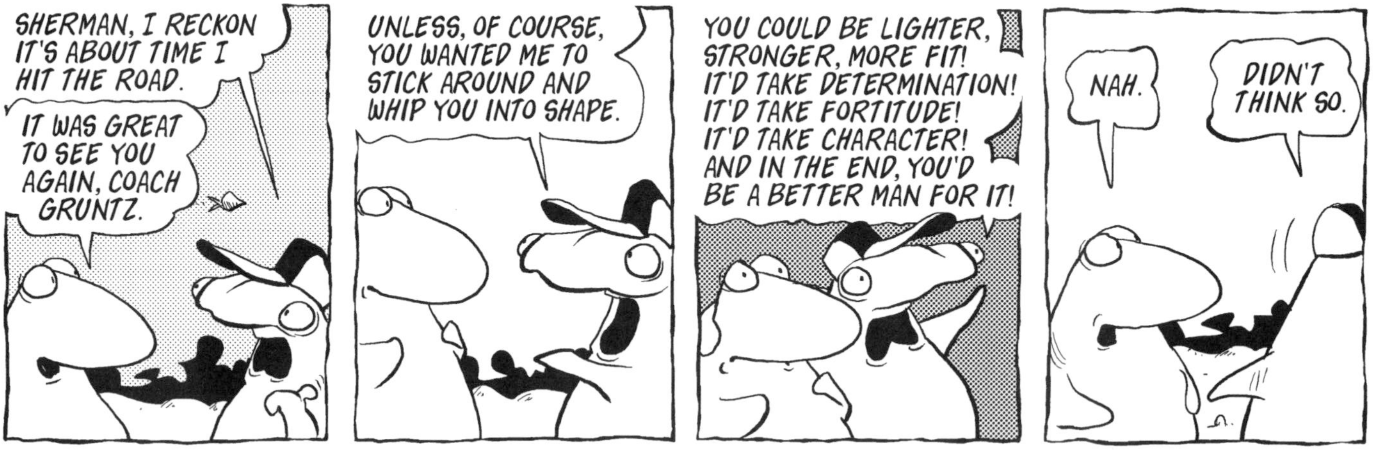
SHERMAN, I RECKON IT'S ABOUT TIME I HIT THE ROAD.
IT WAS GREAT TO SEE YOU AGAIN, COACH GRUNTZ.
UNLESS, OF COURSE, YOU WANTED ME TO STICK AROUND AND WHIP YOU INTO SHAPE.
YOU COULD BE LIGHTER, STRONGER, MORE FIT! IT'D TAKE DETERMINATION! IT'D TAKE FORTITUDE! IT'D TAKE CHARACTER! AND IN THE END, YOU'D BE A BETTER MAN FOR IT!
NAH.
DIDN'T THINK SO.

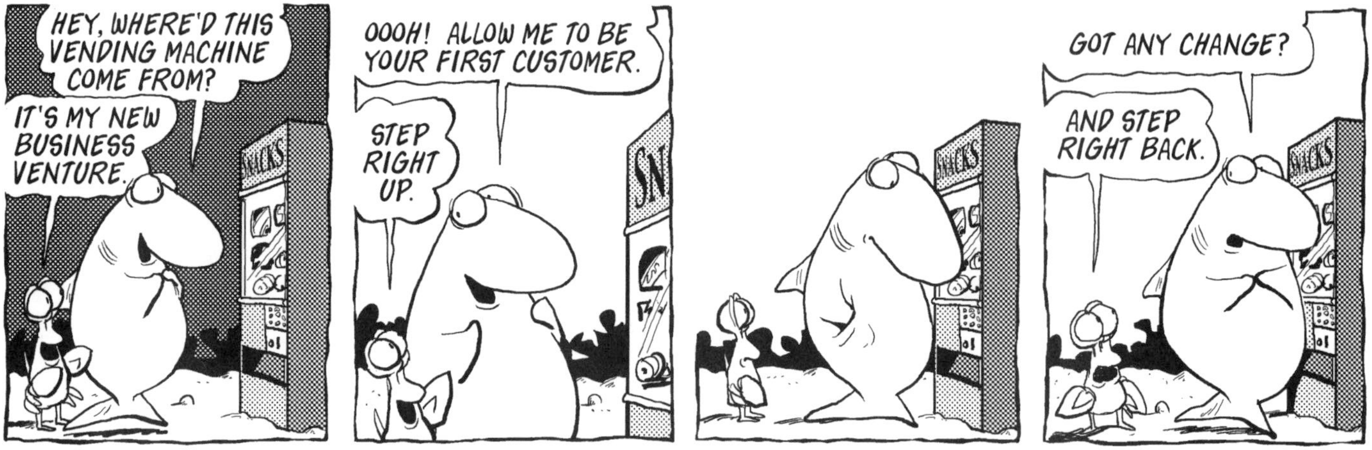
HEY, WHERE'D THIS VENDING MACHINE COME FROM?
IT'S MY NEW BUSINESS VENTURE.
SNACKS
OOOH! ALLOW ME TO BE YOUR FIRST CUSTOMER.
STEP RIGHT UP.
GOT ANY CHANGE?
AND STEP RIGHT BACK.

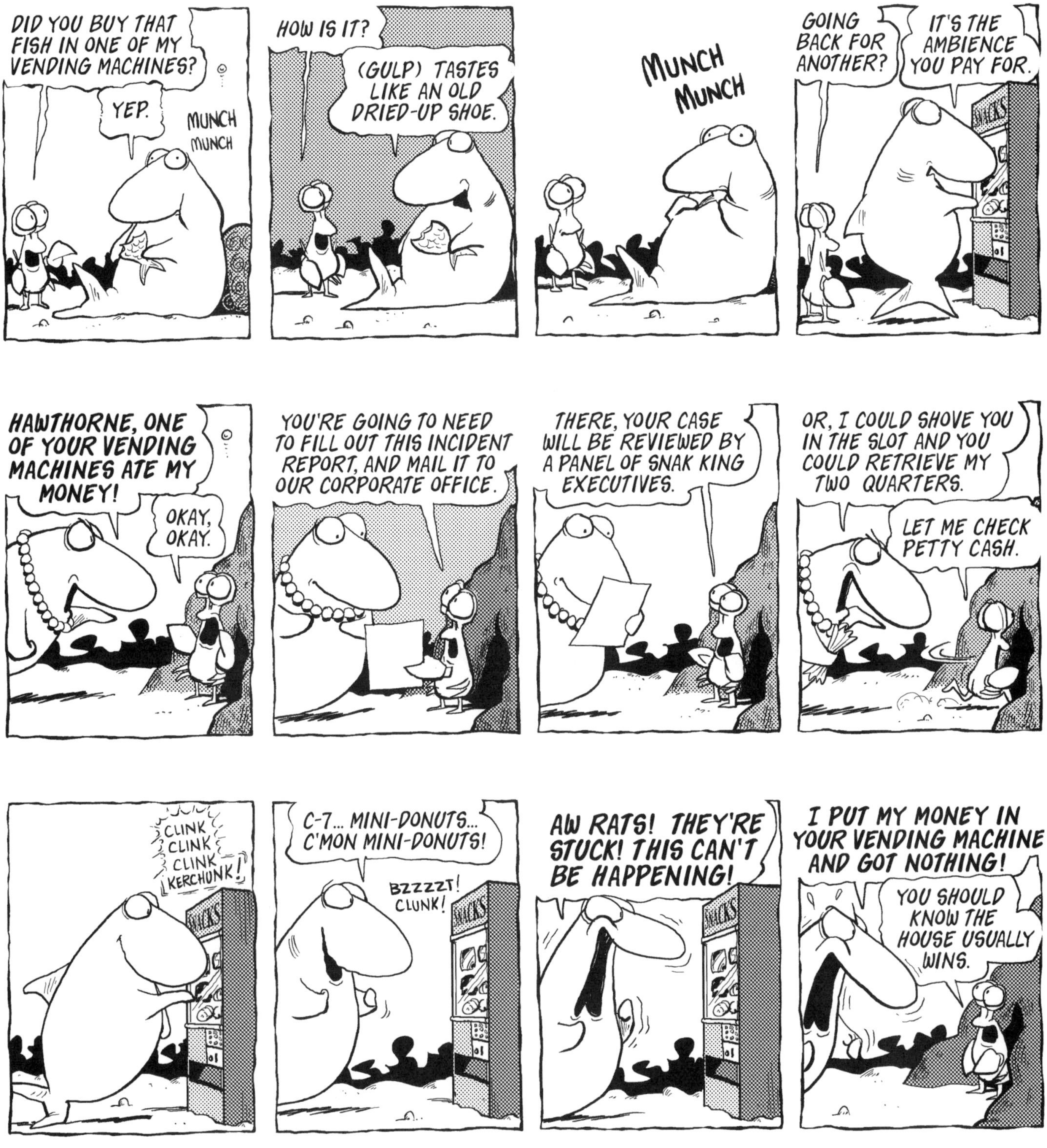
DID YOU BUY THAT FISH IN ONE OF MY VENDING MACHINES?
YEP.
MUNCH MUNCH
HOW IS IT?
(GULP) TASTES LIKE AN OLD DRIED-UP SHOE.
MUNCH MUNCH
GOING BACK FOR ANOTHER?
IT'S THE AMBIENCE YOU PAY FOR.
SNACKS
HAWTHORNE, ONE OF YOUR VENDING MACHINES ATE MY MONEY!
OKAY, OKAY.
YOU'RE GOING TO NEED TO FILL OUT THIS INCIDENT REPORT, AND MAIL IT TO OUR CORPORATE OFFICE.
THERE, YOUR CASE WILL BE REVIEWED BY A PANEL OF SNAK KING EXECUTIVES.
OR, I COULD SHOVE YOU IN THE SLOT AND YOU COULD RETRIEVE MY TWO QUARTERS.
LET ME CHECK PETTY CASH.
CLINK CLINK CLINK KERCHUNK!
SNACKS
C-7... MINI-DONUTS... C'MON MINI-DONUTS!
BZZZZT! CLUNK!
AW RATS! THEY'RE STUCK! THIS CAN'T BE HAPPENING!
I PUT MY MONEY IN YOUR VENDING MACHINE AND GOT NOTHING!
YOU SHOULD KNOW THE HOUSE USUALLY WINS.

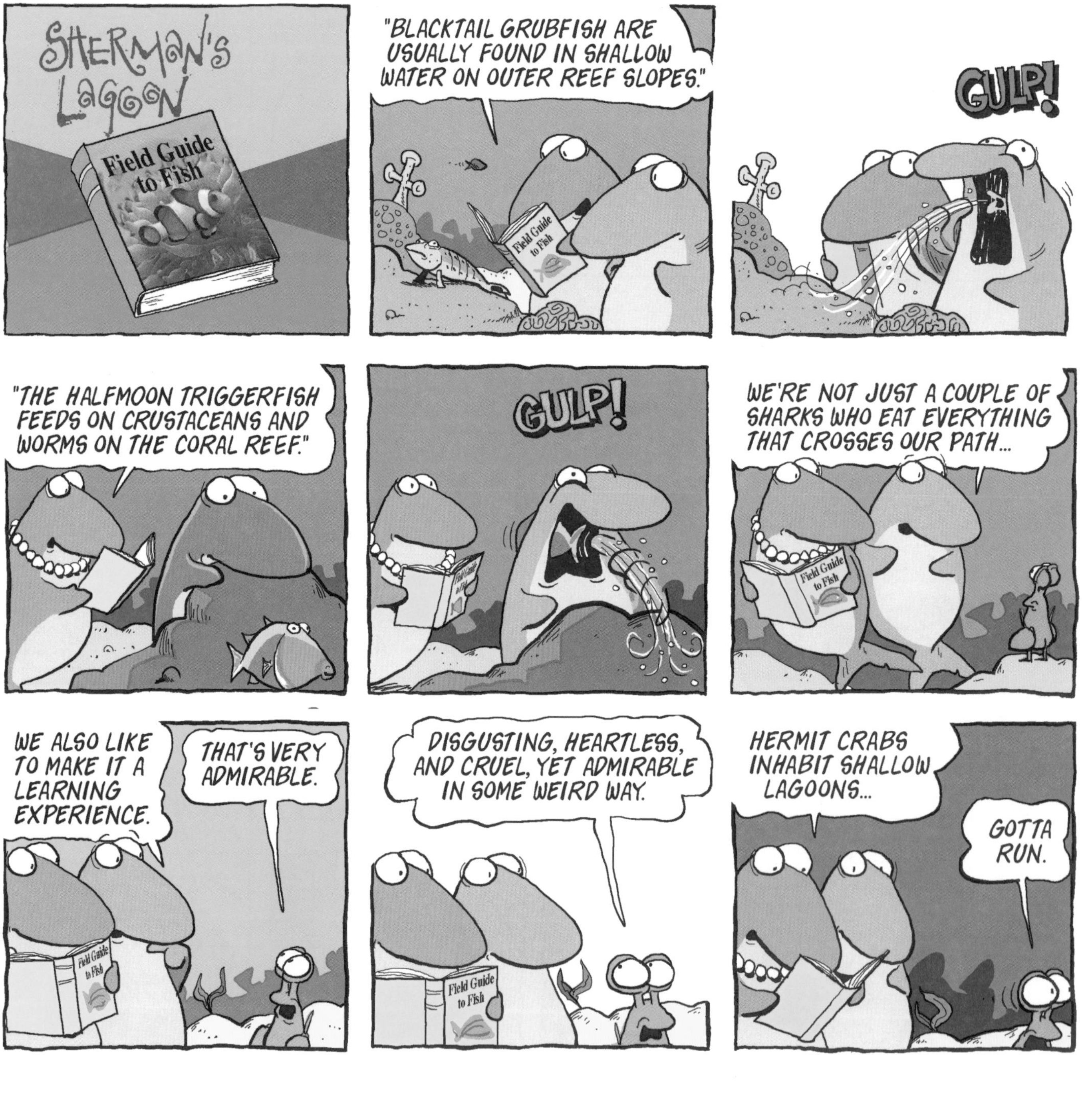
SHERMAN'S LAGOON
Field Guide to Fish
"BLACKTAIL GRUBFISH ARE USUALLY FOUND IN SHALLOW WATER ON OUTER REEF SLOPES."
Field Guide to Fish
GULP!
"THE HALFMOON TRIGGERFISH FEEDS ON CRUSTACEANS AND WORMS ON THE CORAL REEF."
GULP!
WE'RE NOT JUST A COUPLE OF SHARKS WHO EAT EVERYTHING THAT CROSSES OUR PATH...
Field Guide to Fish
WE ALSO LIKE TO MAKE IT A LEARNING EXPERIENCE.
THAT'S VERY ADMIRABLE.
Field Guide to Fish
DISGUSTING, HEARTLESS, AND CRUEL, YET ADMIRABLE IN SOME WEIRD WAY.
Field Guide to Fish
HERMIT CRABS INHABIT SHALLOW LAGOONS...
GOTTA RUN.

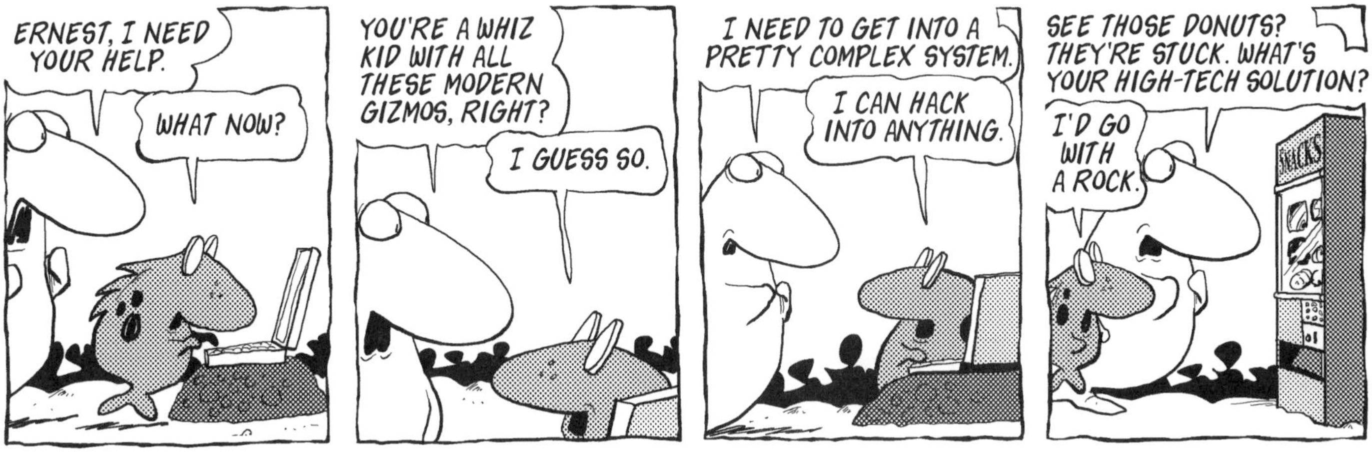
ERNEST, I NEED YOUR HELP.
WHAT NOW?
YOU'RE A WHIZ KID WITH ALL THESE MODERN GIZMOS, RIGHT?
I GUESS SO.
I NEED TO GET INTO A PRETTY COMPLEX SYSTEM.
I CAN HACK INTO ANYTHING.
SEE THOSE DONUTS? THEY'RE STUCK. WHAT'S YOUR HIGH-TECH SOLUTION?
I'D GO WITH A ROCK.
SNACKS

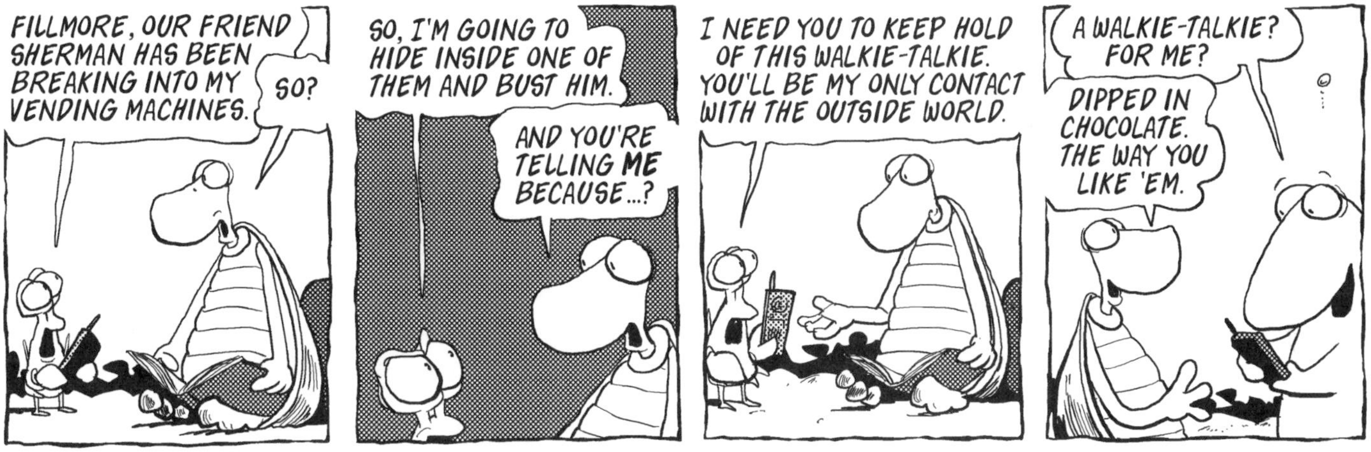
FILLMORE, OUR FRIEND SHERMAN HAS BEEN BREAKING INTO MY VENDING MACHINES.
SO?
SO, I'M GOING TO HIDE INSIDE ONE OF THEM AND BUST HIM.
AND YOU'RE TELLING **ME** BECAUSE...?
I NEED YOU TO KEEP HOLD OF THIS WALKIE-TALKIE. YOU'LL BE MY ONLY CONTACT WITH THE OUTSIDE WORLD.
A WALKIE-TALKIE? FOR ME?
DIPPED IN CHOCOLATE. THE WAY YOU LIKE 'EM.

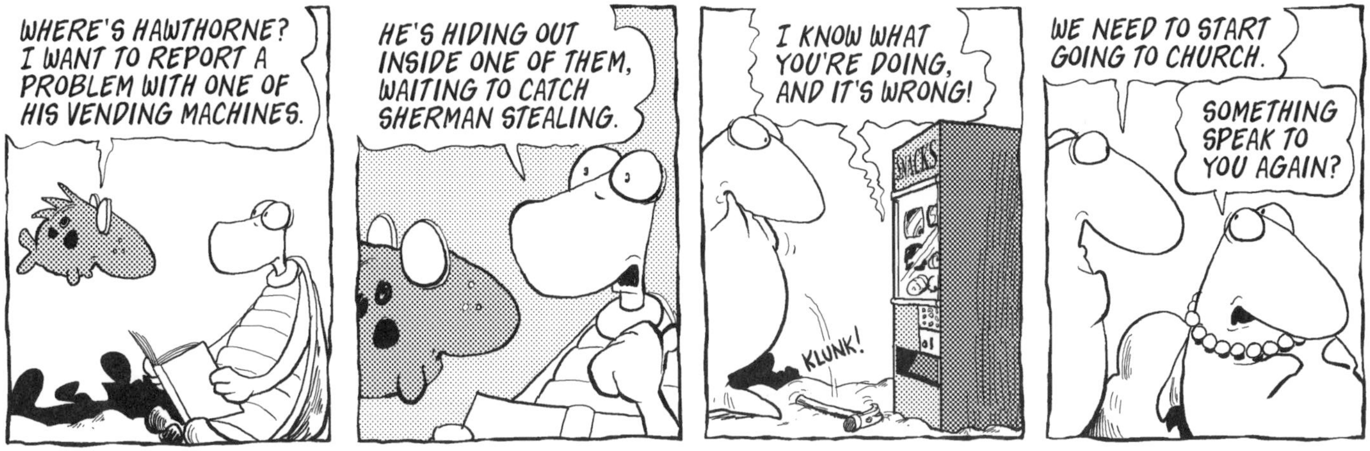
WHERE'S HAWTHORNE? I WANT TO REPORT A PROBLEM WITH ONE OF HIS VENDING MACHINES.
HE'S HIDING OUT INSIDE ONE OF THEM, WAITING TO CATCH SHERMAN STEALING.
I KNOW WHAT YOU'RE DOING, AND IT'S WRONG!
SNACKS
KLUNK!
WE NEED TO START GOING TO CHURCH.
SOMETHING SPEAK TO YOU AGAIN?

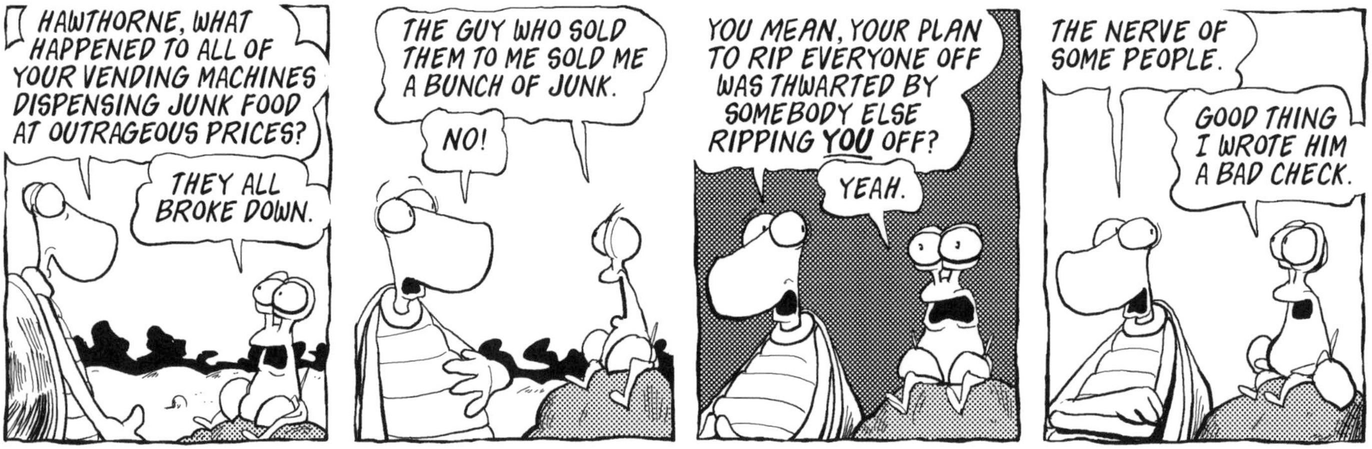
HAWTHORNE, WHAT HAPPENED TO ALL OF YOUR VENDING MACHINES DISPENSING JUNK FOOD AT OUTRAGEOUS PRICES?
THEY ALL BROKE DOWN.
THE GUY WHO SOLD THEM TO ME SOLD ME A BUNCH OF JUNK.
NO!
YOU MEAN, YOUR PLAN TO RIP EVERYONE OFF WAS THWARTED BY SOMEBODY ELSE RIPPING YOU OFF?
YEAH.
THE NERVE OF SOME PEOPLE.
GOOD THING I WROTE HIM A BAD CHECK.

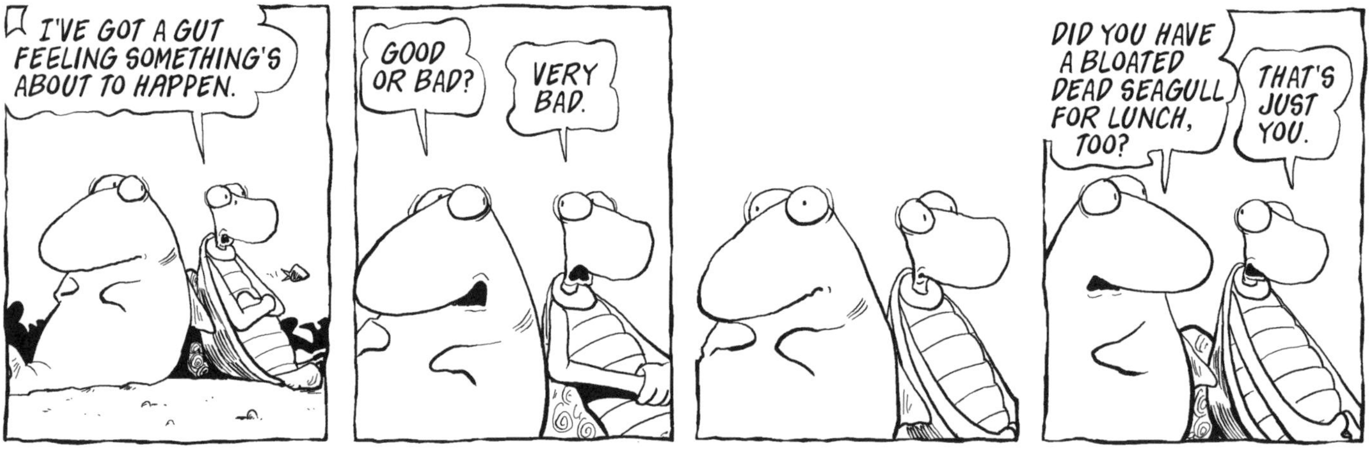
I'VE GOT A GUT FEELING SOMETHING'S ABOUT TO HAPPEN.
GOOD OR BAD?
VERY BAD.
DID YOU HAVE A BLOATED DEAD SEAGULL FOR LUNCH, TOO?
THAT'S JUST YOU.

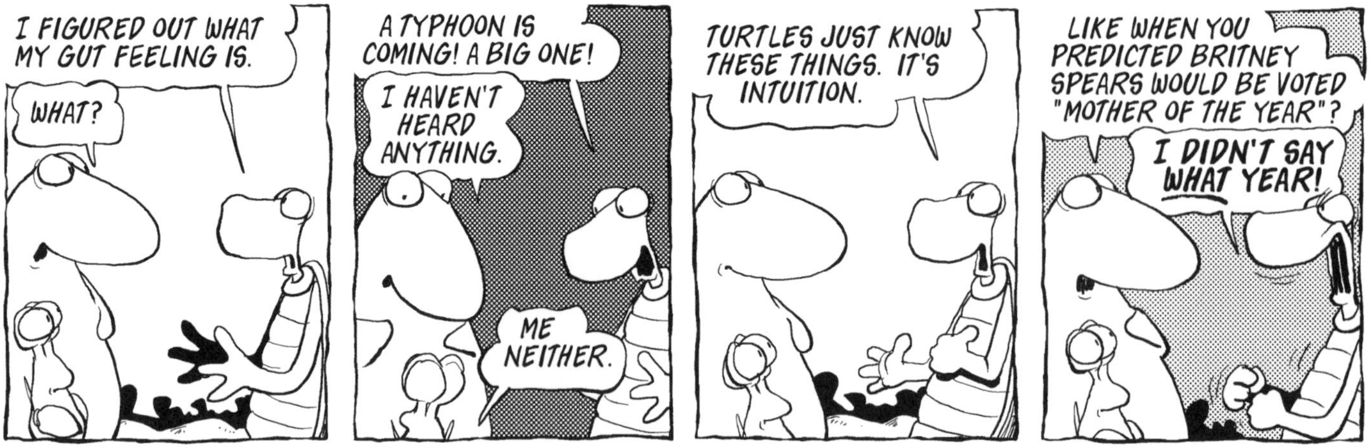
I FIGURED OUT WHAT MY GUT FEELING IS.
WHAT?
A TYPHOON IS COMING! A BIG ONE!
I HAVEN'T HEARD ANYTHING.
ME NEITHER.
TURTLES JUST KNOW THESE THINGS. IT'S INTUITION.
LIKE WHEN YOU PREDICTED BRITNEY SPEARS WOULD BE VOTED "MOTHER OF THE YEAR"?
I DIDN'T SAY WHAT YEAR!

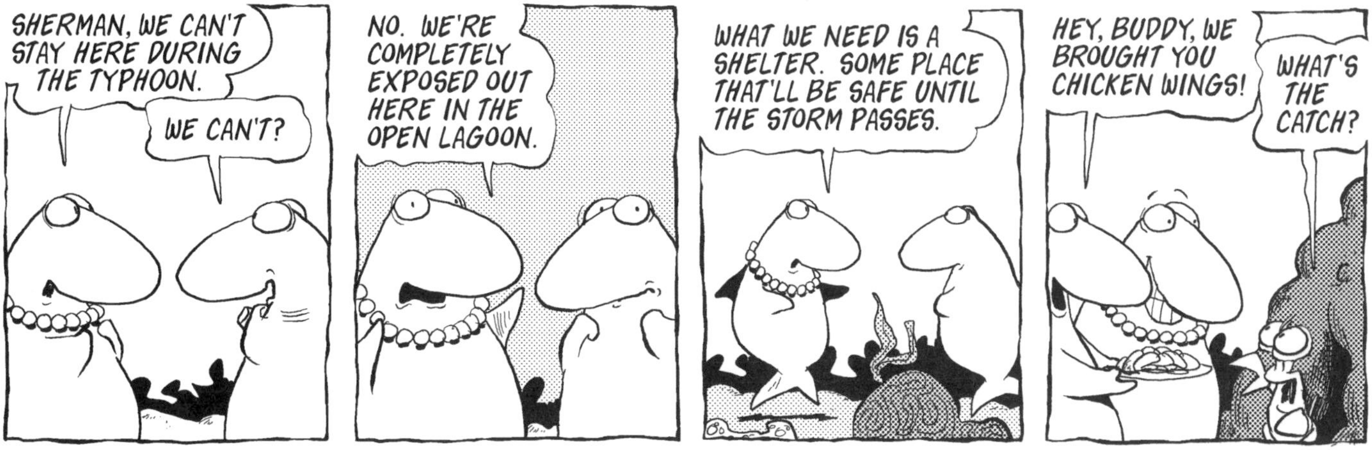
SHERMAN, WE CAN'T STAY HERE DURING THE TYPHOON.
WE CAN'T?
NO. WE'RE COMPLETELY EXPOSED OUT HERE IN THE OPEN LAGOON.
WHAT WE NEED IS A SHELTER. SOME PLACE THAT'LL BE SAFE UNTIL THE STORM PASSES.
HEY, BUDDY, WE BROUGHT YOU CHICKEN WINGS!
WHAT'S THE CATCH?

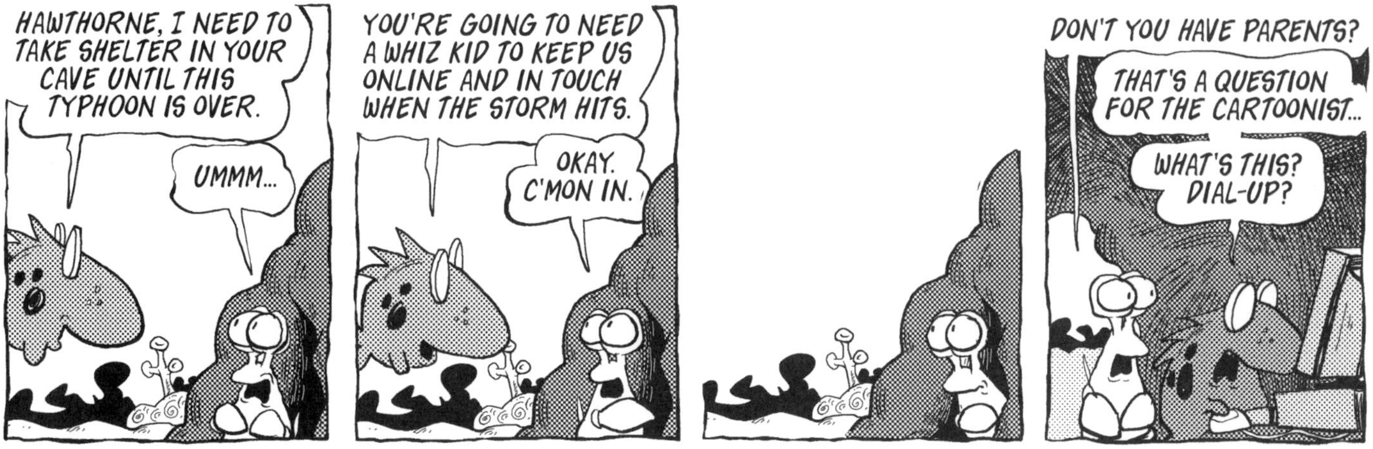
HAWTHORNE, I NEED TO TAKE SHELTER IN YOUR CAVE UNTIL THIS TYPHOON IS OVER.
UMMM...
YOU'RE GOING TO NEED A WHIZ KID TO KEEP US ONLINE AND IN TOUCH WHEN THE STORM HITS.
OKAY. C'MON IN.
DON'T YOU HAVE PARENTS?
THAT'S A QUESTION FOR THE CARTOONIST...
WHAT'S THIS? DIAL-UP?

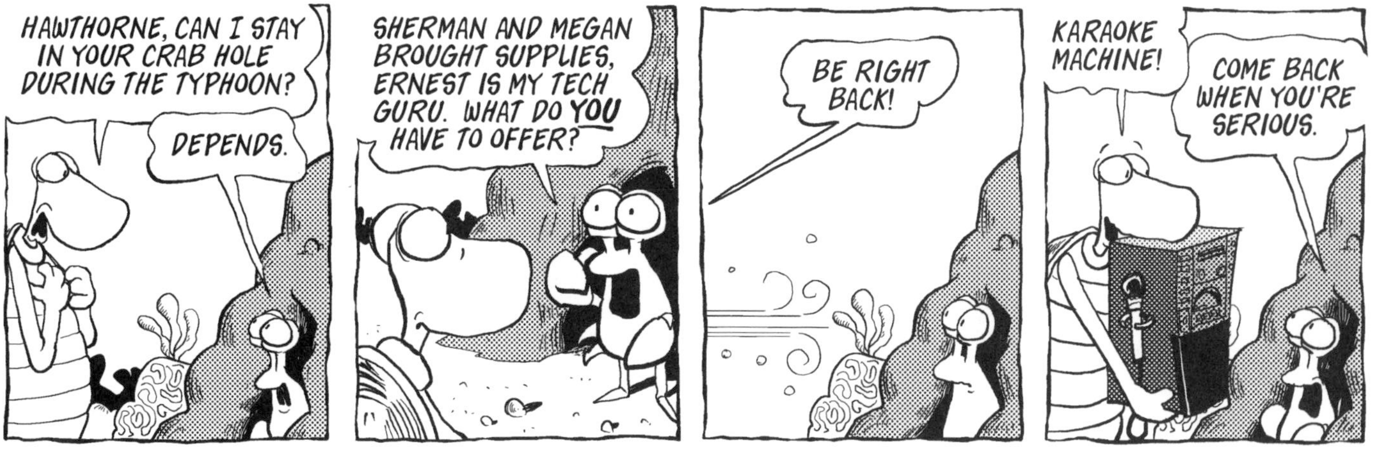
HAWTHORNE, CAN I STAY IN YOUR CRAB HOLE DURING THE TYPHOON?
DEPENDS.
SHERMAN AND MEGAN BROUGHT SUPPLIES, ERNEST IS MY TECH GURU. WHAT DO YOU HAVE TO OFFER?
BE RIGHT BACK!
KARAOKE MACHINE!
COME BACK WHEN YOU'RE SERIOUS.

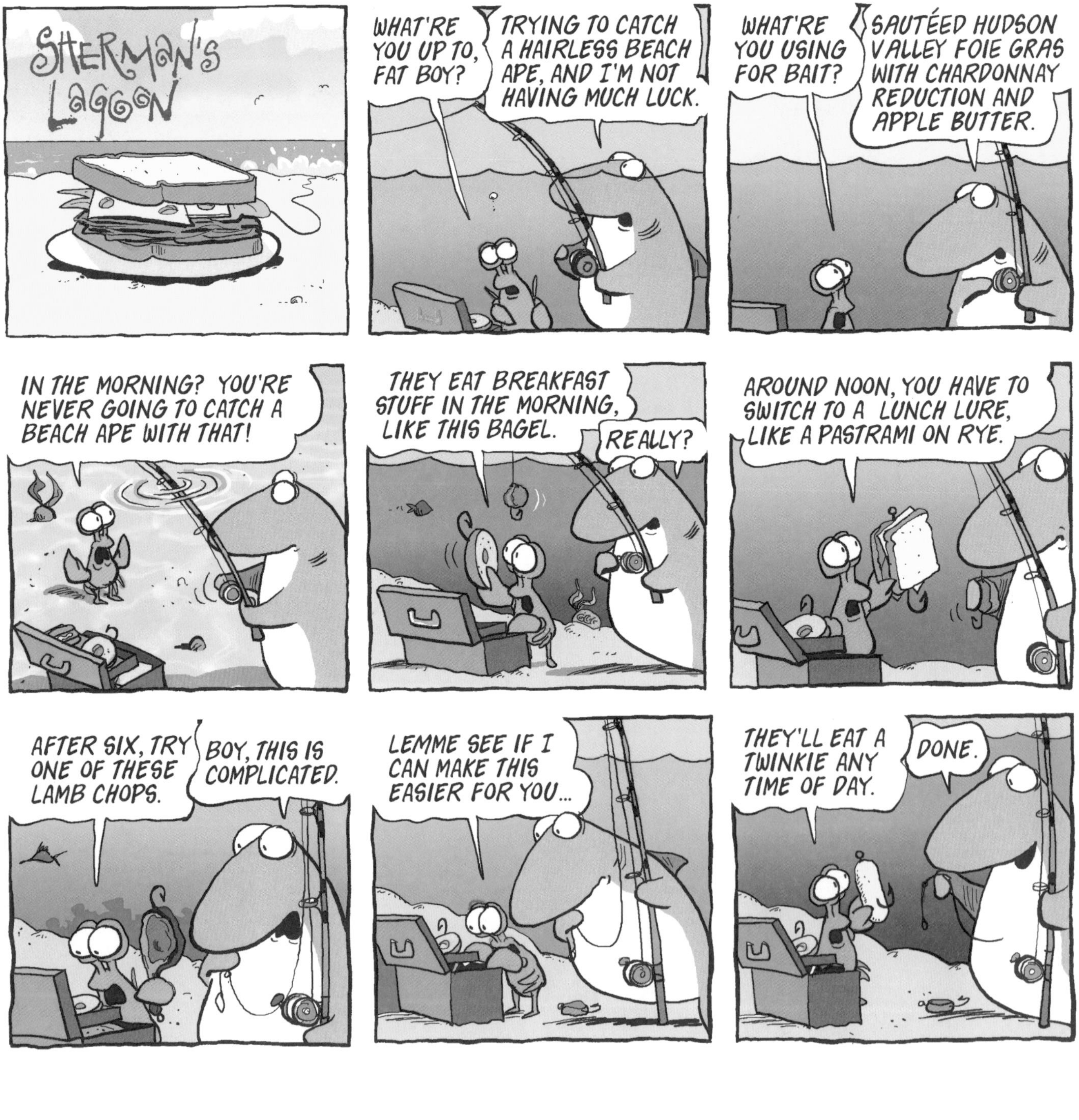
SHERMAN'S LAGOON
WHAT'RE YOU UP TO, FAT BOY?
TRYING TO CATCH A HAIRLESS BEACH APE, AND I'M NOT HAVING MUCH LUCK.
WHAT'RE YOU USING FOR BAIT?
SAUTÉED HUDSON VALLEY FOIE GRAS WITH CHARDONNAY REDUCTION AND APPLE BUTTER.
IN THE MORNING? YOU'RE NEVER GOING TO CATCH A BEACH APE WITH THAT!
THEY EAT BREAKFAST STUFF IN THE MORNING, LIKE THIS BAGEL.
REALLY?
AROUND NOON, YOU HAVE TO SWITCH TO A LUNCH LURE, LIKE A PASTRAMI ON RYE.
AFTER SIX, TRY ONE OF THESE LAMB CHOPS.
BOY, THIS IS COMPLICATED.
LEMME SEE IF I CAN MAKE THIS EASIER FOR YOU...
THEY'LL EAT A TWINKIE ANY TIME OF DAY.
DONE.

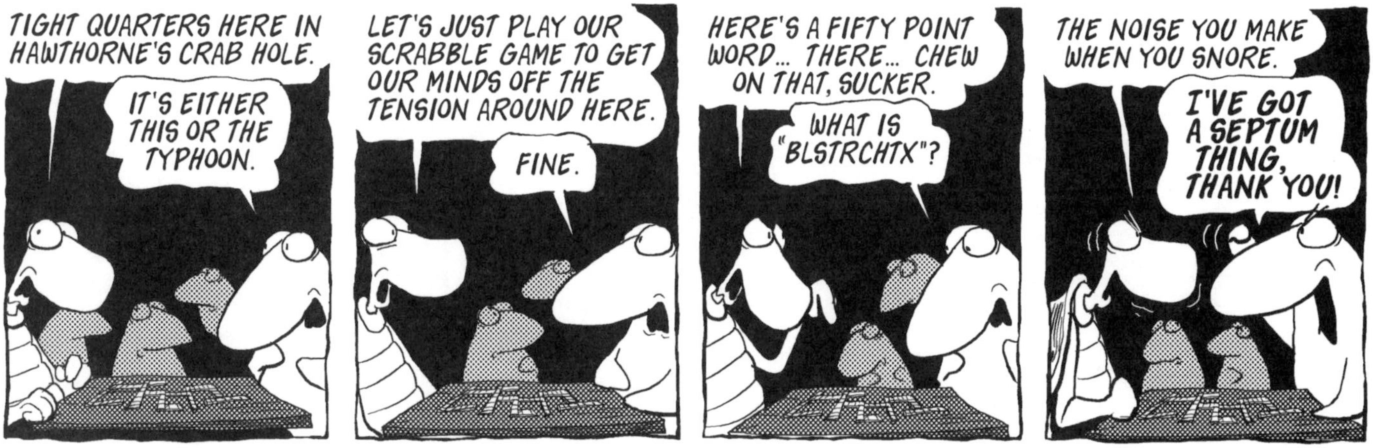
TIGHT QUARTERS HERE IN HAWTHORNE'S CRAB HOLE.
IT'S EITHER THIS OR THE TYPHOON.
LET'S JUST PLAY OUR SCRABBLE GAME TO GET OUR MINDS OFF THE TENSION AROUND HERE.
FINE.
HERE'S A FIFTY POINT WORD... THERE... CHEW ON THAT, SUCKER.
WHAT IS "BLSTRCHTX"?
THE NOISE YOU MAKE WHEN YOU SNORE.
I'VE GOT A SEPTUM THING, THANK YOU!

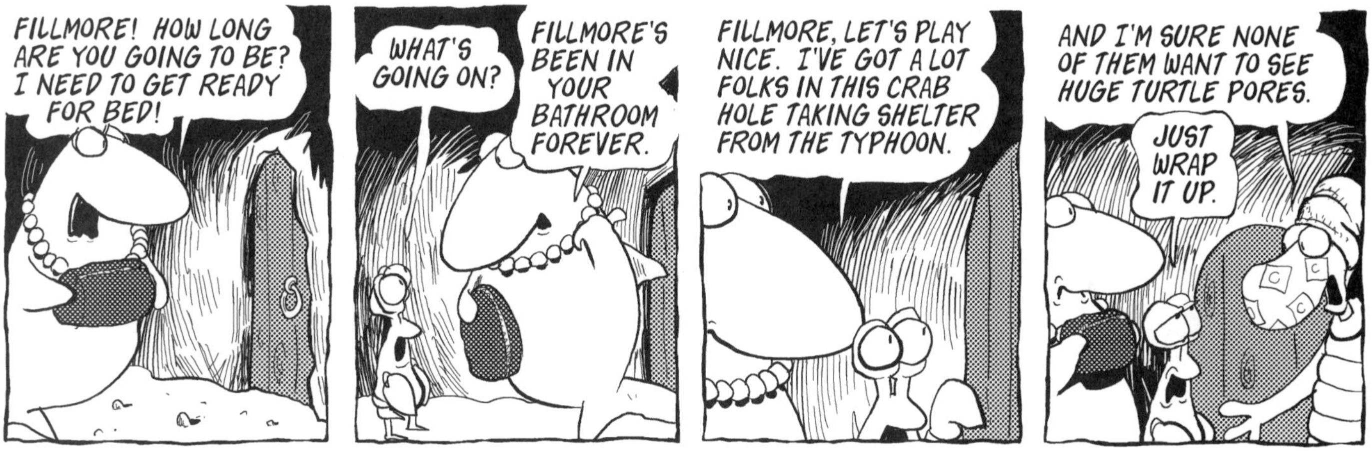
FILLMORE! HOW LONG ARE YOU GOING TO BE? I NEED TO GET READY FOR BED!
WHAT'S GOING ON?
FILLMORE'S BEEN IN YOUR BATHROOM FOREVER.
FILLMORE, LET'S PLAY NICE. I'VE GOT A LOT FOLKS IN THIS CRAB HOLE TAKING SHELTER FROM THE TYPHOON.
AND I'M SURE NONE OF THEM WANT TO SEE HUGE TURTLE PORES.
JUST WRAP IT UP.

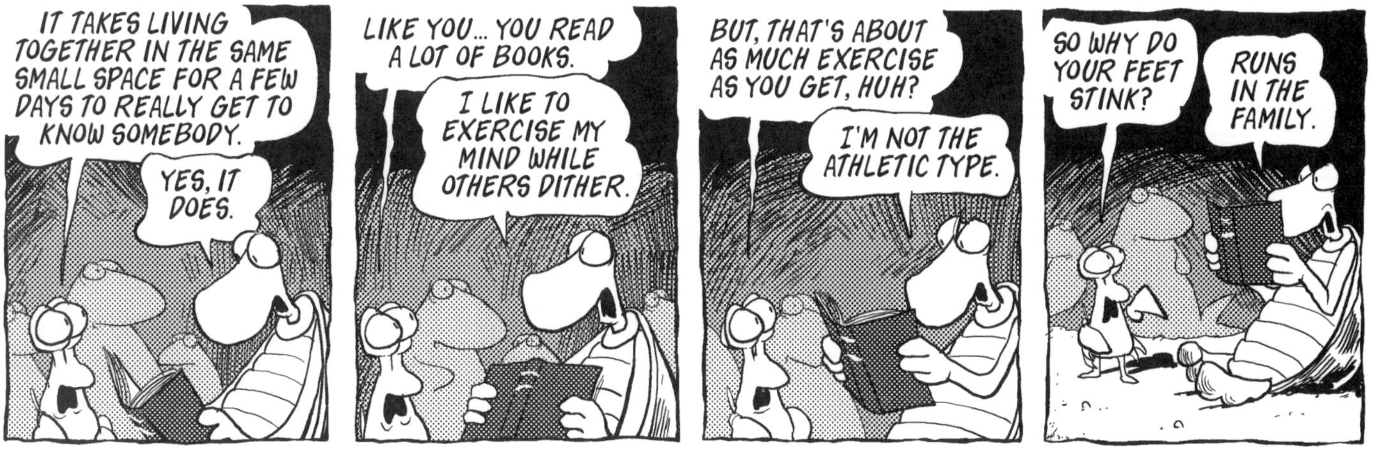
IT TAKES LIVING TOGETHER IN THE SAME SMALL SPACE FOR A FEW DAYS TO REALLY GET TO KNOW SOMEBODY.
YES, IT DOES.
LIKE YOU... YOU READ A LOT OF BOOKS.
I LIKE TO EXERCISE MY MIND WHILE OTHERS DITHER.
BUT, THAT'S ABOUT AS MUCH EXERCISE AS YOU GET, HUH?
I'M NOT THE ATHLETIC TYPE.
SO WHY DO YOUR FEET STINK?
RUNS IN THE FAMILY.

NOW, THERE'S AN ATTRACTIVE SEA TURTLE, FILLMORE. WHY DON'T YOU GO SAY "HI" TO HER?

SHE'S QUITE THE VENUS, ISN'T SHE?

I COULD MARRY HER. WE'D HAVE BEAUTIFUL CHILDREN. WE'D LIVE IN A PRIVATE LAGOON. WE'D...

WHOA!

START WITH LOWER EXPECTATIONS. GOT IT? DOWN HERE.

YOU START WAY UP HERE. GUARANTEED LETDOWN. NO WONDER YOU'RE NEUROTIC.

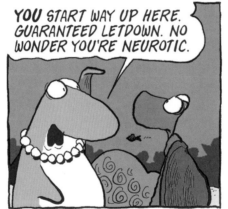

NOW, GO UP TO HER AND SAY SOMETHING WITTY, AND IF SHE DOESN'T THROW UP AND FLEE, THEN CALL IT A SUCCESS. OKAY?

OKAY.

GO.

MAYBE WE NEED TO START LOWER.

SHE GOT ME.

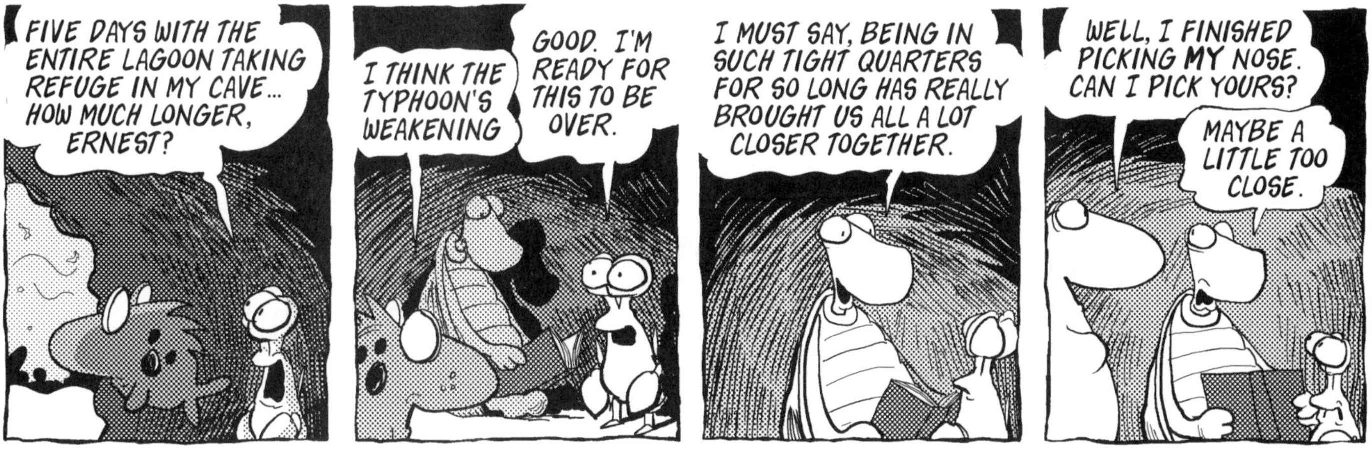
FIVE DAYS WITH THE ENTIRE LAGOON TAKING REFUGE IN MY CAVE... HOW MUCH LONGER, ERNEST?
I THINK THE TYPHOON'S WEAKENING
GOOD. I'M READY FOR THIS TO BE OVER.
I MUST SAY, BEING IN SUCH TIGHT QUARTERS FOR SO LONG HAS REALLY BROUGHT US ALL A LOT CLOSER TOGETHER.
WELL, I FINISHED PICKING MY NOSE. CAN I PICK YOURS?
MAYBE A LITTLE TOO CLOSE.

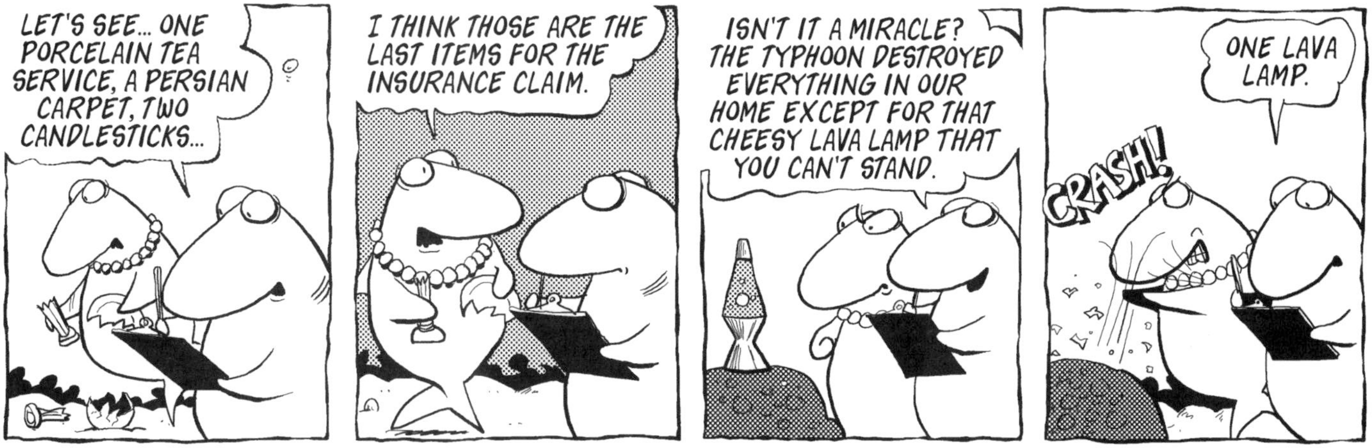
LET'S SEE... ONE PORCELAIN TEA SERVICE, A PERSIAN CARPET, TWO CANDLESTICKS...
I THINK THOSE ARE THE LAST ITEMS FOR THE INSURANCE CLAIM.
ISN'T IT A MIRACLE? THE TYPHOON DESTROYED EVERYTHING IN OUR HOME EXCEPT FOR THAT CHEESY LAVA LAMP THAT YOU CAN'T STAND.
CRASH!
ONE LAVA LAMP.

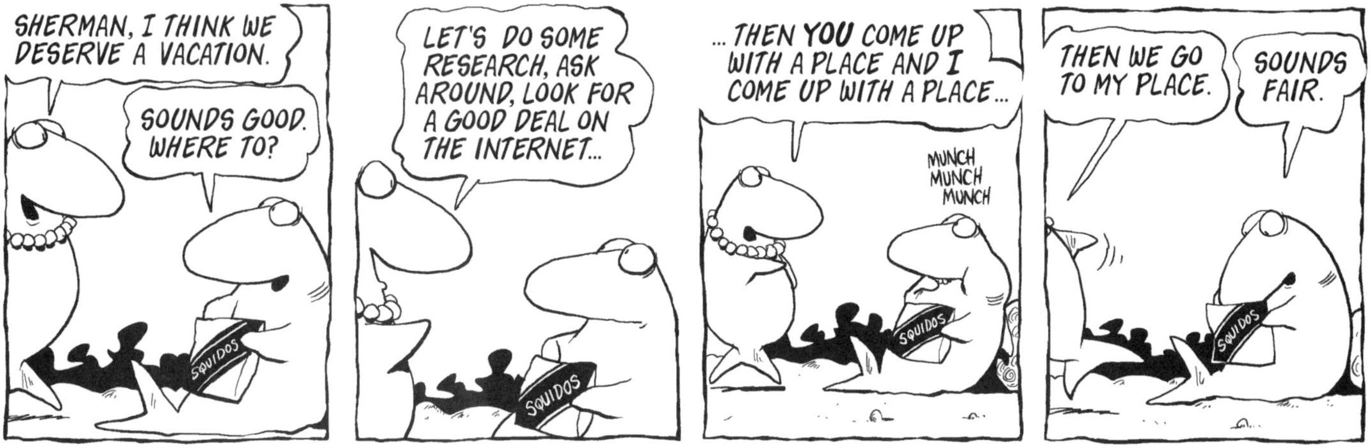
SHERMAN, I THINK WE DESERVE A VACATION.
SOUNDS GOOD. WHERE TO?
SQUIDOS
LET'S DO SOME RESEARCH, ASK AROUND, LOOK FOR A GOOD DEAL ON THE INTERNET...
SQUIDOS
...THEN YOU COME UP WITH A PLACE AND I COME UP WITH A PLACE...
MUNCH MUNCH MUNCH
SQUIDOS
THEN WE GO TO MY PLACE.
SOUNDS FAIR.
SQUIDOS

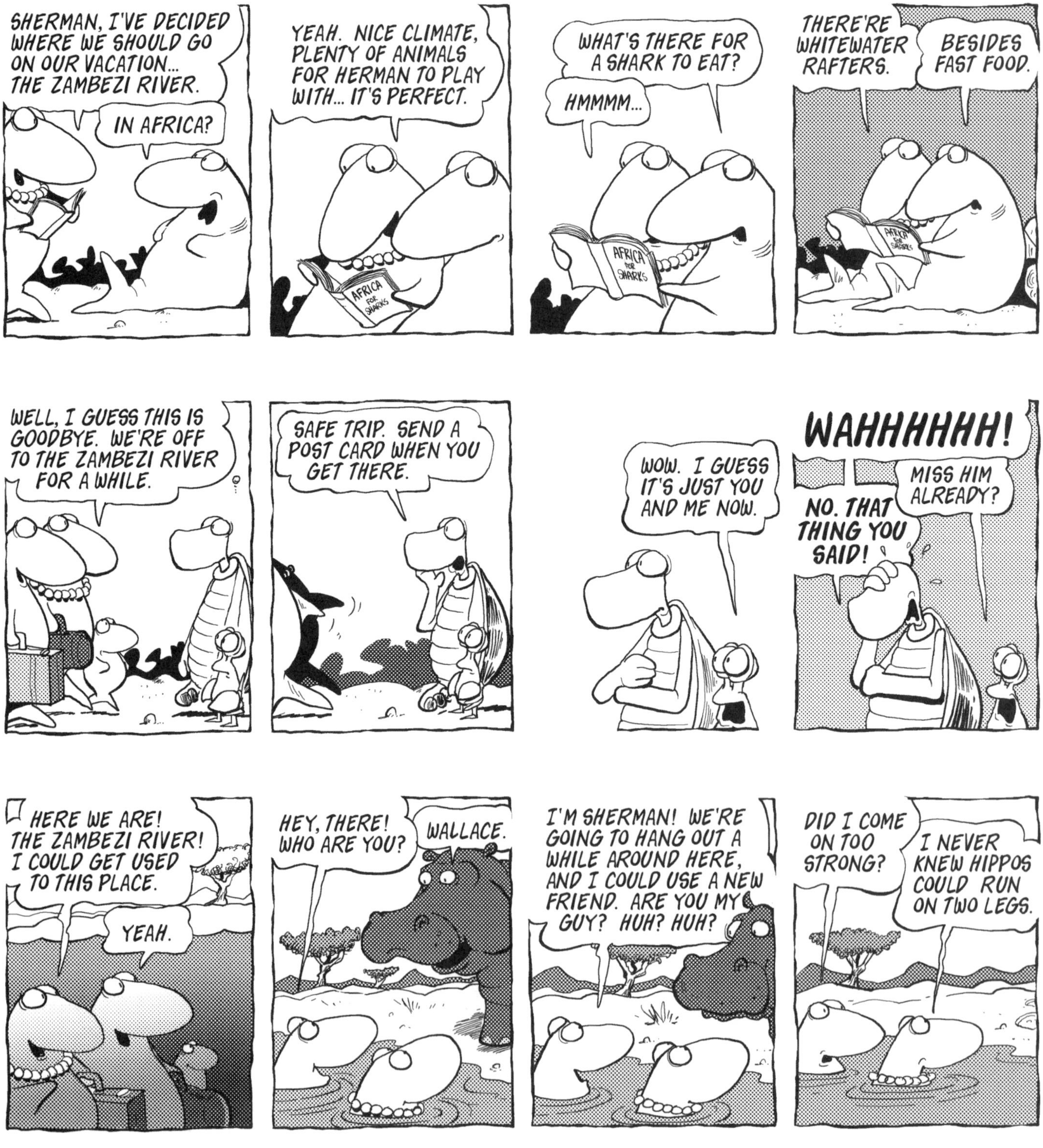
SHERMAN, I'VE DECIDED WHERE WE SHOULD GO ON OUR VACATION... THE ZAMBEZI RIVER.
IN AFRICA?
YEAH. NICE CLIMATE, PLENTY OF ANIMALS FOR HERMAN TO PLAY WITH... IT'S PERFECT.
AFRICA FOR SHARKS
HMMMM...
WHAT'S THERE FOR A SHARK TO EAT?
THERE'RE WHITEWATER RAFTERS.
BESIDES FAST FOOD.
WELL, I GUESS THIS IS GOODBYE. WE'RE OFF TO THE ZAMBEZI RIVER FOR A WHILE.
SAFE TRIP. SEND A POST CARD WHEN YOU GET THERE.
WOW. I GUESS IT'S JUST YOU AND ME NOW.
WAHHHHHH!
MISS HIM ALREADY?
NO. THAT THING YOU SAID!
HERE WE ARE! THE ZAMBEZI RIVER! I COULD GET USED TO THIS PLACE.
YEAH.
HEY, THERE! WHO ARE YOU?
WALLACE.
I'M SHERMAN! WE'RE GOING TO HANG OUT A WHILE AROUND HERE, AND I COULD USE A NEW FRIEND. ARE YOU MY GUY? HUH? HUH?
DID I COME ON TOO STRONG?
I NEVER KNEW HIPPOS COULD RUN ON TWO LEGS.

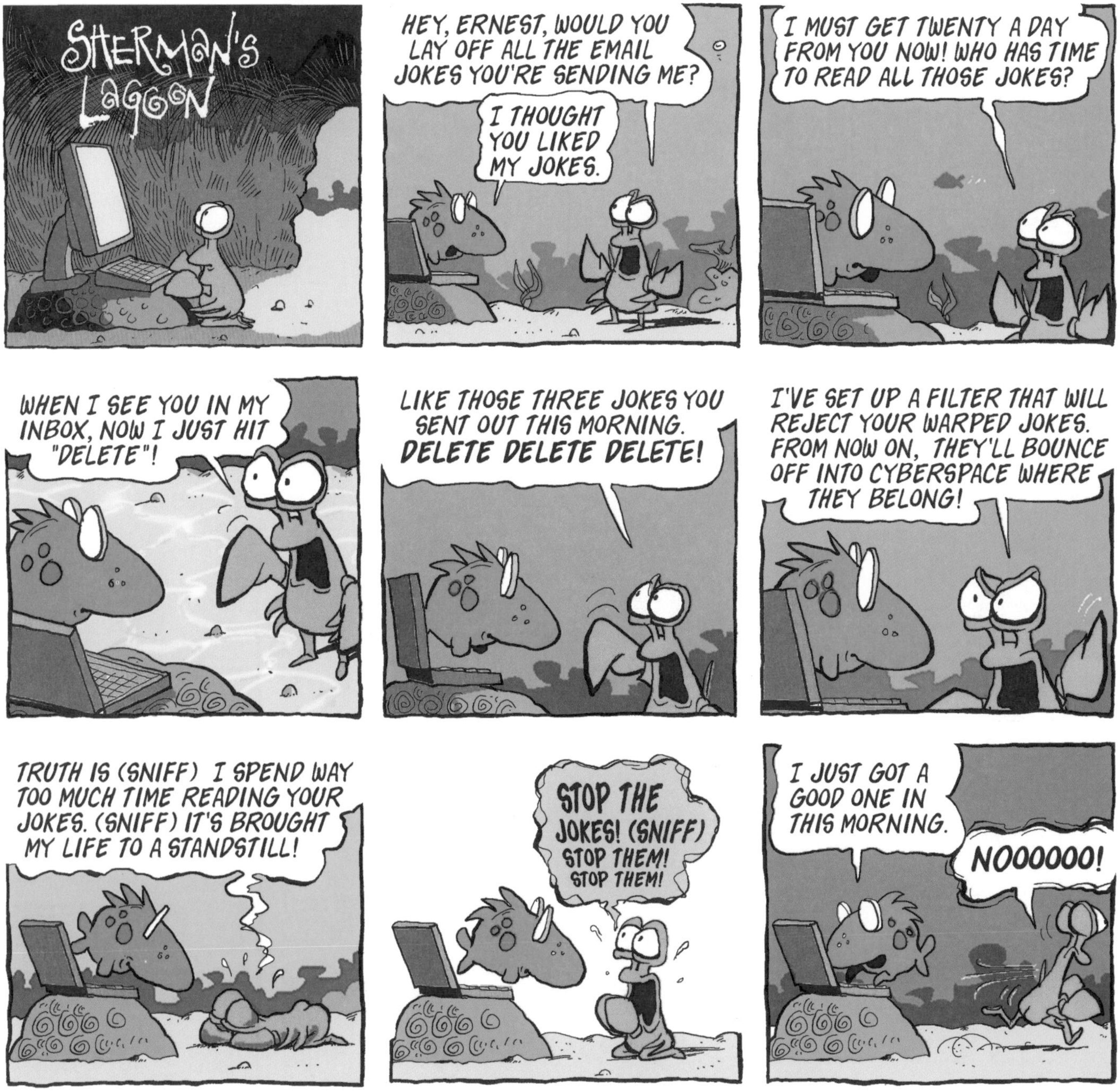
SHERMAN'S LAGOON
HEY, ERNEST, WOULD YOU LAY OFF ALL THE EMAIL JOKES YOU'RE SENDING ME?
I THOUGHT YOU LIKED MY JOKES.
I MUST GET TWENTY A DAY FROM YOU NOW! WHO HAS TIME TO READ ALL THOSE JOKES?
WHEN I SEE YOU IN MY INBOX, NOW I JUST HIT "DELETE"!
LIKE THOSE THREE JOKES YOU SENT OUT THIS MORNING. DELETE DELETE DELETE!
I'VE SET UP A FILTER THAT WILL REJECT YOUR WARPED JOKES. FROM NOW ON, THEY'LL BOUNCE OFF INTO CYBERSPACE WHERE THEY BELONG!
TRUTH IS (SNIFF) I SPEND WAY TOO MUCH TIME READING YOUR JOKES. (SNIFF) IT'S BROUGHT MY LIFE TO A STANDSTILL!
STOP THE JOKES! (SNIFF) STOP THEM! STOP THEM!
I JUST GOT A GOOD ONE IN THIS MORNING.
NOOOOOO!

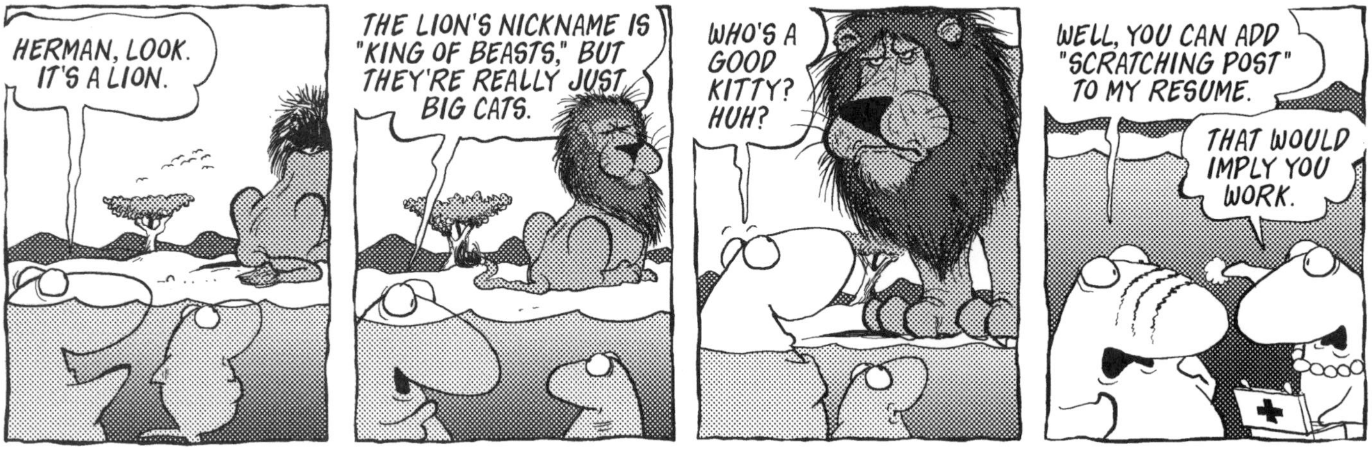
HERMAN, LOOK. IT'S A LION.
THE LION'S NICKNAME IS "KING OF BEASTS," BUT THEY'RE REALLY JUST BIG CATS.
WHO'S A GOOD KITTY? HUH?
WELL, YOU CAN ADD "SCRATCHING POST" TO MY RESUME.
THAT WOULD IMPLY YOU WORK.

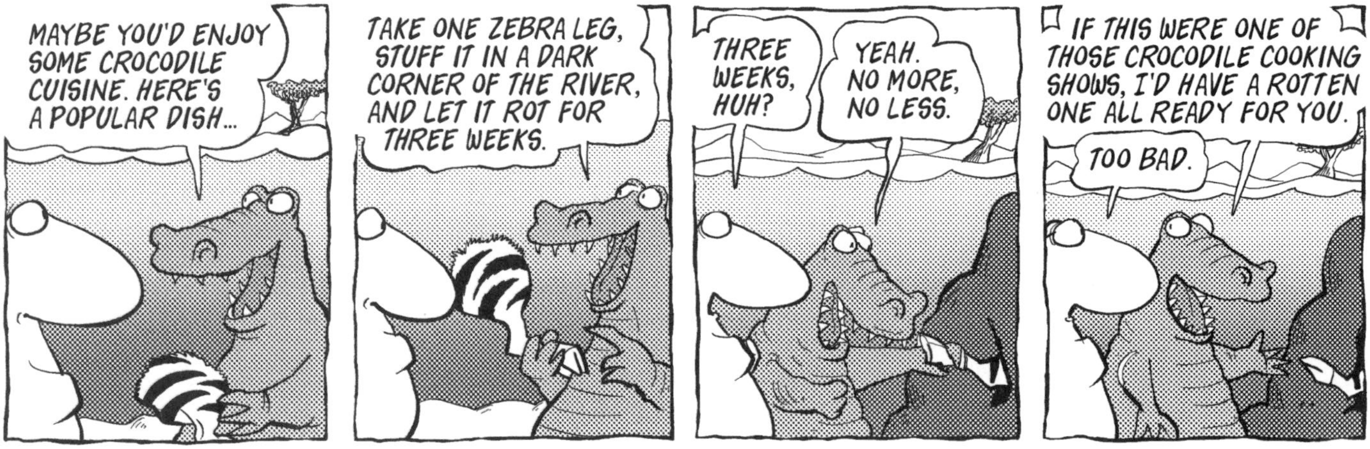
MAYBE YOU'D ENJOY SOME CROCODILE CUISINE. HERE'S A POPULAR DISH...
TAKE ONE ZEBRA LEG, STUFF IT IN A DARK CORNER OF THE RIVER, AND LET IT ROT FOR THREE WEEKS.
THREE WEEKS, HUH?
YEAH. NO MORE, NO LESS.
IF THIS WERE ONE OF THOSE CROCODILE COOKING SHOWS, I'D HAVE A ROTTEN ONE ALL READY FOR YOU.
TOO BAD.

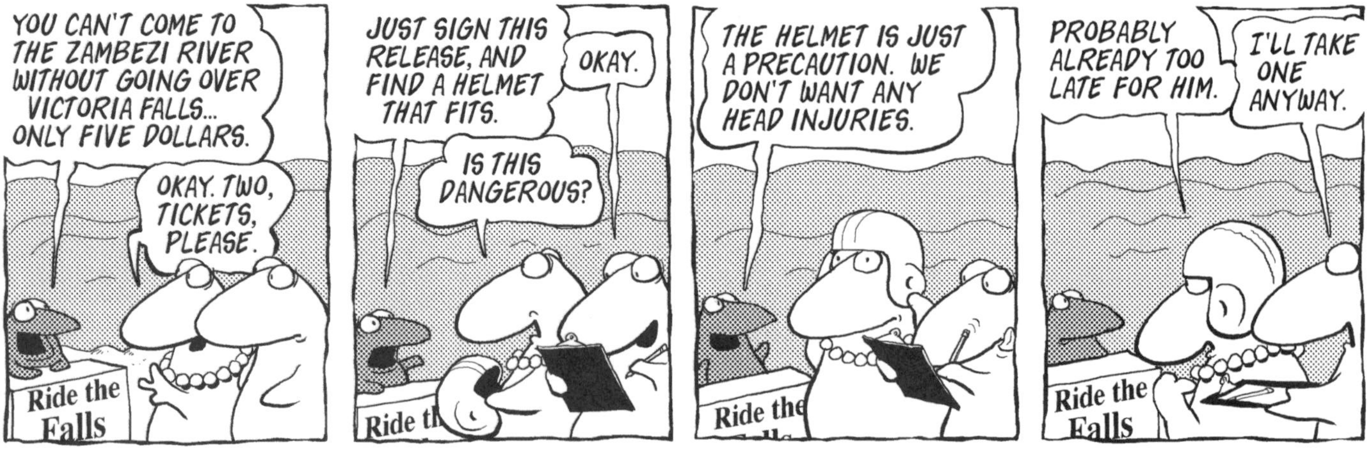
YOU CAN'T COME TO THE ZAMBEZI RIVER WITHOUT GOING OVER VICTORIA FALLS... ONLY FIVE DOLLARS.
OKAY. TWO, TICKETS, PLEASE.
Ride the Falls
JUST SIGN THIS RELEASE, AND FIND A HELMET THAT FITS.
OKAY.
IS THIS DANGEROUS?
THE HELMET IS JUST A PRECAUTION. WE DON'T WANT ANY HEAD INJURIES.
PROBABLY ALREADY TOO LATE FOR HIM.
I'LL TAKE ONE ANYWAY.
Ride the Falls

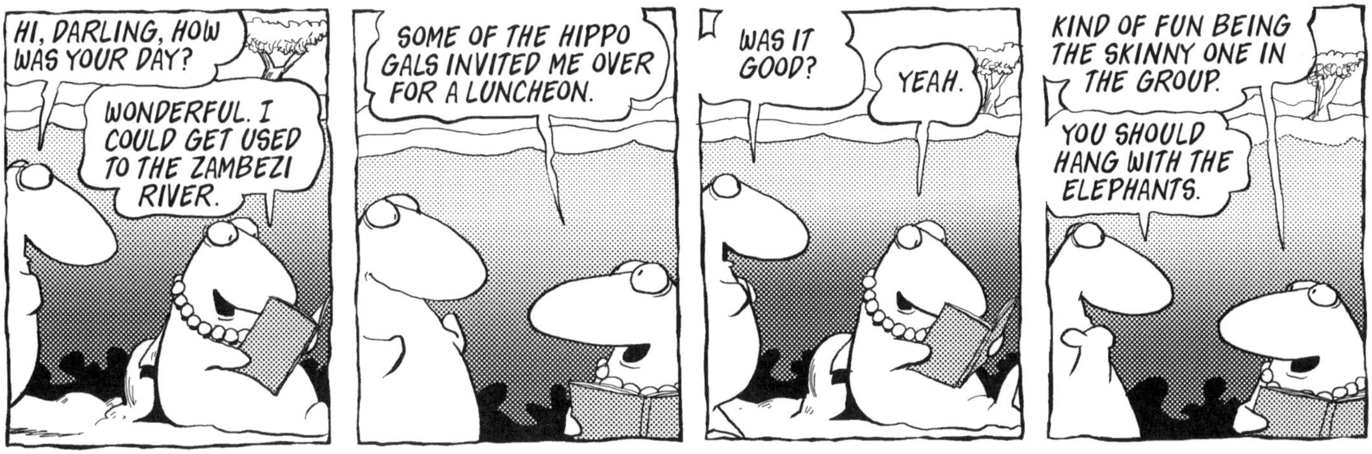
HI, DARLING, HOW WAS YOUR DAY?
WONDERFUL. I COULD GET USED TO THE ZAMBEZI RIVER.
SOME OF THE HIPPO GALS INVITED ME OVER FOR A LUNCHEON.
WAS IT GOOD?
YEAH.
KIND OF FUN BEING THE SKINNY ONE IN THE GROUP.
YOU SHOULD HANG WITH THE ELEPHANTS.

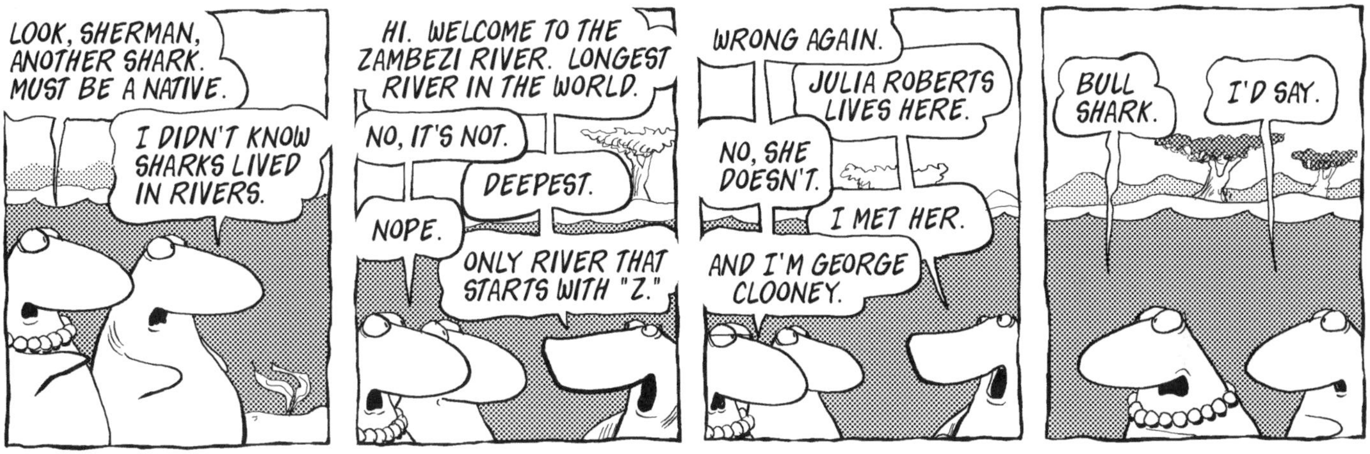
LOOK, SHERMAN, ANOTHER SHARK. MUST BE A NATIVE.
I DIDN'T KNOW SHARKS LIVED IN RIVERS.
HI. WELCOME TO THE ZAMBEZI RIVER. LONGEST RIVER IN THE WORLD.
NO, IT'S NOT.
DEEPEST.
NOPE.
ONLY RIVER THAT STARTS WITH "Z."
WRONG AGAIN.
JULIA ROBERTS LIVES HERE.
NO, SHE DOESN'T.
I MET HER.
AND I'M GEORGE CLOONEY.
BULL SHARK.
I'D SAY.

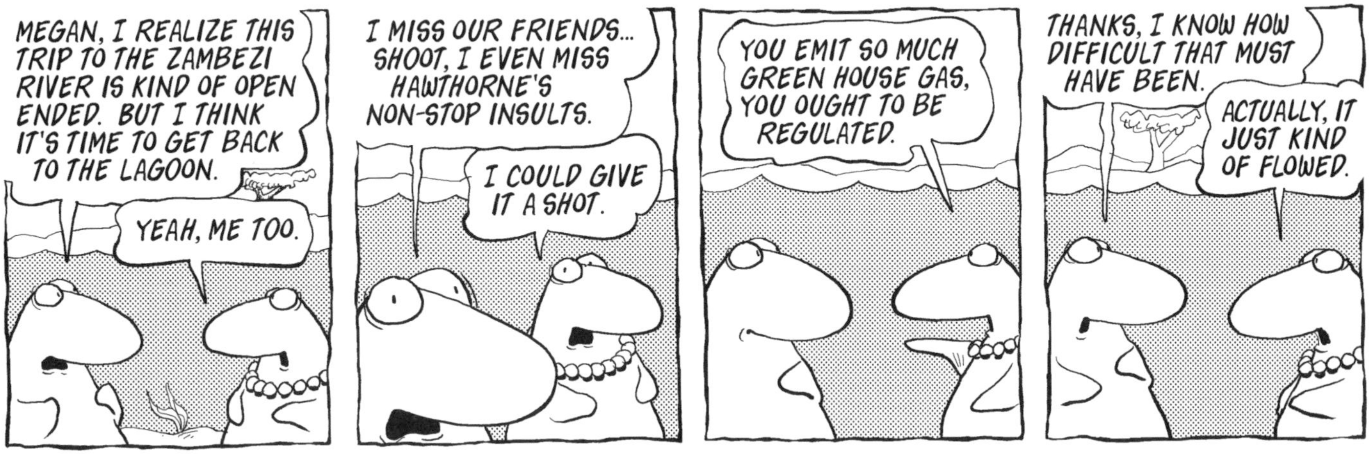
MEGAN, I REALIZE THIS TRIP TO THE ZAMBEZI RIVER IS KIND OF OPEN ENDED. BUT I THINK IT'S TIME TO GET BACK TO THE LAGOON.
YEAH, ME TOO.
I MISS OUR FRIENDS... SHOOT, I EVEN MISS HAWTHORNE'S NON-STOP INSULTS.
I COULD GIVE IT A SHOT.
YOU EMIT SO MUCH GREEN HOUSE GAS, YOU OUGHT TO BE REGULATED.
THANKS, I KNOW HOW DIFFICULT THAT MUST HAVE BEEN.
ACTUALLY, IT JUST KIND OF FLOWED.

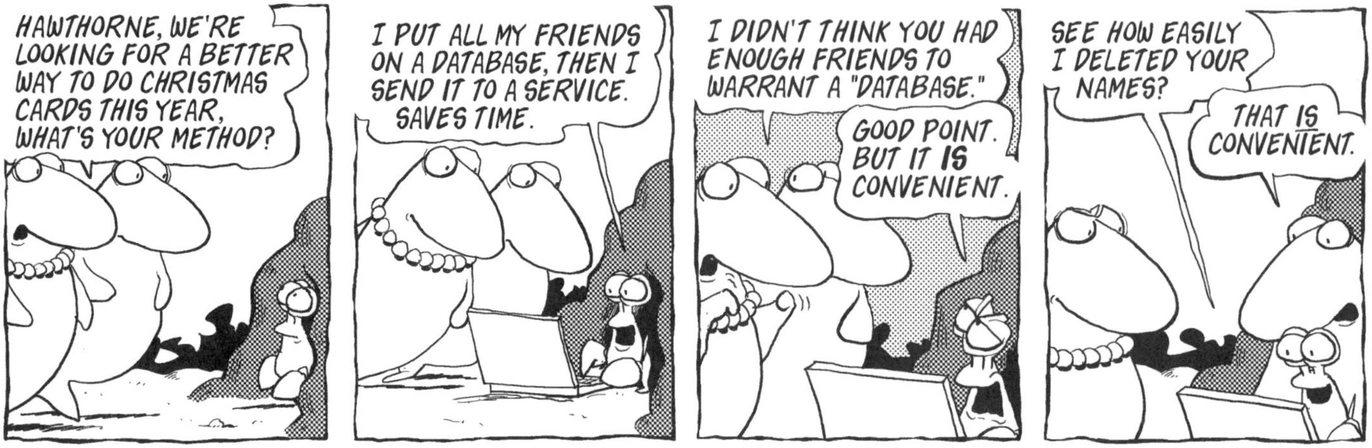
HAWTHORNE, WE'RE LOOKING FOR A BETTER WAY TO DO CHRISTMAS CARDS THIS YEAR. WHAT'S YOUR METHOD?
I PUT ALL MY FRIENDS ON A DATABASE, THEN I SEND IT TO A SERVICE. SAVES TIME.
I DIDN'T THINK YOU HAD ENOUGH FRIENDS TO WARRANT A "DATABASE."
GOOD POINT. BUT IT **IS** CONVENIENT.
SEE HOW EASILY I DELETED YOUR NAMES?
THAT IS CONVENIENT.

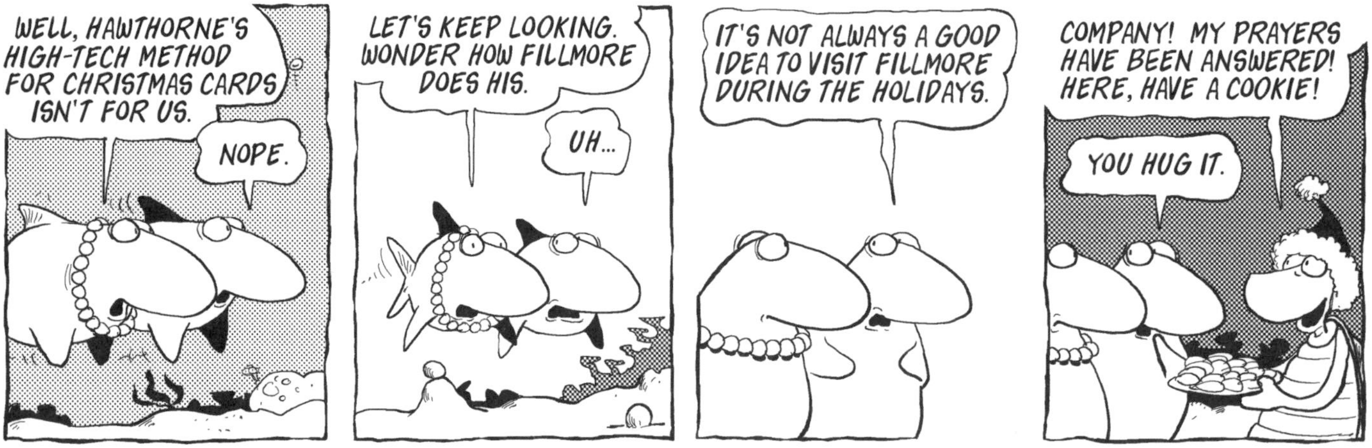
WELL, HAWTHORNE'S HIGH-TECH METHOD FOR CHRISTMAS CARDS ISN'T FOR US.
NOPE.
LET'S KEEP LOOKING. WONDER HOW FILLMORE DOES HIS.
UH...
IT'S NOT ALWAYS A GOOD IDEA TO VISIT FILLMORE DURING THE HOLIDAYS.
COMPANY! MY PRAYERS HAVE BEEN ANSWERED! HERE, HAVE A COOKIE!
YOU HUG IT.

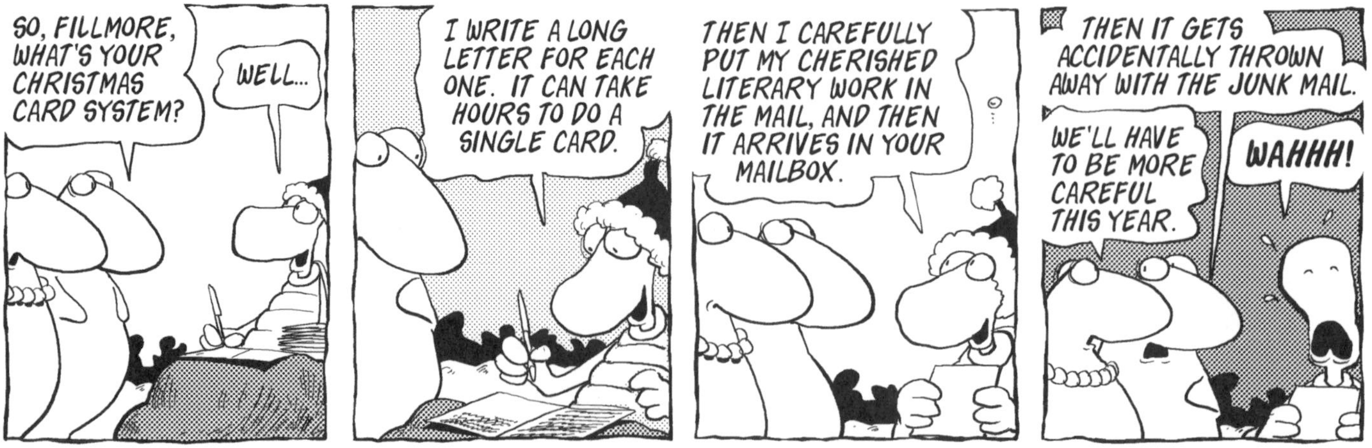
SO, FILLMORE, WHAT'S YOUR CHRISTMAS CARD SYSTEM?
WELL...
I WRITE A LONG LETTER FOR EACH ONE. IT CAN TAKE HOURS TO DO A SINGLE CARD.
THEN I CAREFULLY PUT MY CHERISHED LITERARY WORK IN THE MAIL, AND THEN IT ARRIVES IN YOUR MAILBOX.
THEN IT GETS ACCIDENTALLY THROWN AWAY WITH THE JUNK MAIL.
WE'LL HAVE TO BE MORE CAREFUL THIS YEAR.
WAHHH!

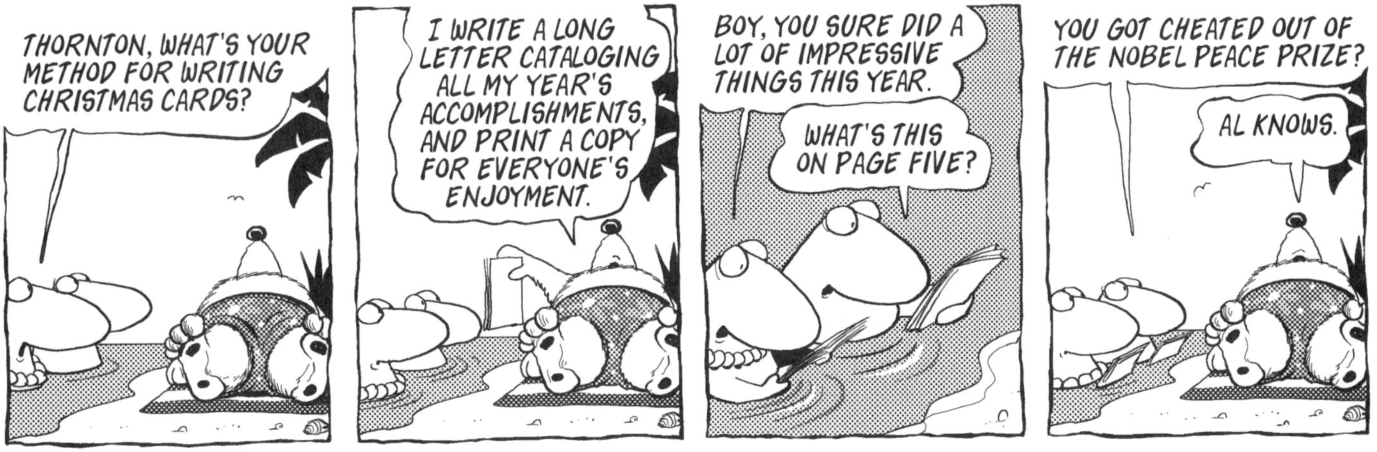
THORNTON, WHAT'S YOUR METHOD FOR WRITING CHRISTMAS CARDS?
I WRITE A LONG LETTER CATALOGING ALL MY YEAR'S ACCOMPLISHMENTS, AND PRINT A COPY FOR EVERYONE'S ENJOYMENT.
BOY, YOU SURE DID A LOT OF IMPRESSIVE THINGS THIS YEAR.
WHAT'S THIS ON PAGE FIVE?
YOU GOT CHEATED OUT OF THE NOBEL PEACE PRIZE?
AL KNOWS.

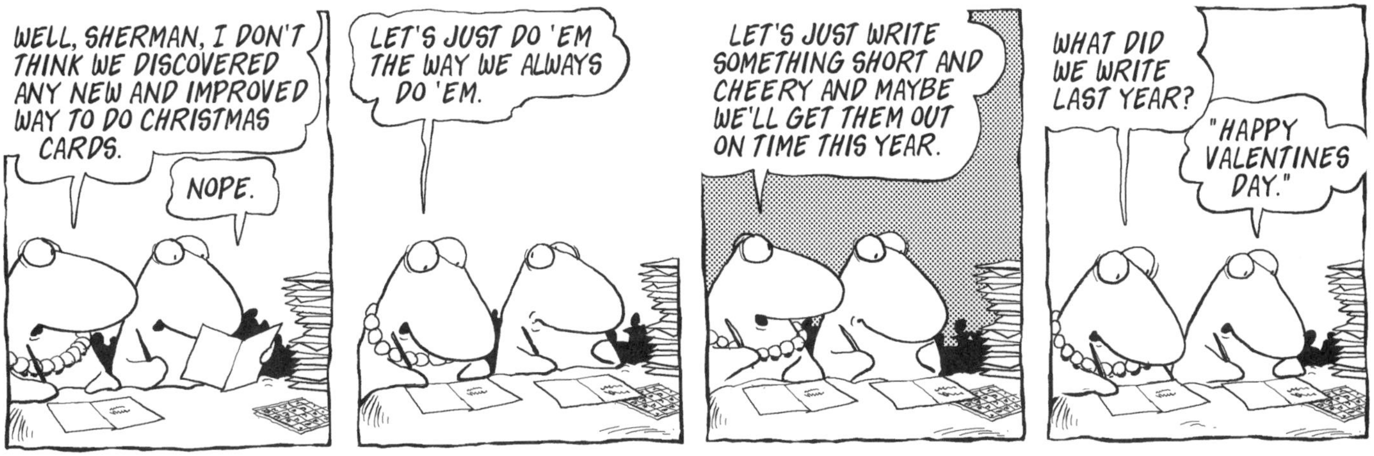
WELL, SHERMAN, I DON'T THINK WE DISCOVERED ANY NEW AND IMPROVED WAY TO DO CHRISTMAS CARDS.
NOPE.
LET'S JUST DO 'EM THE WAY WE ALWAYS DO 'EM.
LET'S JUST WRITE SOMETHING SHORT AND CHEERY AND MAYBE WE'LL GET THEM OUT ON TIME THIS YEAR.
WHAT DID WE WRITE LAST YEAR?
"HAPPY VALENTINES DAY."

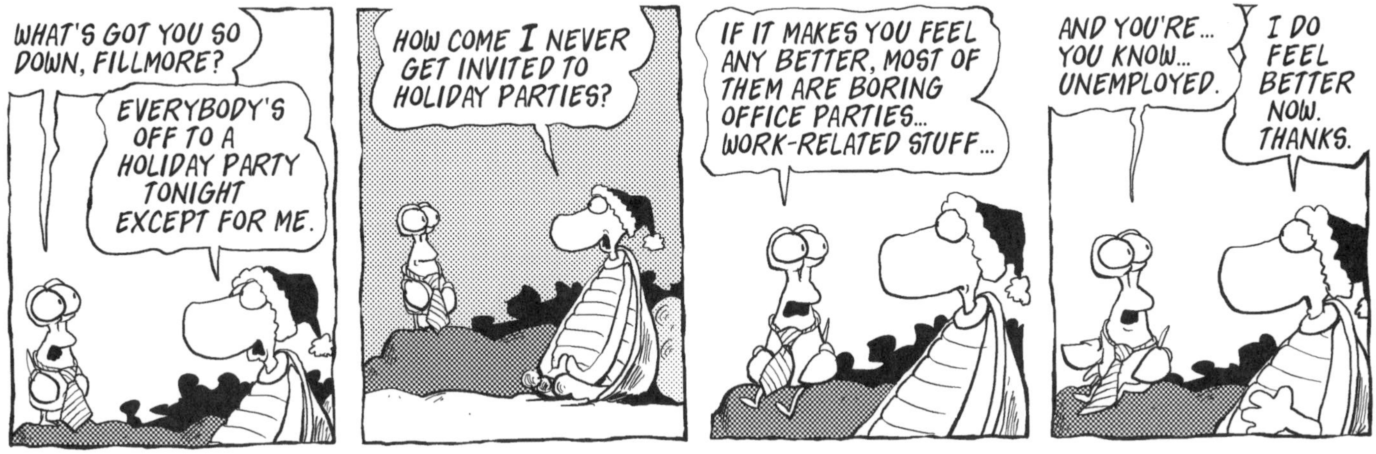
WHAT'S GOT YOU SO DOWN, FILLMORE?
EVERYBODY'S OFF TO A HOLIDAY PARTY TONIGHT EXCEPT FOR ME.
HOW COME I NEVER GET INVITED TO HOLIDAY PARTIES?
IF IT MAKES YOU FEEL ANY BETTER, MOST OF THEM ARE BORING OFFICE PARTIES... WORK-RELATED STUFF...
AND YOU'RE... YOU KNOW... UNEMPLOYED.
I DO FEEL BETTER NOW. THANKS.

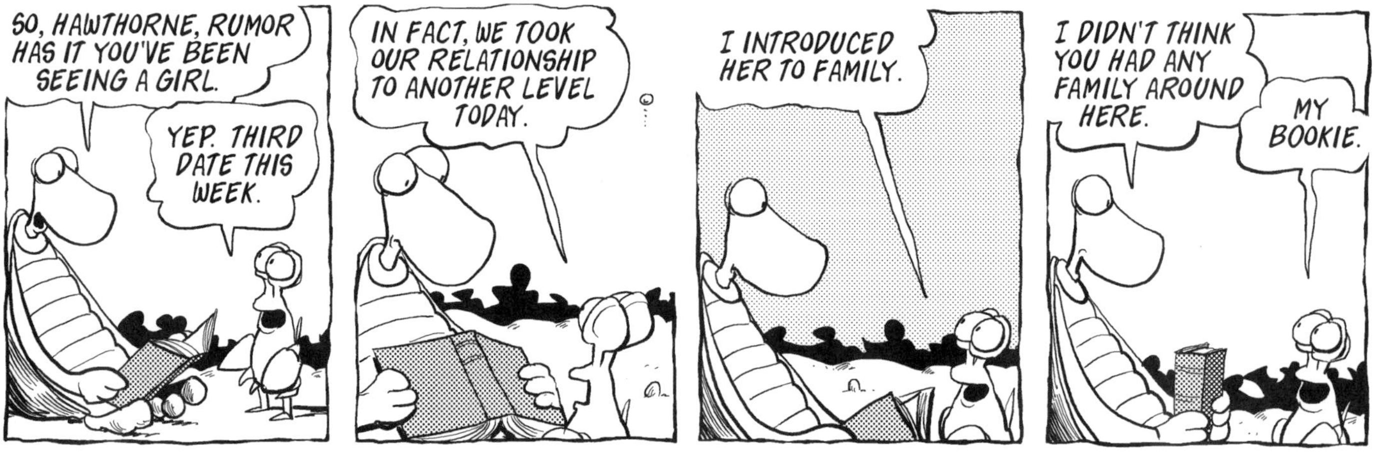
SO, HAWTHORNE, RUMOR HAS IT YOU'VE BEEN SEEING A GIRL.
YEP. THIRD DATE THIS WEEK.
IN FACT, WE TOOK OUR RELATIONSHIP TO ANOTHER LEVEL TODAY.
I INTRODUCED HER TO FAMILY.
I DIDN'T THINK YOU HAD ANY FAMILY AROUND HERE.
MY BOOKIE.

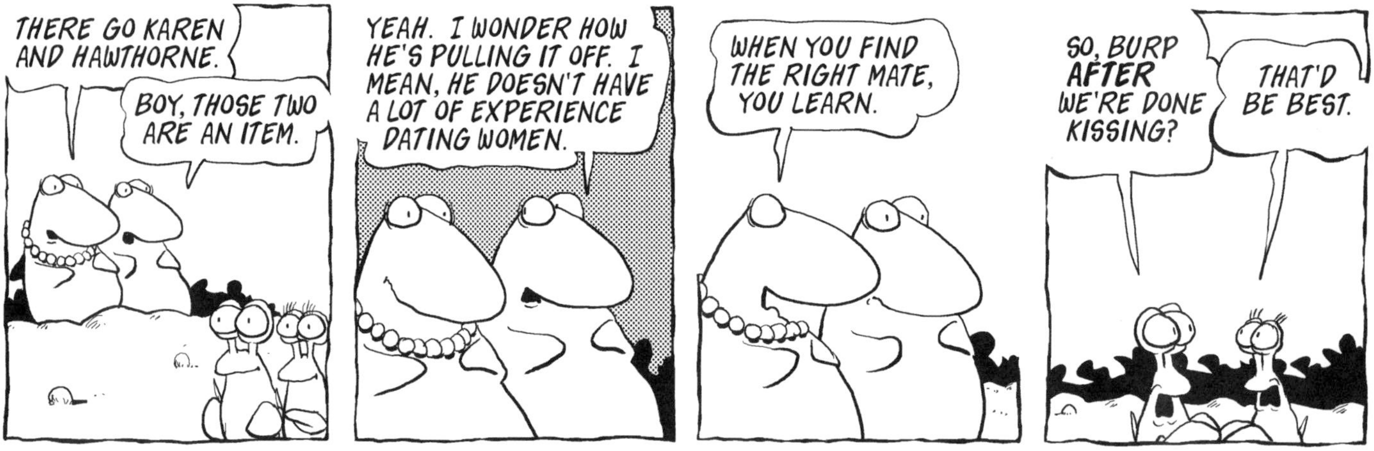
THERE GO KAREN AND HAWTHORNE.
BOY, THOSE TWO ARE AN ITEM.
YEAH. I WONDER HOW HE'S PULLING IT OFF. I MEAN, HE DOESN'T HAVE A LOT OF EXPERIENCE DATING WOMEN.
WHEN YOU FIND THE RIGHT MATE, YOU LEARN.
SO, BURP **AFTER** WE'RE DONE KISSING?
THAT'D BE BEST.

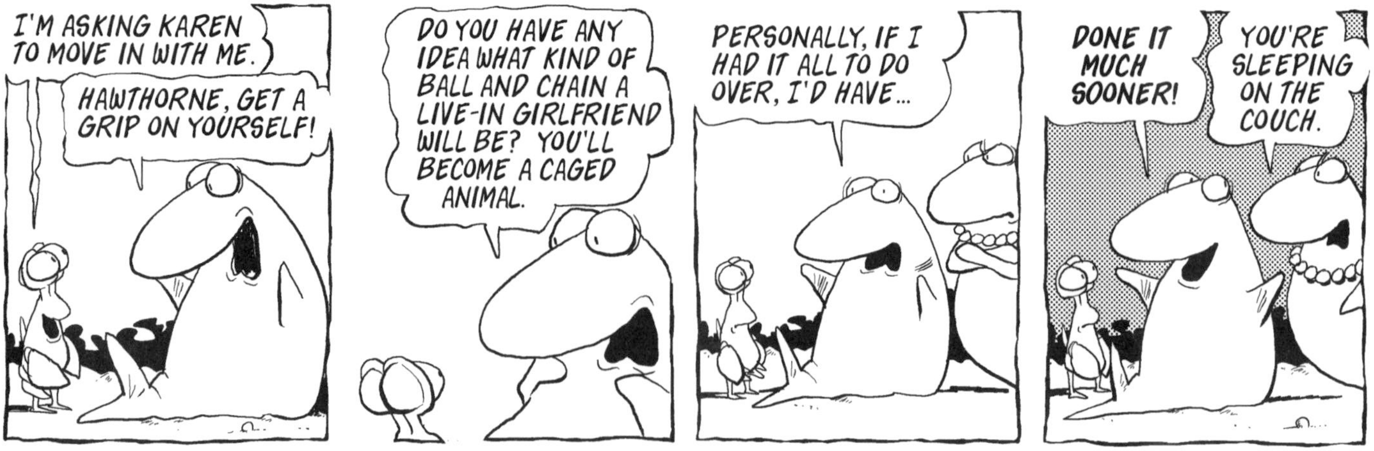
I'M ASKING KAREN TO MOVE IN WITH ME.
HAWTHORNE, GET A GRIP ON YOURSELF!
DO YOU HAVE ANY IDEA WHAT KIND OF BALL AND CHAIN A LIVE-IN GIRLFRIEND WILL BE? YOU'LL BECOME A CAGED ANIMAL.
PERSONALLY, IF I HAD IT ALL TO DO OVER, I'D HAVE...
DONE IT MUCH SOONER!
YOU'RE SLEEPING ON THE COUCH.

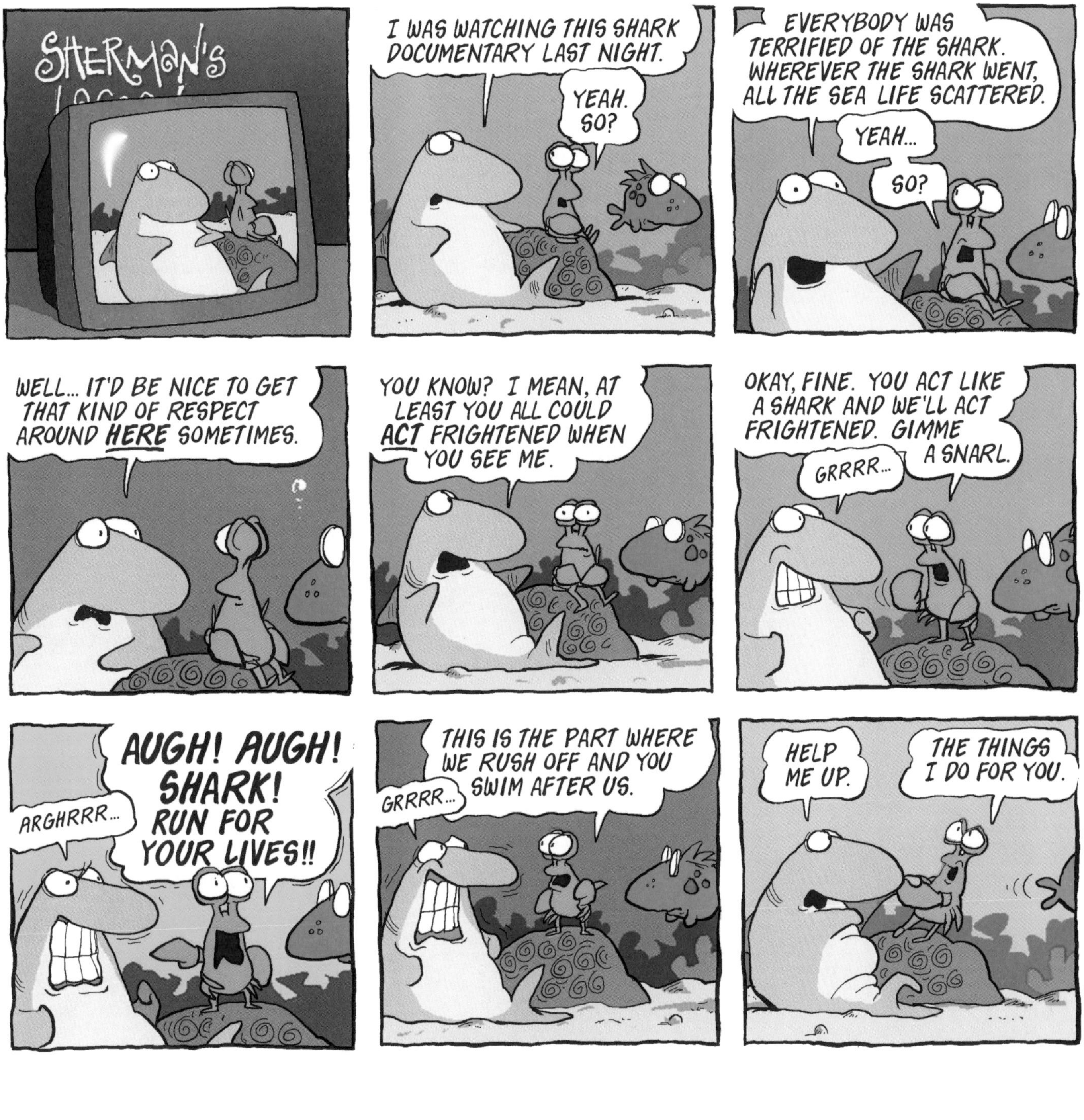
SHERMAN'S
I WAS WATCHING THIS SHARK DOCUMENTARY LAST NIGHT.
YEAH. SO?
EVERYBODY WAS TERRIFIED OF THE SHARK. WHEREVER THE SHARK WENT, ALL THE SEA LIFE SCATTERED.
YEAH...
SO?
WELL... IT'D BE NICE TO GET THAT KIND OF RESPECT AROUND HERE SOMETIMES.
YOU KNOW? I MEAN, AT LEAST YOU ALL COULD ACT FRIGHTENED WHEN YOU SEE ME.
OKAY, FINE. YOU ACT LIKE A SHARK AND WE'LL ACT FRIGHTENED. GIMME A SNARL.
GRRRR...
ARGHRRR...
AUGH! AUGH! SHARK! RUN FOR YOUR LIVES!!
GRRRR...
THIS IS THE PART WHERE WE RUSH OFF AND YOU SWIM AFTER US.
HELP ME UP.
THE THINGS I DO FOR YOU.

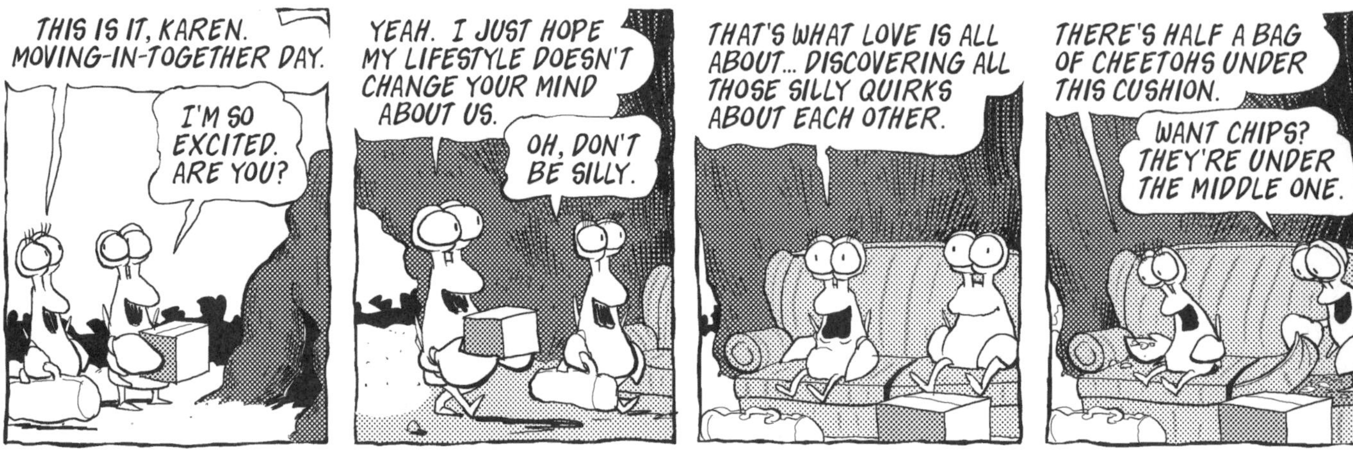
THIS IS IT, KAREN. MOVING-IN-TOGETHER DAY.
I'M SO EXCITED. ARE YOU?
YEAH. I JUST HOPE MY LIFESTYLE DOESN'T CHANGE YOUR MIND ABOUT US.
OH, DON'T BE SILLY.
THAT'S WHAT LOVE IS ALL ABOUT... DISCOVERING ALL THOSE SILLY QUIRKS ABOUT EACH OTHER.
THERE'S HALF A BAG OF CHEETOHS UNDER THIS CUSHION.
WANT CHIPS? THEY'RE UNDER THE MIDDLE ONE.

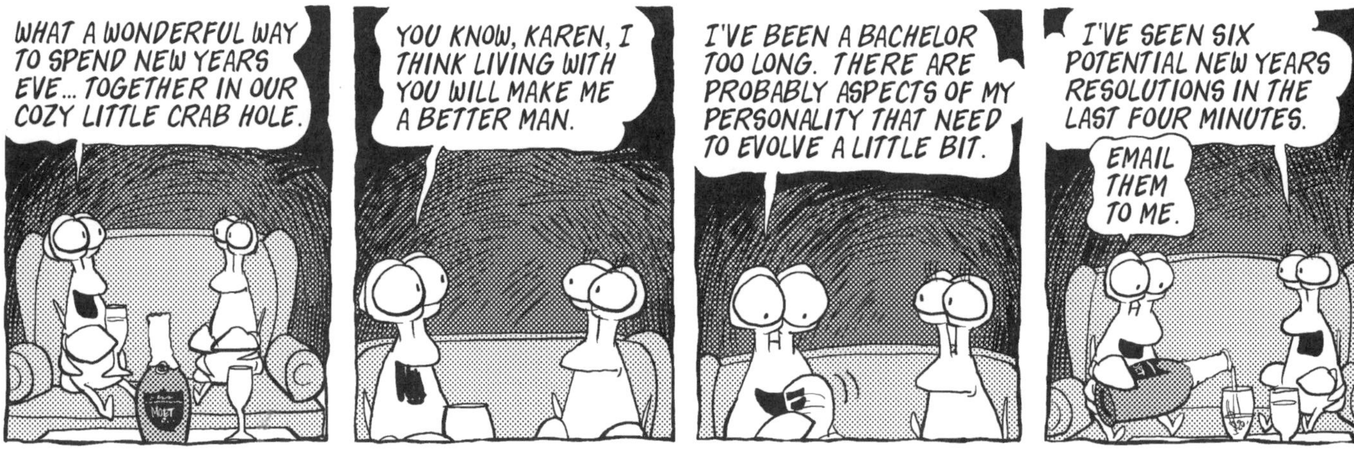
WHAT A WONDERFUL WAY TO SPEND NEW YEARS EVE... TOGETHER IN OUR COZY LITTLE CRAB HOLE.
MOET
YOU KNOW, KAREN, I THINK LIVING WITH YOU WILL MAKE ME A BETTER MAN.
I'VE BEEN A BACHELOR TOO LONG. THERE ARE PROBABLY ASPECTS OF MY PERSONALITY THAT NEED TO EVOLVE A LITTLE BIT.
I'VE SEEN SIX POTENTIAL NEW YEARS RESOLUTIONS IN THE LAST FOUR MINUTES.
EMAIL THEM TO ME.

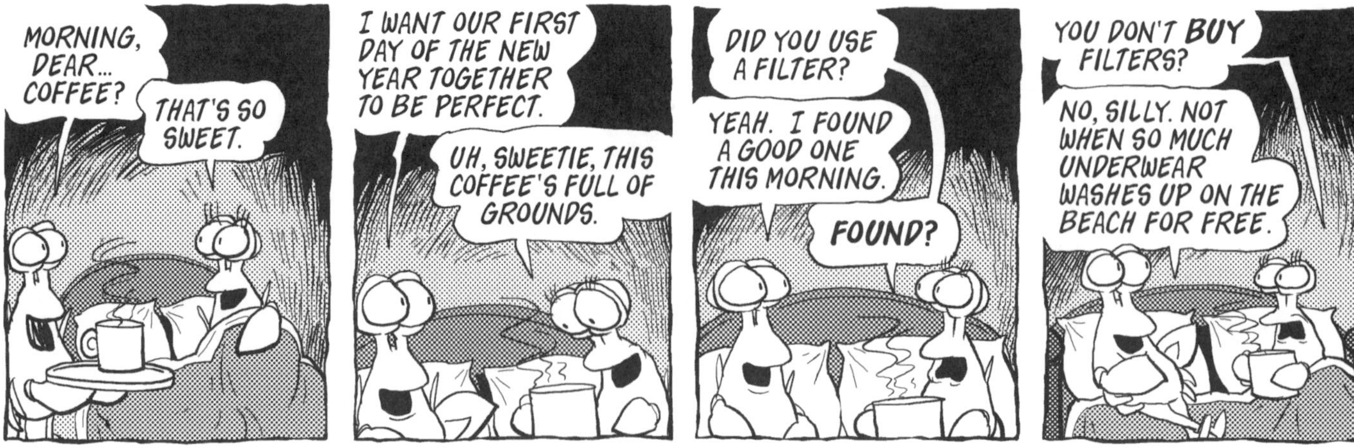
MORNING, DEAR... COFFEE?
THAT'S SO SWEET.
I WANT OUR FIRST DAY OF THE NEW YEAR TOGETHER TO BE PERFECT.
UH, SWEETIE, THIS COFFEE'S FULL OF GROUNDS.
DID YOU USE A FILTER?
YEAH. I FOUND A GOOD ONE THIS MORNING.
FOUND?
YOU DON'T BUY FILTERS?
NO, SILLY. NOT WHEN SO MUCH UNDERWEAR WASHES UP ON THE BEACH FOR FREE.

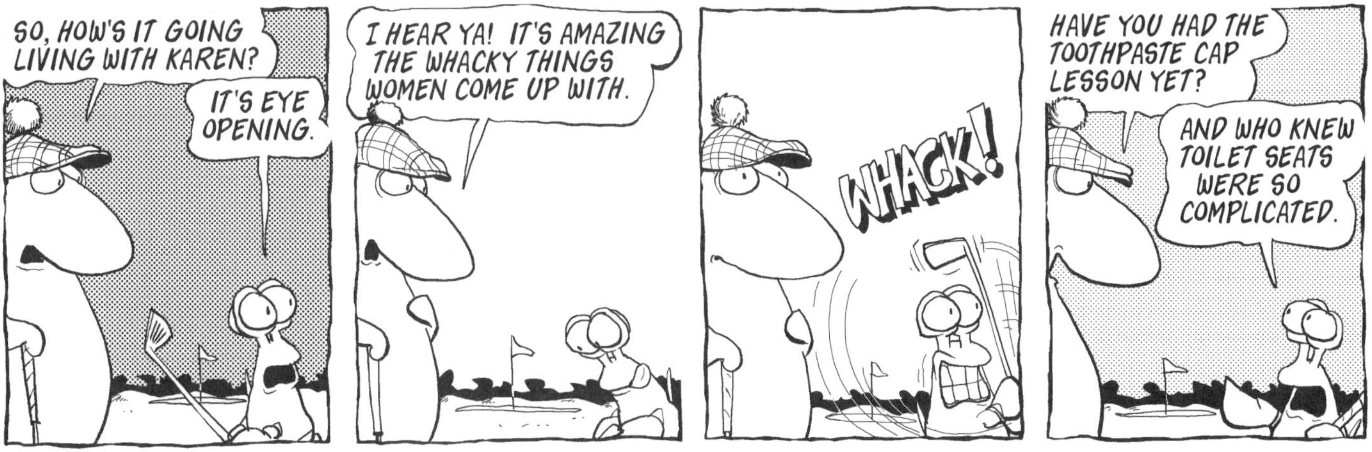
SO, HOW'S IT GOING LIVING WITH KAREN?
IT'S EYE OPENING.
I HEAR YA! IT'S AMAZING THE WHACKY THINGS WOMEN COME UP WITH.
WHACK!
HAVE YOU HAD THE TOOTHPASTE CAP LESSON YET?
AND WHO KNEW TOILET SEATS WERE SO COMPLICATED.

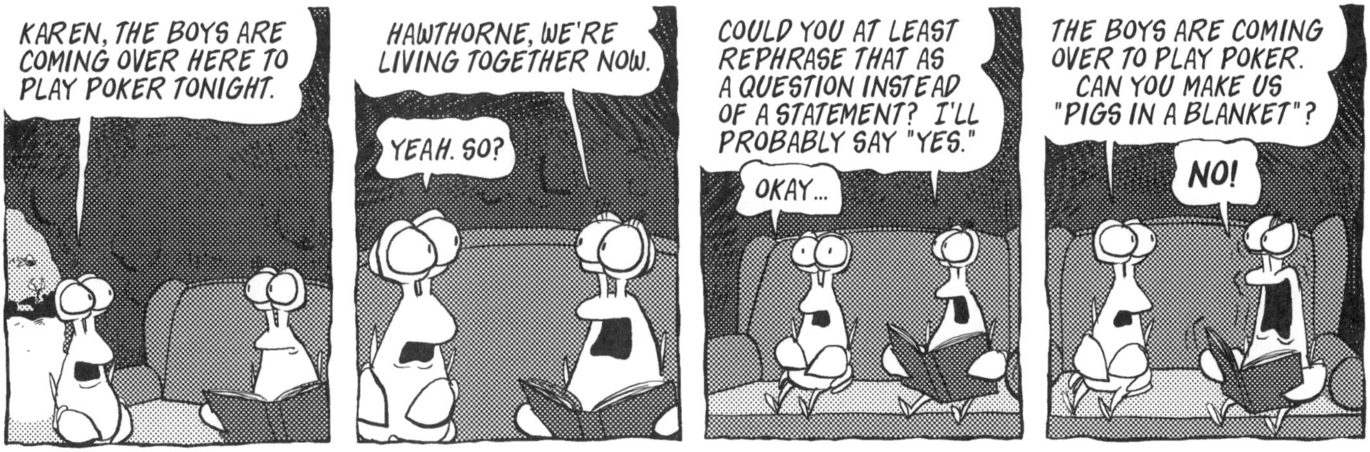
KAREN, THE BOYS ARE COMING OVER HERE TO PLAY POKER TONIGHT.
HAWTHORNE, WE'RE LIVING TOGETHER NOW.
YEAH. SO?
COULD YOU AT LEAST REPHRASE THAT AS A QUESTION INSTEAD OF A STATEMENT? I'LL PROBABLY SAY "YES."
OKAY...
THE BOYS ARE COMING OVER TO PLAY POKER. CAN YOU MAKE US "PIGS IN A BLANKET"?
NO!

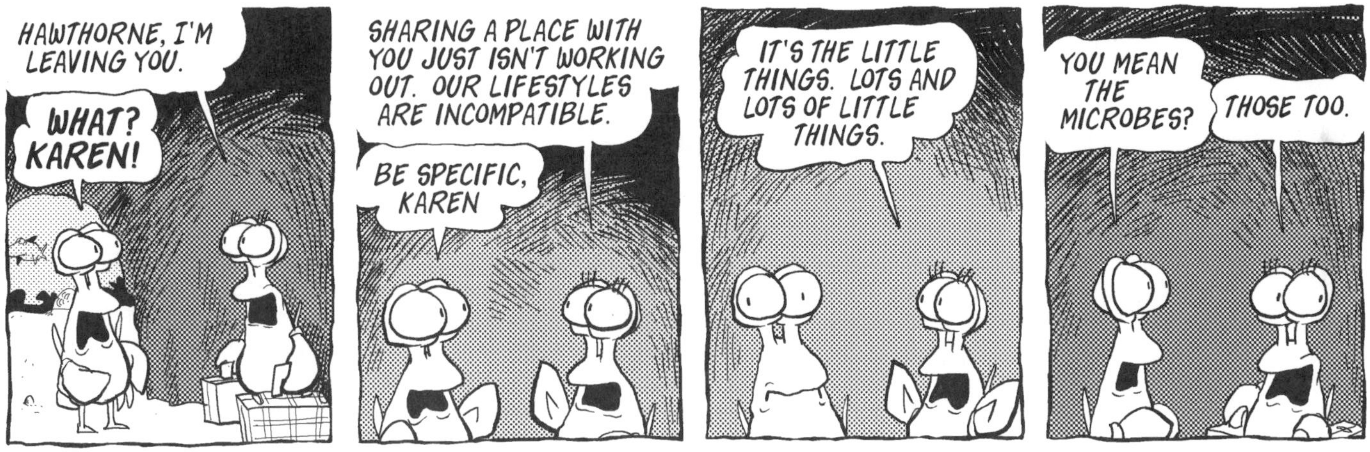
HAWTHORNE, I'M LEAVING YOU.
WHAT? KAREN!
SHARING A PLACE WITH YOU JUST ISN'T WORKING OUT. OUR LIFESTYLES ARE INCOMPATIBLE.
BE SPECIFIC, KAREN
IT'S THE LITTLE THINGS. LOTS AND LOTS OF LITTLE THINGS.
YOU MEAN THE MICROBES?
THOSE TOO.